WORLD BANK LATIN AMERICAN
AND CARIBBEAN STUDIES

*Viewpoints*

# FROM NATURAL RESOURCES TO THE KNOWLEDGE ECONOMY

## *Trade and Job Quality*

*by*

*David de Ferranti*
*Guillermo E. Perry*
*Daniel Lederman*
*William F. Maloney*

**THE WORLD BANK**
Washington, D.C.

© 2002 The International Bank for Reconstruction
and Development / THE WORLD BANK
1818 H Street, NW
Washington, DC 20433

1 2 3 4 04 03 02 01

The findings, interpretations, and conclusions expressed here are those of the author(s) and do not necessarily reflect the views of the Board of Executive Directors of the World Bank or the governments they represent.

The World Bank cannot guarantee the accuracy of the data included in this work. The boundaries, colors, denominations, and other information shown on any map in this work do not imply on the part of the World Bank any judgment of the legal status of any territory or the endorsement or acceptance of such boundaries.

---

**About This Book**
David de Ferranti is vice president and Guillermo E. Perry is chief economist in the World Bank's Latin America and the Caribbean Regional Office. Daniel Lederman is an economist and Willliam F. Maloney is senior economist in the World Bank's Latin America and the Caribbean Regional Office.

For more information on publications from the World Bank Latin America and the Caribbean Region, please visit us at **www.worldbank.org/lacpublications (www.BancoMundial.org/publicaciones).**

Cover design by Jeffrey Kibler, The Magazine Group.
Cover art: *Dialogue with the Universe*, 1999, by Manuel Cunjamá, Mexico. Manuel Cunjamá was born in 1971 in Tuxtla Gutiérrez, Chiapas. He began exhibiting his work in Chiapas in 1992. Cunjamá's work is included in the collection of the World Bank Art Program.

The World Bank Art Program makes particular efforts to identify artists from developing nations and make their work available to a wider audience. The art program organizes exhibits, educational and cultural partnerships, competitions, artists' projects, and site-specific installations.

---

ISBN 0-8213-5009-9

**Library of Congress Cataloging-in-Publication Data**
From natural resources to the knowledge economy : trade and job quality / David de Ferranti . . . [et al.].
    p. cm. — (World Bank Latin American and Caribbean studies)
Includes bibliographical references.
ISBN 0-8213-5009-9
    1. Latin America—Commercial policy.   2. Latin America—Economic policy.   3. Labor supply—Latin America.
4. Occupations—Latin America.   I. De Ferranti, David M.   II. Series.
HF3230.5.Z5 F76 2001
338.98—dc21                                                                                          2001046929

# Contents

## Tables

## Figures

# Acknowledgments

THIS REPORT IS THE PRODUCT OF A COLLECTIVE EFFORT BY A WORLD BANK TEAM COORDInated by the Office of the Chief Economist for the Latin America and the Caribbean Region and led by Guillermo E. Perry. The principal authors by chapter were Guillermo E. Perry (Chapter 1), Daniel Lederman (Chapters 2 and 4), and William F. Maloney (Chapters 3 and 5).

We were honored by the knowledge and talents of specialists (and their numerous coauthors) who wrote background papers: Patricio Aroca, Magnus Blomstrom (Stockholm School of Economics), Eric Bond (Penn State University), John Cuddington (Georgetown University), Pablo Fajnzylber (Federal University of Minas Gerais, Brazil), William Foster (Catholic University of Chile), Rolando Guzmán, Ari Kokko (Stockholm School of Economics), Magdalena Lizardo, Catherine Mann (Institute for International Economics), Patricio Meller (University of Chile), Alex Monge-Naranjo (Northwestern University), Pablo Sanguinetti (Torcuato di Tella University, Argentina), Rodrigo Soares (University of Chicago), J. Edward Taylor (University of California, Davis), Alberto Valdés, Anthony Venables (London School of Economics), and Gavin Wright (Stanford University).

Friends and colleagues from the World Bank made efforts that went well beyond the call of duty. We received important contributions from: Andreas Blom, Wendy Cunningham, Norbert Fiess, José R. López-Calix, Ana María Menéndez, Gabriel Montes, Marcelo Olarreaga, Susana Sánchez, Norbert Schady, Claudia Sepúlveda, Quentin Wodon, and Lixin Colin Xu. In addition, valuable comments were received at various stages of the project from Ian Bannon, Mauricio Carrizosa, Paul Collier, Shelton Davis, Indermit Gill, Marcelo Giugale, Ali Khadr, Paul Levy, Will Martin, Ernesto May, Lee Morrison, Anne Pillay, David Rosenblatt, Carolina Sánchez, Maurice Schiff, Luis Servén, Will Shaw, David Yuravlivker, and Cara Zappala.

Important contributions and guidance were received from Nina Pavcnik at Dartmouth College, and at the initial stages from Ken Sokoloff at the University of California, Los Angeles. We would also like to express our appreciation for the helpful input received from Luther Miller of the Caribbean Tourism Organization (CTO).

The report benefited greatly from discussions with a wide range of civil society organizations and individuals. More than 100 representatives from think tanks, trade unions, community-based organizations, women's movements, Afro-Latino communities, advocacy groups, and development nongovernmental organizations (NGOs)—among others—helped us build a bridge between theory and practice. We conducted a series of consultation meetings in Brazil, Colombia, the Dominican Republic, and Mexico, which provided us with useful information to both formulate and test our hypotheses. In addition, more than 30 participants from several countries in the region were engaged in a productive electronic dialogue, which guided the design of the study. Special recognition should be given to Dr. Ignacio Roman, who arranged further consultation and field visits in Jalisco, Mexico. These consultations could not have taken place without the support of our Civil Society team, especially Kathy Bain and Roberto Senderowitsch.

Any errors or omissions in the report are the sole responsibility of the authors and should not be attributed to any of the above individuals or the institutions they represent.

# Acronyms and Abbreviations

| | |
|---|---|
| ANOVA | Analysis-of-variance |
| CBI | Caribbean Basin Initiative |
| CEO | Chief executive officer |
| CEPAL | Centro Estudios para America Latina |
| CET | Common External Tariff |
| CGE | Computable general equilibrium |
| CINDE | Coalición Costarricense de Iniciativas de Desarrollo |
| CONASUPO | Compañía Nacional de Subsistencias Populares |
| CORFO | Chilean Development Corporation |
| CTA | Centro Técnico da Aeronáutica |
| CTO | Caribbean Tourism Organization |
| ECLAC | Economic Commission for Latin America and the Caribbean |
| EMBRAER | Empresa Brasileira de Aeronautica |
| EMS | Electronics manufacturing services |
| EPZ | Export processing zone |
| ERP | Effective rate of protection |
| FDI | Foreign direct investment |
| FIA | Ministry of Agriculture's research fund |
| FONDECYT | Fondo Nacional de Desarrollo Tecnológico y Productivo, Chile |
| FONDEF | Fondo de Fomento al Desarrollo Científico y Tecnológico, Chile |
| GATT | General Agreement on Tariff and Trade |
| GDP | Gross domestic product |
| GMM | Generalized Method of Moments |
| ICM | Sales tax (Brazil) |
| ICT | Information and communications technology |
| IIT | Intra-industry trade |
| IMF | International Monetary Fund |
| INIA | Instituto Nacional de Investigación Agraria (National Institute of Agricultural Research) |
| IP | Internet Protocol |
| IPI | Industrial products tax (Brazil) |
| ITA | Instituto Tecnológico da Aeronáutica |
| LAC | Latin America and the Caribbean |
| LDC | Less-developed country |
| Mercosur | Mercado Común del Sur |
| MIIT | Marginal intra-industry trade |

| | |
|---|---|
| NAFTA | North American Free Trade Agreement |
| NIC | Newly industrialized country |
| NRP | Net rate of protection |
| NTAE | Nontraditional agricultural exports |
| OECD | Organisation for Economic Co-operation and Development |
| OEMs | Original Equipment Manufacturers |
| PCB | Printed circuit board |
| PROCAMPO | Programa de Apoyos Directos al Campo |
| PROCOMER | Promotora del Comercio Exterior de Costa Rica (The Costa Rican Foreign Trade Corporation) |
| R&D | Research and development |
| RIA | Regional integration agreements |
| SITC | Standard International Trade Classification |
| TFP | Total factor productivity |
| UNESCO | United Nations Educational, Scientific and Cultural Organization |
| USAID | United States Agency for International Development |
| WTO | World Trade Organization |

# CHAPTER 1

# Introduction and Summary

AFTER OVER A DECADE OF REMARKABLE PROGRESS IN TRADE REFORM, OBSERVERS IN Latin America and the Caribbean (LAC) are again asking a question of long standing in the region: Does the way in which the region integrates into the global market promise rapid growth and good jobs for its workers? Indeed, an old and central concern has re-emerged. In most LAC countries their rich natural resource endowments are still determining what they export. This is happening despite earlier predictions that LAC would follow the Asian manufacturing successes, and despite the widely heralded arrival of what we loosely call the "knowledge economy." The worry is that continued specialization in natural resources will leave LAC behind in the slower "old" economy.

More fundamentally, what determines what LAC will export in the 21st century? Traditional concepts of comparative advantage stress endowments of labor, land, capital, and natural resources. However, "new" trade theory stresses that at least as important are other "endowments" such as geography (distance to large markets), technical knowledge, human capital, public infrastructure, quality of institutions, and more generally the ability of firms to provide the right products to the right markets at the right time. Further, the spectacular decline in transport and communications costs over the last century has led to the "fragmentation" of production processes once performed in a single country into multiple stages of production dis-

tributed around the world. This fragmentation may imply that some successful development trajectories are now foreclosed, and may rekindle the concerns of the old dependency school that LAC will be stuck with the nondynamic parts of the global production process. Could natural resources not only be a curse, as some have argued, but now also LAC's inescapable destiny? Or by making increasingly unpredictable the ultimate location of industries, do the new facts and trade theories suggest opportunities for the region that were previously not imaginable?

The parallel concern is that recent decades have seen a diminishing quality of jobs measured in terms of wages, benefits, and working conditions. The most notable fact is the untold personal hardship caused by job loss in industries that could not compete internationally. The longer-term questions are about what can be expected when the dislocations of the transition to the new economic struc-

tures are over; that is, are these emerging jobs—in Export Processing Zones (EPZs), or *maquilas*, long-distance teleservices, nontraditional agriculture, and tourism—good jobs?

These themes are the subject of this, the annual World Bank publication for Latin America and the Caribbean. The report contributes to the debate in two ways. First, it takes stock of where LAC economies are as participants in the global economy by reviewing the trends in the region's exports, drawing lessons from close examination of emerging sectors, and locating the present reality in a historical and international context. Second, it looks at the bottom line of any trade policy: how workers and families have fared, and in particular, how much of the movements in income distribution and informality that took place in the last decade can be attributed to trade, what kinds of jobs are being created, and who benefits from them. The central question we ask is, then, what strategies and policies should a natural resource–rich country follow in order to develop and to improve the quality of jobs?

The report attempts to provide answers to a series of both positive and normative questions related to this fundamental concern. Specifically, we address a series of questions related to trade, natural resources, and growth in Chapters 2 to 4: Will LAC countries continue to specialize in commodities? Is their natural resource wealth their destiny? Can they build comparative advantages in technologically sophisticated economic activities related or unrelated to their natural resource wealth? Is their natural resource wealth a curse for development? Or, on the contrary, are natural resources assets for development? Is there or is there not an inescapable dilemma between the old economy based on natural resources and the new knowledge-intensive economy of the 21st century? Can natural resource–based activities be knowledge-intensive industries that lead development for a long time? In Chapter 5 we also address two questions related to trade and jobs: Are the new jobs emerging from free trade "poor-quality" jobs? Has free trade increased unemployment, informality, and wage inequality?

We attempted to answer these questions through a variety of approaches. We reviewed what new trade theories and recent empirical studies have to say on these subjects. We looked at available quantitative evidence and conducted cross-country panel data and econometric estimations to validate or contradict predictions from theory. We commissioned papers to draw lessons from comparative history (Australia, Finland, Sweden, and the United States compared with LAC), and case studies of recent LAC experiences (for Chile, new agricultural exports; for Mexico, the North American Free Trade Agreement [NAFTA] and the electronic complex in Jalisco; for Brazil, industrial productivity growth and aircraft exports; for Mercosur, export diversification in Argentina and Uruguay; for Costa Rica and El Salvador, foreign direct investment (FDI) and EPZs; for the Caribbean, tourism) by leading experts in the field and well-known local consultants.

We summarize our findings and answers to these questions in the following sections. But before doing so, and because we are a policy-oriented institution, we offer up front a summary of policy recommendations from our answers to the main normative questions related to these concerns: What should countries rich in natural resources do to develop and to improve the quality of their jobs? Should they turn away from their natural resources in attempting to develop new comparative advantages? How

should they bridge their natural resource wealth with the new knowledge economy?

## What Should Countries Rich in Natural Resources Do to Grow Faster and Improve the Quality of Their Jobs?

The policy recommendations that stem from this report can be conveniently grouped into three categories:

- Foster openness to trade, market access, and FDI flows.
- Build new endowments in human capital, knowledge, better institutions, and public infrastructure.
- Play to your strengths: don't turn your back on your natural advantages.

### Deepen Openness to Trade and FDI Flows . . . and Secure Market Access

We find in this report that opening to trade and FDI has led to export diversification (both within and outside natural resource–based activities) and to higher intra-industry trade (IIT) in the region, and we present evidence showing that such developments have been causally related to higher future growth elsewhere. We also find, as many previous studies have, that greater openness and FDI promote innovation and skills, and permit realizing the potential of natural advantages such as natural resource wealth, but also of such factors as location, size, natural beauty, and culture. Finally, we find that new jobs created by trade and FDI flows are "good jobs." Thus, Latin American countries would do well to deepen their efforts toward greater trade integration and attraction of FDI flows that have characterized the latter decade.

At the same time, however, we find that unilateral opening is often not enough. Protectionism in developed countries and developing countries alike limits the potential of export expansion in several activities in which LAC countries possess comparative advantages (agriculture, processing of raw materials, textiles and apparel, and services).[1] Uncertainty about continued market access often inhibits strong FDI and trade flows. In other words, secure market access is crucial for realizing the potential of trade and investment flows. Indeed, this report shows that NAFTA has contributed decisively to a large increase in Mexican trade and to a fundamental change in its production and trade structure, taking advantage of its locational advantages and the opportunities for fragmentation of production opened by the sharp reduction in transport and telecommunication costs. Also, the Caribbean Basin Initiative (CBI) has permitted some Central American and Caribbean countries (such as Costa Rica, the Dominican Republic, and El Salvador) to better exploit their locational advantages, though not to the same degree as Mexico.

Thus, LAC countries could obtain significant gains from a new development round centered in agriculture and services, and from further free trade agreements with Organisation for Economic Co-operation and Development (OECD) countries. The advancement of current negotiations with the United States toward bilateral trade agreements and the Free Trade Zone of the Americas, and with the European Union and Japan, acquire significant importance in this context. However, it should be said that other LAC countries may not benefit as much as Mexico from free trade agreements with the United States, because they do not possess the same locational advantages.

We also find that trade agreements among LAC countries can foster export diversification. Indeed, our study on Mercosur reveals that it has served as a platform for the development of new exports to third markets. It is thus useful to deepen such agreements, though because they may also entail some trade diversion costs, it is important to keep external tariffs low and relatively uniform. Open regionalism continues to be a good policy stance (see Burki, Perry, and Calvo 1997).

Establishing an enabling environment for FDI is an important complement to open trade policies. We find that FDI flows respond to better institutions, human capital, public infrastructure, and knowledge clusters (see below). But we also find that special regimes (like EPZs) can serve a useful purpose in countries with weak institutional infrastructure, because they help reduce transaction costs and enhance the credibility and predictability of policies to attract FDI. Naturally, such regimes must conform with World Trade Organization (WTO) agreements, and thus some of the tax incentive schemes that have been used by some countries will have to be phased out by 2003. Finally, we find some evidence in favor of active promotion programs, such as those developed by the Coalición Costarricense de Iniciativas de Desarrollo (CINDE), a public-private venture in Costa Rica.

## Build New Endowments

A crucial finding of this report is that countries can and do create new comparative advantages through policies that build new endowments. Indeed—validating the predictions of new trade theories—we find that "new" endow-

ments, such as human capital, knowledge, and good institutions and public infrastructure, explain as much, if not more, of the comparative advantages of countries and their evolution over time, as traditional factor endowments such as land, labor, and physical capital. Public policy has a large role in building up such endowments.[2]

- *General Education and Lifelong Learning.* Policies aimed at developing educational systems that provide quality education in general, but that are also focused on lifelong learning and training, are critical to building human capital. This is, in fact, a requirement to ensure that our workers can continuously upgrade *how* they produce in whatever sector they might be employed. It is also a prerequisite for the emergence of strong innovation systems.

- *Research and Development Incentives and Innovation Systems.* Knowledge and technical progress are the main force behind productivity growth and the emergence of new comparative advantages. This is an area where the public sector should be involved, due to the high spillover effects of knowledge that are unlikely to be promoted to their socially optimal level by private firms alone. This report argues that countries should experiment with various types of tax incentives and public subsidies to promote both private and public investments in research and development (R&D). However, the precise design of such policies will depend on the existing institutional capacity of the governments to enforce tax laws and monitor the quality of those investments. Adequate intellectual property rights protection is also essential for the development of innovations. In addition, public policy should promote the establishment of knowledge clusters and networks, encompassing private firms, independent research institutions and universities, and the public sector. Such developments are critically important not just for the so-called high-tech manufacturing sectors, but also for many natural resource–based activities.

- *The Special Role of Information and Communications Technology.* The evidence presented in this report suggests that information and communications technology (ICT) can help reduce coordination costs, which might enable firms to be more effectively plugged into international industrial clusters, ensure the dynamism of the tourism industry, and facilitate access to markets for nontraditional agricultural products. The role of the public sector in this area is to provide the appropriate enabling environment to allow the development of telecommunications infrastructure (for example, telephone lines and cellular telephony). That is, regulations should aim at raising the level of competition and access in domestic economies for the provision of these types of services.

- *Public Infrastructure.* Good public infrastructure is essential to reduce transportation costs and "economic distance" to markets. We find that it is especially important for the development of natural resource–based exports. In this context, improving the regulation of private investment in infrastructure appears as a major policy priority.

- *Good Institutions.* Last but not least, good institutions (rule of law, security, effective property rights, transparency, and doing away with excessive regulatory burdens, and efficiency of public service delivery) are critical for the efficiency of investment and productivity growth in all sectors of the economy, but especially for developing comparative advantages in technologically sophisticated industries.

### Play to Your Strengths: Don't Turn Your Back on Your Natural Advantages

This report finds that a major mistake in LAC's economic history has often been to turn its back to its natural advantages, whatever they may be: natural resources wealth, location, natural beauty, culture. Such attitudes have been largely driven by prejudices about the alleged superiority of manufacturing activities compared to natural resource–based activities. The evidence presented in this report should dispel such prejudices and other concerns about natural resource–based activities.

Indeed, natural resources–based activities can lead growth for long periods of time. This is patently evident in the development history of natural resource–rich developed countries, such as Australia, Finland, Sweden, and the United States. Mining was the main driver of growth and industrialization in Australia and the United States over more than a century, as forestry has been in Finland and Sweden. These countries continue to be significant net exporters of natural resource–based products, along with high-tech products. The recent success of Chile, with the highest growth rate in the region in the last 15 years, has been almost fully led by exports of natural resource–based products.

Natural resource–based activities can be knowledge industries. Mining was the "national learning experience" in the United States that led to building a strong technological system from which modern manufacturing developed. Forestry and forest products are highly knowledge intensive in Finland and Sweden, which explains why they remain competitive compared to countries with much lower wages. Fresh-fruit production and marketing in Chile has a high-tech content. Biotechnology is as high tech as chips and semiconductors, if not more.

Even more, the stock of natural resources themselves can be increased by the application of knowledge. This is especially evident in the case of oil. Just 30 years ago most analysts predicted that supplies from economically viable potential oil reserves would be limiting world growth by the end of the century. Thanks to advances in exploration and extraction techniques, proven oil reserves are today much larger than they were then. Venezuela significantly increased its economic oil reserves through the development of *oriemulsion*, allowing the commercial exploitation of large heavy crude reserves. Today Finland and Sweden have more forests than they did a hundred years ago.

The evidence presented in this report indicates that productivity growth in agriculture has outpaced that of manufacturing in both developed and developing countries. Productivity growth in agriculture in Latin America has increased significantly after trade reform, though in many countries there was an initial period of decrease. In short, natural resource–based activities can have high productivity growth, technical spillovers, and forward and backward linkages, as much as modern manufacturing. Such activities can become knowledge industries. They are in no way incompatible with the new knowledge economy.

What we found is that the key to success is to complement natural resource wealth with good institutions, human capital, and knowledge. Natural resources and knowledge are a proven growth recipe. Developing dynamic natural resource–based sectors is not incompatible, either, with building new comparative advantages in footloose and high-tech manufacturing. We find both sectors coexisting not only in natural resource–rich developed economies, but also in the already highly diversified export structure of Brazil and Mexico, and in small Costa Rica and the Dominican Republic. To what extent successful development will be based more in natural resource–based activities or in footloose manufacturing or service activities will depend largely on other trade advantages such as location or size. Countries close to the United States will more likely develop strong manufacturing links with that market through opportunities for fragmentation of production, especially because they have been able to secure market access through NAFTA and CBI-NAFTA parity. Small economies will not likely evolve as diversified production and trade structures as large Brazil or Mexico. But all of them will integrate successfully into the world economy if they play to their strengths and complement their natural advantages with human capital, knowledge systems, public infrastructure, and good institutions.

## Answering Old and New Concerns about Trade

### *What Determines What We Trade: Traditional and "New" Endowments—Natural Resources Are Not Destiny*

At a very aggregate level, the export profiles of most of the countries of the region have, with few exceptions, changed remarkably little since the early 1980s. The finding that LAC remains an exporter of goods intensive in natural resources is undeniable, and therefore merits special attention. But it is also true that countries like Costa Rica, the Dominican Republic, and Mexico have experienced dramatic changes that are as informative about the possible future trade patterns of the region.

The cross-country evidence presented in Chapter 2 indicates that the structure of trade is, indeed, determined by traditional notions of factor endowments including labor, capital, natural resources, and land. However, the data also show that modern concepts of national endowments emphasized by modern trade theory also have substantial explanatory power. It is not surprising that the comparative advantage in resource-based activities is mostly determined by natural resource endowments, and that labor-intensive manufactures appear where labor is plentiful. In contrast, net exporters of capital-intensive goods, machinery, and chemicals have much higher levels of "modern" endowments, especially knowledge in the case of capital-intensive activities, and knowledge, education, ICT, and quality public institutions in the cases of chemicals and machines. But what is striking is that net exporters of forestry products and cereals also have high levels of these nontraditional factors. Hence, the endowments of the "knowledge economy" also seem to be important for some natural resource–based activities. Overall, the statistical evidence shows

that, especially for manufactures but also for certain agricultural products, the "new" endowments explain a larger share of the international differences in comparative advantage than traditional endowments.

Falling transport and communication costs have spawned new industries such as specialty vegetables in Guatemala, flowers in Colombia, fresh fruits in Chile, teleservices in Jamaica, and tourism in previously isolated locales. They have also enabled the fragmentation of production processes that were previously largely contained in the industrialized countries. Indeed, the statistical evidence shows that comparative advantage in labor-intensive manufactures exhibits a higher over-time variation during the last quarter century than all other commodity groups examined in this report. This fact can be interpreted as indicating that developing a comparative advantage in these types of goods is more likely to occur than for other commodities. Not only do countries like El Salvador and Mexico provide the labor-intensive subprocesses of many globally assembled products, but Guadalajara has become a printer design center for Hewlett-Packard, and Costa Rica now hosts Intel's most recent chip-manufacturing plant, with spillovers in design and software. However, pronouncements of the "death of distance" have been overstated. It is not coincidental that these countries are close to the largest global market.

Trade openness, together with the accumulation of "modern" endowments, has also helped diversify exports and increase IIT (that is, the share of total trade accounted for by exports and imports of similar products). Indeed, there was significant export diversification and an increase in IIT in LAC during the 1990s, the latter encouraged by higher levels of education, openness, better institutions, and infrastructure. Regional integration efforts also contributed to the transformation of the patterns of trade and to increasing export diversification and IIT. This conclusion is supported by the evidence discussed in our case study of the influence of NAFTA on the Mexican economy, and to a lesser extent by our study of the effects of Mercosur on Argentina.

### *Natural Resources Are Not a Curse but an Asset for Development*

However, most countries find themselves again concentrating in natural resource–based products, and this has raised concerns dating back centuries. No less an economist than Adam Smith wrote in 1776 that "projects of mining, instead of replacing the capital employed in them, together with the ordinary profits of stock, commonly absorb both capital and stock. They are the projects, therefore, to which of all others a prudent law-giver, who desired to increase the capital of his nation, would least choose to give any extraordinary encouragement. . . ." The best-known critiques of natural resource–based development in LAC came from Prebisch (1959) and Singer (1950). They were concerned about an apparent long-term deterioration of the prices of these commodities relative to the price of manufactures imported by the region. They also believed that technical progress opportunities were limited relative to those in manufactures. In modern times, Jeffrey Sachs and Andrew Warner (1995a) from the Harvard Center for International Development found that during two decades of the late 20th century, 1970 to 1989, countries rich in natural resources grew more slowly than their counterparts.

This case is not strong. First, the sample period is not historically representative. As Maddison (1994) shows, from 1913 to 1950, resource-rich countries, including LAC countries, grew faster than the then-industrialized countries, and Asia experienced negative growth. Further, Sachs and Warner's period includes the "lost decade" of the 1980s, which resulted from abuse of easy foreign indebtedness in the 1970s, the traumatic demise of the protectionist model of development, and the wrenching transitions to more open economies. Though some of these factors are correlated with natural resource abundance, none are intrinsic to it.

## Lessons from Successful Natural Resource–Rich Countries: Play to Your Strengths

The most convincing evidence is offered by history: it is impossible to argue that Australia, Canada, Finland, Sweden, and the United States did not base their development on their natural resources. In fact, even today they are net exporters of natural resource–based products.

The evidence is now strong that the U.S. industrial success resulted from a gradual transition to resource-intensive manufacturing industries, and only quite late in its development to more knowledge-intensive industries. Canada was the country that inspired "staples theory"—where primary goods exports drive development over an extended period of time through either demand or supply linkages.

Although wool is Australia's most famous staple, extraordinary and continuing success in mining, and the deriv-

ative industries of both, made Australia one of the richest economies in the world by the early 20th century. The discoveries of new deposits and the generation and export of mining-related knowledge—in mineral detection, environmentally sound mining practices, and processing, all based on a massive educational and research infrastructure—may put it near the top of the list again. One of Australia's most famous mining firms, Broken Hill Propriety, Ltd., established long after Chile began copper mining, discovered and manages Chile's largest mine, La Escondida.

The Scandinavian countries that produce aircraft, luxury cars, designer furniture and, most recently, advanced telecommunications products, also built slowly on their strengths in natural resources. Sweden's Volvo and Saab emerged partially as backward linkages of the forestry industry, but perhaps more interesting is how Nokia, originally a wood-pulp producer, became a major player in the global cellular phone industry. The key elements were organizational structures, knowledge networks, and aggressive human capital policies that, though developed to pursue resource processing, were transferable to high-tech industries. In short, the historical record is clear: when managed well and located in the proper institutional framework, natural resources can be vital for development.

### Prebisch Revisited

What happened to Prebisch's twin concerns in light of this historical experience? If anything, the modern literature on decreasing transport costs and agglomeration externalities (Puga and Venables 1999) offers a formalization of dependency theory and possible confirmation of its diagnosis. If manufactures are a more dynamic sector than natural resource–based sectors, either, to paraphrase Prebisch, because of decreasing relative prices or lower possibilities for technological progress, then decreasing transport costs may lead to a "deindustrialization" of the South that reduces its long-term dynamism.

But the emerging literature and several papers commissioned for this study suggest that on both counts Prebisch was too pessimistic. First, the worsening terms-of-trade effect was probably a false alarm. Economic historians have documented increasing relative commodity prices throughout the 19th century. Most recently, Harvard historian Jeff Williamson has argued that Prebisch was probably wrong about their decline at the beginning of the 20th century. Rapidly decreasing transport costs made LAC's commodities appear relatively cheaper in London, where Prebisch measured them, but the reverse would have been true in the Port of Buenos Aires. Finally, a paper by Cuddington, Ludema, and Jayasuriya (2001), commissioned for this project, concludes that from the beginning of the century to 1973, there was no trend in relative commodity prices.

Second and more important, the view that manufacturing has something special (in terms of backward and forward linkages, technological innovation, and other potential externalities), must be called into question—as many contemporaries of Prebisch did (such as Viner 1952 and North 1955). More than what is produced, the important issue is whether there is an enabling environment for adopting technologies. Modern growth literature increasingly stresses the development of "national innovative capacity," or the ability of countries to produce and commercialize knowledge over the long term. This capacity is determined by interrelationships among a variety of social institutions (universities, research centers) and actors (private firms, the public sector).

Evidence is offered by Martin and Mitra (2001), who examine total factor productivity (TFP) growth—the part of growth unaccounted for by the increase in measurable factors such as land, labor, or capital—in agriculture and manufacturing from 1967 to 1992 for a large sample of countries. Not only was TFP growth 50 percent faster in agriculture than in manufactures, but the industrialized countries experienced rates substantially above those of less developed countries (LDCs). In fact, several of the big natural resource success stories—Denmark, France, and Sweden—continue to show the highest TFP growth rates in agriculture.

Work conducted for this book on LAC agriculture confirmed that agricultural productivity increased in all countries after trade reforms. The most successful case in terms of output per worker and export growth during 1980–99 in agriculture was Chile. Part of this successful experience was due to adequate macroeconomic management and, especially, a competitive and relatively stable real exchange rate. As important was Chile's long history of experimenting with various types of sector-specific programs that provided incentives for private investment, for expanding productive capacity, and for promoting research and development in the sector. The main lesson we derive from this case study is that policymakers should be encouraged to experiment with various mechanisms for promoting innovation, especially in

sectors where the country has a clear comparative advantage. R&D policies should not underestimate the innovative potential that can be unleashed in agricultural activities.

Mining or forestry can be a low-innovation sector with few possibilities for long-term growth, but in the cases mentioned above, this was emphatically not the case, nor is it the case today. Tree harvesting, pulp and paper processing, and other downstream industries continue to show productivity gains in Finland and Sweden. As Wright (1999) argues, "mining, in the U.S. case, was fundamentally a collective learning phenomenon," and this applies to the Australian experience as well. Natural wealth itself is not fully exogenous, and the stock of economically useful oil or mineral reserves (or productive land) is a function of knowledge and improvements in exploration and extraction techniques. Brazil's discovery of vast new deposits of iron ore, bauxite, tin, and copper using satellite technologies confirms this insight.

Tourism is a natural beauty–based growth industry worldwide, with expenditures growing by 3.8 percent annually in the last two decades. The case study included here suggests that in several Caribbean countries it supports high living standards and has been an important substitute for the declining sugar and banana industries. LAC has slipped in market share over the last decades, but could increase the sector's dynamism with an aggressive program of product differentiation (ecotourism, historical and cultural tourism, adventure tourism) and infrastructure, enhancing skills, ICT, and marketing research to compete with new locations. Again, a successful strategy requires not only the natural resources, but also complementary inputs in human capital, technical knowledge, and infrastructure.

In a nutshell, both the historical and recent LAC experiences reviewed in this report reveal that what is important is not *what* countries produce, but *how*. In all these cases, a large knowledge network (or cluster) that generates innovation and facilitates the adoption of foreign technologies, stands out as a critical ingredient in sectoral dynamism.

Finally, the concern that natural resource–intensive exports will crowd out other promising industries seems less problematic than often thought. Although Norway and the República Bolivariana de Venezuela do show evidence that their massive development of petroleum or natural gas has precluded other industries, Chile and Sweden do not, and they are arguably more similar to the majority of LAC's economies.

### Lessons from LAC History: Don't Turn Your Back on Your Natural Advantages

Why, then, were LAC countries not as successful in using their natural wealth as a basis for development? Our historical review indicates that several factors prevented such an outcome during most of the 19th and early 20th centuries: political instability, barriers to trade, weak property rights, deficient infrastructure, volatile public finances, and, especially, poor general and technical education and other barriers to innovation explicitly related to knowledge management and generation.

After World War II there was an additional factor: LAC countries turned their backs on their natural wealth. They opted for promoting an import-substitution industrialization strategy that did not play to their endowment strengths, discouraged innovation in manufacturing, and taxed the natural resource sectors in myriad ways. While we do observe a continuum of inefficient interventions in favor of the manufacturing sector to the detriment of the resource-exporting sector in other natural resource–rich countries, neither Australia, Canada, nor Scandinavia had the extreme turn toward inward-looking policies, or the dramatic macrodisequilibria that gave Latin America a special fame. At the extreme end of the continuum, we find Swedish labor unions across all sectors militantly insisting on an open trade stance and energetic pursuit of productivity-enhancing technologies.

The two phenomena were self-reinforcing: recurring balance-of-payment problems led to a greater distrust of the global market and to political instability, and discouraged entrepreneurship and barriers to innovation. Arguably, the measures to coax rapid manufacturing growth out of countries with substantial structural barriers to innovation and without a scientific tradition led to heavy rates of taxation on traditional sectors. In the end, the protected manufacturing industries lacked long-term dynamism, and the potential of the natural resource–based sectors was squandered.

## Building New Areas of Comparative Advantage

Many skeptics of natural resource–led development will accept these historical arguments, but will deny that previously successful experiences of natural resource–based development are replicable under today's conditions. In particular, the sharp reduction in transport costs that took place in the last century eliminated the "natural protection" that some natural resource–rich countries used to

their advantage in developing forward linkages from natural resources. If true, authors of the emerging literature ought to be cautious about urging the promotion of industrial "clusters," and readers should be cautious about believing what they read. The fragmentation process implies large efficiency gains, and forcing uneconomical productive chains may be little more than inefficient industrial policy.

The overall conclusion of both our empirical findings on the determinants of trade specialization and the new theory is that in the current context of globalization, it is difficult to predict where industries will be located in the future. The main reason for this is that international flows of intermediate goods, knowledge, capital, and labor, facilitated by low transport costs and improvements in communications technology, open up opportunities for industries of various degrees of technological sophistication to be established almost anywhere around the globe.

Thus, some Central American and Caribbean economies have been highly successful in attracting FDI and in developing labor-intensive exports to the United States through EPZs. These regimes reduce transaction costs, and provide a stable and reliable regime for FDI (that is, they are efficient and stable institutions) and corporate income tax incentives. Costa Rica has been able to attract more high-tech FDI than other countries in the subregion, and indeed has built an impressive and dynamic cluster in electronics, the well-known Intel plant being the crown jewel. We find that this achievement was possible mainly due to its higher level of human capital, but also to the general quality of its institutions and active promotion policies undertaken by CINDE.

Compared to the rest of LAC, since the mid-1990s Mexico experienced the most impressive transformation of its trade and productive structure. The critical factor is that Mexico finally decided to play to its strength—proximity to the largest and most technologically advanced economy in the world. The case study on the electronics industry, which has been one of the most dynamic in the Mexican economy during recent years, indicates the importance of incipient knowledge clusters and throws further light on the role of public policy. Particularly after the implementation of NAFTA, the computer and telecommunications equipment industry in Jalisco has attracted the providers of electronics manufacturing services and the suppliers of parts and components used in other locations throughout the world. These investments appear to be leading to the creation of integrated supply chains, which could lead to important gains in efficiency, based on both lower costs and better logistics. Overall, this case highlights the possibility of evolving from pure *maquila*-type assembly operations to skill-intensive manufacturing and R&D activities, successfully integrated into global networks.

A case study on Brazil's Empresa Brasileira de Aeronautica (EMBRAER), a major exporter of aircraft, sheds additional light on the possibility of developing industries unrelated to traditional endowments, and on the importance of an outward orientation and knowledge infrastructure. Early on, EMBRAER combined high R&D investments with strategic partnerships with foreign companies in order to achieve its present technological capacity, while always keeping an eye on foreign markets in which it now competes very successfully. It is also clear, however, that the necessary government support to get EMBRAER to this point was substantial, and it is not clear that the net present value of these public subsidies is positive, or that there are major spillovers to other industries. Thus this case raises the issue of how far policy should go in supporting high-tech industries, even when they are commercially successful after many years of government subsidies.

What these experiences, and the teleservices industries in Jamaica, the smelting industry in Trinidad that processes Brazilian ore, and myriad others tell us is that today it is possible for developing countries to build comparative advantages in technologically advanced activities, even if these appear unrelated to their original endowments of natural resources. They need not, and indeed may not be able to, replicate the paths followed by developed countries. But the recipe for success depends more than ever on efficient institutions and investment in human capital, technical knowledge, and infrastructure.

## Are the New Jobs Good Jobs?

The region has seen some disturbing trends in job quality over the last decade. But it is not clear how much these are related to trade liberalization and, if they are, whether they are permanent.

In terms of unemployment, the region has seen some very substantial reallocations of its workforce after trade opening. Large numbers of workers lost their jobs in previously protected industries, and some experienced either very long periods of unemployment, large wage losses, or both. Further, formal sector employment has grown rela-

tively slowly, due either to overall slower growth or to productivity gains that reduce labor absorption.

These dislocations, though extremely costly in human terms, are transitional, and do not imply permanently higher rates of unemployment, as shown by the experiences of Chile and Mexico, the two economies in the region where trade exposure has increased the most. Overall, unemployment rates were not especially higher in the 1990s compared to the 1970s, except in countries with restrictive labor policies, such as Argentina and Colombia.

There is no obvious channel through which greater openness would lead to a degradation of wages. We find that classification of manufactures by increasing sophistication—labor intensive, capital intensive, machinery, and chemicals—is reflected in increasing wages, even after adjusting for human capital. What is not obviously true is that these sectors offer "better" jobs than petroleum, mining, forestry products, and even tropical agriculture in terms of returns to human capital. Further, it appears that in countries as diverse as Argentina, Brazil, Costa Rica, the Dominican Republic, and Mexico, those industries most exposed to international competition pay the highest wages.

Much of the literature, in fact, attributes the observed worsening of wage distribution in many countries to an increased demand for skills as a result of trade liberalization. In fact, the evidence suggests that very little of the observed movements appear to be attributable directly to trade, and supply-side factors, such as long-term movements in education and the dramatic entry of women into the labor force, are easily as important. Nonetheless, it raises the important point that, over the short term, the creation of "better" jobs, in the sense of requiring high skills and better education—the jobs we want—may imply a tradeoff with wage distribution. Strikingly, the increased inequality in northern Mexico is attributed to the fact that the jobs brought through the *maquilas* and NAFTA, while low skilled by U.S. standards, are above average by Mexican standards, and hence have increased the skill premium. Public policy must take advantage of the opportunity that higher skill premiums present (enhanced incentives for families and workers to improve educational levels and skills) to improve the supply of quality education and training. If they do, the end result may be a higher overall level of real wages, with lower (or at least no more) wage disparities than before. In fact, in the two countries with the longest history of liberalization, Chile and Mexico, the trend toward widening wage disparities reversed itself several years after liberalization.

The growth of the "unprotected" or informal sector in the region has been especially noted: the Economic Commission for Latin America and the Caribbean (ECLAC) suggests that 60 percent of new jobs in the 1990s were created in the informal sector. What drives this, and how we should think about it, is not obvious, however. In some cases, such as Colombia after 1997, the traditional dualistic view of formal sector rigidities forcing unwilling workers into marginal informal jobs has merit, although it is not clear that there was any link to trade liberalization. But what is striking is that in Argentina, Brazil, and Mexico, informal self-employment expanded, along with an increase in relative informal incomes in the beginning of the 1990s, at the same time that the exchange rate appreciated. This suggests that the dramatic rise in informality during this period was driven in part by increased opportunities in the nontradeables sector that boomed in many countries of the region following the liberalization of capital accounts and stabilization programs.

A little reflection suggests that there probably should not be a relationship between trade and informality. Aggressive exporters such as Belgium, the Republic of Korea, and Singapore, or resource-intensive economies such as Australia, Canada, Finland, Sweden, and the United States, have low levels of informality. We find no secular trend either in total share of informal salaried workers, or the number of informal microfirms linked to large or exporting firms in Mexico after liberalization or NAFTA. In fact, the share of firms that declare any linkage to large or exporting firms is so small as to suggest that arguments that informality is primarily a way for exporting firms to avoid paying benefits through subcontracts seems without any basis. The macroeconomic fluctuations driven by attempting to stabilize the peso had a far more obvious effect on short-term informality levels than any long-term trend that might be attributed to NAFTA. We argue, in fact, that the problem is not excessive or exploitive integration of microenterprises in the global economy, but rather barriers to more extensive integration posed by onerous registration procedures, deficient credit markets, and poor availability of information.

We also address the concern that the jobs being created are somehow inferior by looking at four new types of jobs in the *maquilas* or EPZs, the teleservice industry, nontra-

ditional agriculture, and tourism. We find the criticism to be overstated. Though wages and benefits are lower than in similar jobs in industrialized countries (that is one of the reasons why some of these jobs are relocating to developing countries), they are higher than for average or comparable jobs in the country in question. Interviews with workers suggest that this is precisely why they take them.

Who ends up employed or benefiting from these new jobs depends on the characteristics of the individual worker. People, like nations, trade based on their comparative advantages. A striking fact that emerges in case after case is that women have dominated the workforce in emerging industries. This is a pattern that was observed in the industrialized countries a century ago as well, and to some degree it arose because most men were already working, and hence women were available to fill the new employment opportunities. But in most sectors a range of gender-linked characteristics ranging from dexterity to reliability and lower incidence of alcoholism appear to motivate employers' choices. For the most part, female-dominated jobs tend to represent opportunities, and may have social repercussions beyond the purely economic.

Significant improvements in job quality over the short term are circumscribed by basic economic constraints. Most of these new jobs tend to be in industries where wage increases not matched by productivity gains might erode competitive advantages and force firms to fail or relocate elsewhere. Over the longer term, better-paying jobs in better conditions can only be achieved by increasing the skills of the workers, and encouraging some degree of differentiation in products, and most fundamentally, by raising productivity. In the end, the process of raising job quality is the process of development.

## Conclusion

We must reiterate that rich endowments of natural resources, combined with the aggressive pursuit and adoption of new technologies, are a proven growth recipe. Further, the evidence strongly indicates that their development does not preclude the development of manufacturing or other activities in the "knowledge" economy. In short, countries that have "played to their strengths" have done well.

An equally important lesson is that what is important is not so much *what* is produced, but *how* it is produced. Taking advantage of global technological progress is essential in every field, and it cannot be done cheaply. The recurrent lesson of the successful natural resource developers, and of contemporary theory, is the necessity of engendering a high level of human capital and developing a capacity for "national" learning and innovation. The present literature on how nations learn and what types of policies are necessary is in its infancy, and we make no pretensions to providing a road map in this area. However, since the knowledge produced by one firm can be applied by others, the road toward the "new" knowledge economy can and should be paved by public policies.

## Notes

1. See a description of the use of protectionist instruments in place (tariff peaks, tariff escalation, subsidies, quotas, antidumping) and their limiting effect on LDC exports in World Bank 2001.

2. Though they are also to some extent endogenous to the process of growth and development.

# CHAPTER 2

# Comparative Advantage, Diversification, and Intra-Industry Trade: Determinants and Consequences

Most countries of the Latin America and Caribbean region liberalized their economies during the late 1980s and early 1990s. This process of liberalization included trade reforms, whereby import tariffs were slashed and nontariff barriers were reduced and simplified, and the welcoming of FDI. Much progress has also been made in other areas of reform, especially in macroeconomic stabilization and privatization (Burki and Perry 1997).

When the reforms were first debated, it was broadly expected that the region would specialize in labor-intensive production of goods and services. However, the evidence presented in this chapter shows that the region's revealed comparative advantage has in fact changed little since the early 1980s. On average, the region has maintained a comparative advantage in the production of commodities that have a relatively high content of natural resources, and it has an advantage in the various types of land used for the harvesting of agricultural goods. It remains a net importer of capital- and labor-intensive manufactures. Despite the lack of structural change in the region's trade patterns, however, there have been significant productivity gains, and consumers also now enjoy greater varieties of high-quality products.

Given the concerns discussed in Chapter 1 about the consequences of different patterns of trade, the first step in the analysis should be to briefly review new trade theories that seek to evaluate the factors that help determine what countries produce. This is done in the next section. The subsequent discussion identifies the revealed comparative advantage of LAC economies during the last two decades of the 20th century, and empirically examines how traditional and modern notions of national endowments affect the structure of international trade and how trade structure in turn affects the rate of economic growth. Special emphasis is placed on the role of public policies. The conclusion is that trade liberalization and the development of modern factors of production can help accelerate the pace of development in the region. What matters is how we produce, not what we export.

## New Trade Theories, New Endowments, and New Patterns of Trade

The theory of international trade has been transformed in recent decades, with the focus of study shifting away from the stylized world of perfect markets, identical technologies across countries, and immobility of factors and inputs of production across borders. Recent literature instead has tended to emphasize the following:

- The role of input trade (Jones 2000; Jones and Findlay 2001)
- Frictions in international trade and investment flows due to geography, institutions, transport, and information costs (Venables 2001; Bond 2001)
- The transmission of knowledge across borders (Grossman and Helpman 1991)

- Technological differences across borders (Trefler 1995; Hakura 2001)
- Monopolistic competition in differentiated products with increasing returns to scale (Krugman 1979; Ruffin 1999).

These new considerations do not mean that the traditional notions of comparative advantage and trade driven by cross-country differences in relative factor endowments are no longer operational. Rather, traditional notions of endowments can be combined with the modern considerations to provide a rich conceptual framework for understanding how and why LAC developed the patterns of trade we observe today.

Perhaps the main lesson from the new theories is that anything is possible. A common pattern of integration in today's global economy is characterized by the fragmentation of the manufacturing of labor-intensive goods (Jones 2000). This structure of trade is observed, for example, in the Dominican Republic, El Salvador, and, to a lesser extent, in Costa Rica and Mexico. The term "fragmentation" tries to capture the idea that the capital-intensive stage of production is conducted mainly in the industrialized, capital-rich economies, while the labor-intensive stage of the production process is conducted in the developing countries, where labor costs are lower.

The main difference between this and the traditional pattern of inter-industry trade is that the transportation of intermediate goods from capital-rich economies to developing countries has now become cheap enough for it to be profitable to export the intermediate good for processing in the developing country. The costs of shipping the finished goods back to the rich consumer markets also must be relatively low for this pattern of trade to be profitable. In sum, the costs of sending the capital input to the developing economy plus the costs of sending finished manufactures back must be lower than the profit gains realized through locating the labor-intensive stage of the manufacturing process in the developing economy. Consequently, it is not surprising that this pattern of trade has emerged in several of the LAC economies located close to the U.S. market. The manufacturing firms in these economies have become part of international industrial clusters, a concept analyzed further below.

A third pattern of trade features linkages between natural resource sectors and domestically manufactured intermediate goods. This is a type of backward linkage, originally analyzed by Hirschman (1958), which is often cited in the literature on industrial clusters (see Bergman and Feser 2001). Perhaps the clearest examples of this pattern of trade have been observed in Finland and Sweden, two economies that have rich forestland and that export forest products (see Chapter 3). Both countries have developed sophisticated, export-oriented, high-tech industries from industries that originally provided inputs for the production of forest products. Similar backward linkages are present in various LAC economies, where mining or agricultural products buy inputs and hire services from other sectors; in Chile, for example, the mining industry hires local engineering services (Meller 2001). These backward linkages do not always result in the development of a separate export industry, however.

Hirschman was also the first to discuss forward linkages from natural resources, such as those observed in the development of the steel industry in the United States during the 19th century (Jones and Findlay 2001). Currently, forward linkages can be seen in the metallurgical industry in Brazil and other developing countries, but low transport costs in the 20th century have reduced the profitability of these types of linkages by fragmenting the stages of production of steel and of other metallurgical industries, with ores now exported for manufacturing to countries that have the know-how, the capital, and other factors needed to most efficiently produce the final products. An additional constraint on LAC countries hoping to develop forward linkages from their agricultural or mining activities is the trade policies of major export markets that favor the export of basic commodities by discriminating against imports of processed raw materials—policies designed to protect domestic industries that process agricultural or natural resources.

The rise of intra-industry trade (IIT)—that is, exports and imports of similar goods—is perhaps the most noteworthy feature of the post–World War II global economy. This type of trade is clearly observed in the case of Mexico, which exports electronics and automobiles to the United States, but which also imports similar products. A key ingredient in Mexico's case is FDI and the importation of capital and other inputs for the production of these goods. The literature on the determinants of IIT (see Krugman 1979) emphasizes that the emergence of such trade depends on product differentiation, in which firms across borders produce similar goods that are distinguished from one another by brand or by other subtle differences. The main driving force of IIT in this context, however, is increasing returns to scale—that is, unit costs of production that decline as the quantity produced increases. In other words, productivity gains are at the center of the competitive process that yields IIT. This pattern of trade can thus emerge when industries benefit from either large initial investments or fixed costs (Ruffin 1999), or when producers become more efficient through experience or through the introduction of technological innovations from abroad or from nearby industries (see Venables 2001, for a literature review.) The next section explores the empirical determinants of IIT.

Agglomeration, or clustering, effects have also received substantial attention (Puga and Venables 1999). The distinguishing feature of such effects is that the production of one type of final good leads to the development of new manufacturing processes as a consequence of learning spillovers; for example, firms in certain knowledge-intensive sectors can learn from the experience of other firms and thus develop new products. The emergence of this type of horizontal cluster has been observed in geographic areas including Silicon Valley in California, and around certain firms in Costa Rica and Mexico. The rapid decline in the costs of information dissemination since the late 20th century suggests that the geographic dimension of industrial clusters might become less important, but the process nonetheless demonstrates that a vibrant manufacturing sector can emerge in formerly agricultural or mining economies as a consequence of foreign investment, input trade, and learning spillovers across firms. As discussed by Puga and Venables, trade liberalization, by reducing the costs of imported inputs, can lead to agglomeration effects that result in significant welfare and productivity gains for developing countries. In contrast, protectionism might lead to much less dynamic industrialization.

The following sections investigate in more detail the formation of industrial clusters and the role of geography and knowledge in fomenting clusters, and include a discussion of the impact of logistics costs in determining trade structure. They also address some issues of measurement and the correlation between ICT and knowledge and the level of development.

## New Factor Endowments: Industrial Clusters, Logistics Costs, and ICT and Knowledge

### Clusters, Geography, and Knowledge

There is a popular specialized literature that emphasizes that national economies, and the world economy more generally, are replete with examples of firms that are linked to each other either as competitors or as parts in a single supply chain (Porter 1990). Sometimes these firms are geographically nearby. Bergman and Feser (2001) state that an "industry cluster may be defined very generally as a group of business enterprises and nonbusiness organizations for whom membership within the group is an important element of each member firm's individual competitiveness." It cannot be overstated that an industrial cluster is held together by the profit objectives of the individual firms—that is, each firm benefits from its relationship or proximity to the other firms in the cluster.

Business administration literature defines a plethora of different types of clusters, of which vertical and horizontal clusters are perhaps the two main categories. Vertical industrial clusters comprise groups of firms that are part of a single supply chain. The textile-apparel cluster, for example, includes firms that supply textiles to other firms, which manufacture clothing and apparel to be sold to consumers. The profitability of firms belonging to such clusters depends to a large extent on their capacity to supply the inputs and the final goods on time. Given that transport costs can help determine the profitability of a firm, geography can thus play an important role in the establishment of these clusters. Coordination and transaction costs are also important, together with transport costs comprising what some analysts call logistics costs (Guasch and Kogan 2001; Bond 2001). It is in large part because transport and coordination costs are likely to be negatively correlated with distance that vertical industrial clusters often appear as regional clusters or as a regional agglomeration of industries.

Horizontal industrial clusters comprise firms that produce similar products, and that learn techniques and management practices from each other. In economic terms, if one firm's activities benefit others, the positive effects of those activities that go beyond the firms' confines are called "externalities." Venables (2001) writes that the "externalities generated in one sector will typically only affect firms in a set of industries, perhaps the same industry or others that are in some way linked to it." The main sort of technological externalities are knowledge spillovers, such as the spillover of research and development activities, technical or managerial know-how, or the knowledge accumulated with experience (that is, learning by doing).

Horizontal industrial clusters sustained by positive knowledge spillovers are often also geographically agglomerated. This is due less to transport costs, which play an insignificant role in the transmission of knowledge, than to the interaction and information exchange between firm managers. Perhaps more important, agglomeration effects can be the result of the existence of trained workers who "job-hop" across firms, taking with them the knowledge and training accumulated while working for different firms (Cooper 2001).

An interesting issue to consider in reference to the agglomeration of firms in a horizontal cluster is whether the recent ICT advances might dilute the advantage of geographic proximity for the sharing of knowledge across firms. The following subsections focus on the role of logistics costs, knowledge, and ICT in determining both economic structure and aggregate performance, with a special emphasis on measurement issues.

### Logistics Costs

Logistics costs can be thought of as the costs of getting the right goods to the right location at the right time.[1] These costs include freight, storage, warehousing, insurance, and administrative costs. They relate both to the selling of final goods and to the purchase of intermediate goods.

There are several factors that affect logistics costs in a country. Geography, the quality of infrastructure, and the management techniques of firms are the most obvious ones. Countries closer to major markets can bring their goods to these markets at lower costs simply because smaller distances have to be traveled to deliver the goods. Also, infrastructure increases the efficiency of the transport system and favors competition on transport networks. Thus, shipping costs may be high because of the inefficient transport system, such as in Mercosur, where three quarters of the overland trade between Brazil and its partners travels over a single bridge. Costs can be reduced by the adoption of more effective management of the supply chain, and higher coordination among firms, as in the just-in-time inventory management techniques that led to substantial productivity improvements in the United States.

These logistics costs are particularly important in analyzing international trade, because a firm dealing in foreign markets faces higher costs than local producers. This difference arises not only because of the transport costs of shipping goods between countries, but also because of the communication and coordination costs of organizing the supply chain at a distance and in a foreign country. Inter-

national Monetary Fund (IMF) statistics indicate that for the countries in the bottom quartile of income distribution (based on per capita gross domestic product [GDP] in 1990), the average transport cost for importable goods was 20 percent of the value of imports. For countries in the top quartile, the average transport cost rate on imports was only 6.3 percent.

This difference in transport cost rates presents a significant barrier for firms in developing countries to entering foreign markets, both in terms of the cost of getting goods to market and in terms of acquiring imported inputs. It also provides protection to relatively inefficient import-competing firms in developing countries. In this sense, the effects of logistics costs are analogous to those of the "effective rate of protection" from the tariff literature: the value added in a particular production activity is changed for given prices of the primary factors of production. The way this change occurs depends on the characteristics of the activity, related to the importance of transportation costs for the final product and for the intermediate goods.

The main determinants of logistics costs are the location of a country and the quality of the infrastructure. Table 2.1 presents several of these measures of logistics costs for different regions of the world. These measures are, from columns (1) to (8): average transport costs (CIF/FOB−1); average air distance to the closest major market (Asia, Europe, and North America); port efficiency index (based on a shipper survey, from 1 [lowest quality] to 7 [highest quality]); average number of days it takes for goods to clear customs (based on the median response from a survey of importers); kilometers of paved roads per square kilometer; kilometers of railroad lines per square kilometer; telephone main lines per capita; and air freight per capita (logarithms for these last four variables).

As can be seen from Table 2.1, the various measures of infrastructure are quite highly correlated. Indeed, high-income countries have values of all infrastructure measures that are from 1 to 1.35 standard deviations above the world average, while Sub-Saharan Africa lags in all measures with quantities from 0.6 to 1 standard deviation below the world average.

The evidence also suggests that logistics costs faced by LAC countries are significantly higher than those of developed countries (see Table 2.2 for values for specific countries). Nevertheless, there seems to be nothing special about LAC: once one controls for the income level, popula-

TABLE 2.1

**Transport Costs and Infrastructure by Country Groups**

| COUNTRY GROUP | AVERAGE TRANSPORT COSTS (CIF/FOB–1) (1) | AVERAGE DISTANCE TO CLOSEST MAJOR MARKET (2) | PORT EFFICIENCY INDEX (3) | MEDIAN CLEARING TIME AT PORT (4) | KM OF PAVED ROADS PER KM² (5) | KM OF RAILROAD LINES PER KM² (6) | TELEPHONE MAIN LINES PER CAPITA (7) | AIRFREIGHT PER CAPITAL (8) | GDP PER CAPITA (9) |
|---|---|---|---|---|---|---|---|---|---|
| Developed Countries | 4.24 | 1,561 | 5.76 | 3.50 | 1.15 | 1.02 | 1.35 | 1.16 | 2.11 |
| South America | 9.83 | 6,528 | 2.84 | 8.81 | –0.65 | –0.65 | 0.16 | –0.12 | –0.12 |
| Central America | 10.96 | 3,086 | 3.59 | 6.56 | 0.09 | –0.04 | 0.24 | –0.33 | –0.37 |
| Middle East and North Africa | 10.12 | 3,512 | 3.77 | 5.50 | –0.09 | –0.32 | 0.20 | –0.11 | –0.08 |
| Sub-Saharan Africa | 19.54 | 6,237 | 4.55 | 12.00 | –0.73 | –0.60 | –1.07 | –0.60 | –0.70 |
| South Asia | 9.74 | 5,121 | 2.79 | n.a. | 0.20 | –0.01 | –1.00 | –0.53 | –0.67 |
| Transition Economies | n.a. | 2,248 | 3.30 | 4.13 | 1.14 | 0.97 | 0.46 | –0.90 | –0.90 |
| East and Southeast Asia | 8.99 | 5,651 | 4.54 | 5.67 | 0.70 | 0.04 | 0.28 | 0.55 | 0.55 |
| Middle-Income Europe | 8.57 | 1,525 | 4.48 | n.a. | 1.10 | 0.76 | 1.11 | 0.69 | 0.69 |

n.a. = Not available.

*Sources:* CIF/FOB is from IMF (1995) except for South America, which is obtained from Hummels (1999); distance from capital city to closest of Rotterdam, New York, or Tokyo (km), obtained from Gallup, Sachs, and Mellinger (1998); port efficiency and clearing time data from Micco and Perez (2001); infrastructure data are from Canning (1999) for 1990 and are expressed as standard normal deviations from the world mean. World Bank measure (1990) from Gallup, Sachs, and Mellinger (1998). The group definitions given in each column heading are provided in the Appendix of Bond (2001).

tion, and size of the country (by regressing the respective infrastructure measure on these variables for a cross-section of countries in 1990), the comparison of the predicted values with the actual values shows no systematic bias associated with LAC. Worse infrastructure and higher logistics costs in Latin America are mainly associated with the characteristics of the countries in the region.

Still, these higher logistics costs are reflected in higher freight rate markups, longer waiting times for goods to clear ports, and higher inventory holdings of raw materials by firms (see Guasch and Kogan 2001). Improvements in the quality of infrastructure have the potential to reduce these

costs. The potential impact of these improvements on the value added in the different sectors within a country will depend on the trade pattern of the final goods and the importance of traded intermediate products in production. To illustrate the importance of these factors, Table 2.3 presents a simulation with the effect of a 1 percent transport cost reduction on the value added by industry, for Argentina, Brazil, and Mexico. The simulation is based on a model of production with logistics costs, assuming constant prices of inputs and nontraded goods, and constant demands for inputs, intermediary goods, and the final good. Thus, the simulation can be seen as an approximation of the immedi-

TABLE 2.2

**Transport Costs and Infrastructure: Selected Latin American Countries**

| COUNTRY | AVERAGE TRANSPORT COSTS (CIF/FOB–1) (1) | AVERAGE DISTANCE TO CLOSEST MAJOR MARKET (2) | PORT EFFICIENCY INDEX (3) | MEDIAN CLEARING TIME AT PORT (4) | KM OF PAVED ROADS PER KM² (5) | KM OF RAILROAD LINES PER KM² (6) | TELEPHONE MAINLINES PER CAPITA (7) | AIRFREIGHT PER CAPITA (8) | GDP PER CAPITA (9) |
|---|---|---|---|---|---|---|---|---|---|
| Argentina | 7.50 | 8,570 | 3.81 | 7.00 | –0.36 | 0.26 | 0.50 | 0.14 | 0.21 |
| Brazil | 7.30 | 7,700 | 2.92 | 10.00 | –0.50 | –0.59 | 0.24 | 0.19 | –0.09 |
| Chile | 8.80 | 8,290 | 3.76 | 3.00 | –0.56 | 0.05 | 0.31 | 0.96 | 0.17 |
| Mexico | 4.50 | 3,360 | 3.34 | 4.00 | –0.03 | 0.33 | 0.31 | –0.54 | –0.06 |
| Paraguay | 13.30 | 7,580 | * | * | n.a. | –1.38 | –0.17 | –0.81 | –0.46 |
| Uruguay | 4.60 | 8,560 | 5.00 | n.a. | n.a. | 0.48 | 0.68 | –0.93 | –0.04 |

* Landlocked country.

n.a. = Not available.

*Sources:* CIF/FOB from Hummels (1999) except for Mexico, which is obtained from the IMF; other variables as in Table 2.1.

TABLE 2.3

**Effect of a 1 Percent Transport Cost Reduction on Value Added by Industry: Argentina, Brazil, and Mexico**

| INDUSTRY | ARGENTINA | BRAZIL | MEXICO |
|---|---|---|---|
| Agriculture, Forestry, and Fishing | 1.11 | −1.33 | −1.10 |
| Food, Beverages, Tobacco | 1.29 | 5.64 | −1.43 |
| Textiles | −1.22 | −1.39 | 2.33 |
| Apparel | −1.08 | −1.47 | 1.69 |
| Leather Products | 1.94 | 3.00 | 2.70 |
| Footwear | −1.72 | 2.56 | 1.56 |
| Wood Products | −1.64 | 2.33 | −1.39 |
| Furniture | −1.05 | −5.61 | 2.53 |
| Paper | −1.47 | 2.35 | −1.31 |
| Printing and Publishing | −1.06 | −2.28 | −1.38 |
| Chemicals | −1.44 | −1.85 | −1.47 |
| Petroleum | 1.22 | −1.55 | −5.32 |
| Rubber Products | −2.05 | 4.22 | −1.33 |
| Nonmetallic Minerals | −1.47 | 2.49 | −1.54 |
| Glass | −1.24 | −1.47 | 1.80 |
| Iron and Steel | −1.50 | 4.74 | −2.02 |
| Nonferrous Metals | −1.30 | 4.25 | 1.68 |
| Metal Products | −1.03 | 1.95 | −1.59 |
| Nonelectrical Machinery | −1.03 | −2.45 | −1.67 |
| Electrical Machinery | −1.02 | −2.34 | 1.92 |
| Transportation Equipment | −1.10 | −3.25 | 2.09 |
| Miscellaneous Manufactures | −1.05 | −1.61 | −1.67 |
| Mining | 1.06 | −1.48 | 1.22 |

*Source:* Bond 2001.

ate impact of the change in the logistics costs given the current allocations in the economy.

The model predicts that, for Argentina, the major beneficiaries of the infrastructure improvements would be the leather, agriculture, food, and petroleum sectors; for Brazil, they would be metal, food products, and rubber; and for Mexico, they would be the leather, textile, transport equipment, electrical machinery, and furniture sectors. It is noteworthy that in these cases the main beneficiaries are agriculture, natural-resource intensive, and labor-intensive sectors.

Overall, there seems to be substantial need for improvement in LAC infrastructure. These improvements will require both investments in new infrastructure and improvements in the regulatory environment. The potential gains from these improvements could be substantial. As an example, a recent World Bank report points to the fact that the costs of handling a container in Brazil could be cut almost in half (from US$4,775 to US$2,614) if multimodal transport reforms were implemented. Cost reductions of this magnitude, amounting to 4.5 percent of the values of shipments for imports, would reduce transport costs on Brazilian goods as reported in Table 2.3 to a level comparable to the rates reported for U.S. trade.

## ICT and Knowledge: Measurement and Correlation with Development

Indicators for knowledge and ICT measure the relative position of each country with respect to others in these key areas of development.[2] Eight indicators were selected. Four reflect innovation activity and R&D in each economy, and four reveal the level of ICT development. The indicators are:

1. Research and development as share of gross national income (GNI)
2. Scientists in R&D per million people
3. Patent applications by residents and nonresidents per 1,000 people
4. Patent applications in the United States by country per 1,000 people
5. Telephone mainlines per 1,000 people
6. Mobile phones per 1,000 people
7. Personal computers per 10,000 people
8. Internet hosts with active Internet Protocol (IP) addresses per 1,000 people.

The definitions and relevance are self-explanatory for most of these variables. Mobile phones and telephones measure the depth of connectivity in a country. The other two ICT variables are personal computers and Internet hosts.[3] In the knowledge area we included R&D as share of gross national income and scientists working in R&D. We also included patent applications filed by nationals and nonnationals as an indicator of both innovation activity and as a measure of the need and ability of the state to protect intellectual property. Patent applications in the United States by country of origin of the inventor was also included.[4] This variable helps control for the variability in the previous variable caused by differences in the institutional development of each country. However, as discussed in Grossman and Helpman (1991), patent applications are also determined by the size of the domestic market where the patented products are sold. Consequently, neither indicator is a perfect proxy for innovation output. All the variables, except patent applications in the United States, come from the *World Development Indicators*. Patent applications in the United States come from the U.S. Patent Office.

Based on averages for 1995 to 2000 or 1990 to 1999, Table 2.4 shows the country variables expressed as a percentage of the U.S. levels. The most striking feature is that

TABLE 2.4

**Indicators of ICT and Knowledge as a Percentage of the United States Levels**

| | INFORMATION AND COMMUNICATIONS TECHNOLOGY | | | | KNOWLEDGE | | | |
|---|---|---|---|---|---|---|---|---|
| | TELEPHONE MAINLINES (PER 1,000 PEOPLE) | MOBILE PHONES (PER 1,000 PEOPLE) | INTERNET HOST (PER 1,000 PEOPLE) | PERSONAL COMPUTERS (PER 10,000 PEOPLE) | R&D AS SHARE OF GNI | R&D SCIENTISTS (PER MILLION PEOPLE) | PATENT RESIDENTS & NON-RESIDENTS (PER 1,000 PEOPLE) | PATENT APPLICATION IN U.S. (PER 1,000 PEOPLE) |
| LAC Countries | | | | | | | | |
| Argentina | 30.04 | 21.56 | 1.41 | 9.12 | 14.25 | 17.79 | 19.34 | 0.52 |
| Bolivia | 8.94 | 6.12 | 0.09 | 1.94 | 18.75 | 4.79 | 1.78 | 0.04 |
| Brazil | 20.38 | 13.00 | 1.04 | 6.12 | 30.88 | 4.53 | 24.36 | 0.19 |
| Chile | 31.09 | 17.05 | 2.09 | 10.58 | 28.88 | 11.69 | 14.24 | 0.24 |
| Colombia | 24.23 | 14.08 | 0.36 | 6.76 | 4.50 | n.a. | 3.98 | 0.07 |
| Costa Rica | 29.96 | 8.65 | 1.40 | 9.45 | 7.13 | n.a. | n.a. | 0.47 |
| Ecuador | 13.00 | 6.36 | 0.13 | 4.06 | 0.53 | 3.42 | 2.99 | 0.06 |
| Mexico | 16.30 | 9.42 | 0.91 | 9.04 | 10.88 | 5.09 | 40.70 | 0.27 |
| Peru | 9.78 | 7.84 | 0.27 | 2.90 | 9.38 | 9.85 | 3.29 | 0.04 |
| Venezuela, R.B. de | 17.06 | 23.47 | 0.32 | 8.90 | 19.00 | 5.70 | 11.22 | 0.35 |
| Average | 16.59 | 18.20 | 1.59 | 7.33 | 23.41 | n.a. | 30.37 | 0.23[a] |
| Asian Countries | | | | | | | | |
| China | 11.73 | 5.02 | 0.02 | 1.34 | 24.85 | 10.33 | 5.50 | 0.03 |
| India | 3.66 | 0.34 | 0.01 | 0.50 | 28.35 | 3.89 | 1.08 | 0.04 |
| Korea, Rep. of | 65.74 | 73.70 | 4.04 | 35.11 | 87.76 | 56.18 | 285.36 | 20.88 |
| Thailand | 12.77 | 16.08 | 0.38 | 4.61 | 5.63 | 3.01 | 9.61 | 0.09 |
| OECD Countries | | | | | | | | |
| Germany | 83.29 | 21.08 | 70.72 | 61.74 | 87.76 | 76.32 | 232.99 | 34.86 |
| Japan | 79.03 | 18.40 | 151.66 | 51.83 | 108.02 | 138.52 | 371.80 | 72.87 |
| United States | 100.00 | 100.00 | 100.00 | 100.00 | 100.00 | 100.00 | 100.00 | 100.00 |
| AVERAGES BY LEVEL OF INCOME | | | | | | | | |
| Low income | 3.05 | 0.67 | 0.03 | 0.86 | n.a. | n.a. | 30.80 | n.a. |
| Middle income | 14.78 | 12.51 | 0.85 | 4.89 | 33.62 | 18.02 | 35.83 | n.a. |
| High income | 84.04 | 111.29 | 65.60[a] | 69.52 | 89.35 | 86.13 | 334.78 | 69.24[a] |

n.a. = Not available.

a. Average of the corresponding countries included in this table.

for all developing countries except Korea, development in knowledge and ICT is very shallow. Korea spends almost as much as the United States on R&D, but the number of scientists in R&D in Korea is about half that in the United States. The indicators of connectivity (phones and mobile phones) are about 65 percent of those in the United States. The penetration of personal computers is about 35 percent of that in the United States, and the level of Internet hosts (4 percent) and the number of patent applications by Koreans in the United States (20 percent) are much lower. On the other hand, the number of patent applications in Korea when controlled by population is three times that of the United States, suggesting a relevant system of property rights and innovational activity in the country.

On the other hand, the other three Asian countries (China, India, and Thailand) show very low levels of knowledge and ICT development. In fact, their figures are closer to those of the selected LAC economies. In China and India, knowledge and ICT are almost exclusively led by R&D, which in both cases is about 25 percent of that in the United States. China has about 10 percent of scientists in R&D, which for a big country amounts to a large contingent of engineers.

Even though the LAC countries have a much lower level of knowledge and ICT development than Korea and the United States, there are special characteristics worth mentioning. Brazil and Chile have relatively more R&D than China and India, which in their own structure of "knowledge" depended strongly on R&D. LAC countries also have higher connectivity levels (phones and mobiles), especially Argentina, Chile, Costa Rica, and República Bolivariana de Venezuela. Nonetheless, these variables are 30 percent of the level achieved in the United States. The penetration of personal computers is similar for most LAC countries, but Argentina, Chile, Costa Rica, and República Bolivariana de Venezuela are the leaders (around 10 percent of the United States). Argentina has a relative strength in the number of scientists per 1,000 people, even though it is only 19 percent of the level in the United States. Patent applications in the United States are minimal for all the countries, but patent applications in Mexico are 40 percent of those in the United States, and this is the only area of "knowledge" where Mexico has a relative strength. On average, LAC countries are above middle-income countries in ICT, but are lagging behind on the components of knowledge.

In the following section we use knowledge and ICT composite indexes to analyze the determinants of trade patterns. These indexes are generated using the principal components of the variables described herein. Figures 2.1 and 2.2 show the relationship of each one of the composite indexes and GDP per capita. It is evident that there is a positive and nonlinear relationship between knowledge and ICT and the level of development across countries during 1976–99. The fit of the regression is high for the ICT index ($R^2$=0.8). Thus, communications, computer penetration,

and access to the Internet are, according to this basic result, highly correlated with income per capita. The relationship for the knowledge index and development is also high. GDP per capita explains about 60 percent of the variance in the knowledge index ($R^2$=0.6).

Thus far, the evidence is clear concerning the impact of logistics on the structure of trade, and ICT and knowledge are key correlates of the level of development. The following section explores more broadly the determinants of trade structure around the world, with a special focus on the role of "new" endowments, including ICT and knowledge. However, a brief discussion of measurement issues is necessary prior to analyzing the patterns of trade in LAC countries.

## Comparative Advantage: Facts from LAC

The concept of "comparative advantage" is one of the best understood by academic economists, and the least accepted by society. When economists mention "comparative advantage" they are referring to economic activities that an economy can produce at lower relative costs than others. In other words, it means that countries have certain strengths, and the resulting patterns of trade and production should reflect those strengths, rather than policy distortions.

This report relies on indicators proposed by Edward Leamer of the University of California at Los Angeles, who is one of the leading world experts on international trade

FIGURE 2.1

**Development and Knowledge Index**

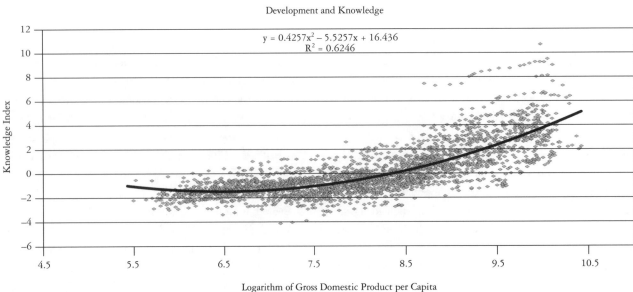

Development and Knowledge

$$y = 0.4257x^2 - 5.5257x + 16.436$$
$$R^2 = 0.6246$$

Logarithm of Gross Domestic Product per Capita

FIGURE 2.2

## Development and ICT Index

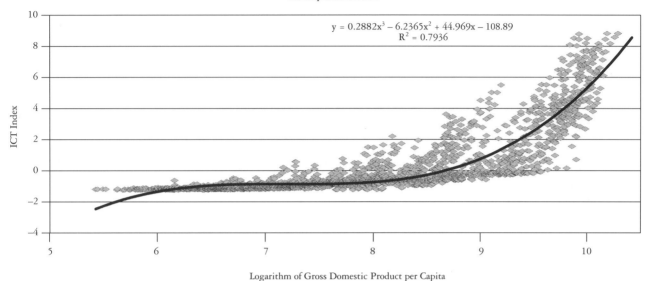

Development and ICT

$$y = 0.2882x^3 - 6.2365x^2 + 44.969x - 108.89$$
$$R^2 = 0.7936$$

Logarithm of Gross Domestic Product per Capita

analysis. In several important professional publications, Professor Leamer proposed using a set of 10 industrial clusters, which are aggregates of over 2,200 products traded internationally (see Leamer 1984, 1987, and 1995). The distinguishing feature of each commodity group is that empirical analyses conducted by Leamer (1984, 1995) show that the products included in each cluster tend to be exported by similar countries in terms of their endowments of different types of labor, land, and natural resources. For reference, Table 2.5 shows the components of Leamer's 10 commodity aggregates, based on the widely used Standard International Trade Classification (SITC).

As a precursor for further analysis of the evolution of patterns of trade around the world, Figure 2.3 shows the shares of world merchandise exports of the four clusters of manufactures, plus the sum of the shares of petroleum and raw materials, and the sum of the four agricultural sectors during 1976–99. The cluster of machines has had the lion's share of the world market, and also experienced a surge during the 1990s. In the companion Table 2.6, it is evident that the growth of machines was not even for all products during the last decade, although all products in this cluster had positive growth rates. The fastest-growing products were electrical equipment, office and automatic data processors, and telecommunications equipment. There are no surprises in these numbers.

The other three clusters of manufactured products (labor intensive, capital intensive, and chemicals) maintained a relatively stable share of the world market during the 1990s. In contrast, the agricultural and mining commodities experienced a noticeable decline in their corresponding shares. However, these data should not be interpreted as indications that agricultural and mining commodities are zero-growth industries. In fact, world exports of cereals grew, on average, by 2.6 percent per year during the 1990s, exports of animal products by 3.2 percent, raw materials by 3.6 percent, petroleum by 4.1 percent, agriculture by 4.4 percent, capital-intensive manufactures by 4.6 percent, labor-intensive products by 6.7 percent, and chemicals by 7 percent. The rising share of world exports of machines reflects the fact that machine exports grew even faster than the others—its overall average growth rate was about 8.2 percent per year.

The theoretically rigorous measure of comparative advantage is net exports, the difference between the value of exports and the value of imports of each of these product aggregates. The mathematical derivation of this conclusion comes from Leamer (1984) and is presented in Box 2.1. The intuition, however, is quite clear: countries will export products that are produced with the strong aspects of their economies, which could be large endowments of natural resources or highly skilled labor, or any other type of

TABLE 2.5

## Components of Leamer's 10 Commodity Clusters

| AGGREGATES | SITC | AGGREGATES | SITC |
|---|---|---|---|
| Petroleum | | Labor Intensive | |
| Petroleum and derivatives | 33 | Nonmetal minerals | 66 |
| | | Furniture | 82 |
| Raw Materials | | Travel goods and handbags | 83 |
| Crude fertilizers and minerals | 27 | Art apparel | 84 |
| Metalliferous ores | 28 | Footwear | 85 |
| Coal and coke | 32 | Miscellaneous manufactured articles | 89 |
| Gas, natural, and manufactured | 34 | Postal packaging, not classified | 91 |
| Electrical current | 35 | Special transactions, not classified | 93 |
| Nonferrous metal | 68 | Coins (nongold) | 96 |
| | | | |
| Forest Products | | Capital Intensive | |
| Lumber, wood, and cork | 24 | Leather | 61 |
| Pulp and waste paper | 25 | Rubber | 62 |
| Cork and wood manufacturers | 63 | Textile yarn and fabric | 65 |
| Paper | 64 | Iron and steel | 67 |
| | | Manufactured metal n. e. s. | 69 |
| Tropical Agriculture | | Sanitary fixtures and fittings | 81 |
| Vegetables | 5 | | |
| Sugar | 6 | Machinery | |
| Coffee | 7 | Power generating | 71 |
| Beverages | 11 | Specialized | 72 |
| Crude rubber | 23 | Metalworking | 73 |
| | | General industrial | 74 |
| Animal Products | | Office and data processing | 75 |
| Live animals | 0 | Telecommunications and sound | 76 |
| Meat | 1 | Electrical | 77 |
| Dairy products | 2 | Road vehicles | 78 |
| Fish | 3 | Other transportation vehicles | 79 |
| Hides and skins | 21 | Professional and scientific instruments | 87 |
| Crude animals and vegetables | 29 | Photographic apparatus | 88 |
| Processed animal and vegetable oils | 43 | Firearms and ammunition | 95 |
| Animal products n. e. s. | 94 | | |
| | | Chemical | |
| Cereals, etc. | | Organic | 51 |
| Cereals | 4 | Inorganic | 52 |
| Feeds | 8 | Dyeing and tanning | 53 |
| Miscellaneous | 9 | Medical and pharmaceutical products | 54 |
| Tobacco | 12 | Essences and perfumes | 55 |
| Oil seeds | 22 | Fertilizers | 56 |
| Textile fibers | 26 | Explosives and pyrotechnics | 57 |
| Animal oil and fat | 41 | Artificial resins and plastics | 58 |
| Fixed vegetable oils | 42 | Chemical materials n. e. s. | 59 |

n. e. s. = Not elsewhere specified.
SITC = Standard International Trade Classification.
*Source:* Leamer 1995.

endowment. The precise definitions of the types of endowments that could be considered as sources of strengths for any given economy at a particular point in time were discussed in the previous section of this chapter.

Another advantage of using net exports as an indicator of revealed comparative advantage, rather than other measures that focus only on the structure of exports, such as those discussed in Balassa (1989), is that theoretically countries should be net exporters of products that intensively use the resources and economic strengths they have at their disposal. This is so because an exclusive focus on exports will ignore the possibility that countries import a substantial amount of goods that they also export, which could indicate that the hypothetical country is a net

FIGURE 2.3

**Shares of World Merchandise Exports, 1976–99**

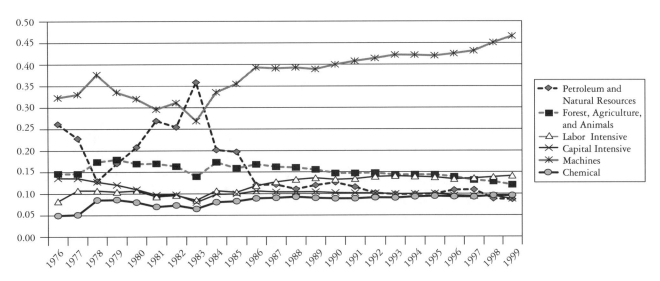

TABLE 2.6

**Growth of World Machine Exports, 1990–99**

(Percent)

| PRODUCT | ANNUAL GROWTH RATE |
|---|---|
| Arms | 0.3 |
| Metalworking | 3.7 |
| Specialized | 3.9 |
| Photography | 4.4 |
| General Industrial | 6.8 |
| Road Vehicles | 7.0 |
| Other Vehicles | 7.6 |
| Power Generating | 8.0 |
| Professional and Scientific Instruments | 8.8 |
| Telecommunications and Sound | 9.7 |
| Office and Data Processing | 10.7 |
| Electrical | 11.9 |
| TOTAL | 8.2 |

importer of the factors of production used in the elaboration of those products. In other words, the indicator of net exports provides adequate information concerning the products in which an economy has strengths relative to the rest of the world. Hence, the rest of the analysis in this chapter focuses on the pattern of net exports for the regional average, and for a set of LAC countries.

## The Regional Average since the Early 1980s

As mentioned earlier, in Latin American countries that experimented with protectionist regimes roughly since the interwar period (the 1920s and 1930s) until the early 1980s, the move to trade liberalization was meant to bring about a change in the structure of trade in favor of labor-intensive sectors. However, the region's average pattern of international trade, as reflected in the net exports per worker across Leamer's (1984 and 1995) clusters of commodities, has remained dependent on and even increased the net exports of land- and natural resource–intensive commodities, as shown in Figure 2.4. By 1997, the regional average of *net exports* of raw materials per worker was about US$250; the number for petroleum and tropical agriculture was about US$210; while net exports of animal products per worker was almost US$50. In contrast, in 1997, *net imports* per worker of machines were almost US$800. The hopes of structural change were perhaps misguided, because neoclassical trade theory predicts that countries with abundant land and natural resources will specialize even more in these sectors after liberalization. Nevertheless, the increased dependence on such products has again raised eyebrows and instigated recent calls for reevaluating the structural effects of development strategies based on liberal trade policies (see, for example, Katz 2000; and Ramos 1998).

### Specific Country Experiences since the Early 1980s

The regional averages discussed above, however, are misleading in that they do not show the rather large differences that exist within the region. Figures 2.3 through 2.10 show the evolution of the composition of net exports for our core

BOX 2.1

**Net Exports as an Indicator of Comparative Advantage Driven by Endowments**

Assuming Leontieff technology, the framework in Leamer (1984) begins with the system of equations that relate factor supplies to factor demands as follows:

$$K = a_{K1}Y_1 + a_{K2}Y_2, \text{ and} \qquad (1)$$
$$L = a_{L1}Y_1 + a_{L2}Y_2 \qquad (2)$$

K and L are the amounts of two factors of production, call them capital and labor, available in a given country. These amounts are country specific and are assumed to be internationally immobile. The $Y$'s denote the quantity produced in the given country of two commodities (labeled $_1$ and $_2$). The $a$'s are the traditional factor intensities determined by the available production technologies in each sector, and they represent the units of each factor required to produce a unit of output. Equations (1) and (2) represent a system that can be solved for outputs $Y$ as a function of the inputs $K$ and $L$ and the factor intensities.

In matrix notation, this setup can be generalized to a model with multiple products and multiple factors of production as long as the latter do not exceed the number of products, or as long as the model is just identified or underidentified. Then:

$$Y = A^{-1}V \qquad (3)$$

where $Y$ is the vector of product outputs and $V$ is the vector of endowments. The $A$ is the vector of factor intensities, which is invertable as long as the production technologies are different across sectors so that the ratios of factor intensities across sectors are not identical.

Still following Leamer (1984), the production of the world economy as a whole can also be written in the same format:

$$Y_W = A^{-1}V_W \qquad (4)$$

Assuming that countries consume commodities in the same proportions, the country consumption levels can be expressed as:

$$C = sY_W \qquad (5)$$

where $Y_W$ is the world's output vector and $s$ is the proportion consumed by each country.

The proportional-consumption assumption is rather implausible and is used for the sake of simplicity, but it is not a fundamental part of the argument. Deviations from this assumption do not change the substance of the analysis (see Leamer 1984). Hence the vector of net exports is simply the product of the inverse of the vector of factor intensities across product clusters and the difference between each country's vector of endowments and the world's vector of endowments. An often forgotten step in the derivation of testable hypotheses is that the key dependent variable is net exports, not gross exports or gross imports. This is clear after considering the fact that net exports are the difference between domestic production and consumption:

$$NX = Y - C = A^{-1}(V - sV_W) \qquad (6)$$

In principle, empirical models of neoclassical trade theory should be estimated with net exports as the dependent variable, and excess factor endowments as the explanatory variables. In turn, the signs of the estimated coefficients on the endowment variables, or the values inside the inverted $A$ matrix, reflect the factor intensities of production.

At this point, it is important to note that the inverted vector $A$ contains factor intensities across product clusters, not relative factor abundances across countries. However, each country's consumption share (relative to the world) is a weighted average of its factor shares (also relative to the world's endowments), so that $s$ is:

$$K/K_W > s > L/L_W, \text{ or, } K/K_W < s < L/L_W \qquad (7)$$

That is, a capital-abundant country will have $K/K_W > s > L/L_W$, while a labor-abundant country will have $K/K_W < s < L/L_W$.

set of six countries. Of these, only *Costa Rica* and *Mexico* (Figures 2.8 and 2.10, respectively) show a significant change in their trade structure in the sense that at some point between 1980 and 1999 they became net exporters of new products. In the case of Mexico, this occurred in 1995,

right after the implementation of NAFTA (January 1994), and after the currency devaluation of December 1994. Beginning in 1995, Mexico became a net exporter of machines. More disaggregated data reveals that, within the cluster of machines, Mexico is an important exporter of

FIGURE 2.4

**Average LAC Net Exports per Worker by Commodity Groups, 1982–97**

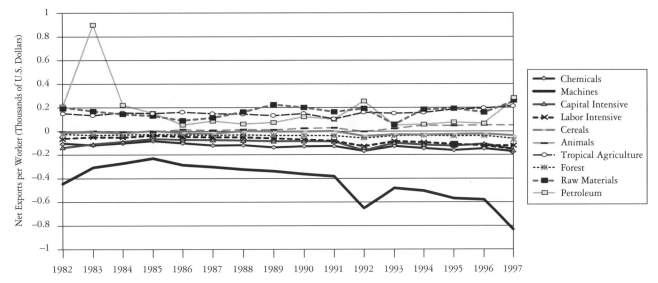

*Note:* Sample of 22 countries: Argentina, Barbados, Belize, Bolivia, Brazil, Chile, Colombia, Costa Rica, Ecuador, El Salvador, Guatemala, Honduras, Jamaica, Mexico, Nicaragua, Panama, Paraguay, Peru, the República Bolivariana de Venezuela, Suriname, Trinidad and Tobago, and Uruguay. To see this figure in color, refer to Figure A.1 in the Annex.

FIGURE 2.5

**Argentina: Structure of Net Exports, 1980–99**

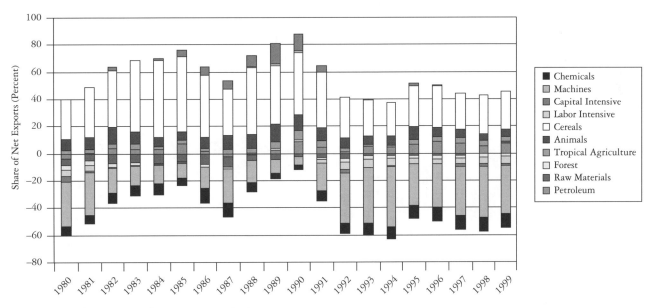

*Note:* To see this figure in color, refer to Figure A.2 in the Annex.

telecommunications equipment, transport equipment (including vehicles and auto parts), and office equipment. In 1999, *Costa Rica* became a net exporter of machines, and this result is driven by exports of computer chips produced by the newly installed Intel plant in that country, which

began its operations in 1998. Both of these cases will be discussed in more detail in the rest of the report.

The picture for *Argentina* (Figure 2.5) reflects the fact that it is rich in agricultural endowments. It maintained a considerable comparative advantage in cereals and animal products, and to a lesser extent in other agricultural commodities, throughout this period. In addition, this economy benefits from substantial petroleum reserves. Argentina seems to have lost an incipient capital-intensive industry since the early 1990s, which has raised concerns about the impact of economic reforms implemented during 1991–94 on the process of industrialization. On the other hand, the establishment of the Common Market of the Southern Cone in 1991 might have helped maintain some domestic industrial production, which nevertheless at first sight does not seem to have helped to develop a comparative advantage in these products relative to the rest of the world (see Yeats 1998). These issues are analyzed in greater detail in Chapter 3.

The case of *Brazil* is also interesting, but for different reasons. The structure of net exports of this economy is remarkable throughout the period shown in Figure 2.6, largely due to the diversity of products that it exports. For example, Brazil is a net exporter of tropical agriculture, cereals, animal products, and forestry, but it also exports capital- and labor-intensive manufactures. Moreover, an interesting trend emerged after the implementation of the *Real* macroeconomic stabilization plan in mid-1994. That is, during 1994–97 the trade balance deteriorated, which is reflected in the downward move of the bars shown in Figure 2.6. During this period, machine imports rose much faster than exports, and thus the share of net exports of this cluster of products,

which includes transport equipment, fell precipitously. Given the international success of **EMBRAER**, Brazil's small-aircraft producer privatized in 1994, this downward trend in machine net exports is remarkable. Further disaggregation of the trade flows in this cluster shows that, as of 1999, Brazil remained a net exporter of transport vehicles, which includes aircraft. We will return to the Brazilian experience later in this report.

As is well known, *Chile* was a leader in the implementation of economic reforms prior to the 1980s. Hence it is the country in the region that has had the longest experience with liberal trade and investment policies. Consequently, it is an important case to consider, because it might offer insights about the long-term effects of liberal policies. Since the early 1980s, in spite of a temporary reversal of its trade policies during 1982–84 (see Lederman 2001 for a detailed analysis), its structure of net exports has remained quite stable, as shown in Figure 2.7. It is an economy that exports natural resource–intensive commodities, such as copper, and agricultural and animal (including fisheries) products. It is a net importer of petroleum and of all types of manufactured goods. This pattern raises the issues concerning the dependence on natural resources and land. Moreover, it has been one of the best-performing economies during the last 15 years in terms of economic growth in the region, and perhaps in the developing world, and thus

FIGURE 2.6

**Brazil: Structure of Net Exports, 1981–99**

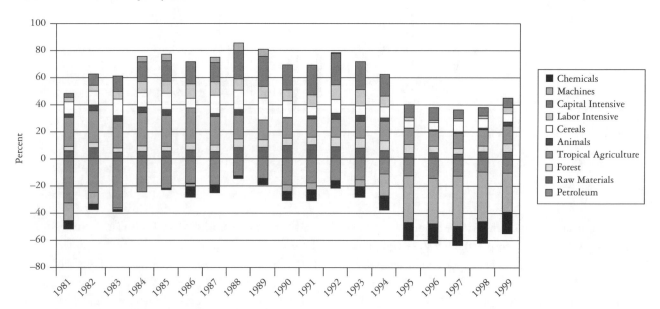

*Note:* To see this figure in color, refer to Figure A.3 in the Annex.

FIGURE 2.7

## Chile: Structure of Net Exports, 1981–98

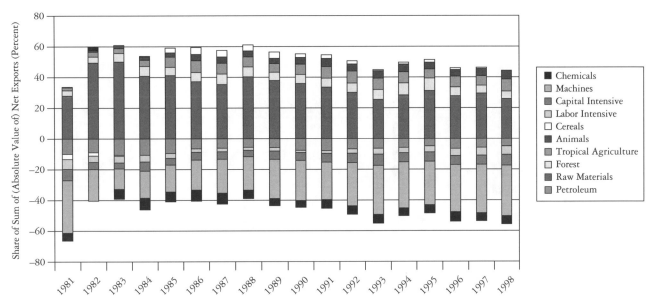

*Note:* To see this figure in color, refer to Figure A.4 in the Annex.

illustrates the fact that economic development and poverty reduction need not be hampered by the existence of natural wealth. This report will cover not only the experience of Chile in the agricultural and mining sectors, but also the historical development experiences of now-industrialized economies such as Australia, Canada, Finland, Sweden, and the United States, in order to evaluate the factors and policies that aided the development of these economies.

The *Dominican Republic* (Figure 2.9) is an example of an economy that, on the merchandise side, has maintained a clear comparative advantage in tropical agriculture and labor-intensive manufactures. Its comparative advantage in

FIGURE 2.8

## Costa Rica: Structure of Net Exports, 1981–99

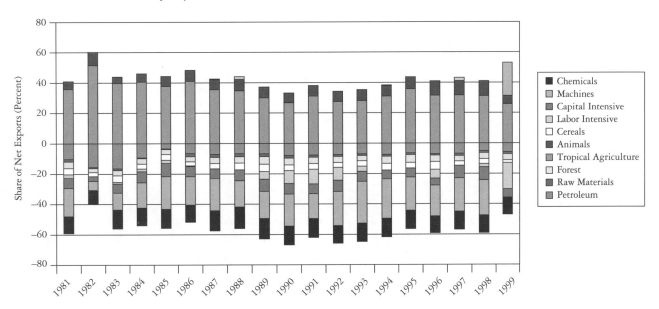

*Note:* To see this figure in color, refer to Figure A.5 in the Annex.

FIGURE 2.9

**Dominican Republic: Structure of Net Exports, 1981–99**

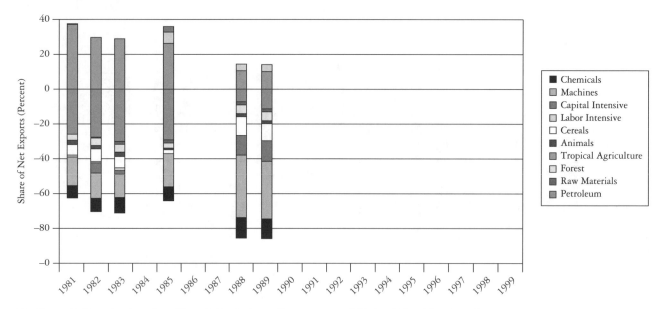

*Note:* To see this figure in color, refer to Figure A.6 in the Annex. Data were not available for 1984, 1986, 1987, and 1990–99.

FIGURE 2.10

**Mexico: Structure of Net Exports, 1981–99**

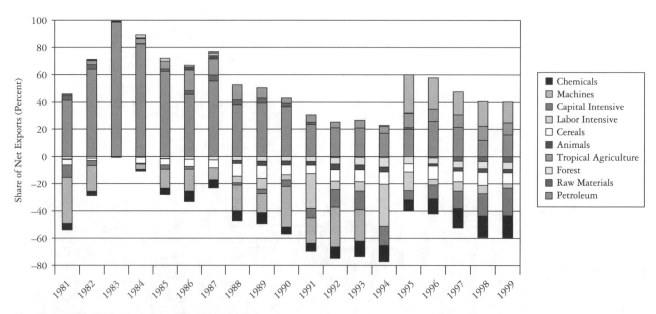

*Note:* To see this figure in color, refer to Figure A.7 in the Annex.

agricultural products has persisted for a long time, clearly due to its relatively high endowment of arable land relative to its labor force and capital stock. As discussed below, exports of labor-intensive manufactures from the Dominican Republic and several Central American countries were stimulated by policies establishing EPZs. Like northern Mexico, the manufacturing sector of this country has benefited from its proximity to the large consumer market of the United States. Later in this report, the role of communications technology, including the Internet, and international transport costs will be analyzed in terms of their importance for attracting FDI in manufacturing activities that are vertically linked with a broader manufacturing production process. That is, countries like the Dominican Republic, which are close to large consumer markets and to the source of more capital-intensive inputs for production, will tend to attract foreign investment to take advantage of both their geographic location and their competitive labor force.

Observers of the global economy, especially of flows of manufactured products, recognize that firms that export certain goods are facing the pressure of competition from other large developing countries, especially countries such as China, India, and Korea. In particular, there are fears that the opening of China and India, with their large pools of competitive labor, pose significant challenges for exports of labor-intensive manufactures such as apparel and footwear. Box 2.2 reviews the structure of trade in these large developing countries.

An interesting issue explored below emerges from the comparison of Costa Rica and the Dominican Republic. Costa Rica succeeded in attracting major investment in the relatively more "sophisticated" industrial cluster of machinery (that is, computer chips), while the Dominican Republic has maintained a comparative advantage in labor-intensive manufactures. It is likely that this qualitative difference is mainly due to the difference in the quantity and quality of the countries' human capital. The case of the Dominican Republic is also interesting due to its dynamic tourism sector. Hence we will cover this sector in Chapter 4.

The main issue raised by the recent evolution of the patterns of trade of LAC countries is the concern about the remaining, and in some cases rising, dependence on export revenues provided by natural wealth, such as mining and petroleum reserves and arable land. The following section tries to clarify the potential determinants of the observed patterns of trade, and then discusses statistical evidence based on international comparisons from throughout the globe.

---

BOX 2.2

### The Structure of Trade in Large Developing Countries: China, India, and Korea

Figures 2.11, 2.12, and 2.13 show the evolution of net exports per worker of manufactures for three large developing countries: China, India, and Korea. China shows a continuous increase in its net exports of labor-intensive goods since the late 1980s, when the process of economic liberalization was launched. India also has a comparative advantage in labor-intensive goods, but remains relatively closed. The emergence of these international powerhouses in the export of labor-intensive manufactures poses a challenge for other developing economies wishing to expand their labor-intensive exports.

Korea is the most open economy of the three. During the entire period from 1976 to 1999 Korea maintained a clear comparative advantage in manufactures, especially labor- and capital-intensive manufactures. However, since 1992, Korea's net exports of machinery increased dramatically, while since 1989 its net exports of labor-intensive manufactures declined steadily. This structural change in its pattern of trade is probably a consequence of Korea's success in terms of raising real wages and moving up the ladder of manufacturing processes. This case

illustrates how an economy integrated into the global marketplace can naturally change its comparative advantage as development progresses.

What do these comparisons imply for Latin America and the Caribbean? First, the emerging patterns of trade in these economies indicate that labor-intensive manufactures will continue to be a very competitive sector of the world economy, especially as the process of liberalization continues in China and India. Consequently, the survival of labor-intensive industries in LAC will depend on the extent to which they are able to compete with Chinese and Indian exports by playing to their strengths, mainly their close proximity to the United States. Moreover, as discussed later in this chapter, the adoption of ICT can also help enhance the performance of labor-intensive firms. This consideration is particularly important for the Dominican Republic and some Central American countries that have managed to develop labor-intensive industries oriented toward foreign markets. Korea's pattern of trade is similar to the one emerging in Mexico. Consequently, we can expect stiff competition in machines by Korean firms.

FIGURE 2.11

**China: Net Exports per Worker, 1984–99**

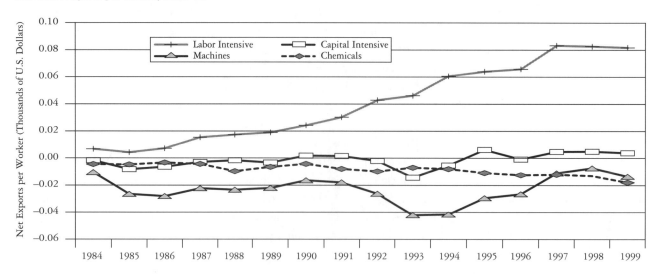

FIGURE 2.12

**India: Net Exports per Worker, 1978–98**

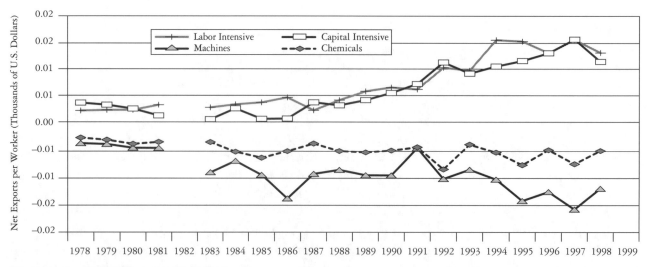

*Note:* Data were not available for 1981, 1982, and 1999.

## Are Traditional Endowments Destiny?

The short answer to this question is "no," having natural riches does not mean that a country will only produce and export commodities based on the exploitation of natural resources, land, or both. It turns out that other types of "endowments" also matter a great deal in the determination of trade patterns. Furthermore, several of the factors that help explain why some countries are net exporters of manufactures, while others export agricultural commodities, are quite sensitive to social and economic policies. The following analysis discusses statistical evidence that shows the importance of modern notions of factor endowments.

### Determinants of Trade Structure:
### International Evidence

Given that the previous casual discussion of various patterns of trade simply established that all patterns are theoretically possible and that natural wealth (that is, in terms

FIGURE 2.13

**Republic of Korea: Net Exports per Worker, 1976–99**

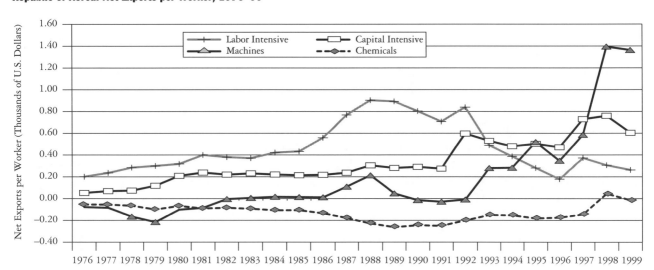

Of land and mining reserves) are not necessarily destiny in terms of trade patterns, what do data actually show?

## Trade and Endowments

In this section we discuss empirical evidence based on data for over 55 countries during 1976–99. Box 2.3 explains the data. Greater detail can be found in the background paper by Lederman and Xu (2001). Our objective here is to compare the influence of traditional concepts of factor endowments (that is, land, labor, and capital) to the effects of modern notions such as education, knowledge, ICT, institutions, infrastructure, and volatility.

Table 2.7 shows in dicators of the patterns of trade and their potential determinants for our sample of countries. Column (1) shows the standard deviation of the variables across countries; column (2) shows the average standard deviation within countries (that is, over time); and column (3) shows the ratio of the first divided by the second. This last set of numbers is interesting because it provides a sense of how much each indicator varies across countries relative to its variation within countries (that is, over time).

An interesting finding is that the value of net exports of labor-intensive manufactures and the probability of being a positive exporter of these goods are the trade indicators with the lowest relative variance across countries, when compared to the variation over time. For example, the probability of being an exporter of these goods varies only 2.2 times more across countries than over time. Hence it

seems that for any given country, developing a comparative advantage over time in this type of manufactured goods is more likely than for other commodity groups. It is likely that this finding is due to the possibility of attracting FDI in search of competitive labor. More generally, most indicators related to net exports of manufactured goods tend to vary more over time than indicators related to agricultural commodities. The only exceptions to this rule are the probabilities of being a positive exporter of animal products and cereals, which have a relatively low ratio in column (3).

The fact that changing comparative advantage over time seems to be relatively difficult (as shown by the relatively low variation of the trade variables within countries) does not mean that nothing can be done. Indeed, the data discussed so far show that it is possible to experience structural changes over time even if this is relatively rare when compared to the variation that exists across countries. The real issue is, therefore, what can be done either to enhance the performance of the industries in which a developing country has a comparative advantage or to change its structure of trade. Figures 2.14, 2.15, and 2.16 shed some light on this question.

Each graph contains the difference between the average value of each endowment indicator for countries (and years) that have a comparative advantage (that is, positive net exports) minus the average for those countries (years) that do not have a comparative advantage. Each one corresponds

BOX 2.3

**Data: Traditional and New Endowments**

The traditional explanatory variables of comparative advantage are the endowments of crop- and forestland (hectares per worker) and capital (per worker). The "new" variables considered here include our index of institutional quality (a composite index based on data from the *International Country Risk Guide*), ICT, domestic land transport infrastructure (a combination of the length of paved roads and railways), the index of knowledge (R&D expenditures, technical workers as a share of the labor force), the average years of education of the adult population, and the volatility of the real effective exchange rate. The data cover 1976 to 1999 for over 55 countries. The regressions were conducted after dropping the top and bottom 1 percent.

As mentioned, the explanatory variables were divided into two categories; those that determine comparative advantage and those that determine the value of net exports per worker. Table 2.7 shows the standard deviations for the dependent (the sign and value of net exports) and explanatory variables. Column (1) shows the standard deviation of the variables across countries; column (2) shows the average standard deviation within countries (that is, over time); and column (3) shows the ratio of the first divided by the second. The first obvious observation is that the cross-country variance for all variables is greater across countries than within countries. However, the trade

data, namely the value of net exports and the condition of being a positive net exporter, both change much less over time than many of the explanatory variables. The cross-country variance of the value of net exports is two to nine times greater than the within-country variance. The condition of being a net exporter has an even higher relative cross-country variance than the value of net exports for most sectors, except animal products, and to a lesser extent labor-intensive manufactures and cereals.

All the variables chosen as explanatory variables in the comparative advantage equation—that is, those listed in bold letters—are relatively more stable over time than the value of net exports. The only exception is the index of ICT, whose over-time variance is surprisingly high. This is due primarily to the very fast growth of the number of registered Internet hosts in the late 1990s, when many countries went from having zero to having positive numbers. Therefore, we opted to include it in the comparative advantage together with the other endowment variables that change little over time. All characteristics of neighbors were put in the trade intensity function, thus limiting the variables in the comparative advantage equation to relatively stable home-country characteristics. (For more detailed information on the data and methodology, see Lederman and Xu 2001.)

to a given agricultural or manufacturing industrial cluster, again based on Leamer's commodity aggregates. Some interesting generalizations can be drawn from these pictures.

An interesting similarity exists between countries with a comparative advantage in tropical agriculture and those with a comparative advantage in labor-intensive manufactures. The countries that export these goods seem to have relatively low levels of virtually every endowment, except land in the case of tropical agriculture. In contrast, countries with a comparative advantage in forestry and cereals have higher endowments of all types than countries that import those goods. Countries with a comparative advantage in forestry have particularly high levels of infrastructure; those with a comparative advantage in cereals have particularly high levels of education and infrastructure. Finally, countries that export capital-intensive exports, machines, and chemicals have higher than average endow-

ments of all types, except for land. But these countries have particularly high levels of the "modern" endowments. This is especially the case of knowledge for capital-intensive exports; knowledge, education, ICT, and institutions for both machines and chemicals. Hence it is clear that having land resources does not automatically mean that a country cannot develop a comparative advantage in manufactures. More important, countries that export certain agricultural commodities tend to be very sophisticated in terms of their level of technological and institutional development.

The main weakness of the analyses presented so far is that they ignore the fact that all these endowments interact to produce particular patterns of international trade. In other words, the simple correlations presented here should not be interpreted as evidence about the precise determinants of comparative advantage. The following econometric analysis is required to ascertain the extent to which the

TABLE 2.7

**Variance of Variables of Interest across and within Countries**

| VARIABLES | (1): BETWEEN S.D. | (2): MEAN WITHIN S.D. | (3): (1)/(2) |
|---|---|---|---|
| **Net exports of:** | | | |
| Raw materials | 0.40 | 0.07 | 5.71 |
| Forestry | 0.54 | 0.08 | 6.75 |
| Tropical agriculture | 0.17 | 0.05 | 3.40 |
| Animals | 0.48 | 0.08 | 6.00 |
| Cereals | 0.19 | 0.05 | 3.80 |
| Labor intensive | 0.31 | 0.13 | 2.38 |
| Capital intensive | 0.21 | 0.07 | 3.00 |
| Machines | 0.85 | 0.27 | 3.15 |
| Chemicals | 0.31 | 0.10 | 3.10 |
| **Probability of being a positive net exporter of:** | | | |
| Raw materials greater than 0 | 0.46 | 0.06 | 7.67 |
| Forestry greater than 0 | 0.44 | 0.05 | 8.80 |
| Tropical agriculture greater than 0 | 0.46 | 0.05 | 9.20 |
| Animals greater than 0 | 0.43 | 0.15 | 2.87 |
| Cereals greater than 0 | 0.43 | 0.12 | 3.58 |
| Labor intensive greater than 0 | 0.42 | 0.19 | 2.21 |
| Capital intensive greater than 0 | 0.40 | 0.10 | 4.00 |
| Machines greater than 0 | 0.30 | 0.06 | 5.00 |
| Chemicals greater than 0 | 0.34 | 0.05 | 6.80 |
| **Explanatory variables:** | | | |
| Annual rate of change of the real exchange rate | 0.33 | 0.25 | 1.32 |
| **ICT Index** | 1.79 | 1.27 | 1.41 |
| Institutions Index | 1.55 | 0.44 | 3.52 |
| **Capital per worker** | 1.29 | 0.30 | 4.30 |
| Income per capita | 1.03 | 0.22 | 4.68 |
| Adjusted Openness Index | 47.09 | 8.39 | 5.61 |
| **Years of schooling** | 2.67 | 0.46 | 5.80 |
| Knowledge | 2.49 | 0.38 | 6.55 |
| **Cropland per worker** | 0.72 | 0.07 | 10.29 |
| **Forestland per worker** | 1.43 | 0.10 | 14.30 |
| **Land Transport Index** | 1.48 | 0.10 | 14.80 |

*Note:* See Box 2.3 and Lederman and Xu (2001) for details on the data. Variables in bold were used as determinants of comparative advantage in the econometric exercises.

endowments affect the likelihood that any given country at any given time will have a comparative advantage in a certain industry.

## Econometric Evidence

Perhaps the most important message from the discussion of the various patterns of integration is that, in the current context of globalization, it is difficult to predict where industries will be located in the future. The main reason for this is that international flows of intermediate goods, knowledge, capital, and labor, facilitated by low transport costs and improvements in communications technology, open up opportunities for industries of various degrees of technological sophistication to be established almost anywhere in the world. Furthermore, agricultural and economic activities based on the discovery, extraction, and processing of natural resources offer opportunities for the

emergence of sophisticated manufacturing activities, which in the future might become completely detached from the aforementioned sectors.

The main question posed in this section was whether natural endowments are destiny in terms of determining the pattern of comparative advantage across countries and over time. The empirical evidence presented above indicates that land and capital per worker do play an important role in determining comparative advantage. However, they are not destiny, because other country-specific characteristics, which are arguably more sensitive to public policies, also play an important role. This general conclusion comes from the descriptive evidence. However, the previous analysis was based on an examination of the characteristics of countries that have positive net exports of the various types of goods, which cannot establish the precise impact of the various country endowments on comparative advan-

FIGURE 2.14

**Characteristics of Countries with a Comparative Advantage in Tropical Agriculture, Raw Materials, Petroleum, and Labor-Intensive Manufactures**

(Compared to the Rest)

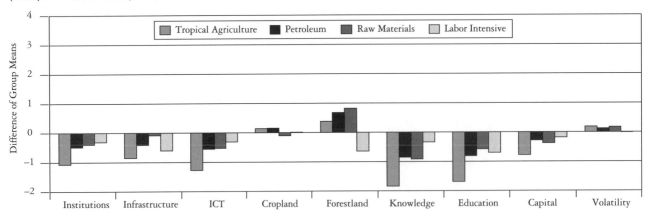

FIGURE 2.15

**Characteristics of Countries with a Comparative Advantage in Forestry, Cereals, and Animals**

(Compared to the Rest)

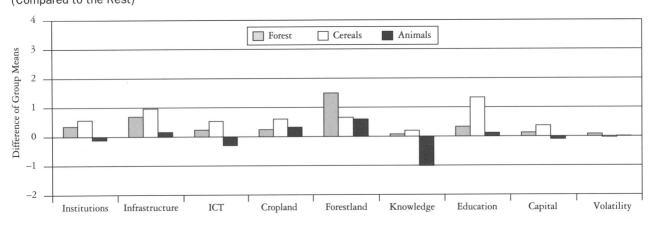

FIGURE 2.16

**Characteristics of Countries with a Comparative Advantage in Capital-Intensive Manufactures, Machines, and Chemicals**

(Compared to the Rest)

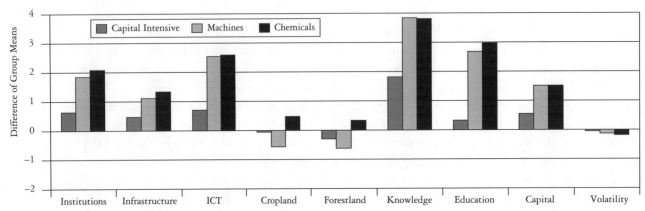

FIGURE 2.17

**Marginal (Average) Effects of Country Characteristics on Comparative Advantage**

(Comparative Advantage = Probability of Positive Net Exports; Only Statistically Significant Effects Shown)

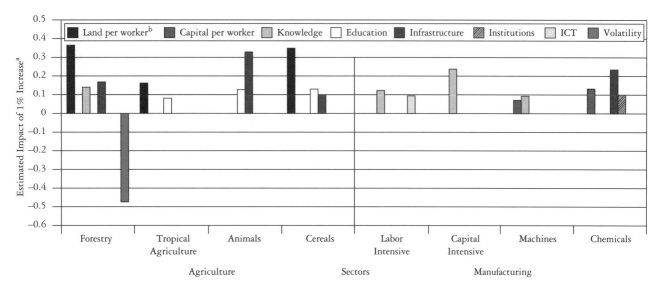

a. Except knowledge, infrastructure, institutions, ICT; impact of one standard deviation, which are indexes.
b. Either forestland or cropland; the stat. Significant one used.
*Note:* Education is general; knowledge includes technicians/patents/R&D. Sample: Over 55 countries, 1976–99.
*Source:* Lederman and Xu 2001.

tage because many of these characteristics move together. Hence further econometric analysis that examines the "marginal" effects of each of the country endowments can be a useful complement.

The main econometric results concerning the determinants of comparative advantage are summarized graphically in Figure 2.17; the methodology is discussed in Box 2.4. Each bar shown in the graph indicates the impact of the corresponding country endowment on the probability of comparative advantage in the agricultural and manufactured-goods sectors.

For given endowments, small increments in forestland, knowledge, and infrastructure have significant effects on the likelihood of having a comparative advantage in forestry exports. These results are driven by several Scandinavian countries, such as Finland and Sweden (see Chapter 3), which invest in R&D and have developed important technologies in a variety of areas, including forestry. Likewise, these countries also have advanced domestic infrastructure. Furthermore, some developing countries that export forestry products, such as Chile, also have relatively more advanced infrastructure than other developing countries. Finally, comparative advantage in forestry is impeded by macroeconomic volatility.

On average, small improvements in education (besides cropland) can have significant positive consequences for net exports of tropical agricultural products. In interpreting this result, readers should be aware that this product category includes commodities, such as fresh fruits, which are exported by relatively (compared to developing countries) educated countries, such as Chile and New Zealand. Likewise, net exports of cereals benefit from small increases in cropland, general education, and infrastructure. These results for cereals clearly reflect the influence of countries such as Australia, Canada, and the United States, which have highly educated populations and extensive roads and railways. Also, on average, countries that raise their general education and transport infrastructure on the margin will increase their chances of developing a comparative advantage in animal products.

All else remaining constant, countries that raise their endowments of knowledge and ICT will increase their chances of developing a comparative advantage in labor-intensive manufactures. This result is strikingly consistent with the trade theories that emphasize the role of coordination costs, and logistics costs more generally, in stimulating the fragmentation of production across borders. That is, the labor-intensive stages of production are made more

BOX 2.4

## Econometric Methodology: Heckman Selection Models

In using the Heckman selection model (Heckman 1976, 1979), we simultaneously estimate a model of the determinants of comparative advantage with another of export (and separately, import) intensity. Factor endowments, broadly defined, determine whether the country is a net exporter (or a net importer); then trade policy (that is, "adjusted openness"), the institutional environment, infrastructure, and economic size (of the domestic economy and of its principal neighboring countries) determine the value of net exports (imports). Formally,

$$I_{it}^* = X_{it}^c \beta_c + \varepsilon_{it}$$
$$I_{it} = 1 \text{ if } I^* > 0$$
$$NX_{it} = X_{it}^E \beta_E + u_{it}$$
$$\text{where cov } (\varepsilon_{it}, u_{it}) \neq 0$$

where $I_{it}^*$ represents the index function for exports (imports); a positive value of the function leads to the status of net exporter (importer). The $NX_{it}$ function represents the value of net exports (imports) per worker. Note that the unobservables for the selection equation and the main equations are allowed to be correlated. The equation of the determinants of export (import) status is the "comparative advantage equation." The equation of the determinants of net export values is the "trade intensity equation." In estimating the import and the export segments separately, we have allowed the coefficients for the net export equation to differ across the net-export and the net-import subsamples, which provides an intuitive way to allow for nonlinearities in our estimates of the determinants of trade intensity.

Due to data limitations, the analysis does not include deposits of minerals and petroleum. To correct this omission, we conducted additional statistical exercises, using the condition of being a net exporter of raw materials and petroleum as a proxy. The results discussed in the main text for agricultural and manufacturing products did not change significantly. Another caveat is that the "endowments" might be "caused" by trade. Hence the econometric models used the lagged values of the endowments in the analysis discussed here.

profitable when countries raise their levels of ICT development, which helps producers coordinate their activities better with their input suppliers located in the developed (capital-rich) countries.

Small improvements in knowledge have even greater effects on comparative advantage in capital-intensive manufactures—more so than for labor-intensive goods. Also, marginal increments in knowledge and in the amount of capital per worker have significant impacts on the comparative advantage in machines. For a given level of knowledge, tiny improvements in institutional quality favors comparative advantage in chemicals, which are also exported by countries with high endowments of capital per worker and land-transport infrastructure. As discussed earlier in this chapter, the knowledge index used for this analysis is composed largely of outcome indicators of R&D expenditures and the number of patent applications. The fact that the quality of institutions has a large (marginal) impact on comparative advantage in chemicals indicates that a proper institutional framework for the creation of knowledge can be greatly improved with (statistically) small efforts to reform domestic institu-

tions, especially those involving the enforcement of intellectual property rights, and even those regulating the incentives for R&D expenditures. The good news is that small improvements in institutional quality might have large positive effects on these sectors. More generally, the results show that since the mid-1970s, new endowments have had significant effects on the patterns of trade around the world.

To finalize the discussion about whether traditional endowments are destiny, Table 2.8 reports the possible ranges of the variance of comparative advantage attributable to traditional notions of endowments (land and capital per worker) and to the modern notions of endowments (knowledge, schooling, infrastructure, institutions, ICT, and so forth). The table shows the plausible ranges estimated with various analysis-of-variance (ANOVA) exercises, which had the predicted probabilities from the previous models as the dependent variable.

The evidence shows that only the variance of comparative advantage in raw materials and forest products explained by the conventional factor endowments are greater than the variance explained by the modern concepts, which are more

TABLE 2.8

**The Role of Conventional and New Factors in Accounting for Patterns of Comparative Advantage across Countries during 1976–99**

| | SHARE OF VARIANCE EXPLAINED BY: | |
| --- | --- | --- |
| COMPARATIVE ADVANTAGE IN: | "CONVENTIONAL" FACTORS: CROPLAND, FORESTLAND, AND CAPITAL PER WORKER | "NEW" FACTORS: INSTITUTIONS, ICT, INFRASTRUCTURE, VOLATILITY, EDUCATION, AND KNOWLEDGE |
| Raw Materials | 0.35–0.78 | 0.19–0.62 |
| Forestry Products | 0.52–0.76 | 0.19–0.40 |
| Tropical Agricultural Products | 0.09–0.55 | 0.40–0.87 |
| Animal Products | 0.11–0.35 | 0.65–0.89 |
| Cereals | 0.25–0.54 | 0.42–0.72 |
| Labor-Intensive Manufacturing | 0.15–0.35 | 0.62–0.83 |
| Capital-Intensive Manufacturing | 0.02–0.12 | 0.86–0.96 |
| Machinery | 0.06–0.62 | 0.38–0.94 |
| Chemicals | 0.22–0.61 | 0.39–0.78 |

*Note:* The dependent variable in the ANOVA exercises for each row is the predicted probability of exporting the specific product; the underlying model is the selection equation of the Heckman model. The reported number in the cells are the share of the variance attributable to each group of variables. Since the share depends on the "ordering" of the explanatory variables in the ANOVA equation, we report the range of shares under different combinations.

malleable through public policies. More precisely, for raw materials, the minimum and maximum shares of the conventional factors are higher than the corresponding shares of the new factors. In the case of forest products, the minimum share of the conventional factors is greater than the maximum of the modern factors. However, as mentioned earlier, we acknowledge that the explanatory power of traditional factors would probably be slightly higher if we included mining and petroleum reserves, although our additional estimations using rather imperfect proxies for these variables yielded very similar results.

There are some surprising results concerning comparative advantage in agricultural and animal products. The share of the global pattern of comparative advantage in tropical agricultural products and cereals explained by the new factors could be as much as 87 to 89 percent of this variance. The conventional factors could explain no more than 54 to 55 percent. In the case of animal products, the evidence is even stronger in favor of the new factors, because the minimum possible share of the variance explained by these factors is almost twice as high as the maximum variance possibly explained by the more traditional notions of factor endowments. In our view, these results are surprising because agricultural products obviously require land, but we have already discussed the influence of domestic infrastructure and general education on agricultural comparative advantage.

It is perhaps less surprising that the new factors explain relatively high shares of the global variation in comparative advantage in manufactured goods. The evidence shows that this is especially strong in labor- and capital-intensive manufactures. In the latter, the new factors explain between 86 and 96 percent of the variance. In the cases of machinery and chemicals, the maximum share reaches 94 percent for machines and 78 percent for chemicals.

From a public policy standpoint, the overall results are encouraging. It cannot be overemphasized that land endowments and other natural riches are not destiny. Developing countries can develop comparative advantage in manufacturing activities through sustained efforts to raise the quality of domestic institutions, improve the public transport infrastructure, and help the private sector adopt new information and communications technologies. Perhaps more important, policymakers should not underestimate the role played by general education and knowledge in determining the global patterns of trade. Although we have emphasized that for any given level of educational attainment of the adult population, knowledge creation is a key factor in the performance of most manufacturing activities, you cannot have knowledge without general education; engineers and innovation are not created in a vacuum. Yet knowledge by itself seems to have strong and independent effects on the capacity of countries throughout the globe to export manufactured goods.

The following sections explore the causes and consequences of other structural features of international trade, namely the degree of export diversification and IIT. These features have important consequences for the pace of economic development, and their determinants are somewhat different from the factors discussed thus far.

## Export Diversification and IIT: Where Are We, and Does It Matter?

A recurrent preoccupation of LAC policymakers is that their natural riches produce a highly concentrated structure of export revenues, which then leads to economic volatility and lower growth. This section examines the evidence concerning export revenue concentration. It first compares the region's degree of export revenue concentration with those of other parts of the world. The evidence indicates that the region enjoyed declining export concentration during the 1990s, after the trade reforms. This declining trend is also evident in the set of LAC countries. After presenting these facts, we explore the relationship between export revenue concentration and economic growth. The evidence is clear: concentration reduces subsequent economic growth, and only a fraction of this effect is explained by the correlation between export concentration and macroeconomic volatility. It is likely that a large portion of the remaining negative effect of concentration on growth is due to the negative relationship (but not necessarily causation) that exists between concentration and the incidence of IIT (that is, the share of total trade that is composed of imports and exports in the same product class).

IIT is correlated with the pace of economic development because it is driven by productivity gains. Much of the recent literature on trade has focused on scale economies in production, which can produce patterns of trade that are unrelated to factor endowments. Thus, economies of scale provide an explanation for trade flows among countries with similar endowments and that export similar products to each other. Regarding the relationship between IIT and economic growth, IIT is more likely to be driven by product differentiation, productivity gains, and/ or the life cycle of product development (see, for example, Krugman 1979).[5] That is, IIT is driven by economies of scale and productivity gains, which in turn should be reflected in a country's growth rate.

To determine the stylized facts about the recent evolution of the incidence of IIT in the region as a whole, and for our core set of countries, we studied the determinants of IIT across the globe, using annual data from 1970 to 1997. We found that public policies can affect the incidence of IIT. Among the most important policies to consider are increasing the rate of education of the population so that the region can catch up with the rest of the world, maintaining an open trade regime, and improving domestic institutions and infrastructure to ameliorate the impact of geographic distance from the major world markets.

This report links sectoral comparative advantage with the issues of export concentration and IIT. It looks at the evidence concerning the relationship between comparative advantage in the 10 industrial clusters discussed previously and the degree of export concentration and IIT. We attempt to answer the question of whether sectoral policies can help reduce export concentration and raise IIT. The data show that there is no clear relationship between the degree of concentration and IIT across sectors. Consequently, we conclude that sectoral policies that aim at addressing export concentration and IIT by "changing" a country's comparative advantage might have unexpected results. Indeed, attempts to increase exports of manufactures might actually reduce export diversification and IIT.

## Export Diversification and IIT in LAC

There are various ways to measure the degree of concentration of any economic variable. For example, the menu of indicators for measuring the degree of concentration of income across households is quite large, and includes the Gini index, the Theil index, and the Herfindahl index. For the moment we rely on the Herfindahl index to examine recent trends in export concentration in LAC. The case of Argentina is examined in Chapter 4 and alternative measures of concentration are used therein. The advantage of the Herfindahl index is that it is not sensitive to the incorporation or elimination of product lines.[6]

Figure 2.18 shows the evolution of the median (or typical) index of concentration of export revenues for the region compared with the rest of the world. The export concentration of the typical LAC country experienced a secular decline since 1981. Nonetheless, the degree of concentration is still higher than in Asia, Eastern and Central Europe, and the industrialized countries of the OECD. Another interesting aspect of these indicators is that the higher they are the more volatile they are. This is revealed in Figure 2.18, where the corresponding indexes for Sub-Saharan Africa and the Middle East and North Africa are quite volatile. This is expected because a high concentration of export revenues in a few products will also result in a high sensitivity of the index to particular variations in the international prices of those commodities. Thus we cannot say much about the relative position of Sub-Saharan Africa to Latin America and the Caribbean in the last three obser-

FIGURE 2.18

**Median Herfindahl Index of Concentration of Exports by Regions**

(Minimum of 11 Country Observations per Year; Calculations Based on over 2,000 Product Lines, Four-Digit Standard International Trade Classification [SITC])

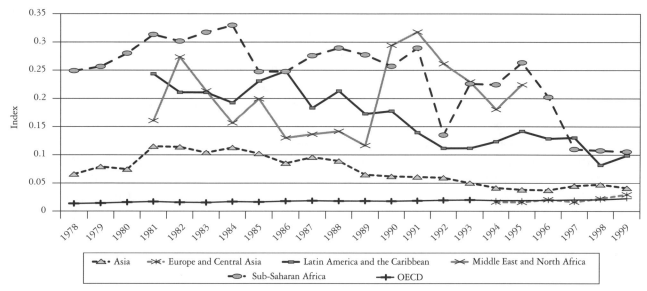

*Note:* Data were not available in all years for all countries.

FIGURE 2.19

**Herfindahl Index of Merchandise Export Revenue Concentration**

(Calculations Based on 2,208 Product Lines, Four-Digit SITC)

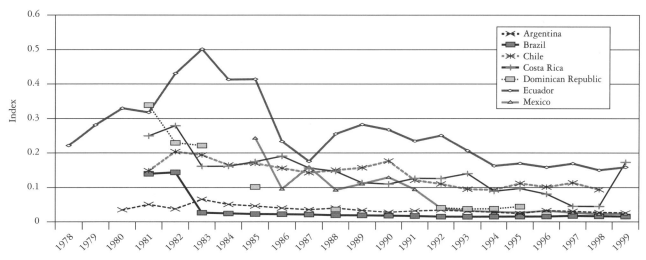

*Note:* Data were not available in all years for all countries.

vations in the chart. That is, we do not know whether this was due to, for example, a temporary decline in the price of Africa's major commodity exports. In contrast, as mentioned, LAC did experience a secular decline in its concentration of export revenues. The question that remains is

whether this declining trend is also present in our core set of countries.

Figure 2.19 shows the indexes of export concentration for a set of LAC economies. Of the sample, Brazil has the most diversified export structure, which is reflected in the relatively low values of its concentration index. It has been diversified for some time, especially when compared to the rest of the sample. Argentina also has a diversified export structure, and has experienced a decline in concentration since 1991. This experience is examined in detail in Chapter 3. Mexico experienced the most dramatic decline in export concentration. In fact, since 1990 (which was not the year of Mexico's highest level of concentration) the Mexican index declined from about 0.13 to 0.02 in 1999. By the end of the 1990s Mexico had reached the Brazilian level of diversification of exports.

Chile also experienced an important decline of export revenue concentration, but it remains relatively concentrated, especially when compared with the aforementioned countries of South America and Mexico. Costa Rica's experience is also interesting. Like the rest of the sample, it experienced a steady process of diversification during the 1990s, until the very end. In 1999, after Intel began exporting computer chips from Costa Rica, the country's export structure experienced a dramatic increase in the level of concentration. It remains to be seen whether this degree of concentration will prove to be transitory as the economy begins to develop new potential export products. For now, however, this case raises the issue that strong foreign investment and the emergence of a new manufacturing industry will not automatically lead to greater diversification of export revenues. Indeed, Costa Rica will probably face macroeconomic challenges in attempting to manage swings in the international price of computer chips. However, the volatility of high-tech product prices might be lower than that of agricultural commodities, and it is possible that the country will quickly develop new export industries, in part due to potential dynamic effects of having Intel. At the moment, it is clear that Costa Rica's high-tech sector is composed not only of Intel, but also includes a variety of domestic firms that are providing inputs to Intel, plus other foreign firms that have expansion plans in the country partly as a result of the signal sent to foreign investors by Intel's decision. This experience will be examined more closely in Chapter 4 (see also Rodríguez-Clare 2001).

Quality data for the Dominican Republic were not available for every year. However, the scattered evidence shown in Figure 2.19 seems to indicate that this country also experienced a process of export diversification since the early 1980s. Finally, Ecuador clearly has the highest level of export revenue concentration, except for Costa Rica in 1999. This is to be expected from a small economy that is highly dependent on oil exports. But it also experienced a process of diversification or falling export concentration. In sum, the region as a whole and most individual countries experienced an increase in export diversification after trade liberalization.[7] The discussion in the following section suggests that these trends are good news for the future development of the region.

Regarding the share of IIT, Figure 2.20 shows that LAC's IIT rose between 1980 and 1998, but it is still behind other regions. Nevertheless, the regional upward trend of IIT also appears in the individual LAC countries examined in this report (Figure 2.21). Overall, the upward trends in export diversification and IIT in LAC countries coincided with the implementation of trade liberalization throughout the region. Whether these trends represent good news for the region is an empirical issue addressed in the following section.

### Export Diversification, IIT, and Growth

Why should the concentration of export revenues hamper economic growth? There are various plausible channels through which the concentration of export revenues in a handful of commodities can affect growth performance. First, the concentration of exports could be associated with macroeconomic volatility. This might happen because countries that rely on a few commodity exports can face more severe and sudden variations in their terms of trade. In turn, economic uncertainty can hamper domestic investment (Pyndick 1988; Servén 1998; Lederman and others 2001a) and stifle other business decisions such as whether to sell goods abroad or for the home market, thus negatively affecting trade (Maloney and Acevedo 1995). Second, export concentration can be a symptom, rather than a cause, of poor economic growth due to low incidences of IIT. As discussed, IIT is driven by product differentiation and competition among firms with monopoly power in their respective product niches of the international market. An important consequence of IIT is that it is driven by productivity gains, which could be reflected in greater aggregate growth rates. Finally, high degrees of export concentration might be related either to civil conflicts (Collier and Hoeffler 1998) or to other forms of institutional failures due to the existence of large supplies of natural riches. This has been coined the "voracity effect" by Lane and Tornell (1999).[8]

FIGURE 2.20

**Grubel-Lloyd Index of IIT by Regions, 1980 and 1998**

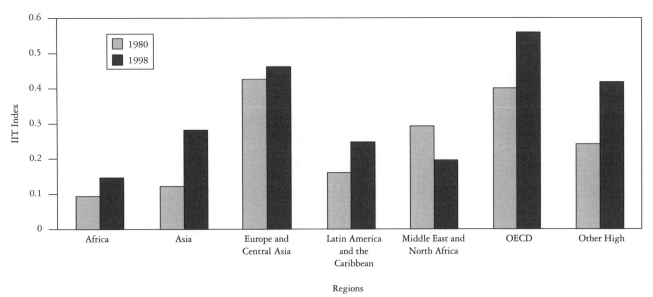

FIGURE 2.21

**IIT in LAC Countries Since the Early 1980s**

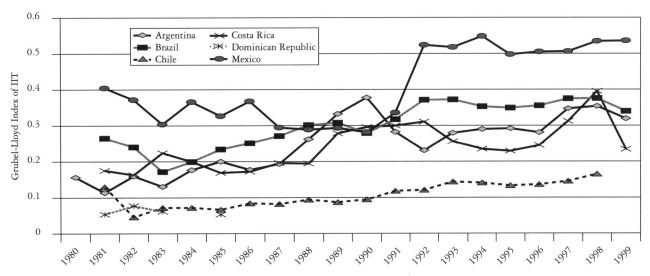

*Note:* Data were not available in all years for all countries.

So, what do the data say? As a preliminary incursion into the relationship between export concentration and economic growth, Figure 2.22 shows clearly that export concentration is negatively correlated with subsequent growth. The graph contains the fitted line from a linear regression. At first sight, the data show that countries with higher levels of export concentration tend to grow slowly. However, this evidence is not enough to be convincing because this simple correlation could be spurious. For instance, it could be the result of other variables that produce both low growth and high export concentration. The simple correlation is also not convincing because Figure 2.22 itself reveals that although the negative correlation is statistically significant, by itself it explains a very small portion of the cross-country and over-time variation of growth rates, thus indicating that there are many other fac-

FIGURE 2.22

**Export Concentration and Subsequent Growth**

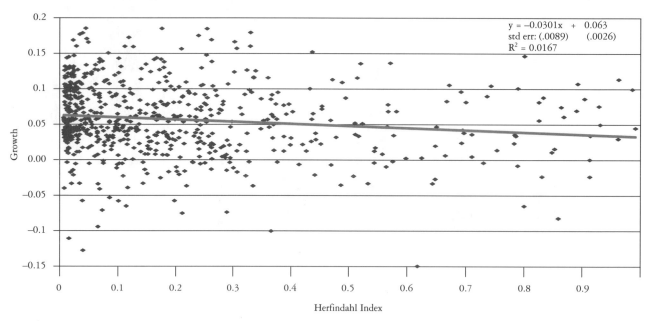

tors that affect growth. This issue, unfortunately, cannot be addressed without more sophisticated statistical analysis. A discussion on multivariate regression results follows.

Table 2.9 shows the results of two econometric models, where the dependent variable is the average real-GDP growth rate during three-year periods corresponding to 1976 to 1999 (the same data used in Figure 2.22). These exercises include several explanatory variables suggested by the existing literature on economic growth (see, for example, Barro and Sala-I-Martin 1995). In addition to the standard controls, we include our indicator of export-revenue concentration, and the results appear in column (1). The results suggest that a 1 percent increase in the concentration of exports is associated with a 0.5 percent decline in the growth rate of real-GDP per capita.

The studies by Sachs and Warner (1995a, 1997) find that the exports of raw materials as a share of GDP are negatively correlated with growth. In additional econometric estimations (not presented here) we reproduced the estimates by Sachs and Warner. The results suggest that once we controlled for the degree of export concentration, the statistical significance of raw materials exports vanished.[9] It is likely, therefore, the Sachs-Warner result operates through the export concentration channel.

Still, a policy-relevant question is what are the channels through which export-revenue concentration affects the pace of economic growth? This question is addressed empirically

in column (2) of Table 2.9. The regression results correspond to an exercise similar to the one discussed above, but with explanatory variables of interest that might represent channels through which export concentration affects growth. The results indicate that roughly 50 percent of the previously estimated impact of export concentration on growth is due to the volatility of the exchange rate, the incidence of IIT, and the quality of domestic institutions.[10] When the volatility of the exchange rate, the incidence of IIT, and the quality of domestic institutions are included in the regression, the direct effect of export concentration on growth is reduced to half of the previous estimate. In other words, about half of such estimated effect is due either to the effects of export concentration on the volatility of the exchange rate, the incidence of IIT, and the quality of domestic institutions, or to exogenous differences in these variables.[11]

### Export Diversification and IIT: Can Anything Be Done?

We have already seen that since 1976 the degree of export diversification and IIT has been positively correlated with subsequent economic growth across countries.[12] Again, to inform policy it is important to understand the determinants of these phenomena. We now shed some light on what can be done by LAC policymakers to raise export diversification and the share of IIT.

To understand export diversification in LAC countries during the 1990s, we conducted additional empirical analy-

TABLE 2.9

**Does Export-Revenue Concentration Affect Economic Growth? Econometric Results**

| DEPENDENT VARIABLE | ANNUAL GROWTH RATE (1) | ANNUAL GROWTH RATE (2) |
|---|---|---|
| Initial GDP per Capita | −0.343 | −0.304 |
| | (11.15)[a] | (12.63)[a] |
| Education | 0.041 | 0.025 |
| | (2.69)[a] | (2.27)[b] |
| Government Expenditures (% of GDP) | −0.001 | 0.001 |
| | (0.24) | (0.27) |
| Investment Rate | 0.011 | 0.006 |
| | (4.55)[a] | (3.36)[a] |
| Population Growth | −0.031 | −0.016 |
| | (2.11)[b] | (1.57) |
| Trade over GDP | 0.001 | −0.000 |
| | (0.70) | (0.64) |
| Export Concentration | −0.508 | −0.254 |
| | (2.24)[b] | (1.90)[c] |
| Import Concentration | | −1.028 |
| | | (2.46)[b] |
| Real Exchange Rate Volatility | | −0.251 |
| | | (3.14)[a] |
| IIT Index | | 0.389 |
| | | (2.27)[b] |
| Institutions Index | | 0.004 |
| | | (0.32) |
| Constant | | |
| Observations | 475 | 475 |

a. Significant at 1 percent.
b. Significant at 5 percent.
c. Significant at 10 percent.

*Note:* Econometric methodology: GMM. T-statistics in parentheses. The variables are in first-differences to get rid of country-specific effects. The instrumental variables are the lagged levels of the endogenous variables, and the differences of out-of-system instrumental variables (that is, those included in the determinants of the export Herfindahl index but not in the growth equations). The overidentifying restriction tests suggest that our instruments are largely valid. Results from fixed- and random-effects models produced results that are consistent with those presented in this table.

ses in two stages. The first stage entailed the estimation of statistical models where the index of export concentration was explained by GDP per capita and its squared term for LAC countries in the 1990s. The second stage entailed the same analysis but with data for the 1980s. The results from these two exercises revealed that the relationship between development and export concentration was different during the two periods. This counterfactual analysis clearly shows that if LAC countries had not liberalized, and thus would have behaved like they did in the 1980s (after controlling for their per capita income levels), the degree of concentration of export revenues would have been higher. Hence the first clear policy implication concerning export concentration is that for the vast majority of LAC countries, trade liberalization was associated with reductions in the concentration of export revenues. This was due primarily to the reduction of the anti-export bias of protectionist policies. Regional integration also helped to diversify exports. This particular hypothesis is examined in detail in Chapter 4 with reference to the case of Argentina's participation in Mercosur. Additional econometric exercises indicated that factors that reduce transaction costs, such as the quality of domestic institutions, also are negatively correlated with export concentration.

Since the early 1970s specialists have devoted much effort to trying to understand the determinants of IIT. On one hand, studies that use data from industries within countries have emphasized the role of economies of scale, product differentiation, and imperfect competition. In this context, industries produce a variety of similar goods with similar factor intensities. Cross-country studies, on the other hand, have focused almost exclusively on bilateral trade flows among industrialized countries.

For this study, we conducted an empirical analysis using cross-country annual data covering 1970 to 1997. These trade data were then used to construct the widely used Grubel-Lloyd (1975) index of the incidence of IIT, which is the indicator used in the previous sections of this report.[13] Following the existing literature, the analysis focuses on five types of explanatory variables. First, an important set of variables concerns the degree of similarity between the country and its partners. In this case, we use trade with the world, and consequently the indicators of similarity used herein are constructed with reference to world characteristics. More specifically, this analysis studies the effect of the "stocks" of education (total years of schooling of the population), capital, and labor in each country on the incidence of IIT. The log of the country-level stocks are differenced with respect to the world's total stocks of these variables, thus producing an indicator of the similarity of each country relative to the rest of the world. Second, we study the impact of the size of the domestic economy (that is, GDP) on IIT, in order to capture the potential effects of so-called economies of scale. Third, the analysis considers the potential effects of the level of development on IIT, because it is thought that consumers from rich societies tend to prefer product varieties, more so than consumers in the least-developed countries. Finally, we consider indicators of the extent of international transport and transaction costs and the level of overall international trade (as a share of GDP) as potential determinants of IIT.

Table 2.10 contains the results of the econometric analysis. The three indicators of similarity are significant determinants of IIT, as are the size of the domestic market and the level of development. This set of findings indicates that large and rich economies with high levels of education tend to have higher IIT indexes. The policy implication is clearly related to the education variables, which is the most policy sensitive of the lot. Countries should emphasize efforts to increase the provision of general education, so that poor LAC countries can at some point reach the levels of education of the industrialized countries. In other words, the pace of education improvement should be faster in the poor countries than in the rich countries for the poor countries to increase their IIT.

The rest of the explanatory variables are related to trade orientation, geographic distance from major markets (Brussels, Tokyo, and Washington), the quality of domestic institutions, and the existence of currency unions. The trade orientation is meant to capture the theoretical proposition that more trade (relative to domestic production) leads to higher IIT, where one of the gains for domestic consumers is the

increase in product variety (Krugman 1979). The other variables are meant to broadly capture the potential effects of international transaction and transport costs. The corresponding results show that high ratios of trade to GDP tend to be associated with higher IIT; geographic distance (which is related to transport costs) tends to reduce IIT; and currency unions (which eliminate international transaction costs related to currency exchanges) tend to increase IIT.[14] The index of domestic institutions has the expected effect of increasing IIT, but it is not statistically significant.

This analysis provides a handful of policy propositions, and the results are consistent with those found in the literature (see, for example, Stone and Lee 1995; Clark and Stanley 1998). Perhaps the most important propositions are related to trade orientation, education, and international transport and transaction costs. The policy implications of the first two are quite clear: trade liberalization will lead to higher IIT, and we have already mentioned the need for poor countries to "converge" to the levels of education of the industrialized world. The latter proposition can take a long time to come to fruition, but it cannot be overemphasized that general education plays an important role in determining trade patterns, as is mentioned throughout this report. The policy implications related to transport and transaction costs are also interesting. Perhaps more important, policymakers wishing to raise their country's level of IIT should consider improving the institutions related to customs administration and the infrastructure related to international commerce (ports, railways, roads), which play an important role in reducing the effects of geographic distance from the major export markets of the world.

The following section conducts further policy analysis about the relationship between sectoral comparative advantage and export concentration and IIT. The objective is to assess the potential of reducing export concentration, raising the incidence of IIT by focusing on sector-specific policies, or both.

### Export Concentration, IIT, and Comparative Advantage: Can Sectoral Policies Help Reduce Concentration and Raise IIT?

Another policy-oriented analysis is to examine the correlation between comparative advantage in the 10 sectors discussed in this chapter and the indexes of export diversification and IIT, both of which are correlated with economic growth. Many LAC analysts and policymakers believe that

TABLE 2.10

**What Can Be Done to Raise IIT? Econometric Results**

| EXPLANATORY VARIABLES | (1) | (2) | (3) |
|---|---|---|---|
| FACTOR ENDOWMENT SIMILARITY | | | |
| Capital | 0.027[a] | 0.031[a] | 0.034[a] |
| Labor | 0.020[a] | 0.023[a] | 0.024[a] |
| Education | 0.002[a] | 0.001[a] | 0.003[a] |
| | | | |
| SCALE ECONOMIES | | | |
| GDP | 0.047[a] | 0.048[a] | 0.049[a] |
| | | | |
| CONSUMER PREFERENCES | | | |
| GDP per Capita | 0.058[a] | 0.054[a] | 0.055[a] |
| | | | |
| TRADE IMBALANCE | 0.130 | | |
| | | | |
| TRADE ORIENTATION | | | |
| (X+M)/GDP | 0.018[b] | 0.017[a] | 0.019[a] |
| | | | |
| TRANSPORT AND TRANSACTION COSTS | | | |
| Geographic Distance | −0.014[a] | −0.012[a] | −0.013[a] |
| Institutions | 0.032 | 0.025 | |
| Currency Union | 0.002[b] | 0.001[a] | 0.001[a] |
| | | | |
| NO. OF OBSERVATIONS | 1,873 | 1,873 | 1,873 |

a. Significant at 5 percent level.
b. Significant at 10 percent level.
*Note:* Methodology: Tobit regressions with panel data. Dependent variable is the Grubel-Lloyd index. Regional and time dummies were included, as was a constant.

countries that export manufactured products automatically have higher diversification and IIT. If we find that certain patterns of comparative advantage are associated with higher levels of export diversification and IIT, then the policy recommendations discussed will also apply to the issues of export diversification and IIT.

Figures 2.23a, 2.23b, and 2.23c provide this analytical perspective. They show the differences among averages of country characteristics, and tell us whether countries with

a comparative advantage in a particular sector will tend to have higher (positive difference) or lower (negative difference) levels of export concentration and IIT than countries without a comparative advantage in the specified sectors. Figure 2.23a contains the estimates of the differences of the averages for countries with a comparative advantage in petroleum and raw materials. Net exporters of these products tend to have higher indexes of export concentration and lower indexes of IIT than other countries.

FIGURE 2.23a

**Export Concentration and IIT by Sector**

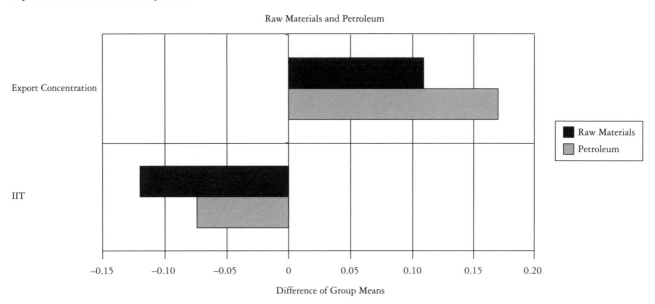

FIGURE 2.23b

**Export Concentration and IIT by Sector**

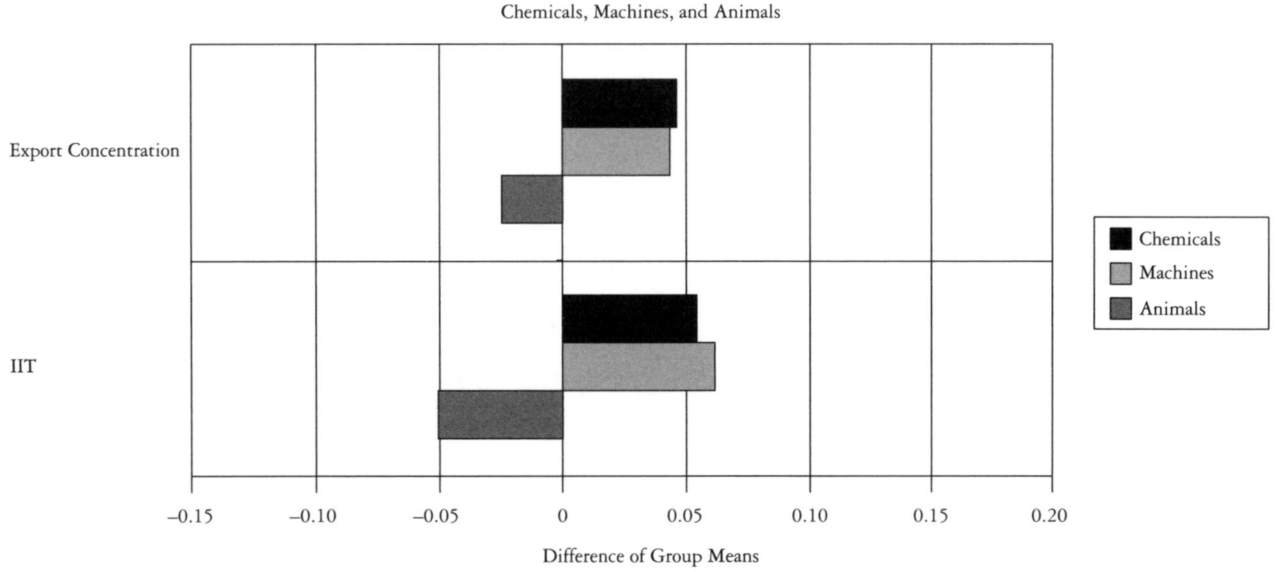

FIGURE 2.23c

**Export Concentration and IIT by Sector**

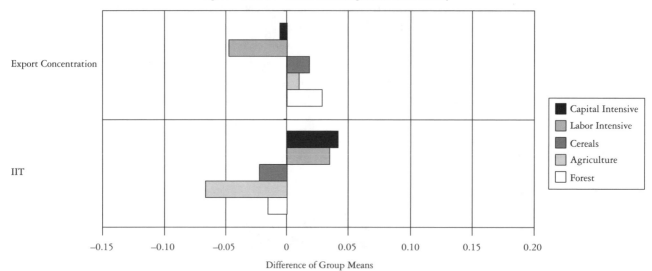

Capital and Labor Intensive, Cereals, Agriculture, and Forestry

Difference of Group Means

Figure 2.23b shows the estimates for countries with a comparative advantage in chemicals, machines, and animals. These groups share the characteristic that their bars for export concentration and IIT point in the same direction: Countries with a comparative advantage in chemicals and machines have higher export concentration than other countries, but they also have higher IIT indexes. Net exporters of animals have the opposite characteristics— lower export concentration, but also lower IIT.

Finally, Figure 2.23c contains the calculations for capital-intensive and labor-intensive manufactures, and for cereals and agriculture and forestry products. Countries with a comparative advantage in these products share the characteristic that their averages of export concentration and IIT point in different directions. Those that are net exporters of capital- and labor-intensive manufactures tend to have both low export concentration and high IIT, while the reverse is true for the agricultural exporters.

Overall, the evidence presented in Figures 2.23a, 2.23b, and 2.23c indicates that comparative advantage in some sectors is associated simultaneously with high export concentration and high IIT (machines and chemicals), while others are associated with low export concentration and low IIT (capital- and labor-intensive manufactures). Moreover, some agricultural sectors behave similarly to some manufacturing sectors.

Should a country implement policies to develop a comparative advantage in capital- or labor-intensive manufac-

tures, both of which seem to have the desirable qualities of low export concentration and high IIT? The answer must be a cautious one: yes, unless the particular policies have other undesired distortionary effects. For instance, a public program designed to improve the infrastructure and regulatory framework to aid the adoption of new information and communications technology will help develop a comparative advantage in labor-intensive manufactures. The goal of this type of program should be to increase the adoption of new information and communications technology for the economy as a whole, including reviewing the regulatory framework for communication and helping to develop the necessary infrastructure (see Mann 2001). These policies, in turn, are likely to enhance the competitiveness of labor-intensive industries that belong to a broader manufacturing process that has been fragmented across borders. This impact is likely to be stronger for this type of industry than for others, but this does not mean that the rest of the economy will not benefit from these policies. On the contrary, there are likely to be beneficial economywide effects.

## Summary of Findings about Comparative Advantage, Diversification, and IIT

The analyses in this chapter provide several conclusions that might be useful for policymakers and analysts.

On average, the LAC region has maintained a comparative advantage in petroleum, raw materials, tropical agriculture (including fruits and vegetables), and animal products. While there has been a lack of structural change, this has nonetheless been accompanied by productivity and welfare gains for consumers due to trade reforms. Perhaps more interesting, the regional average masks important differences across countries. Some countries, especially Costa Rica and Mexico, have moved into the fast-growing global market in machines, while Brazil has maintained a diversified structure of net exports by exporting agricultural commodities and several types of manufactures.

New trade theory indicates that anything is possible in the world economy of the 21st century. The evidence shows that "new" endowments, such as knowledge, ICT, quality domestic institutions, and domestic infrastructure, plus volatility, explain a large share of the trade patterns observed around the globe. Hence natural resources are not destiny.

LAC countries experienced a significant diversification of merchandise export revenues in the 1990s, and a rise in the share of IIT. Both were partly due to trade reforms. These trends are encouraging because the statistical evidence shows that export diversification and IIT are positively correlated with subsequent economic growth. The region's dependence on natural resources has clearly not prevented these trends, thus indicating that natural resources are not necessarily a curse for future development.

Chapter 3 further explores this last point by reviewing the evidence concerning how natural resources can be used to promote fast productivity growth. Certain industrialized countries developed successfully by tapping the potential for productivity growth offered by their abundant natural resources. Some of the world's fastest-growing economies in the long run had rich endowments of natural resources, but they accumulated knowledge while maintaining an outward orientation. Chapter 4 looks at the specific experiences of LAC countries, showing in detail how trade reforms, regional integration, the promotion of FDI, and the use of modern endowments have improved the economic performance of both the emerging natural resource and manufacturing sectors.

## Notes

1. This subsection is based on Bond (2001).

2. Ana María Menéndez (World Bank) wrote an initial draft of this section.

3. A caveat regarding the data for Internet hosts is that all hosts without a country code are assumed to be located in the United States, inflating the figure for that country and reducing it for all the other countries.

4. The U.S. Patent Office files the nationality of the first inventor in the patent application.

5. This is especially true when IIT is driven by horizontal rather than vertical IIT (Thom and McDowell 1999). Horizontal IIT is trade in products coming from the same stage in the production process, whereas vertical IIT is trade among products, some of which can be inputs in the production of the other products. For example, trade in automobiles is horizontal, while trade in automobiles and auto parts is vertical.

6. The Herfendahl index is defined as $H = \sum_i^n \left( x_i \Big/ \sum_i^n x_i \right)^2$, where $i$ stands for a particular product and $n$ is the total number of products. When a single export product produces all the revenues, $H = 1$; when export revenues are evenly distributed over a large number of products, $H$ approaches 0.

7. Econometric exercises not presented in this report also showed that export diversification was higher in the 1990s in LAC, after controlling for the level of development.

8. Sachs and Warner (1995a, 1997, 1999) argue that dependency on exports of natural resources and agriculture hurt economic growth through its negative Dutch Disease effect on manufacturing industries, which they argue theoretically can have unexploited economies of scale. Hence when manufacturing falls, aggregate productivity growth falls as well. This is an argument distinct from the ones being discussed here about export-revenue concentration on any type of commodity.

9. In fact, when using the Generalized Method of Moments (GMM) estimates with instrumental variables, the Sachs-Warner variables sometimes have a positive and significant sign.

10. The incidence of IIT is the Grubel-Lloyd index, which is a measure of the share of imports and exports of identical products (at the four-digit level of the SITC, Revision 2) with the world.

11. The concentration of imports appears with a significant sign in Table 2.9. However, this variable was not significant on its own, and was not robust to the choice of econometric technique. Thus we downplay its potential role.

12. Claudia Sepúlveda (World Bank) conducted the econometric analysis of IIT.

13. The index is defined as $IIT = 1 - \dfrac{\sum_i^n \left| X_i - M_i \right|}{\sum_i^n (X_i + M_i)}$, where $i$ indicates a product category and $n$ is the total number of products. This index varies between 0 and 1, and it shows the share of total trade that is conducted among identical products (that is, imports and exports of the same product category).

14. The data on currency unions come from Glick and Rose (2001). These authors also provide an empirical analysis of the impact of currency unions on the magnitude of trade flows.

# CHAPTER 3

# It's Not Just What You Produce, But How: Lessons from Comparative History

CHAPTER 2 MADE TWO KEY OBSERVATIONS. FIRST, PATTERNS OF TRADE ARE DETERMINED NOT only by traditional factors of production—land, labor, capital, and natural resources—but equally or more by "new" factors—knowledge, education, ICT, and the quality of institutions. The ability to create these factors, combined with the historical decrease in transport and communications costs, offers the opportunity for the region to move into industries that were heretofore unimaginable. The second observation is that, while some countries—Costa Rica and Mexico, for example—have experienced dramatic changes in their production structures, most countries remain largely exporters of natural resource–based goods.

This second finding could be a concern for two reasons. First, some may interpret it as evidence that there have been few of the promised efficiency gains of trade liberalization. Second, recent literature, in particular Sachs and Warner (1997), appears to confirm a traditional Latin American suspicion that resource-rich countries underperform.

This chapter answers both concerns with the same finding: It is not so much *what* is produced, as *how* it is produced. The estimated static efficiency gains of eliminating trade distortions—eliminating the famous Harberger triangles—have never exceeded more than a few percentage points of GDP. It is the

dynamic process of productivity growth arising from innovation and adoption of new technologies that propels development. This, as much as any reallocation of factors among industries, is the promise of trade liberalization. Further, the evidence reviewed in this chapter shows that natural resource sectors have as much or more potential for gains in productivity as the manufacturing sectors.

## The Lesson from History: Play to Your Strengths

History offers numerous examples of how sustained and dynamic growth is possible based on any number of patterns of export specialization. The manufacturing success of Japan and the Asian newly industrialized countries (NICs) is one route. However, many of the world's most developed countries—Australia, Canada, Scandinavia, and the United States—have successfully developed on the basis of, and not in spite

of, their resource base. In fact, as Figures 3.1 through 3.4 show, their net exports are heavily resource intensive.

The evidence is now strong that the U.S. industrial success must be considered that of a natural resource–rich nation that made a gradual transition to resource-rich manufacturing industries (see Irwin 2000). The United States was the richest country in terms of natural resources, and its transformation into the global manufacturing leader, while somewhat technology driven, was sparked by the discovery of iron ore reserves in Minnesota that reduced the cost of iron-intensive manufactures below those of the competition. Even today, it remains first and foremost a net exporter of foodstuffs.

Innis (1933) and Watkins (1963) had Canada in mind when they developed their "staples theory." They saw primary good exports, beginning with fur and fisheries and then progressing to forestry and wheat—through either

FIGURE 3.1

**Australia: Structure of Net Exports in Selected Industrialized Countries**

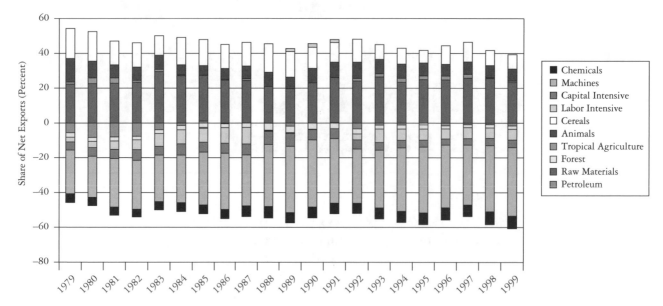

*Note:* To see this figure in color, refer to Figure A.8 in the Annex.

FIGURE 3.2

**Canada: Structure of Net Exports in Selected Industrialized Countries**

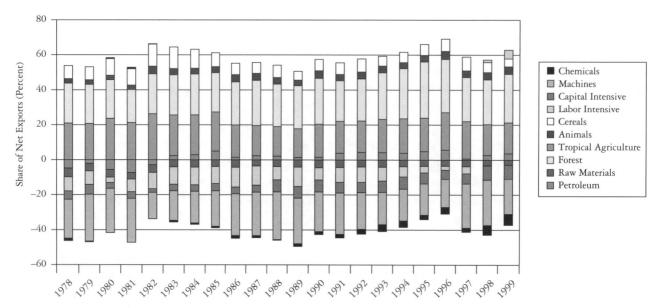

*Note:* To see this figure in color, refer to Figure A.9 in the Annex.

demand or supply linkages—as driving subsequent industries in wood, pulp, and metal refineries. Canada remains principally a net exporter of forest products. Although wool is Australia's most famous staple, extraordinary and continuing success in mining and the derivative industries

of both made the country one of the richest economies in the world in the early 20th century, and discoveries of new deposits might put it near the top of the list again.

The Scandinavian countries that produce aircraft, luxury cars, designer furniture, and most recently, advanced tele-

FIGURE 3.3

**Finland: Structure of Net Exports in Selected Industrialized Countries**

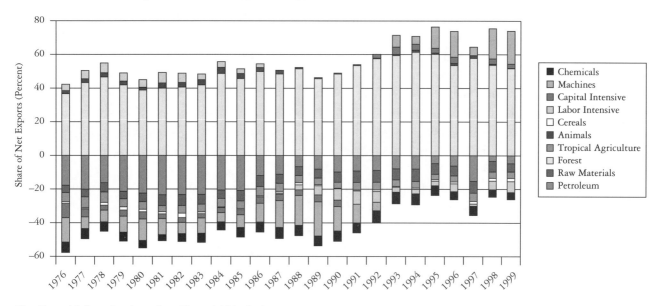

*Note:* To see this figure in color, refer to Figure A.10 in the Annex.

FIGURE 3.4

**Sweden: Structure of Net Exports in Selected Industrialized Countries**

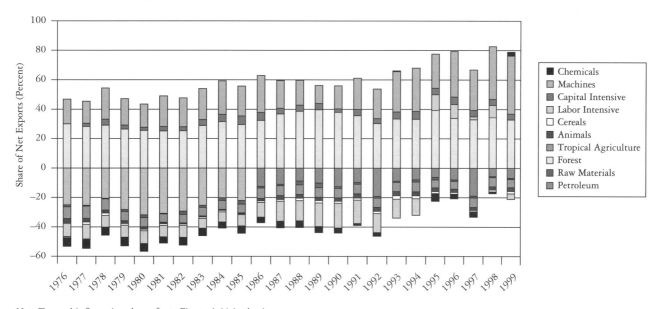

*Note:* To see this figure in color, refer to Figure A.11 in the Annex.

communications products, again built slowly on their strengths in natural resources. The forest and metal industries together still employ 20 percent of the industrial labor force in Sweden, and constitute 25 percent of exports, with even larger numbers in Finland. However, the most striking feature is the rapid growth of the Swedish and Finnish world market shares in the high-tech sector. As late as 1990, computer and telecommunications products accounted for less than 7 percent of Swedish and Finnish exports. By 2000, this share had increased to nearly 20 percent in Sweden and 30 percent in Finland, and high-tech firms like Ericsson and Nokia had become household words.

Latin America also offers its success stories. Mexico's dynamic industrial city, Monterrey, emerged from the mining boom of the 19th century as a processor of iron ore and steel. Colombia's Antioquia, with its epicenter Medallin, was also originally based on mining, and then coffee, before becoming an important industrial center. As is frequently noted, São Paolo, if taken alone, would have the GDP of Belgium, and it too was built on mining and coffee.

The bottom line is that it is impossible to argue that these economies did not base their development on their natural resources.

How, then, do we square these success stories with Sachs and Warner's (1997) findings that for two decades of the late 20th century, 1970 to 1989, countries rich in natural resources grew relatively more slowly? Most important, their data sample probably is not representative of the past and, hence, is probably not able to answer questions about long-term growth. As Maddison (1994) shows, during 1913–50, Latin America was one of the fastest-growing regions, as were other resource-rich countries like Canada, Finland, Sweden, and the United States, while resource-poor areas like Japan, the Republic of Korea, and Asia more generally had negative growth (Table 3.1). Second, Sachs and Warner's period encompassed a "lost decade" when resource-rich countries in Latin America and elsewhere were forced to take wrenching adjustment measures to deal with unmanageable debt.[1] This period was also one in which Latin America was grinding to the end of its import substitution policies that were, in themselves, partially an unsuccessful reaction to perceived natural-resource dependence.

The failure of the import substitution industrialization (ISI) strategy, and the fact that Australia, Canada, and the Scandinavian countries succeeded by playing to their resource strengths, suggests that success has less to do with what a country produces in particular, and everything to do with the way in which it produces it. In particular it depends on establishing an environment that enables innovation and the adoption of technologies.

## Total Factor Productivity Growth and Development

The engine of growth is not only the accumulation of capital and labor, but the process of innovation and, more specifically increasing total factor productivity (TFP)—the part of growth that cannot be explained by factor accumulation. The recent literature suggests that it is primarily differen-

TABLE 3.1

### Rates of Growth of GDP per Capita, 1820–1989

(Annual Average Compound Rate of Growth)

| | 1820–70 | 1870–1913 | 1913–50 | 1950–73 | 1973–89 |
|---|---|---|---|---|---|
| *The European capitalist core and its offshoots* | | | | | |
| Austria | 0.6 | 1.5 | 0.2 | 4.9 | 2.3 |
| Belgium | 1.4 | 1 | 0.7 | 3.5 | 2.0 |
| Denmark | 0.9 | 1.6 | 1.5 | 3.1 | 1.7 |
| Finland | 0.8 | 1.4 | 1.9 | 4.3 | 2.8 |
| France | 0.8 | 1.3 | 1.1 | 4.0 | 1.9 |
| Germany | 0.7 | 1.6 | 0.7 | 5.0 | 1.9 |
| Italy | 0.4 | 1.3 | 0.8 | 5.0 | 2.6 |
| Netherlands | 0.9 | 1.0 | 1.1 | 3.4 | 1.3 |
| Norway | 0.7 | 1.3 | 2.1 | 3.2 | 3.1 |
| Sweden | 0.7 | 1.5 | 2.1 | 3.1 | 1.7 |
| United Kingdom | 1.2 | 1.0 | 0.8 | 2.5 | 1.9 |
| Australia | 1.9 | 0.9 | 0.7 | 2.4 | 1.7 |
| Canada | | 2.3 | 1.5 | 2.9 | 2.4 |
| United States | 1.2 | 1.8 | 1.6 | 2.2 | 1.6 |
| **Average** | **0.9** | **1.4** | **1.2** | **3.5** | **2.1** |
| | | | | | |
| *European periphery* | | | | | |
| Czech Republic | 0.6 | 1.4 | 1.4 | 3.1 | 1.3 |
| Greece | | | 0.5 | 6.2 | 1.7 |
| Hungary | | 1.2 | 1.2 | 3.5 | 1.2 |
| Ireland | | | 0.7 | 3.1 | 2.9 |
| Portugal | | 0.3 | 1.4 | 5.6 | 1.7 |
| Spain | 0.6 | 1.4 | 0.2 | 5.1 | 1.8 |
| Former Soviet Union | | 0.8 | 2.3 | 3.6 | 1.0 |
| **Average** | **0.6** | **1.0** | **1.1** | **4.3** | **1.7** |
| | | | | | |
| *Latin America* | | | | | |
| Argentina | | 1.9 | 0.7 | 2.1 | −1.2 |
| Brazil | 0.2 | 0.3 | 2.0 | 3.8 | 1.7 |
| Chile | | | 1.7 | 1.2 | 1.5 |
| Colombia | | | 1.5 | 2.1 | 1.8 |
| Mexico | 0.4 | 1.1 | 1.0 | 3.1 | 1.0 |
| Peru | | | 1.4 | 2.5 | −1.2 |
| **Average** | **0.3** | **1.1** | **1.4** | **2.5** | **0.6** |
| | | | | | |
| *Asia* | | | | | |
| Bangladesh | | | −0.3 | −0.7 | 2.2 |
| China | 0.0 | 0.3 | −0.5 | 3.7 | 5.7 |
| India | 0.0 | 0.3 | −0.3 | 1.6 | 2.7 |
| Indonesia | 0.2 | 0.5 | −0.2 | 2.1 | 3.4 |
| Japan | 0.1 | 1.4 | 0.9 | 8.0 | 3.0 |
| Korea, Rep. of | | | −0.2 | 5.2 | 6.4 |
| Pakistan | | | −0.3 | 1.8 | 2.8 |
| Taiwan (China) | | | 0.4 | 6.2 | 6.1 |
| Thailand | | 0.4 | 0.0 | 3.2 | 5.2 |
| **Average** | **0.1** | **0.6** | **−0.1** | **3.5** | **4.2** |

*Source:* Maddison 1994.

tials in TFP, not resources or education, that account for the vast income differences among countries, and that it was the convergence of TFP, not of factor accumulation, that was the central force behind the catch-up of the OECD countries to the United States in the 1960s and 1970s.[2]

The outstanding question appears to be why certain nations are able to tap into the existing external stock of know-how and why others cannot or, more specifically, why some countries, for example, the Nordic countries, caught up while others, like Argentina and the Philippines, fell behind (see Baumol, Nelson, and Wolff 1994; and Amsden and Hikino 1994).

The search for the barriers to innovation and the adoption of technology is an old pursuit.[3] Most recently, Parente and Prescott (2000) argue that the reason cross-national TFP differences persist, in spite of an immense stock of global knowledge that offers ready quasi-rents to any LDC entrepreneur, is the existence of monopolistic structures that prevent new entry and ratify labor's intransigence in the face of job-threatening new technologies. Their simulations suggest that the impact of such barriers far exceeds the few percentage point differences in GDP accounted for by counting the Harberger triangles of traditional static models or, for that matter, differences in education.[4]

Their analysis echoes Albert Hirschman's (1958) broader point that in an uncompetitive situation such as the one posed by the guild system, "an innovation in producing a given commodity could only be introduced by someone who was already engaged in its production by the old process. . . . [T]his fact would, in itself, militate against many innovations that might render painfully acquired skills useless and valuable equipment obsolete . . ." (p. 57). Similar effects can appear due to concentrated credit markets that lend only to insiders, foreign exchange shortages that simply inhibit access to technology, and any explicit trade barrier.

But contemporary theory and economic history also suggest the importance of factors that actually encourage and facilitate the adoption of new technologies by developing national "innovative" or "learning" capacity.[5] It was the ability to develop this national innovative capacity, and the elimination of the barriers posed by trade protection, rigid labor codes, and concentrated financial systems, that differentiates Sweden, for example, from Latin America (see Boxes 3.1 and 3.2). The lesson that emerges from Blomström and Kokko's (2001) work on Scandinavia, and Irwin's (1996) and Wright's (1999) work on the United States is that development took place in a context of rich networks of universities, research institutes, and high levels of human capital that led to an incessant process of innovation. Focusing on these types of linkages, rather than the more mech-

anistic conceptions of clusters (see Ramos 1998, for example) based on product similarity, is what allowed Nokia, Finland, to move from trees to telecommunications (see Box 3.3).

## Knowledge and Natural Resources: A Proven Recipe for Growth

One of Raul Prebisch's (1959) concerns was that the potential for technical progress was limited in raw material–intensive products compared to industry, and his concern resonates today, including in Sachs and Warners' work.[6] However, even in that era, future Nobel Prize winner Douglass North argued that "the contention that regions must industrialize in order to continue to grow . . . (is) based on some fundamental misconceptions," and the pioneer trade economist Jacob Viner stated that "There are no inherent advantages of manufacturing over agriculture, or, for that matter, of agriculture over manufacturing" (Viner 1952, cited in North 1955). Both recent econometric work and experience in other regions suggest that Prebisch was wrong about the potential for TFP growth, but was perhaps correct in his view of the Latin American case he was studying.

Numerous recent studies support Viner's views on agriculture.[7] Martin and Mitra (2001) offer the most comprehensive study of TFP growth in agriculture and manufacturing from 1967 to 1992 for a broad cross-section of countries. They estimate that average LDC manufacturing productivity growth was around 1 percent compared to agricultural growth rates of roughly double. (See Figure 3.5.) This relative performance holds for the industrialized countries as well, which, as Figure 3.5 shows, also had consistently higher TFP growth in both areas. In fact, several of the big natural resource success stories—Denmark, France, and Sweden—continue to show the highest TFP growth rates in agriculture. The question is, again, why LDCs adopt technologies so slowly, especially since their great distance from the knowledge frontier implies large gains.

The Scandinavian experience with forestry highlights not only another case of sustainable growth based on natural resources, but also the vital importance of knowledge networks or clusters to generate productivity growth, competitiveness, and new ideas. Forestry offered downstream demand for both paper and pulping technologies, as well as transport products developed by Saab and Volvo in Sweden. However, as Box 3.2 and Table 3.2 show, even in the paper and pulp sector, there is a large and established network

BOX 3.1

### The Swedish Growth Secret: Innovation Networks and Aggressive Labor

Sweden did many things recommended by mainstream development economics: its early land reforms stimulated agricultural productivity and provided capital and labor to emerging downstream industries. Its stable politics and reliable institutions minimized risk. Its efficient capital markets channeled resources to promising growth sectors. But the critical difference lay in the environment of learning, research, and innovation in which the process of resource-led development was embedded. The introduction of a mandatory school system in 1842 was crucial for the creation of a skilled human capital base and for the dissemination of technologies, and literacy rates reached nearly 100 percent within one generation.

Universities in Uppsala and Lund date from the 15th and 17th centuries, with technical schools being established in the early 1820s. Other institutions, such as the Swedish Academy of Science, date to 1739, and the Swedish Ironmaster's Association to 1747, which published a mining science journal in 1817 and financed foreign study trips made by Swedish engineers and scientists. New engineering workshops established for the construction of iron bridges and lock-gates of the Göta Canal served as training centers. Swedish engineers were often trained and educated in Great Britain and Germany, and important contributions were made by several British engineers that immigrated to Sweden. In sum, due to a high level of technical skills and competence, Sweden possessed the fundamentals of a modern engineering industry by about 1850, and as Harvard historian David Landes (1998) argues about Scandinavia more generally, "They were equal partners in Europe's intellectual and scientific community." The intellectual infrastructure, both at an abstract and applied level, were there to absorb new ideas and apply them to their strengths, primarily based in the natural resource area.

The impetus to Swedish industrialization was the boom in demand for cereals from the 1850s and 1910s that provided capital for industrial expansion and forest production. Demand for raw and sawn wood by English urbanization maintained high demand for these products. Swedish inventors led the development of pulp technologies and established the world's first chemical pulp factory in 1872, and by 1913 Sweden became the largest exporter of pulp and paper. The forest industry progressively expanded into more and higher value-added goods, including prefabricated housing, furniture, and refined paper products, and acquired numerous subsidiaries throughout Europe to further process products. Its high phosphorous content of iron ore made processed iron weak, but adopting the foreign Bessemer process permitted the emergence of a domestic industry.

As in Britain and the United States, Swedish mechanization was a slow process that implied ongoing accumulation of know-how and continuous interaction with the outside world. To a significant extent the expansion of manufacturing during the first decades of the 20th century was based on Swedish innovations—steam turbines, centrifugal separators, ball bearings, the adjustable spanner, the safety match, air compressors, automatic lighthouse technique, various types of precision instruments, techniques for precision measurements, and so forth (Lindbeck 1974). The great companies known today were built on innovations in these areas—Ericson (1876, the telephone), Alfa Laval (1879, the separator), ASEA (1890, electrical equipment), and SKF (1907, bearings) (Amsden and Hikino 1994). The exceptional long-term performance of firms established during this period, Blomstöm and Kokko (2001) note, "has been based on the ability of Swedish industry to create, adapt and disseminate new technologies." And throughout, a high degree of research continues. Even the long-established pulp industry dedicates 4 percent of value added to research in the industry's institutes. Despite the emergence of new producers in Brazil, Chile, and Indonesia, the network of organization or institutional framework or knowledge clusters remains the main strategic and competitive asset of the Swedish forest industry. In sum, Scandinavian development looks like a slightly accelerated version of U.S. development: high levels of innovation applied to and building on a generous resource base, but all embedded in an enabling network of educational, legal, financial, and corporate institutions.

But the final ingredient, Hjalmarsson (1991) argues in *The Scandinavian Model of Industrial Policy*, is the enlightened attitude of Swedish Trade Unions which, "as early as the 1920s strongly promoted a productivity enhancing industrial policy, emphasizing the rationalization of firms" that placed a premium on continual renewal of technology, plant organization, and machinery. The 1951 policy document of the Confederation of Trade Unions stressed competition to increase productivity and force less-efficient firms out of the market, combined with active labor market policies to reallocate displaced workers. In the

1950s, the confederation was resolutely free trade, strongly criticized government protectionist measures, and "argued that tariffs would decrease productivity growth since it would protect stagnating and less competitive industries." In short, whether due to earlier land reforms or alternative transfer mechanisms, Swedish labor unions were not concerned about distribution and could focus purely on raising TFP.

BOX 3.2

## And More Specifically, Knowledge Clusters: The Swedish Pulp and Paper Industry

The forestry sector is often characterized as a mature low-technology industry facing bleak prospects arising from increased competition from Brazil, Chile, and Eastern Europe. Blomström and Kokko (2001) disagree. Not only is there likely to be continuing high demand, but Sweden's continued investment in knowledge clusters in what can be a very high-tech industry will ensure forest products remain an important Swedish export. Swedish industry has managed to overcome the disadvantages caused by high raw material and labor costs by mechanizing production processes, and by moving into operations with higher value added. At the same time, product development is generating new uses for forest resources, new types of industrial products, and the development and leadership of environmentally correct forestry practices. Many of these opportunities are available because the forest industry has created dynamic networks of institutions and organizations involved in the production and dissemination of the knowledge and skills that are needed to remain competitive. This network of organizations—or knowledge clusters—is perhaps the main strategic and competitive asset of the Swedish forest industry (see Table 3.2).

Most companies in the pulp and paper industry devote considerable resources to R&D activities, and to in-house education. Yet, the network of institutions permeating the industry is essential for maintaining and developing international competitiveness, not least concerning education and the dissemination of skills from universities and research organizations to the industry. As an example, university training of engineers specializing in pulp and paper processing, biotechnology, and related fields is

provided by the Royal Technical University in Stockholm, and the Chalmers Technical University in Gothenburg, and the University of Karlstad. The industry's leading research institution, the Swedish Pulp and Paper Research Institute, finances student research projects, arranges guest lectures, and provides lecture rooms and equipment. A major share of postgraduate education was managed jointly by the Swedish Pulp and Paper Research Institute and the technical universities. The Research Institute also accounted for a major share of the research and development activities taking place in the cluster. With 250 employees, half of whom were qualified researchers, it was one of the largest research institutions of any kind in Sweden, and was recognized internationally as one of the leading centers, as well.

In addition to the activities that took place in each of the research institutes, there were collaborative research projects involving several of the industry's institutions. One example is a multidisciplinary research program entitled Paper-Color-Print, the goal of which was to develop Swedish competence in paper processing, paper coating, and printing technology. The project was conducted jointly by the Royal Technical University, the Swedish Pulp and Paper Research Institute, the Institute of Surface Chemistry, the Graphical Research Laboratory, and the Swedish Newsprint Mills' Research Laboratory, with financing from the participating institutions, independent research foundations, and the government. Launched in 1993 and planned to run for six years,

(continues on next page)

BOX 3.2

**Continued**

employing on average 40 full-time researchers, the project was estimated to result in 5 doctoral dissertations, 20 licentiate dissertations, 50 graduate engineering degrees, and 100 to 150 scientific publications and lectures. More generally in the industry, during the 1990s some 20 new full professor positions in the forestry sector—each with a connected assistant professor, graduate students, and support—were established at the main research institutions to boost academic competence. The Royal Institute of Technology and the Chalmers Technical University

have chairs in pulp technology, paper technology, wood chemistry, forest industrial chemistry, wood chemistry, packaging technologies, printing technologies, and environmentally oriented pulp production technologies.

In short, the forestry industry in Sweden is very high tech and prosperous, but without question requires ongoing investment in human capital and research capacity.

*Source:* Blomström and Kokko 2001.

TABLE 3.2

**Participants in the Knowledge and Skills Clusters in the Swedish Paper and Pulp Industry**

| CLUSTER | GENERATION | DISSEMINATION |
|---|---|---|
| Skills (Education) | Royal Technical University<br>Chalmers Technical University<br>University of Karlstad<br>Swedish Pulp and Paper Research Institute | Swedish Pulp and Paper Research Institute |
| Knowledge (Research) | Royal Technical University<br>Chalmers Technical University<br>University of Karlstad<br>Swedish Pulp and Paper Research Institute<br>Institute of Surface Chemistry<br>Graphical Research Laboratory<br>Swedish Packaging Research Institute<br>Swedish Newspaper Mills' Research Laboratory | Swedish Pulp and Paper Research Institute<br>Institute of Surface Chemistry<br>Graphical Research Laboratory<br>Swedish Packaging Research Institute<br>Swedish Newspaper Mills' Research Laboratory |

*Source:* Blomström and Kokko 2001.

of public and private research institutes and universities that engage in an unrelenting pursuit of productivity growth. This enables Sweden to confidently face producers in Brazil or Chile. As Box 3.3 explains, the human capital and knowledge clusters that prepared Finland for unforeseeable technological opportunities were what linked Nokia's former excellence in forestry to its present leadership role in telecommunications.

Wright (1999) offers an analogous argument that mining is much more than simple extraction. The stock of minerals is, to some degree, endogenous, and as with manufacturing, major increases in productivity both in discovery and exploitation could be reaped by the application of knowledge

and the supporting intellectual networks such as schools of mining. "Mining," he argued about the U.S. success, "was fundamentally a collective learning phenomenon" (p. 308), from the initial investments in exploration techniques to training mining engineers and geologists, in fomenting a metallurgical revolution. For instance, the development of electrolytic processes in the 1890s was essential to the development of copper and aluminum. Before World War I, the United States had the world's highest level of human capital and boasted the world's best mining institutions, with the University of California at Berkeley and the Columbia Mining School preeminent. He identifies many resource "under-achievers"— those with significant but heretofore undiscov-

BOX 3.3

## Finland: From Trees to Telecommunications

In 1869, Fredrik Idestam expanded his ground-wood mill to the nearby village of Nokia where the river Emäkoski provided the energy to propel Nokia Ltd. to become Finland's largest pulp and paper mill. By 1930, Nokia, along with Finnish Rubber works (also in Nokia) and Finnish Cable works (based in Helsinki), formed a single conglomerate. All segments drew heavily on imported technology and all benefited from access to the large Russian market as a Grand Duchy under Russian rule, and all grew in strength over the next half-century.

Finnish Cable Works in particular benefited from war reparations to the Soviet Union after World War II. The demanded manufactures exceeded the capacity of Finnish industry, and the shortage of hard currency forced output increases through productivity rather than capacity expansion. The existence of a secure market in the former Soviet Union was a strong incentive to increase capacity after postwar currency restrictions were lifted, and diversification seemed attractive: an electronics department with a group of R&D engineers was established in 1960, and resulted in the development of a variety of electronic goods. In 1962, Finnish Cable Works developed a prototype radiotelephone at the request of the army (in competition with the country's two other leading electrical engineering firms, Salora and Televa, and the Swedish producer Sonab). Cuts in the defense budget forced the companies to find other markets, including the Soviet oil and gas industry.

In 1966, the three companies were formally merged and divided into four divisions: paper, cable, rubber, and electronics, the last being the smallest, with only 3 percent of turnover. Though profitability was low or negative for years, Nokia's chief executive officer (CEO) ensured that the electronics workshop had access to the latest technology. In 1977, the new CEO, Kari Kairamo, decided to transform Nokia from largely a producer of paper, tires, and cable to a leading high-tech company. The foundation had been laid in the electronics division, which had expanded with the public radiotelephone system in the early 1970s, and had been marketing foreign computers (Bull and Honeywell Elliot), and had found a market adapting foreign computer equipment into pack-age solutions for domestic industrial customers. By the late 1970s, learning had progressed far enough for it to develop its own computer terminals and cash registers, and a portable computer that competed well with the Apple in the Nordic Market.

Kairamo wanted to expand beyond the Nordic market, but knew Nokia lacked the necessary skills and experience to compete with established American, European, and Japanese incumbents in the global electronics market. With an early commitment to compete in all markets, alliances with European and American firms were essential to Nokia's transformation from a raw material–based to a knowledge-based high-tech company. But Blomström and Kokko (2001) also cite an aggressive human resource development program that encouraged work abroad in foreign affiliates. Karaimo also worked to modernize the public education system and to support broad international student-exchange programs, continuous lifelong learning, and close collaboration between industry and academia. The most tangible fruit was Nokia University, a comprehensive and ambitious education program managed by several Finnish Universities in collaboration with Nokia to raise the formal competence of all Nokia employees by one level: bachelors to masters, masters to doctorate. "The increase in the level of human resources was essential for Nokia's ability to absorb and diffuse the skills and knowledge that were obtained through acquisitions and strategic alliances during this stage of Nokia's development.

Though the leap from a raw material–based industry to high-tech activities seems large, Blomström and Kokko argue that success in both areas has similarities. In both cases, knowledge and human resource development—in the form of well-developed knowledge clusters, like in the mature forest industry, or in the form of in-house assets, like in the early stages of Nokia's and Ericsson's breakthroughs—have been essential for success in both sectors. They argue that while it is not possible to systematically create innovations, it is possible to systematically prepare for those commercial and technological opportunities and challenges that will occur.

*Source:* Blomström and Kokko 2001.

FIGURE 3.5

## Percent Annual TFP Growth (1967–92)

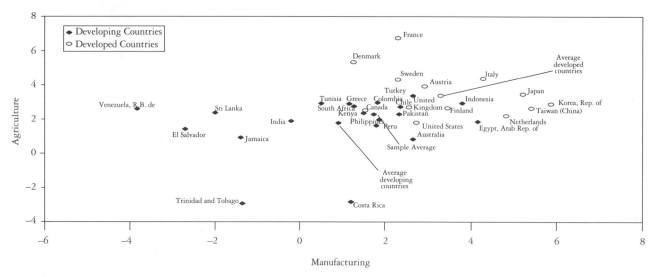

*Source:* Based on Martin and Mitra (2001).

BOX 3.4

### How Did Australia Come to Run Chilean Mines?

Chile's largest producer of copper is run by Broken Hill Proprietary Company (BHP), hailing from Australia, a country roughly the size of Chile and with a shorter tradition of copper mining. Though Australia's mining policy has fluctuated dramatically across time, one explanation for its ability to export mining expertise lies in the buildup of human capital in this area over time. Engineers and metallurgists were recruited to Australia in 1886 and this firmly linked the country to the innovations generated in the United States (Wright 1999). Duncan and Fogarty (1984) argue that "geological knowledge and mining expertise became part of the Australian heritage enriched by schools of mines of world class and the industry has been in the forefront in the development and application of mining and treatment technology." In fact, Australia lagged behind the United States until after 1920—with 47 engineers per 100,000 people compared to 128 per 100,000—but would reach 163 by 1955. Further, several important universities could offer local beachheads for foreign research. The Sydney Mechanics Institute was established in 1843 and the Sydney Technical College in 1878, both with the goal of the diffusion of scientific and special knowledge; Sydney University was established in 1850;

and a School of Mines was established in Ballarat in 1870 and in Bendigo in 1873. The University of New South Wales (UNSW) was founded in 1949 on the campus of the Technical College, with the Massachusetts Institute of Technology and the Berlin University of Technology as models, and a core focus on research and teaching in science and technology. The UNSW School of Mining Engineering now ranks as one of the largest educators of mining engineers in the world. These institutions rest on a commitment to universal education beginning with the Victoria Education Act of 1872 that established free, secular, and compulsory education in that state—this in a country that until the 1840s had been a penal colony of the United Kingdom.

Out of this context emerged one of Australia's most influential mining companies and industrial conglomerates. In 1883, a boundary rider on a sheep station in New South Wales discovered lead and silver and formed a syndicate with other local workers, leased the mine, and in 1885 floated BHP. Called by those of the region "the cradle of Australian industrialization," mines and smelters would expand, and when easy-to-access oxide zones were exhausted, BHP metallurgists and engineers introduced the flotation process that, as a residual, allowed the expansion of zinc production by new firms. BHP diversified into manufactured steel products, coal and iron ore, petroleum, and shipping and shipbuilding, and eventually severed its ties completely with its birthplace. BHP and similar conglomerates became modern corporations, with vertical control from mining to blast furnaces to wire rope factories to shipping lines with links to foreign capital through joint ventures. BHP would gain a global reach, acquiring mines in Canada and in the state of Utah in the United States, and would eventually discover and undertake the development of *La Escondida* copper mine in Chile. Australians now lead the world in mineral detection technology embodied in their "transparent earth" initiative, and in mine-closing techniques and mining-related environmental knowledge, and export more mining know-how than their famous wines.

The Australian case suggests several lessons. First, mineral wealth was a blessing. Second, literate and free everymen can be an important source of entrepreneurship and innovation. Third, the ready adoption of mining and metallurgical expertise allowed local exploitation of the mines and, eventually, the export of mining knowledge.

ered mineral deposits—with having deficient capacity in these areas.

The case of Australia, discussed in Box 3.4, suggests that a similar process of collective learning could be replicated later in a small peripheral economy. Australia's BHP company found *La Escondida* in Chile, one of the world's largest deposits of copper. Something similar appears to have occurred in Brazil. Baer (2001) argues that modern satellite surveying techniques radically increased Brazil's known endowments over those known in the late 1960s. Previously, most mineral reserves were thought to lie in the mountain ranges of Central Brazil, especially in the state of Minas Gerais. However, massive deposits of iron ore were discovered in 1967 in the Serra dos Carrajas in the Amazon, which was also found to contain large deposits of bauxite. Tin reserves now appear to exceed those in Bolivia, copper was found in Bahia, and offshore oil exploration vastly expanded available reserves of oil. In Peru, mining exports doubled between 1992 and 1999, making it the world's second-largest silver, bismuth, and tin producer, the world's sixth-largest copper producer, and eighth-largest gold producer. Still, Wright argues, this is far below Peru's potential.

All three sectors suggest that Latin America's challenge is not necessarily getting out of what it presently produces well, but taking advantage of the possible productivity gains. The question emerges of why it is foreign technology that is exploiting Chilean ores, and why it is Australia that exports more mining know-how than wine, and not Chile, which started copper mining over a century earlier. (See Box 3.5.) We argue that much of the reason may have to do with both explicit barriers to adoption, and to a lack of an environment that facilitates innovation.

## Two Final Concerns

Two concerns that are found in much of the literature on natural resource–rich countries merit comment.

First, another of Prebisch's concerns was that a declining share of world income accounted for by commodities would lead to worsening terms of trade: Latin America's exports would buy progressively fewer manufactured imports. Recent literature has called this diagnosis into question. As part of a larger challenge to what he depicts as a weak and scientifically unsound dependency literature, Stanford historian Stephen Haber (1997) reviews the work of numerous scholars and finds that during the 19th century the region's terms of trade actually rose. He concludes that "the weight of the evidence points to the conclusion that there has been no secular deterioration in Latin America's terms of trade, but rather that there have been cyclical swings with no discernable long-term trend." Hadass and Williamson (2001) reexamine evidence on the Prebisch-Singer hypothesis, constructing estimates of the terms of trade for 19 developing and industrialized countries, and find that the terms of trade actually *improved* for *all* regions. This is due largely to rapidly declining transport costs during the sample period: the decline in the relative price of Latin America's exports that Prebisch's 1870 to 1950 U.K. data showed would have been reversed in any port in Latin America. In a sense, everybody's terms of trade improved, and up to World War I, the

BOX 3.5
## Why Didn't Chileans Find La Escondida?

Chile's largest mine was discovered and managed by Australia's BHP, as discussed in Box 3.4. Why didn't Chile follow a similar trajectory? Chile's mining sector became a classic foreign-owned enclave with relatively few linkages. In *Chile, A Case of Frustrated Development*, Pinto Santa Cruz is only the best read of Chile's historians who point to the willingness to live passively off natural wealth, a culture of conspicuous consumption, and deficient entrepreneurship among the Chilean elite. But in other areas, Chileans were very entrepreneurial. Exports boomed after the elimination of Spanish restrictions on trade. Copper production by Chileans increased four-fold from 1844 to 1860. In response to increased demand arising from the gold rush in California in the United States, Chilean wheat exports rose ten-fold in value from 1848 to 1850, and area under wheat cultivation more than tripled between 1850 and 1870 (Conning 2001).

An alternative cause may lie in the historical lack of an infrastructure for scientific learning and innovation. Until the 20th century, Chilean governments remained ambivalent about universal primary education, and higher studies required going to Lima until the establishment of the University of San Felipe in 1758. Most students studied theology and law; medicine was considered unsuitable for the upper class, and mathematics was particularly neglected. A major break occurred in 1797 with the establishment of the Academy of San Luis, which attempted to introduced more practical courses in languages, arithmetic, geometry, and drafting, all of which its founder saw as essential to the development of the colony's agriculture, industry, and commerce. But this remained an uphill battle in a society where traditionally the Inquisition enforced, albeit incompletely, religious orthodoxy, and where the largest collection of books at the time was the 5,000 at the University of San Felipe, which focused on theology, canon law, and the lives of the saints, none of which had been printed within the previous half-century. In 1819, revolutionary leaders would establish the *Instituto Nacional*, an amalgam of the existing institutions that would focus on, in addition to theology, engineering, natural sciences, and medicine. In 1813, the first *Sociedad Economica*, patterned on those that took root in Spain after

1775, was established, and sought to improve the country's agriculture and industry by the diffusion of industrial arts and the promotion and adoption of useful inventions. But even a century later, in 1915, only 19 of the 970 students graduating from the National University would complete work in engineering (Will 1957). Chile's rich culture would produce two Nobel Prize winners in literature, a major surrealist painter, and first-class musicians. But it lagged behind in engineering sciences.

Arguably this weakened Chile's capacity for innovation and adoption of new technology. Pinto (1959) spectacularly underlines the foregone power of a gradual accumulation of know-how to the maintenance of competitive position and generation of new areas of comparative advantage:

... the technological demands of the [earlier] period, in contrast to what is occurring today in some areas of mining or industries, were relatively modest and thus not too costly. What could and had to be done in the national mining companies and in agriculture ... was perfectly compatible with the resources accumulated in the long periods of bonanza. If the process had been initiated and maintained adequately, without doubt, it would have created the means to confront more challenging tasks, such as those posed by copper mining when it was necessary to exploit less rich veins. However, faced with the technological revolution, the local mining companies had behind them neither sufficient accumulated resources, nor the organizational or administrative capacity that were indispensable. In these circumstances, there was no other option but the introduction of foreign capital and expertise.

Chilean copper mines were seen as inefficient, poorly managed, and lagging behind technically. The big and visible advances were in the Guggenheim mines at El Teniente and Chuquicamata. In the end, rather than any lack of entrepreneurial spirit, there may have been an implicit acknowledgment that technically, Chileans could not manage their resources as well as the British and later the Americans could. But the path chosen meant that no indigenous mining universities or institutions would emerge, and there would be limited indigenous capacity developed for innovation or analysis. Meller (2001) argues that "in the 1950s one could have learned more about Chilean copper in foreign libraries than in Chilean ones. Neither was there training of Chilean engineers and technicians specializing in copper." The fact that in 1952 the Controller General admitted that he had no idea of what went on in the companies suggests that part of the feeling of vulnerability and dependency must be attributed to the lack of technical capacity to monitor and confidently critique the actions of the *Gran Mineria*. It was not until 1955 that the Copper Department was created to oversee U.S. firms' copper operations, and a bureaucracy established of Chilean professionals, engineers, and economists, as the basis for local Chilean expertise. "In short," Meller argues, "it took about 40 years, from 1925 to 1965, to develop a domestic capacity to analyze the role of copper and to educate Chilean professionals and technicians in the management of the [large copper firms]." This is a striking statement in a country that began exporting copper long before the United States or Australian firms that would dominate the industry in Chile. Even today, there is relatively little interaction between the copper companies and universities or other think tanks.

Lagos (1997) argues that one way to continue development of the North after the inevitable decline in mining production is for the region to transform itself into a regional service center for the mining industry of neighboring countries Argentina, Bolivia, and Peru. A crucial aspect of this is the development of advanced science in the fields of the environment, production, and exploration technologies, markets, applications, and other key issues. Lagos suggests that a possible starting point would be for the state to create a research fund directed to strategic research projects, not only in Chile, with the target of positioning copper globally in all these fields. There may also still be a chance to be a player in the emerging lithium industry that is central to developing batteries for electric cars. In both cases, it may be necessary to cultivate more of a knowledge cluster.

periphery improved more than the center. Finally, for this report, Cuddington, Ludema, and Jayasuriya (2001) use modern time series econometric techniques and find no downward trend across the century before 1973 (see Box 3.6 and Figure 3.6). Even if the post 1973 downward trend were permanent, Meller argues that, measured in terms of the quality of manufactures, purchasing power may have risen: a Chilean can buy four times the number of computers in 2001 than he could in 1981.

Second, there is no overwhelming evidence of Dutch Disease effects that would crowd out other desirable activities. Competition for capital or labor or, alternatively, appreciation of the exchange rate due to large inflows of foreign capital, are probably not as severe as sometimes argued. The literature is not convincing on this point, however. A 1996 study by Ilades–Georgetown University estimated that the impact of the copper mining boom amounted to about 2 to 4 percent of crowding out of investments and some labor from other sectors. Overall, the negligible crowding-out effects and increases in both aggregate production and new resources show that "the copper boom is closer to a full blessing than to a mixed bless-

ing" (cited in Lagos 1997), and Lagos concludes that a Dutch Disease scenario is not likely to occur in Chile. Gylfason (1999) also suggests that though there is some evidence of Dutch Disease emerging in Iceland and Norway, the same is not true for Denmark, Finland, and Sweden. Given the strength in automobile, machinery, and telecommunications exports, it seems difficult to argue that a high share of natural resource–intensive exports was an insuperable obstacle in these latter cases.

## Why Was Latin America's Experience So Disappointing?

Latin America clearly did not follow the lead of these countries, arguably for two reasons: (a) the poor foundation for technological progress laid in the colonial period, and (b) the cultivation of inefficient manufacturing sectors to the detriment of the resource sectors in the post–World War II period.

### Initial Conditions

During the initial phase of export growth, the foundations were not laid for dynamic innovative economies, as they were elsewhere. Economic historian David Landes (1998)

BOX 3.6

**Prebisch Redux: Are LAC's Terms of Trade Declining?**

In a paper written for this report, Cuddington, Ludema, and Jayasuriya (2001) take a more rigorous econometric approach. They find breaks in the underlying data-generation process in 1921 and 1974, and until the latter date, they cannot reject a random walk with no trend in relative commodity prices. After 1974 they cannot reject a secular decline of roughly 1 percent per year (see Figure 3.6).

FIGURE 3.6

**Segmented Trends in Real Commodity Prices, 1900–2000**

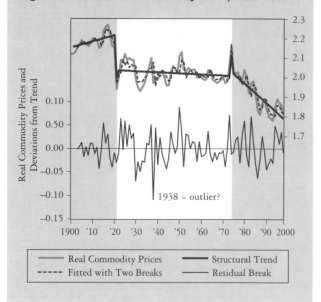

1938 = outlier?

Real Commodity Prices
Fitted with Two Breaks
Structural Trend
Residual Break

suggests that the slow adoption of technological advances in the southern European countries relative to their rapid adoption in Scandinavia was a legacy of a period of being intellectually closed following the *reconquista* in Spain. Numerous authors refer to a *rentier* mentality of living off the income from the new world mines that discouraged the emergence of entrepreneurship and the pursuit of scientific knowledge. Though trading mining riches for manufactured goods is consistent with comparative advantage, Landes argues that it did not encourage a tinkering or entrepreneurial culture at the core of the industrializing nations, which is essential to developing new areas of comparative advantage. These traits were inevitably communicated to a greater or lesser extent to the Spanish colonies, along with the stifling institution of the Inquisition.

While these more cultural themes emerge in much of the Latin American historical literature, we choose to focus on more structural conditions, in particular those that impeded the generation of a dynamic, innovative society. Many of these are familiar: barriers to trade, imperfect property rights, deficient infrastructure, unsound public finance, and deficient market size. We focus particularly on issues of education, technical capacity, and other barriers to innovation explicitly related to knowledge management and generation.

The first were barriers to trade and explicit barriers to diversification. The Spanish and Portuguese both forbade trade with other nations and enforced trading monopolies (Baer 2001). The vast expansion of trade in Chile after independence testifies to the lost dynamism of the previous decades. Further, fear of competition for manufactured products led Portugal to order the destruction of all smelting furnaces to make iron implements throughout the mid 18th-century, thus short-circuiting a potentially important backward linkage (Baer 1969).

Second, Latin America's birth as independent states was violent, and the transition to stable, consensual states difficult. This implies that, while Australia, Canada, Scandinavia, the United Kingdom, and the United States were able to quickly establish stable, legitimate governments and could forge ahead in promoting—at the very least—stability, education, infrastructure networks, and often direct nurturance for emerging industries, the principal job of Latin states in the 19th century was nation building. Mexico offers a particularly striking example of the roots of the lost half-century after independence (see Box 3.7). Mining, which had powered Mexican development for most of the 18th century, fell 60 percent and remained depressed for decades. Mines flooded, most expertise fled, emerging downstream industries and transport networks stalled, and national finances were thrown into chaos (Cardenas 1997). In Colombia, independence and then numerous civil wars extending into the present constantly interrupted construction of railroads and the consolidation of the national economy or local finances. In few ex-colonies of the 19th century was there a government capable of implementing a sustained and coherent vision of economic development.

These setbacks were critical factors in the delay of growth. Recent literature supports Coatsworth's early arguments that the lack of good roads and canals, and the delay in the construction of railroads, were two of the most impor-

62

BOX 3.7

## Canada and Mexico: So Far from God, So Close to a Huge Market

Canada and Mexico both share a border with a vast market and the principal source of innovation in the 20th century. For both countries, this implied both dependency and opportunity. Yet Canada's per capita income has expanded roughly three times more than Mexico's since the 1870s, and its industries are thought to be as efficient as those in the United States. Why would these outcomes be so different?

Mexico's beginning was hampered by the factors that would delay the development of much of Latin America. The first factor was a violent search for independence that would cost it 50 years. Further, poor roads and few railroads delayed integration of its market with the exterior, and weak educational and technological infrastructure impeded increasing the human capital of its people. The Canadian government early on made a commitment to railroads and farming infrastructure, and to universal public education.

Industrialization in Mexico in the late 19th century would be undertaken almost entirely by the resident Americans, English, Germans, Spanish and, particularly, the French (Hansen 1971), and would drive the growth boom of the *Porfiriato*. Using machinery from the homeland, the French started the textile industries in Veracruz and Puebla (Buffington and French 1999). Foreigners also started Mexico's first iron and steel plant, the *Fundidora de Fierro y Acero de Monterrey*, in 1903, that would build on the region's ore deposits and anchor its industrial development (Hansen 1971). Hansen argues that there were entrepreneurial spillover effects that drew many Mexicans into the capitalist ranks. However, this would also lead to substantial foreign ownership of production.

Canada also struggled with foreign control. The percentage of the value of production in minerals controlled by U.S.-controlled and affiliated companies in 1932 ranged from 39 percent in iron to 63 percent in nonferrous metals, including electrical apparatus (Wylie 1990). Canada maintained "defensive" tariffs since the turn of the century, although they would never be of the magnitude of those in Mexico. Dehem (1962) cited the fact that most

of Canada's important industries were tariff-jumping affiliates of foreign firms as the key factor inhibiting growth. In fact, many successful countries—Australia, Canada, Finland, and Norway—were dominated by large economies in such a way that Latin America's dependency literature could apply there with force as well (Maloney 2001a). But as Cortes Conde (1985) notes, compared to Latin American countries, Canada took advantage of the large market to the south, beginning with exports of newsprint, and was aggressive in adapting foreign technologies (Wylie 1990).

Technological progress was hampered in Mexico by several factors. First, there were distributional issues. Haber (1992), for example, suggests that the *Fundidora de Fierro y Acero de Monterrey* adopted modern technologies, but the plant never operated at more than 30 percent capacity due both to the thinness of the market and to, perhaps, a workforce unsocialized as modern salaried workers. Canada inherited the equal distribution of lands and an educated populace that allowed the emergence of indigenous industry that would grow to form large, vertically integrated corporations.

Second, due to concentration in the credit markets and other forms of economic and noneconomic pressure, newcomers to the market tended to avoid established industries and hence did not put on the pressure to further innovate. Unlike in Brazil and the United States, most investment capital came from a tight clique of national financiers who grew to control the most important manufacturing companies. Haber's study of the paper manufacturing industry in Mexico and the United States finds that both the *San Rafael y Anexas* paper company and the International Paper Company (IPC) came to control their respective markets by the 1890s through mergers and consolidations to capture economies of speed, and cut off the supply of raw materials to would-be competitors. However, monopoly rents attracted competitors financed by the stock and bond markets in the United States, and drove IPC's market share from 64 percent in 1900 to 48 percent by 1905. No such challenge would occur in Mex-

*(continues on next page)*

BOX 3.7
**Continued**

ico, and San Rafael would not lose its monopoly position until 1936, when it was nationalized by the state as a strategic industry.

Third, few captains of industry had any technical experience. Of the nine men on the board of directors of *Fundidor Monterrey*, only one had any relevant technical experience. "These were not the tinkerers of the English Industrial Revolution or the production-orientated engineers of U.S. industry. They were financiers whose princi-

pal talents lay in making deals to maintain their monopoly positions and in manipulating the economic apparatus of the state to provide them with protection from foreign and domestic competition" (Haber 1992:24).

Finally, beginning at the end of the *Porfiriato*, Mexico increasingly insulated itself from foreign competition, and not until the mid-1980s did it embrace the degree of openness to U.S. technology, markets, and innovation that Canada did.

---

tant factors in retarding Mexico's economic growth (Cardenas 1997; Haber 1997). Their eventual appearance integrated the market, making it easier for local industry to reach scale economies, and also made possible the new exports of copper, zinc, lead, cotton, coffee, tobacco, and sisal. Summerhill (1997) estimates that by 1900 the static social savings in terms of greater specialization and freight costs was as much as one-quarter of Brazilian GDP, and 20 percent of Mexico's, rising to 40 percent by 1920.

Weak financial sectors not only prohibited financing of railroads, but also, as Haber notes in the case of Mexico, prevented the entry of competing firms that might have stimulated innovation. The small markets, the politicized nature of defending property rights and enforcing contracts, and the lack of appropriate legislation delayed the emergence of a banking system in Mexico (Cardenas 1997), and frequent government defaults on the debt impeded the development of equity markets. Haber attributes the vastly more rapid expansion and technological sophistication of the Brazilian compared to the Mexican textile industry to the presence of a more developed, less "insider"-based capital market in Brazil.

Weak public finances partially explain the lower commitment to both education and infrastructure in the postcolonial states, extending into the 20th century. Cortes Conde (1985) argues that Argentina's loss of market in wheat had to do with a lack of commitment to infrastructure, agricultural extension, and quality control that were critical in Canada and were recognized as such by Argentines at the time. Australians see similar policies in their

country as responsible for the far greater success of the merino sheep industry in Australia compared to Argentina, introduced in the same year in both countries.

## Distribution

Another major difference with the successful natural resource exporters is found in the unequal distribution of wealth, land, financial capital, and education. The Scandinavian countries did not start with an egalitarian tabula rasa. In the 18th century, Danish land was in the hands of a few thousand families on large estates tilled by serfs, and only 23 percent of rural households owned land in Finland. What laid the foundation for the Scandinavian transformation to modern wealthy societies was the agrarian reforms that ranged in timing from Denmark's precocious beginnings in 1788 to Norway's and Sweden's reforms in the 1850s and later Finland's in the 1920s, which created small- and medium-size privately owned farms or plots of forestland (Blomström and Meller 1991). In fact Blomström and Kokko (2001) argue that "it is hardly possible to overemphasize the importance of the improvement in agricultural productivity for Swedish industrialization," which facilitated transfer of labor and savings, and made possible exports that generated capital for investment in forestry and manufacturing, providing a market for local craft-based production. Similar importance has been attached to the homestead-style settlement of the plains of Canada and the United States for the emergence of local industries. A Latin American analogue can be found in the even landholdings of Antioquia, Colombia, that numerous authors find provided the initial demand that jump-started Medallin (Palacios 1979; Urrutia 1979).

Recent thinking suggests that Latin America's persistent inequality may have had even further-reaching effects. In "Inequality, Institution, and Differential Paths of Growth Among New World Economies," Engerman and Haber (1997) argue that the period of sustained economic growth during the 18th and early 19th centuries that distinguished Canada and the United States from the other New World economies was fundamentally due to the patterns of settlement and crops that led to a relatively unequal distribution of income in the slower-growing areas. This concentration preserved the political influence of the advantaged elites and marginalized much of the population, thus losing their potential contributions, particularly through lower access to the franchise, restricted access to primary schooling and natural resources, use of financial institutions, and property rights.[8]

## Education and Technical Capacity

This marginalization is particularly striking in education. The Colonial period enforced a negative intellectual bias in many ways. Most countries had a local franchise of the Inquisition and, largely for reasons of political control, the icon of intellectual discourse, the printing press, was banned in Brazil until the head of the Portuguese empire was moved to Rio de Janeiro in 1809 (Baer 2001).[9] The same concerns with control, extreme inequality of income, weak public finance, and perhaps an intellectual commitment to a small state, all led to dramatically smaller efforts toward universal education than the successful natural resource exporters made. By 1870, more than 80 percent of the population age 10 or above in Canada and the United States was literate, over three times the percentage in Argentina, Chile, Costa Rica, and Cuba, and four times the percentage in Brazil and Mexico. By 1925, Argentina, Chile, Costa Rica, and Uruguay attained literacy rates of over 66 percent, while the literacy rates in Bolivia, Brazil, Colombia, Guatemala, Honduras, Mexico, Peru, and Venezuela hovered at 30 percent until much later (Mariscal and Sokoloff 2000) (see Figure 3.7).

As Engerman and Haber (1997) note, this proves particularly important given that early industrialization reflected the cumulative impact of incremental advances made by individuals throughout the economy, rather than being driven by progress in a single industry or the actions of a narrow elite. As one manifestation critical to the development of innovation, they note that the greater equality in human capital accounted partially for the high rates of invention in the United States overall, but also that the more general concern with the opportunities for extracting the returns from invention contributed to a patent system which was probably, at the time, the most favorable in the world to common people. This stands in stark contrast to Mexico and Brazil, "where patents were restricted by costs and procedures to the wealthy or influential, and where the rights to organize corporations and financial institutions were granted sparingly, largely to protect the value of rights already held by powerful interests."

FIGURE 3.7

**Literacy Rates in Selected Countries (1870–1925)**

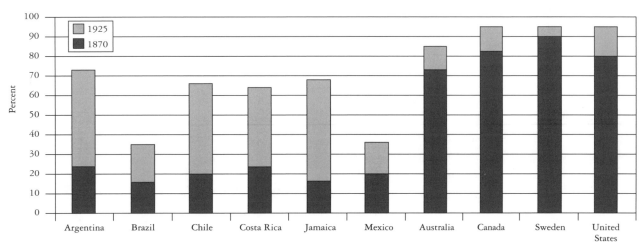

*Sources:* Mariscal and Sokoloff 2000, and Meridith 1995.

In addition to the poor distribution of education, the nature of education in Latin America was less technical than that found elsewhere, and this may have been central to how the resource sectors developed in Latin America. Spanish higher education was largely religiously based and focused on law, philosophy, and theology, and this pattern was replicated in the colonies. The Spanish enlightenment after 1750 saw the establishment of groups of autonomous *sociedades economicas* that sought to diffuse technology from abroad and establish libraries throughout the country, and of some Royal Societies emphasizing applied science. These had spillovers for the colonies: in both Chile and Colombia specific royal initiatives gave the initial impetus to scientific inquiry in the last decades of colonization (see Will 1957; Safford 1976). But Spain itself lagged behind; it began training engineers seriously only in the 1850s, and by 1867 had only one *Escuela de Ingenieros Industriales*, located in Barcelona (Riera i Tuebols 1993). When Latin Americans began to look for innovation, they followed the Spanish in looking to the British, the French, the Germans and, eventually, the Americans. This needs to be compared to Sweden, which had technical schools in the 1820s, a modern engineering industry by 1850, and was exporting engineers and innovations to the United States by 1900. By that year, serious research in chemistry was being carried out at the University of Oslo that laid the foundation for the dominant fertilizer, electrochemical, and electrometallurgical industries in Norway (Hveem 1991).

Latin America lagged behind Spain. Chile's first *sociedad economica* was established in 1813, and schools teaching engineering and the natural sciences were established in 1819, but even a century later they were not producing serious numbers of engineers. The birth of Colombia's technical corps was also long and difficult, and highlights an additional dynamic of development that has perhaps been overlooked. As Box 3.8 suggests, not only was it the recurring violence and political instability that silenced prominent scientists and undermined fledgling universities, or fiscal instability that made financing of the sciences unreliable, but a lack of demand for engineers prevented the career from being feasible. The building of railroads provided a vital source of employment for the scientific profession; however, frequent work stoppages due to war or public finance problems made such employment unreliable.

But the lack of technical capacity arguably had two major impacts. First, it prevented the development of the kinds of knowledge clusters that characterize the Scandinavian forestry sectors and the Australian, Finnish, and North American mining sectors. Hence the kind of dynamic expansions of those sectors, and knowledge spillovers that occurred there, were less likely to appear. For example, despite a primitive tradition of iron smelting dating from the mid-16th century, Brazil's capacity was hampered by limited technical expertise and, arguably as a result, low adoption of new technologies that impeded competition with British goods.[10] Baer (1969) sees as a critical event for the development of the steel industry the foundation in 1879 of the School of Mines at Ouro Preto, Minas Gerais that led to the establishment of the first new blast furnace since the failures of the beginning of the century. Much like the Antioquia School of Mining, graduates of the *Escola de Engenharia do Exercito*, established in 1930, led the steel industry as it developed through the 1960s. Again, this must be compared to Sweden, which was *exporting* engineers by the turn of the century.

Second, the lack of technical capacity established a dependency not only on foreign know-how, but on foreign adaptations of know-how to local circumstances. Chilean historian Anibal Pinto Santa Cruz is very clear that one reason that Chileans left copper development to foreigners (and this may also be the case with nitrates earlier) was simply that the incremental learning process that would have enabled them to adapt or develop techniques to mine lower-grade ores never took place. Chile did not develop the capacity to even monitor the *gran mineria* until the 1950s.

In sum, a variety of structural problems, ranging from poor distribution of income, weak property rights, volatile public finances, political instability, and the very late development of a structure that fomented the adoption of foreign technologies and stimulated domestic innovation impeded the full development of Latin America's economies and, in particular, the natural resource sectors in which they were strongest. Some of these, particularly the knowledge-related factors, may have been less critical in the 19th century when Latin America was still growing extensively toward the "frontier." However, as the next section argues, they may well have become so when growth became more dependent on appropriating the quasi-rents of technological progress.

## Disruptive Industrialization in the Postwar Period

The second major determinant of Latin America's poor performance as a natural resource–rich region lay in the very self-conscious and deliberate process of fomenting manu-

BOX 3.8

## Obstacles to Technical Development in Nueva Granada

Colombia offers insights into the difficulties of establishing the type of technical education central to the success of Australia, Scandinavia, and the United States. Safford (1976) documents the barriers due to political instability and the vagaries of public finances that plagued much of the region. As suggestive, however, is the feedback from economic expansion to the growth and specialization of the technical base.

An early and seminal vector of the Spanish Enlightenment in Colombia, José Celestino Mutis arrived in 1761 to serve as personal physician to the Viceroy. An accomplished botanist, Mutis also taught mathematics and astronomy from 1762 to 1776 at *El Colegio del Rosario*, one of the two principal universities for the Colombian elites. He ran afoul of the Inquisition over issues surrounding the teaching of the Copernican system, but later viceroys promoted his idea of a public university with more science and "useful knowledge" in the curriculum. In 1783, they also financed astronomical, meteorological, and geographical research that included the collection of potential export crops, indigo, and nutmeg. In 1805 Mutis turned over the Bogotá astronomical observatory to another accomplished scientist, Francisco José de Caldas, who also took over the professorship of mathematics at *El Rosario* upon Mutis' death. From 1808 to 1810 Caldas published articles of an emerging group of science enthusiasts in the *Semanario del Nuevo Reino de Granada*, a journal dedicated to science and the promotion of material progress. These beginnings of this fledgling scientific community floundered on the recurring obstacles of Colombian history. A shortage of immediately practical employment possibilities kept attendance of Caldas's mathematics class extremely low. More tragically, most of the contributors to *El Semanario* were also active in the independence movement and were shot in the Spanish Pacification of 1815.

A series of transitory military schools from 1848 to 1885 contributed to the science focus of Colombian universities and to developing a source of engineers, partially by guaranteeing a source of employment. The technically oriented National University was established in 1868. However, in the 1890s, the Faculty of Mathematics and Engineering had enrollments of 22 to 52, while enrollment at the School of Natural Science and Medicine ranged from 144 to 197, and at the School of Law enrollment never fell below 100. This may have been due to the traditional biases in Spanish culture, but it was probably also due to the multiple civil wars that, among other things, slowed railway construction and hampered general growth that would have provided employment. Further, the *Sociedad Colombian de Ingenieros* complained that changes in political parties and personalities so often changed the focus of the school, from being the "brains of industry" to simply designing military ordinance, that the teaching of engineering had failed to develop permanence or solidity. Further hampered by the lack of a permanent location, labs, or equipment, the school would finally close during the War of the Thousand Days (1899–1903). Nonetheless, by the 1880s, Colombia would develop a class of engineers up on the latest in Western engineering and capable of some innovation.

During this period agriculture would gain more attention. The first *Sociedad de Agricultores Colombianos* was founded in 1878, and the Trujillo government soon after embarked on a broad program of agricultural research and development, the establishment of experiment stations, and extensive data collection, all patterned on the U.S. Department of Agriculture. Agricultural programs existed at the National University since the 1870s, and Trujillo sought to extend education by offering subsidies for agricultural instruction in primary and secondary schools, and created the National Institute of Agriculture. Public finance problems would undermine the whole program, however. The Institute lacked a chemistry laboratory, suffered from deficient professorial ability, and lasted for only five years. Professional instruction in agronomy was not attempted again for 20 years, and was not firmly established until 1916. During the fiscal emergencies of the 1890s, subsidies to primary education were suspended, plans to send samples of local plants to international expositions abandoned, and funding of the experimental stations cut.

The legendary Antioquia School of Mining, modeled after the University of California, Berkeley, possessed in

*(continues on next page)*

BOX 3.8
**Continued**

the 1880s a French chemist, a Belgian metallurgist, and an Antioqueño mining engineer trained at Columbia, but it was terminated in the civil war of 1895. When revived after 1904, along with a mining degree it offered separate programs in civil engineering, industrial chemistry, and electrical and mechanical engineering. Alumni would play a critical role not only in both large mining enterprises and railways, but also in the development of Medallin's renowned manufacturing sector in the early years of the 20th century. However, it was also the case that deficient demand would force engineers to serve a variety of markets and specializations, and hence innovation in any narrow field was impossible.

Technical schools and public works projects in the last third of the 19th century generated a proficient technical class in Colombia. However, the problems of political, economic, and fiscal instability endemic to much of Latin America delayed its emergence and made less secure its roots, necessarily reducing its contribution to the overall growth of the country.

*Source:* Safford 1976.

facturing in the mid-20th century that dealt a double blow to possibilities for innovation and growth. Not only did it create a sector with limited potential for long-term productivity gains, but to finance it the traditional or potential sources of growth in the resource sector were undermined.[11] In effect, it was Latin America's reluctance to play to its natural resource strengths, and its embarking on an inefficient industrialization strategy, that led to low growth in both sectors where countries like Sweden and the United States saw rapid gains in both.

### The Siren's Call of Industrialization[12]

Latin America saw import substitution of manufactured goods as an alternative to its traditional resource-intensive sectors. But, again, arguably, it is not just what is produced but how it is produced that is critical. In the long term, the sector must not only be a source of jobs, but also of dynamic gains in productivity. The Argentine economist Guido Di Tella (1985) sees the critical development juncture to be whether countries moved beyond a state of exploiting the pure rents of a frontier or extraction of mineral riches into exploiting the quasi-rents offered by innovation, or whether their entrepreneurs became hooked on "collusive rents" offered by state-sanctioned or otherwise imposed monopoly (see Box 3.9). As the most extreme case, we can think of the Asian NICS as examples of the former. Whatever dynamism emerging in the economy came from manufactures, as the TFP figures show, they were among the greatest adopters of technology in the postwar period. Scandinavia and the United States evolved industrial structures that played to the strengths of their natural resources and can be seen as pursuing productivity growth in both, and they too are near the TFP growth frontier. As a dramatic contrast, Blomström and Meller (1991) argue

> When Latin America decided to force industrialization by import substitution, it was not an industrialization based on the countries' endowments that was supported. While the Scandinavian countries slowly and gradually filled in the empty slots in their input-output tables, the Latin American countries filled in all the numbers at the same time; and even worse, they tried to fill in the U.S. numbers! Suddenly there were several small Latin American economies with production structures similar to that of the United States.

Chile and Ecuador had as many car producers in the 1960s as the United States. Not only did Latin American countries want to accelerate the growth process, but they chose paths unrelated to their comparative advantage. And they did it behind high tariff walls that institutionalized the barriers to innovation discussed by Hirschman, Prescott, Parente, and others.

To varying degrees, many of the late-developing, resource-based economies faced similar junctures, and in fact Australian observers see far more similarities than differences in the goals of mid-century technocrats of the two regions. In *Opening Late-Industrializing Economies: Lessons from Argentina and Australia*, Wynia (1990) sees both regions as attempting "more merciful and less costly industrial revolu-

BOX 3.9

### Where Do You Go at the End of the Frontier?

Referring to the closing of the Argentine frontier, Di Tella (1985) argues:

This kind of area of new settlement was bound to see its rates of growth falter after initial colonization. Argentina behaved, to some extent, in this fairly predictable fashion. But the same was not true for the other countries. It must be acknowledged that the ability of the United States, Canada and Australia to continue a process of vigorous growth even at the end of the expansion of the frontier has been a most extraordinary feat, and one that could not be taken for granted. At that point the successful cases were able to move to a quasi-rent based stage—early for the most successful of all, the United States, less so for Canada and Australia, and rather later for Argentina; further development for the United States and Canada was more clearly based on innovation and less so in Australia. For Argentina it arose exclusively from collusive quasi-rents. To the extent that development was based on innovation, these countries were switching to an alternative and unlimited source of growth. To the extent that it was based on collusion, it opened up a limited, alternative path."

The distinction between industrialization driven by the appropriation of quasi-rents arising from adopting innovations abroad versus exploiting artificially created rents, is critical. Again, it is not that you have a manufacturing sector, but the *way* in which you have a sector, that defines whether the country has created a source of growth, or a drag on growth. The Asian NICs could not afford the latter for long. Korea and Taiwan (China) built sunset clauses into their infant industry protection to ensure competitiveness, and established export targets to ensure efficient scale and technology. Brazil's informatics industry not only became addicted to protection and proved undynamic, but it dragged downstream industries such as the automobile industry with it.

tions, guided by sentiments of nationalism and the need to reduce dependency on large economies. Governments in both countries sought to do it by relying heavily on government regulations and controls, contrived economic rents and applied the best minds to managing this 'rent seeking approach to economic modernization.' "[13]

But prolonged rent-seeking policies had similar effects everywhere. Observers in Australia and Canada cite the stifling and dependency-increasing effects of protection on their industrial sectors. Australia, for example, had an indigenous automobile industry of some promise, and BHP-type conglomerates with solid roots, but it also nurtured import-substituting industries that were neither of efficient scale nor appropriate, given comparative advantages. At the furthest extreme from this pattern is Sweden which, despite equivalent levels of unemployment during the depression, maintained low tariffs and an aggressive outward orientation throughout the postwar period, largely at the insistence of organized labor. The significance of this case is that it shows that it was not preordained that resource-rich economies had to turn inward.

Latin America is thus not sui generis in adopting the policies it did, and it should be seen as lying at the extreme end of a continuum that extends through Canada and Australia to the United States and Sweden at the opposite and most successful end. Acknowledging the similarities is vital since it prevents us from isolating the region as some sort of rare and unredeemable case operating under separate economic laws. Indeed, the persistent Australian interest in Argentina stems precisely from its perceived kinship and a desire to avoid its fate.

### A Turning Away from Natural Resource Strengths

What this implies is that, far from being a dynamic growth sector with strong incentives to raise TFP through tapping the growing world knowledge base, the manufacturing sector requires transfers from the traditional sectors to be viable. The U.S. and Swedish economies found organically emerging industrial sectors that added value to their abundant natural resources. Latin America was highly suspicious of its natural resources sectors, both because of the external dependency implied, and because of Prebisch's argument of declining terms of trade. In the end, however, the hothouse industrial sectors were more dependent than ever on natural resource–based sectors that, at the same time, were being dramatically undermined.

Australian observers see the degree of this turning away from the natural resource base as critical to explaining their country's relatively better performance compared to Argentina's. As Australia encouraged investment in petroleum and refining and electrical equipment in the postwar period, it initially neglected the rural sector, which expanded at only half the rate of population growth. But this policy was reversed in 1952 with the granting of investment subsidies, extension of credit, price stabilization programs, and expansion of research and extension programs. This led to a doubling of production over the next decade due to the "clover revolution," improved crop and wool yields, and the introduction of myxomytosis in 1950 as a way of eliminating the plague of rabbits. Australia continued to suffer from mild cycles of boom and balance-of-payments crises, and required IMF assistance in 1952. But a rebirth of interest in traditional mining sectors in the 1960s led to increased dynamism in the resources sector that might in the near future lead Australia to have the fifth-highest per capita income (Wright 2001). It also diverted attention away from the inefficiencies of the import substitution industrialization strategy. In a sense, the manufacturing sector continued to be a drag on the natural resource sector, but the increasing productivity and dynamism of the natural resource sector was such that it was able to overcome it.

During the same initial inward-looking period of the 1940s and 1950s, Argentina inflicted deep damage on its traditional leading sector, driving output growth to 0.2 percent per year and leaving the country perilously close to ceasing to export foodstuffs. In Chile, continuing tensions with foreign copper companies led to, among other things, a steady decline in copper-generated foreign exchange reserves, the lifeline of the manufacturing sector. Massively negative rates of protection prevented the emergence of exports in natural resource–based areas that, after liberalization, surged as dominant sectors (see Box 3.10). The combination of inefficient industrialization and the demise of its traditional export sectors left the countries exceptionally vulnerable to the cycles of boom and bust that characterized the region.

In sum, while there is a continuum of inefficient interventions in the manufacturing sector, to the detriment of the resource-exporting sector, neither Australia, Canada, nor

Scandinavia had the extreme turn toward inward-looking behavior, nor the dramatic macrodisequilibria that gave Latin America a special fame. The two phenomena are self-reinforcing: recurring balance-of-payment problems led to a greater distrust of the global market, to political instability, to discouraged entrepreneurship, and to barriers to innovation. Arguably, the measures to coax rapid manufacturing growth out of countries without a scientific tradition and with substantial structural barriers to innovation led to heavy rates of taxation on traditional sectors. In the end, manufacturing lacked long-term dynamism, and the natural resource sector lost the potential it had. Sweden stands as the road not taken. The openness to foreign trade, the insistence on technological upgrading by its labor unions, and playing to its natural resource strengths led to a gradually accumulated capacity to innovate in both the natural resource and manufacturing sectors.

## Are the Successful Models Replicable? The Death of Distance, Fragmentation, and First-Mover Advantages

Can the experiences of Australia, Canada, and Scandinavia be replicated in the early 21st century? The answer is not obviously yes. In particular, transport costs offered a measure of protection to fledgling downstream industries, even to industries with low tariffs, which have since fallen to a fraction of their turn-of-the-century levels. As Chapter 2 discussed, Jones and Kierzkowski (1990) and Jones (2000) show that decreasing transport costs can lead to the fragmentation of production structures that in the past would have constituted what some term a "vertical cluster." They argue that various *production blocks* in a vertically integrated process are connected by *service links*. As the scale of the activity expands, the firm may find it profitable to outsource some blocks to other countries in which differences in factor prices or productivities lower the marginal cost of production of the fragments. Transport, communication, and coordination costs between blocks are the cost of such fragmentation, and these are precisely the costs that have decreased so dramatically over time.

Another way of phrasing this is that the increasingly globalized world may be leading to fewer forward and backward linkages. The traditional view of primary exports driving development in other sectors, originally formulated in staples theory to explain the Canadian case, can be short-circuited. As Puga and Venables (1999) show, this is not

BOX 3.10

## The Costs of Chilean Industrialization: Frustrated Development in Fishing, Fruit, and Forestry

While mining remains Chile's primary export, the recent success stories that resonate most with the United States and the Scandinavian experience are in the fishing, forestry, and agriculture sectors. The Promethean efforts of the Chilean Development Corporation (CORFO), founded in 1939, were financed by a 15 percent tax on copper, and by the 1950s grew to control 30 percent of investment in plants and equipment. CORFO's efforts would lay the foundation for the dynamic export industries of the next half-century. To develop the fishing industry, CORFO contracted technical assistance missions, established a marine biology station near Valparaiso in 1945, granted sizable tax exemptions in 1952, and joined the army and the University of Chile in surveying the coastal waters in 1954. It took the first inventories of forest stocks, and contracted the 1944 Haig technical assistance mission, which revealed "the indisputable truth that an adequate management of our forests could become the basis for a . . . great industry of forest products." In 1953 it financed processing plants for cellulose and newsprint. In the fruit industry CORFO financed technical assistance missions, extended credit for cultivation and experimental plots, and invested in supporting infrastructure. In 1941 it financed efforts to promote exports of wood products and wine. During the 1950s and early 1960s CORFO established an experimental fishing station in Arauco, financed construction of modern boats and dock facilities in Tarapaca and Valdivia, and founded fish canneries and fishmeal mills. The World Bank–financed Paper and Carton Manufacturing Company in Bío Bío stimulated paper- and cellulose-related forestry activities after 1957.

CORFO may have been correct in boasting, on its 20th birthday, of Chilean history being divided into two eras—one before the construction of the Huachipato iron works near Concepción in 1947, and one after, which transformed the region into an important center of manufacturing in Latin America, hosting peripheral industries in steel wires, ferrous alloys, zinc and tin recovery plants, electrical equipment, and tools and machinery. But early on, local observers wondered at the costs. A compilation of seminars given in the business commu-

nity in 1954 entitled *Negative Aspects of Economic Intervention: Failures of an Experiment*, praised CORFO's irreplaceable role in creating the electricity and fishing industries, but derided the gross inefficiency of Huachipato and the National Petroleum company, and saw the capriciousness of exchange controls as the overriding disincentive to needed foreign investment. The halving of export volume over the previous decade, the stagnation of agriculture, and the frustration of Chile's tremendous potential in vegetable and fruit exports were laid at the feet of irrational intervention in the price mechanisms and the persistently overvalued exchange rate.

In the 1960s, recurrent balance-of-payments crises would lead the government of Eduardo Frei to seek to promote nontraditional and traditional exports. Yet, Chile's areas of natural comparative advantage were stymied by the gross protection and inefficiencies that were the logical culmination of a system of protection and incentives that had mutated into literally incomprehensible degrees of distortion. A researcher at the Catholic University noted that in 1965, "the multiplicity of instruments used, and the frequency with which they were modified, had arrived at such extremes that it was humanly impossible to have a clear vision of their final impact by sector or for the economy as a whole" (Jeanneret 1972). She found effective rates of protection extreme by global standards, ranging from –100 to 650 compared to –50 to 500 for Brazil, –25 to 200 for Malaysia, and –17 to 106 for Norway. These heavy negative rates of protection implied that 10 of 21 industries studied could export only at a loss, and that "some of these sectors, principally wood, paper, paper products, fish and other minerals, would have become, perhaps, significant exporters. A contemporary observer, Marko Mamalakis, also wondered at the inability of the agro-export industry to grow, given that export demand for raw or processed Chilean fruit, seafood, oils, wine and so forth [was] almost unlimited" (Mamalakis 1976).

That these disincentives to invest and innovate were critical is borne out by subsequent history. As is well

(continues on next page)

BOX 3.10
**Continued**

known, the history since 1975 was one of relentless pursuit of integration with the world economy and a correction of the distortions accumulated in the previous decades. In the next 20 years, noncopper exports increased by a factor of 10, essentially eliminating the traditional foreign exchange bottleneck to industry. The traditional dependence on copper fell as its export share fell

to 45 percent, and exports of fruit, fishmeal, lumber, and wood furniture rose from 2 percent to peaks of 9 percent, 8 percent, and 6 percent, respectively; paper and cellulose rose from 4 percent to 11 percent; and chemicals rose from 1 percent to 4 percent.

*Source:* Maloney 1997.

problematic unless there are scale economies, market imperfections, or other externalities implicit in the downstream process that a country would benefit from were these processes retained in-country. In particular, if industry can benefit from agglomerating in one area, then as transaction costs fall we may see the "south" deindustrializing. As industry is less constrained by location near market or inputs, it agglomerates in the "north." If it is true that the greatest productivity gains will be realized in manufacturing, (we have argued that it probably is not), then the traditional bifurcation of dynamic north and stagnant south common in the dependency literature will emerge.

The phenomena of decreasing transport and communication costs and fragmentation are historical facts. By 1920, transport costs had already fallen to a quarter of their

1800 levels (O'Rourke and Williamson 1999), and as Figure 3.8. shows, the trend has continued dramatically since then, and even more dramatically in communications. History suggests that fragmentation was a fact before the turn of the 20th century, and that it had the potential to break apart downstream linkages. As one example, Findlay and Jones (2001) argue that, compared to Lancashire, United Kingdom, New England textile mills required both more labor and higher raw material per unit of output. However, lower prices of U.S.-produced cotton would have given the United States an advantage in the presence of barriers to trade in cotton. Unfortunately, the reverse was true. Cotton transport costs were very low, and as Bils (1984) argues, the American cotton textile industry would probably not have been viable without the protection it received.

FIGURE 3.8
**Transportation and Communication Cost (1920–90)**

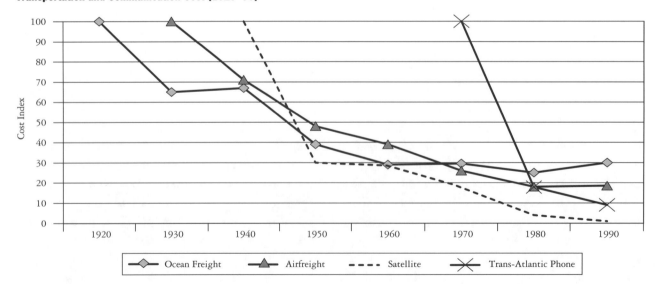

*Source:* Branson.

The same is likely true in the mineral-based industries discussed earlier. High ore transport costs effectively gave downstream U.S. industries a price advantage over foreign processors. But these same industries also maintained a cartel prohibiting exports to ensure that this was the case. As early as 1910, Australian minerals were being processed across the world in Germany, and the coming of World War I made it far easier for BHP's processing capacity in Newcastle to become established as a forward linkage in that country.

Pressures toward fragmentation of the processes underlying "staples" models of development were thus strong a full century ago, and are only stronger today. This can be seen, for example, in the few linkages to industry arising from the expansion of the Chilean pulping capacity from 1987 to 1992. The Nacimiento plant was built by a Finnish company specializing in pulp-mill engineering, Jaako Pöyry, and the Mininco plant by the Canadian firm Simons and the Swedish firm IPK. The machinery was imported from Canada, Finland, Sweden, and the United States. Saab and Volvo may have had their start in providing transport to the forest industry, but Chile's path would be different.

### New Opportunities Appear

However, though certain paths are made difficult, as Chapter 4 will show, the situation is not at all bleak.

First, as discussed above, natural-resource-based industries can be very knowledge intensive and have the potential for very high growth rates. Further, falling transport costs have allowed the emergence of natural-resource-intensive industries such as flowers in Colombia and Ecuador, specialty vegetables in Guatemala, and fresh fruits in Chile that were not possible before. Far-flung locales can now take advantage of the expanding market in tourism.

Second, this ability to fragment production allows global efficiency gains, but does not imply that all industries move to the industrialized world. Krugman (1979) and Venables (2001) argue that as transport costs continue to fall, benefits from agglomeration lessen. Puga and Venables (1999) show that as this happens, wage differentials between countries may cause many manufacturing or other fragments to again be relocated to poorer countries. With the Asian development experience in mind, they envision a process where intermediate processes move in a cascading fashion from one country to another as wages rise. Hence, Korea took over

some manufactures from Japan until wages became too high, and then they were relocated to China or Malaysia.

This pattern was not observed in the early part of the 20th century, and as the next chapter shows, it offers new possibilities for Latin America: plummeting Internet connectivity and communications costs make Jamaica a center for telemarketing and design consulting. Guadalajara and Costa Rica became important parts of cutting-edge information technology industries.

The potential efficiency gains implicit in the fragmentation process also offer an important caveat to the emerging literature promoting "clusters," envisioned as sequences of related products. If the blocks were more efficiently broken up, keeping them together may create an inefficient industry. As an example, BHP originally calculated that smelting copper in Chile was not cost-effective, partly due to higher energy costs, and now ships the ore elsewhere for processing. There may be externalities emerging from keeping smelting near the point of extraction, but if not, the country will lose overall. Focusing on production chains where comparative advantage does not dictate can begin to look like inefficient industrial policy.

Arguably, a more efficient policy might use the income from present natural resources to create comparative advantage in new areas, for instance, by creating a well-educated workforce, or investing in communication or physical infrastructure. Chile may never produce forestry or mining equipment, but lower communication costs, a well-trained workforce, and a network of universities and research institutes could make it an exporter of mining and forestry expertise, or computer software.

The next chapter examines in more detail the successful development and necessary supporting conditions of industries playing to the region's traditional strength in natural resources, and those in new areas.

### Notes

1. It may be argued that natural resource collateral may have permitted excessive indebtedness and ill use of readily available lending funds. However, the Asian NICs had the same response to higher oil prices, and similar debt-to-GDP ratios. The big difference for LAC was that the more open and dynamic export economies of the Asian NICs were able to manage debt service in ways that Latin America could not.

2. Parente and Prescott's (2000) simulations suggest that a TFP level one-third that of the United States can explain GDP differences of 1:27, or roughly the difference between the incomes of the highest- and lowest-income countries in the world. Colombia, they simulate,

has TFP levels of 64 percent of the United States, and 59 percent of Paraguay (Dollar and Wolff 1997).

3. We use "innovation" not only to refer to the process of generating new knowledge, but to making the necessary adaptations to externally developed techniques.

4. Hall and Jones (1999), after controlling for differing levels of education, still find differing levels of log TFP highly correlated with log of output per worker with a correlation coefficient of .89.

5. See Stern, Porter, and Furman (2000); Romer (1990); Nelson (1993); Wright (1999). All seek to explain the factors determining the flow of innovation in terms of the interrelationships of a variety of social institutions and actors.

6. Most recently Matusayama (2000), Sachs and Warner (1995a, 1997, 1999), Rodriguez and Sachs (1999), and Rodrik (1996, 1997) have argued that agriculture has few prospects, and as Wright (2001) notes, there is a bias toward seeing mineral sectors as pure extraction, with few possible gains from technology.

7. Looking across the 1970s and 1980s, Bernard and Jones (1996) find TFP growth of 2.6 percent in agriculture compared to 1.2 percent in industry, and in only one of their 14 sample countries was TFP growth in industry. Lewis, Martin, and Savage (1988) find productivity growth higher in agriculture in the Australian economy than for the rest, and Martin and Warr (1993) find similar evidence for Indonesia.

8. These arguments also apply to Brazil. As Baer (1969) notes, education remained virtually nonexistent until 1776, and even after that "the few schools that functioned had little impact on the cultural level of the population."

9. This section based on Maloney (2001b).

10. Baer (1969) reports that the techniques used at the end of the 19th century were primitive. Of the 30 ironworks in the headwater region of the Rio Doce in 1879, seven used Italian forge methods and the rest used the old African cadinho technique.

11. This section based on Maloney (2001).

12. With apologies to Duncan and Fogarty (1984).

13. "None of this is confined to Latin America. Rent-seeking economics is not derived from that region's patrimonial political traditions or Hispanic affection for corporatist ways of conducting politics. Rather, it was a strategy chosen by authorities in nations that were, at the time that economic modernization was accelerated, already too activated socially and politically to permit less politically self-conscious approaches to economic renovation. . . . The Australians were not radically different from the Argentines in their approach to the protection of industry and labor. . . . They were guided by sentiments of nationalism and nativism, stressing the nation's defense against competition from cheaper labor and/or more powerful foreign economies" (Wynia 1990: 187–8).

# CHAPTER 4

# Recent LAC Experiences: The Role of Knowledge and Institutions

THIS CHAPTER FOCUSES ON COUNTRY EXPERIENCES, MOST OF THEM DEALING WITH SPEcific sectors. The role of nontraditional endowments, such as geography, knowledge, institutions, ICT, and foreign direct investment (FDI), seems to be key for the performance of emerging economic activities in LAC. This is true for a variety of production processes, ranging from fruits in Chile to computer electronics in Costa Rica and Mexico, and tourism in the Caribbean. Moreover, it is also clear that trade liberalization and regional integration also helped diversify the structure of exports in most countries. NAFTA was particularly important for Mexico, while Mercosur was important for Argentina.

The EPZs in Central America and the Caribbean have helped these countries take advantage of their close proximity to the United States. It seems that such arrangements can provide an institutional safe haven in terms of relatively stable regulations for FDI, although corporate tax incentives need to be reviewed in the near future. In both Costa Rica and Mexico, however, human capital and FDI have jointly stimulated the emergence of knowledge-intensive manufacturing activities. Hence the role of knowledge and human capital cannot be overestimated in the promotion of dynamic FDI. The experience of Costa Rica's CINDE also shows that proactive FDI promotion policies undertaken jointly between the private and

public sectors can yield handsome rewards for development. In the future, ICT development might enhance the performance of industries ranging from the *maquila* sector in Mexico and Central America to the tourism business in the Caribbean.

In addition, support from the public sector for research and development was a key ingredient in Chile's agricultural success story, and in the recent commercial success of Brazil's EMBRAER. The case of agriculture in Chile also indicates that macroeconomic management was a key ingredient for the success of the sector after the mid-1980s.

The case studies that follow provide specific examples of how policies can affect economic structure with desirable consequences. In the end, the path from the use of natural resources to the knowledge economy is aided by intelligent policies, combined with the types of new

endowments discussed in the recent scientific literature (see Chapter 2). The dynamic potential of combining national strengths, such as geography, abundant natural resources, natural beauty, and even cultural heritage, with other modern factors of production such as sound institutions, ICT, and knowledge is a good recipe for growth and development.

There is thus a clear similarity between the recent LAC experiences discussed in this chapter and the historical experience of the industrialized countries reviewed in Chapter 3: in both instances the emergence of new industries depended on how countries played to their strengths, ranging from abundant natural resources to geographic factors, by progressively applying new technologies and knowledge to their production processes, while strengthening ties with the global economy.

## Chile's Agricultural Performance: The Case of Fresh Fruits Exports

Economic reforms in Latin America have been followed by concerns regarding the impact of trade reforms on the performance of the agricultural sector. These doubts encompass several issues, ranging from the dynamism of the sector to its effects on poverty (see Foster and Valdés 2001).

In this section, we focus mainly on the case of Chile, but we begin by analyzing the productive performance of the agricultural sector in LAC countries before and after the reforms. We investigate whether economic reforms brought improvements in the productivity and export performance of agriculture. But even after the reforms, Chilean agricultural performance was still outstanding compared to the rest of the region. We find that part of the explanation is the long history of applying knowledge to the development of new exportable agricultural products.

### Economic Reforms and the Performance of the Agricultural Sector in LAC

Table 4.1 presents some basic information for several LAC countries.[1] It indicates the year in which economic reforms were adopted in the different countries, according to the independent analysis of Sachs and Warner (1995a). The table also summarizes the behavior (average annual growth rates) of agricultural labor productivity and exports per worker, before and after the reforms.

A quick glance at Table 4.1 reveals that Chile was the top agricultural performer during 1980–99. Furthermore, in the vast majority of cases, the performances of productivity and exports per worker were better in the period after the reforms. Nevertheless, for individual countries, the difference in performances is statistically significant only for a handful of cases, probably due to the limited number of observations in the different periods. Table 4.1 suggests that with respect to efficiency, the reforms tended to benefit agriculture. More detailed empirical analyses of the impact of the economic reforms on the performance of the agriculture sector is presented in Lederman and Soares (2001). In general, the evidence indicates that reforms tended to have an immediate effect of reducing the productivity growth in agriculture relative to Chile, and this reduction was recovered after approximately three-and-a-half years. This result is illustrated in Figure 4.1. On average, at the time of the implementation of reforms, LAC countries were underperforming relative to Chile by about 3 percent. After the initial decline, the gap between LAC agricultural productivity and Chile became less severe with time. Also, on average, reforms tended to have an immediate positive impact on the growth of exports, and this impact tended to be progressively intensified over time.

## Econometric Results

The country-by-country analysis discussed in Lederman and Soares (2001) shows that the general pattern observed in the

TABLE 4.1

**Date of Economic Reform, Growth of Labor Productivity and Exports per Worker in Agriculture, Selected Latin American Countries, 1980–99**

| COUNTRY | YEAR OF REFORM | PREREFORM PRODUCTIVITY | EXPORTS | N | POSTREFORM PRODUCTIVITY | EXPORTS | N |
|---|---|---|---|---|---|---|---|
| Argentina | 1991 | 0.15% | −3.32% | 11 | 0.84% | 0.01% | 8 |
| Bolivia | 1985 | −1.28% | −31.61% | 5 | −0.30% | 11.14%[a] | 14 |
| Brazil | 1991 | −0.63% | −8.67% | 11 | 1.59% | 1.63%[b] | 8 |
| Chile | 1976 | — | — | 0 | 2.58% | 4.39% | 19 |
| Colombia | 1986 | −2.28% | −5.15% | 6 | −0.88% | −7.90% | 13 |
| Costa Rica | 1986 | −1.69% | −4.71% | 6 | 0.97% | −0.64% | 13 |
| Ecuador | 1991 | 0.81% | −3.15% | 11 | −1.47% | −1.05% | 8 |
| El Salvador | 1989 | −4.37% | −19.53% | 9 | −1.48%[a] | −0.75%[a] | 10 |
| Guatemala | 1988 | −1.87% | −8.98% | 8 | −0.21%[a] | −2.09% | 11 |
| Honduras | 1991 | −0.45% | −8.29% | 11 | −2.73% | −9.72% | 8 |
| Mexico | 1986 | −1.87% | −1.53% | 6 | −2.00% | 0.98% | 13 |
| Peru | 1990 | −1.11% | −8.74% | 10 | 2.16% | 4.41% | 9 |
| Uruguay | 1990 | −1.67% | −1.40% | 10 | 1.68% | −1.07% | 9 |
| Total | | −1.16% | −8.20% | 123 | 0.16%[b] | 0.47%[b] | 143 |

a. Postreform average is significantly larger than prereform average at 10 percent.
b. Postreform average is significantly larger than prereform average at 5 percent.
*Note:* Variables are growth rates (difference in natural logarithms) of value added in agriculture, forest, and fishing per worker (labor force); and total exports (FOB) of agricultural products per worker (labor force), both in 1990 U.S. dollars.
*Source:* Reform dates from Sachs and Warner (1995b).

FIGURE 4.1

**After Reforms, LAC Countries Caught up with Chile:
An Illustration of Econometric Results**

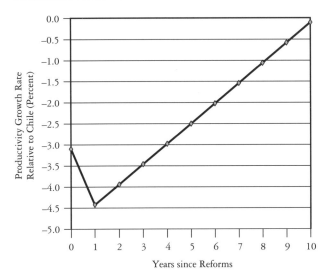

aggregate for productivity could also be seen in each individual country. Overall, the results suggest that, with respect to efficiency, the reforms tended to bring long-term benefits to the agricultural sector. In this respect, concerns about the impacts of economic liberalization on the performance of agriculture seem to be misplaced. Yet Chile still outperformed the other LAC economies due to its long history of reforms, its adequate macroeconomic management, and its historical investments in knowledge and innovation in agriculture. In the following paragraphs we look more closely at the Chilean experience, with a special focus on the role of macroeconomic management and knowledge creation.

*Reforms and Changes in Incentives in
Chilean Agriculture*

The trade reforms most immediately affected the incentives facing producers through changes in the prices of tradable goods.[2] This yielded incentives to move resources from import-competing goods toward the export-oriented and nontraded sectors. A central goal of reform in general, and especially with respect to agriculture, was to reduce the explicit and implicit anti-export bias that existed previously. Imported input prices also fell as tariffs decreased with liberalization, which was a significant element in determining the effects of reform for some countries.

In addition to the changes in direct price incentives brought about by freer trade, there were other price effects induced by deregulation and privatization and other as-

pects of the reform process. Perhaps more important for the farm sector were the indirect effects of exchange rates and interest rates, two key prices to which the sector is particularly sensitive. By now it is well recognized that the exchange rate is the most important "price" affecting the agricultural economy (Valdés 1986). We now examine the effects of reform on sector prices.

## Net Rates of Protection

To examine the long-term trends in the evolution of incentives in the farm sector, the most general measure is the value added of agricultural activities relative to nonagricultural activities. Most trade and price policies are restricted to tradable goods in the case of agriculture, and most agricultural goods in LAC countries are tradables. Box 4.1 reviews the algebra of a relevant indicator of relative price incentives—the net rate of protection (NRP). The rest of this section reviews the evidence concerning NRPs for various agricultural commodities in Chile.

As the NRPs in Table 4.2 show, prior to 1974 Chile favored export-oriented crops (apples and grapes) and most import-competing commodities (beef, maize, milk, sugar beets, and wheat). Immediately following 1974, the NRPs for exportables fell to very low rates, and since the initiation of the second phase of reforms in the early 1980s, NRPs have effectively been zero. For import-competing crops the story is notably different. The NRPs for milk and wheat were relatively high in the decade of the 1960s. Measured NRPs during the early 1970s are not very meaningful, given the regime of price controls, hyperinflation, shortages, and rampant black markets. NRPs were relatively high during 1984–89 due to the government's response to the strain on the traditional farmer sector arising from low international prices and a strong appreciation of the currency between 1979 and 1982. Chile instituted price bands for wheat, sugar, and oilseed, and minimum import prices for milk during that time. Although there was a currency depreciation in the late 1980s, protections remained. During the 1990s, the currency again appreciated, and the already instituted price bands cushioned traditional producers.

Table 4.2 shows the decomposition of real domestic prices for selected Chilean agricultural products for the period from 1960 to 1993 or 1995. For example, during 1975–83 the average 0.18 percent decrease in the real price of milk is the result of a 2.39 percent decrease in the real border price, a 46.47 percent increase in the real exchange rate, and a 44.26 percent decrease in price supports.[3] As the

BOX 4.1

### Effective and Net Rates of Protection: Some Algebra

The algebraic expression that captures the returns to primary factors may be written as the value added of agriculture relative to an average value added in nonagriculture (tradables and home goods):

$$\frac{VA_A}{VA_{NA}} = \frac{VA_A}{\alpha VA_r + (1-\alpha)VA_H}$$

Although this has been used occasionally for the case of specific commodities (for example, Hurtado, Valdés, and Muchnik 1990), more commonly relative prices substitute for value added measures:

$$\frac{P_A}{P_{NA}} = \frac{P_A}{\alpha P_T + (1-\alpha)P_H} = \frac{P_A/P_H}{\alpha P_T/P_H + (1-\alpha)}$$

The effects of trade and price policies are captured by the effective and net rates of protection (ERP and NRP), which compare prevailing domestic price ratios with those that would exist with free trade. The ERP is the most relevant to capture the impact on incentives; the NRP is better suited to measure the effects on prices paid by consumers. It should be noted that most studies on agricultural protection measure ERP and NRP by direct comparisons between border and domestic prices,

adjusted for internal transport costs, quality difference, and other factors, because traditionally, especially in agriculture, there were several forms of intervention (nontariff barriers) and not simply tariffs. With a simple tariff (export taxes) as the only instrument restricting importables (exportables), these measures should reflect the explicit tax charged.

What these measures do not capture is the effect of what is called indirect protection (Krueger, Schiff, and Valdés 1988), which includes possible misalignment of the exchange rate and the effects of industrial protection on domestic relative prices. The net and effective rates of protection (positive or negative) can be adjusted accordingly. The total adjusted NRP (incorporating direct and indirect interventions) may be expressed for a specific agricultural good $i$:

$$NRP_i^T = \frac{P_i/P_{NA}}{P_i^*/P_{NA}^*} - 1$$

where the $P_i^*$ is the counterfactual border price adjusted for exchange rate misalignments, and $P_{NA}^*$ is the counterfactual price of nonagricultural goods adjusted for both industrial protection and exchange rate misalignment.

table demonstrates, there were increases in real domestic prices for fruits and wheat during the initial phase of reforms, 1975 to 1983.

During the second phase of the reform, 1984 to 1989, real domestic prices declined for all products, except beef and apples.[4] The declines in real domestic prices for wheat, maize, and fruits, in spite of a steady depreciation of the real exchange rate, were due to a decline in border prices. After 1990 there was a cumulative decline in all real domestic prices, except for grapes, due to an appreciation of the Chilean currency and, for four of the selected products, due to a decrease in real border prices. To the extent that the changes in the real domestic prices of these selected products crudely approximate the changes in the returns to farming, one can say that in the case of Chile the main forces behind agriculture's price incentives were beyond the control of policy. The main factors were the border prices.

## Research and Development in Chilean Agriculture

While many reformers have tended to retreat from development-oriented institutions concerned with the farm sector, it has been broadly accepted that the unsuccessful delivery of supportive services of such institutions can impede the achievement of reforms. The ability of R&D services to contribute to productivity growth, especially in the case of poor farmers, can ameliorate the negative and enhance the positive effects of trade liberalization (Tabor 1995). This in turn can make the implementation of agricultural reforms more palatable. In addition, strengthening the growth of the agricultural sector through technical change and productivity growth can improve overall employment, income growth, and food price levels, thus easing the costs of adjustment more generally. In particular, strengthening export agriculture can directly earn for-

TABLE 4.2

## Decomposition of Producer Price Changes in Chilean Agriculture

| | | CUMULATIVE PERCENTAGE CHANGE IN: | | | | |
|---|---|---|---|---|---|---|
| PRODUCT | PERIOD | REAL DOMESTIC PRICES | REAL BORDER PRICES | REAL EXCHANGE RATE | (1 PLUS THE) TARIFF RATE | OTHERS |
| **Exportables** | | | | | | |
| Apples, Red | 1960–70 | 133.77 | 41.02 | 30.94 | 17.14 | 44.67 |
| | 1971–74 | –2.4 | –21.22 | 44.77 | –10.38 | –15.58 |
| | 1975–83 | 6.4 | –8.4 | 46.47 | –6.77 | –24.9 |
| | 1984–89 | 30.48 | –4.1 | 36.11 | 0 | –1.53 |
| | 1990–93 | –429.1 | –64.88 | –14.79 | 0 | –349.43 |
| Grapes, Thompson | 1960–70 | 99.29 | 21.53 | 30.94 | 17.14 | 29.67 |
| | 1971–74 | 54.35 | 4.37 | 44.77 | –0.59 | 5.8 |
| | 1975–83 | 41.51 | 20.91 | 46.47 | –16.55 | –9.31 |
| | 1984–89 | –4.7 | –30.47 | 33.67 | 0 | –7.91 |
| | 1990–94 | 22.24 | 21.37 | –16.8 | 0 | 17.67 |
| **Importables** | | | | | | |
| Beef | 1960–70 | 41.2 | 9.57 | 30.94 | 0 | 0.69 |
| | 1971–74 | 87.27 | 42.14 | 44.77 | 0 | 0.36 |
| | 1975–83 | –51.72 | –76.06 | 46.47 | 0 | –22.12 |
| | 1984–89 | 136.69 | 64.93 | 33.67 | 13.98 | 24.12 |
| | 1990–95 | –30.05 | 16.88 | –26.84 | –3.54 | –16.54 |
| Maize | 1960–70 | n.a. | n.a. | n.a. | n.a. | n.a. |
| | 1971–74 | n.a. | n.a. | n.a. | n.a. | n.a. |
| | 1975–83 | n.a. | n.a. | n.a. | n.a. | n.a. |
| | 1984–89 | –4.24 | –45.12 | 25.27 | –7.84 | 23.46 |
| | 1990–93 | –22.18 | –23.84 | –16.25 | –3.54 | 21.44 |
| Milk | 1960–70 | 3.29 | –5.37 | 30.94 | 0 | –22.28 |
| | 1971–74 | 77.44 | 14.27 | 44.77 | 0 | 18.4 |
| | 1975–83 | –0.18 | –2.39 | 46.47 | 0 | –44.26 |
| | 1984–89 | –6.25 | 9.46 | 33.67 | 13.98 | –63.35 |
| | 1990–93 | –16.51 | –19.66 | –16.25 | –3.54 | 22.94 |
| Sugarbeets | 1960–70 | n.a. | n.a. | n.a. | n.a. | n.a. |
| | 1971–74 | n.a. | n.a. | n.a. | n.a. | n.a. |
| | 1975–83 | n.a. | n.a. | n.a. | n.a. | n.a. |
| | 1984–89 | –1.35 | 39.16 | 25.27 | –7.84 | –57.93 |
| | 1990–93 | –7.57 | 18.72 | –16.25 | –3.54 | –6.5 |
| Wheat | 1960–70 | 6.33 | –13.15 | 26.76 | 0 | –7.28 |
| | 1971–74 | 53.81 | 80.13 | 9.89 | 0 | –36.21 |
| | 1975–83 | 35.51 | –88.39 | 81.35 | 0 | 42.55 |
| | 1984–89 | –0.42 | –32.83 | 37.84 | –7.84 | 2.41 |
| | 1990–95 | –27.8 | –12.84 | –26.84 | 7.84 | 4.04 |

n.a. Not applicable.

*Source:* Foster and Valdés 2001.

eign exchange and indirectly finance imports. Yet, to some extent, the private sector usually replaces public support by opening new avenues for the agricultural sector to achieve technological and managerial advances (Umali 1991). In terms of who its "clients" are, however, private support is more likely to be oriented toward larger, commercial farmers than the public sector, especially toward those in growth sectors, which are often the export sectors in the case of LAC.

In the case of Chile, the role of R&D in agricultural performance is most clearly observed in the fruit sector. This experience is narrated in Box 4.2. The rest of this section reviews the role of R&D policies more generally.

Prior to 1973, agricultural research in Chile was concentrated in the Agriculture Ministry's parastatal Instituto Nacional de Investigación Agraria (INIA). The agency was responsible for all scientific specialties, crops, and regions. In terms of both funding and personnel, other institutions,

BOX 4.2

**R&D Policies and the Emergence of the Fruit Sector in Chilean Agriculture**

The most dramatic story occurs in the fruit sector where exports grew at a rate of 20 percent annually in the first 20 years since the reforms of 1974. Areas planted to commercial orchards almost tripled and fruit production quadrupled. Jarvis (1992) attributes this success to the speed with which Chileans were able to transfer, adapt, and extend fruit technologies initially developed for California and other fruit-growing regions to Chile. He argues that private initiative in these areas was driven by changes in price relationships and industry structure that increased returns to private R&D. The Corporación de Fomento (CORFO) played an important role in the early 1960s in surveying existing fruit orchards, analysis of potential demand in foreign markets, elaboration of production goals, introduction and screening of new varieties, establishment of nurseries to propagate disease-free plants, construction of cold-storage facilities at strategic locations to promote postharvest care, phytosanitary inspection of exported fruit, establishment of favorable credit lines and working capital, and "drawback" payments for fruit exports. In 1965 a 10-year program of cooperation between the University of California and the University of Chile was established to permit technical cooperation and improve graduate training. This helped the University of Chile develop a first-rate faculty in fruit-related sciences and to begin modern fruit research. Spillover effects strengthened government agencies and other universities. As one crude measure, Jarvis documents that the number of theses on fruit issues submitted for the Agricultural Engineering degree increased by 2.5 percent and as a share from 13 to 31 percent from 1976–80 to 1986–1990. In 1964 Chile established the National Institute of Agricultural Research (INIA), which paid relatively high salaries and attracted skilled researchers. The agency initiated a fruit research program from the start. By these means, Chile developed the scientific personnel and knowledge to achieve technological

transfer, identified and began to plant new varieties suitable for foreign markets, improved orchard and postharvest management, upgraded fruit research and teaching, and developed the infrastructure necessary to export fruit to foreign markets. Jarvis notes that the bulk of these developments were carried out by the public sector. Exports rose slowly across this period and several export companies emerged that gained experience with foreign markets. Chilean firms achieved the volume needed to charter special fruit cargo ships. Fruit handling, better cold-storage management, and reduced transit times allowed improvements in fruit quality at destination.

Significant barriers remained. Uncertainties surrounding land reform and macropolicy of the late 1960s and early 1970s deterred private investment. Import quotas and high tariffs, slow and inefficient transport and port handling, and bureaucratic red tape slowed progress. With the policy reforms of the early 1970s, quota restrictions on imported inputs were reduced, and in 1976 import tariffs were cut to a uniform 10 percent from the previously high average level of 96 percent. Export procedures were streamlined and labor unions were proscribed. Strong world prices for fruit and a competitive peso raised returns to capital in the range of 25 to 50 percent.

Chile improved technology at all levels of the production chain—domestic transport, port operation, international shipping, banking, and telecommunications—and in all aspects of fruit production, packing, and cold storage. Jarvis examines in detail particular gains in planted varieties, management, and transport, and the private channels of technology dissemination. The number of fruit entrepreneurs increased four-fold. Jarvis further concludes that there were strong spillovers to other sectors that saw the possibilities of exporting. Most of the innovation was carried out by the private sector, although Jarvis wonders about the need for public provision as fruit markets have become tighter.

including universities, contributed a small proportion to the overall system of agricultural research. Private sector efforts were relatively slight; research investments in 1973 represented only 2 percent of the annual budget of INIA

(Venezian and Muchnik 1994). With the introduction of reforms, while direct public funds remained at a level of less than a half percent of agricultural GDP, the development of other funding sources led to at least a doubling of total support for agricultural research—from 0.4 percent of sector GDP to 0.9 percent between 1973 and 1992.

In the spirit of the economic reforms after 1975, several institutions were created to promote private sector participation and competition in research and development. The operation of these institutions required the use of either collaborative funding or research (or both) originating in the private sector. Moreover, the support of these institutions was for the most part open to rivalry across regions and between researchers in any economic sector. Except for the Ministry of Agriculture's research fund (Fondo de Investigación Agrícola, FIA), research directed toward the farm sector had to compete for resources available to all types of investigations.

A national fund for science and technology (Fondo Nacional de Desarrollo Tecnológico y Productivo, FONDECYT) was established in 1982, and the national development corporation created a research fund (FONTEC) in 1984. More important for university-based research, a 1989 law introduced tax incentives for research donations to institutions of higher education, and 1992 saw the implementation of the development fund Fondo de Fomento al Desarrollo Científico y Tecnológico (FONDEF), in support of R&D, which was underwritten with an Inter-American Development Bank loan. By 1990 private expenditure on agricultural research had increased 19 times its 1973 level, and represented approximately 13 percent of total spending on research in the sector. Within a few years following the introduction of FONDEF, private spending nearly doubled to about 20 percent of total farm sector research expenditures. The greater diversification of institutions and sources of financial support for farm sector R&D was accompanied by a shift in the nature of funding for the largest research institution, INIA. Prior to the reforms, INIA relied on taxpayer monies for 90 percent of its budget, the remainder coming from sales of services and seeds and other farm products. Following 1975, government policy pushed INIA toward self-financing. By 1985 the institution was earning 40 percent of its income from sales and another 20 percent from grants, loans, and other nongovernment sources.

The increased availability, diversification, and private direction of funding sources was associated with a greater weight given to research on exportable crops and the investigation of postproduction technologies, product characteristics and quality, and other topics important to commercial agriculture. While the previous emphasis on traditional crops by INIA was continued by that institution, the private sector and universities adapted quickly to the new incentives generated by reforms. Magnifying the effect of domestic research activities related to commercial agriculture generally, and to export agriculture especially, was the easy availability of proven crops and technologies from abroad, most notably from California. For-profit research activities proliferated, especially where the returns to the identification and adaptation of new varieties and methods were more easily internalized.

The human capital and experience officially located in INIA, but put to use by private enterprises, were important elements in the initial identification and evaluation of varieties and technologies accessible from abroad. As R&D in the service of private interests gained in stature and funding, INIA expanded its area of responsibility and replaced in part previous government services that had been unable to survive in the political environment following the initiation of reforms. Moreover, the political adherence to market-based solutions, and the obvious successes of commercial farmers, exporters, and processors, called into question public support for activities that otherwise might be sustained by private interests. As a result, INIA's role evolved toward a focus on smaller-scale agriculture. Nevertheless, one consequential benefit to all agricultural interests that followed the institution's adoption of a development role was the enhanced coordination of research with the demands of farmers.

The Chilean experience related to the contributions of agricultural research and development reinforces the importance, within the context of overall reform, of deregulation and privatization in the provision of more-reliable and lower-cost services. The climate that permitted these contributions, however, has also tended to de-emphasize longer-term research questions and the institutional infrastructure that supports scientific research, development, and training leading to benefits not easily internalized by private concerns. The net cost or benefit of such a shift in the balance of agricultural research and development policy away from long-term issues is not obvious.[5] It is also worth noting that the successes of the Chilean system in responding to the incentives brought about by the reforms were made possible not merely by the similarity of Chile's natural resources to those of regions in more economically advanced countries. Regardless of its deficiencies, the pre-reform agricultural research system had sustained a pool of human capital that, however inefficiently employed, was available for use when the reforms shifted the emphasis onto private efforts. Box 4.3 discusses more general issues concerning the design of R&D incentive programs.

## Argentina's and Uruguay's Export Diversification after Liberalization

### A Unilateral and Regional Liberalization in Argentina and Uruguay

Argentina's and Uruguay's trade liberalization was accomplished by policies applied unilaterally and regionally, and within the multilateral negotiations under the auspices of the General Agreement on Tariff and Trade/World Trade Organization (GATT/WTO).[6] The process of trade liberalization in Argentina started as a unilateral policy in 1988, with the so-called Canitrot Reform. At the beginning of 1991, trade liberalization was pushed even further; the average tariff fell to an unprecedented level of 12.2 percent in mid-1991. Overall, this unilateral liberalization reduced the average tariff in Argentina from 45 percent in 1987 to around 13 percent in 1994 (Berlinski 1998).

The process of trade liberalization in Uruguay also received a strong push in the early 1990s, but trade liberalization had been pursued without major interruptions since the end of the 1970s. The tariff reduction in Uruguay was accelerated after 1990. The average nominal protection declined from 30 percent in 1990 to 17 percent in 1993, and reached 13 percent in 1995.

From 1995 onward, trade policies in Argentina and Uruguay were set within Mercosur. This integration initiative was established among Argentina, Brazil, Paraguay, and Uruguay in 1991 with the signing of the Asunción Treaty. In its first article this treaty states that the aim of the agreement is to achieve "the free circulation of goods, services and productive factors among the member countries, through the elimination of the tariff and nontariff restrictions to the circulation of merchandises and of any other equivalent measure." It also established a Common External Tariff (CET) and a common commercial policy toward the rest of the world.[7] The full implementation of free trade within the region and the establishment of the CET were scheduled for 1995. These objectives were partially achieved with significant exemptions (for details, see Bouzas 1996; Terra 2000; and Sanguinetti, Pantano, and Posadas 2001).

By 1996, the member countries were, on average, pretty close to the liberalization objectives. While the external tariff in Argentina and Brazil converged from above toward the CET, those of Paraguay and Uruguay approached the CET from below, thus reflecting the relatively lower level of protection that those countries had initially, compared to their big neighbors. Regarding the tariff levels observed for the exempted items, the small countries set very high tariffs for the excluded items. On the other hand, the big countries, in particular, Brazil, have high tariffs on the external excluded items (21.39 percent). This fact could potentially play an important role in encouraging exports from Argentina and Uruguay to the Brazilian market. This hypothesis is explored further below.

### Diversification Indicators

In this section we investigate the precise nature of the changes outlined above. Particularly, we focus on the degree of export diversification. Following Sapir (1996) we construct the Gini coefficient and the Theil Coefficient to measure the extent of diversification of exports and imports in both countries. The Gini Coefficient ranges between 0 and 1. For example, a high Gini Coefficient is associated in the income distribution literature with high-income inequality. In our context, it will be an indicator of a highly concentrated trade structure. Different indicators weight differently changes in the distribution of export and import shares, so it is a good practice to check the robustness of results to different indicators.[8] Table 4.3 presents the Gini and Theil Coefficients for Argentina and Uruguay.

Several observations can be made. First, the evolution of diversification does not depend on the indicator we use.[9] Second, as one would have expected for a small country like Argentina, exports are more concentrated than imports throughout the period. Third, imports and exports show a consistent decline toward greater diversification. However, export concentration declined steadily and continuously while the import concentration indexes show a structural change around 1991 and 1992, when trade liberalization was implemented.

For Uruguay, exports are also more concentrated relative to imports, and both indicators decline in the period (greater diversification). Again, as in the case of Argentina, the concentration of imports declined sharply at the beginning of the 1990s, reflecting the deepening of trade liberalization policies taking place in those years. Indeed, this

BOX 4.3

## Incentives for R&D: Some Policy Issues

R&D has long been recognized as an important factor determining the pace of economic development. They reduce production costs of existing products and create new ones, thus contributing to sustained growth and enhancing economic welfare. Recent microevidence for Ireland also shows that, at the plant level, R&D-active firms are usually associated with plants with higher survival rates and higher job quality (Kearns and Ruane 2001). But there are externalities and public good features of investments in R&D that tend to make decentralized solutions—market outcomes—inefficient. These are related to the generation of knowledge that can be publicly used, and to externalities typical of human capital investments. For these reasons, governments usually use incentive devices to increase R&D investments and to try to attain a socially optimal allocation of funds for R&D.

The most common incentive takes the form of tax credits for investment in R&D. The rather scarce evidence suggests that these incentives increase investments in research, and that each additional dollar in tax credit for R&D stimulates roughly one additional dollar of R&D (Hall and Van Reenen 2000). The impact is relatively small, and does not seem to have a multiplier effect on private investment decisions. Considering that firms usually adapt their accounting practices to tax laws and incentives, this figure implies that each dollar given away through tax exemptions is probably associated with less than one additional dollar really spent on R&D. The natural question, therefore, is whether these resources would be better allocated if directly managed and invested by the government in specific R&D programs.

One alternative is a subsidy in the form of cost sharing of R&D investments between the private and public sectors. In this case, the public sector would add a defined amount for each dollar invested by private firms. In terms of instruments, and of the impacts on government accounts and R&D expenditures, a scheme like this would probably be equivalent to a tax credit system, since the tax incentive can be set at any percentage of the total R&D investment by private firms. Hence it is always possible to reproduce the fiscal and R&D impacts of a given cost-sharing system with some specific tax credit structure. But there are operational differences between these two systems. Table 4.4 summarizes some of the issues to be considered when discussing incentives for R&D.

The cost-sharing scheme allows the government to partially control the composition of investments in R&D, which in principle can be used to enhance welfare. It also assigns the monitoring of programs to special public institutions (such as development agencies), which are possibly more capable of checking the appropriate use of resources than a tax agency restricted to looking at the accounting statements, as in the tax credit system. But the cost-sharing mechanism also has its drawbacks. In principle, it is questionable whether the public sector has a better ability than the private sector to decide what are the investments with higher social return. The decision process inside the government is certainly affected by rent-seeking and political lobbying, thus increasing the uncertainty in relation to the optimality of the outcome. Also, although development agencies already exist in most countries, a system of public subsidies would possibly overload the existing institutions and increase operational costs. All these factors have to be weighed against the problems of the tax credit system. These include the fact that, in this case, the whole decision process remains delegated to the private sector. The effectiveness of tax credits is limited by the possibility of its use for tax-evasion purposes and the increased complexity of the resulting tax structure.

Therefore, the choice between the two systems, or the ideal design of any of them, is far from clear. Which of the factors mentioned above is the most important one probably depends on the specific productive and political structure of each country. In this sense, there seems to be space for experimentation, using pilot programs and the institutional structures already in place in the different countries. This would reveal the differential impacts of the alternative structures in different environments, giving a more solid guide for policy decisions. In any case, the issues mentioned here should be kept in mind, because they are factors that will determine the costs and benefits of R&D incentive programs, including their fiscal impact, the response of private R&D expenditures, the composition of R&D expenditures across sectors, the monitoring mechanisms, and the potential political and institutional constraints.

TABLE 4.3

## Indicators of Trade Concentration, Argentina and Uruguay, 1986–99

| | ARGENTINA | | | | URUGUAY | | | |
| | IMPORTS | | EXPORTS | | IMPORTS | | EXPORTS | |
| | GINI | THEIL | GINI | THEIL | GINI | THEIL | GINI | THEIL |
|------|------|-------|------|-------|------|-------|------|-------|
| 1986 | 0.76 | 1.2 | 0.89 | 2.0 | 0.76 | 1.4 | 0.92 | 2.4 |
| 1992 | 0.64 | 0.8 | 0.86 | 1.7 | 0.72 | 1.1 | 0.90 | 2.1 |
| 1999 | 0.64 | 0.8 | 0.83 | 1.4 | 0.65 | 0.8 | 0.85 | 1.8 |

*Source:* Sanguinetti, Pantano, and Posadas 2001.

increase in the varieties of imports was great news for consumer welfare in both countries.

### Decomposition of Concentration by Sectors and Regions

In this subsection we present a more detailed analysis of the driving forces behind the evolution of concentration of exports. The analysis first uses variants of the Theil Coefficient to determine the extent to which trade diversification in Argentina and Uruguay occurred either *within* product groups or *between* product groups. In turn, the analysis explores the impact of Mercosur on trade concentration in Argentina.

### Decomposition of Export Concentration by Sectors

The Theil decomposition analysis allows us to check whether diversification occurred either within or between product aggregates. Figure 4.2 presents the results for Argentina.[10] The main conclusion is that a large share of the diversification of exports of Argentina is accounted for by within-group diversification. Almost 80 percent of the decline in the Theil Coefficient is explained by within-group

TABLE 4.4

## Issues in R&D Incentive Policies

| ISSUES | TAX CREDIT | COST-SHARING SUBSIDY |
|--------|------------|----------------------|
| 1. Fiscal impact | Possibly equivalent | Possibly equivalent |
| 2. R&D expenditures | Possibly equivalent | Possibly equivalent |
| 3. Composition of investment | 100 percent privately determined | Shared decision |
| 4. Monitoring and administrative responsibility | Tax collection agency | Special public institutions |
| 5. Challenges | Tax evasion, complex tax structure | Rent-seeking for subsidies, public sector's decisionmaking ability, institutional overload |

diversification, and this proportion remained stable during the entire period. On the import side (not shown), we observe an increase in the participation of between-group diversification since 1991 (around 40 percent), suggesting a significant effect of trade liberalization on the composition of imports at a very aggregate level of products.

Figure 4.3 shows the calculations for Uruguay. The results are similar to those obtained for Argentina in the sense that most of the diversification is explained by within-group diversification. The main difference is that we find a stable behavior of the participation of within-group (and between-group) diversification during the entire period for both exports and imports (not shown).

### Diversification Indicators by Region: Mercosur and the Rest of the World

A final important aspect of the behavior of the diversification indicators is to check whether diversification was different across trade flows within Mercosur and with the rest of the world. If this is so, part of the overall diversification process could be attributed to the increase in regional trade. Figure 4.4 shows Theil concentration indexes for Argentina's exports.

Exports to Mercosur are less concentrated than those to the rest of the world. On the import side (not shown), imports coming from the rest of the world are more diversified. Regarding the dynamics of the concentration indicators, the export indicator for Mercosur behaved more erratically compared to the export indicator corresponding to the rest of the world. More important, export diversification within Mercosur increased over time, though some diversification occurred even before 1991. This may reflect that on the export side considerable market access was obtained prior to 1991 through the partial agreements signed among Argentina, Brazil, and Uruguay. On the other hand, import concentration declined significantly after 1991, showing the effect of across-the-board regional (and unilateral) trade liberalization that has taken place since that year.

FIGURE 4.2

**Concentration Index Decomposition by Main Aggregates, Argentina Exports, SITC**

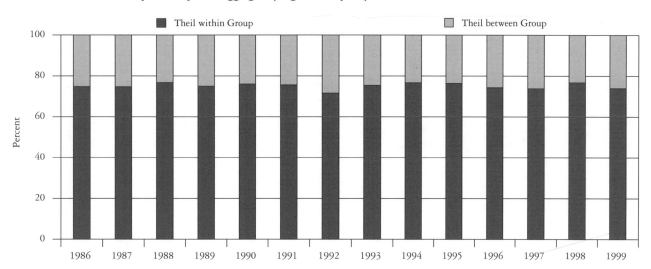

*Source:* Sanguinetti, Pantano, and Posadas 2001.

FIGURE 4.3

**Concentration Index Decomposition by Main Aggregates, Uruguay Exports, SITC**

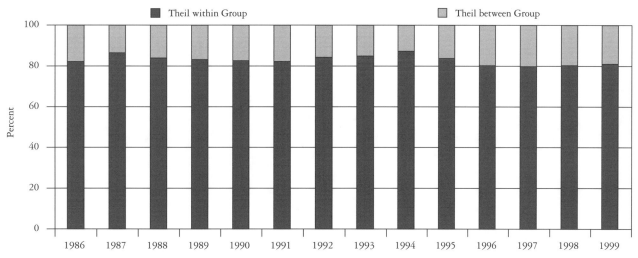

*Source:* Sanguinetti, Pantano, and Posadas 2001.

The evidence for Uruguay (see Sanguinetti, Pantano, and Posadas 2001) shows that on the export side we also observe a greater level of diversification of those going to Mercosur. The differences in the level of the concentration indicators across destinations seem to be less significant (and have declined over time) than those found for Argentina. Still, when we calculate the Herfindahl concentration index (see Figure 4.5) the data show a significant and relatively stable difference in export concentration where those geared to Mercosur are less concentrated than those going to third markets. The remaining issue is how Mercosur aided trade diversification.

### Regional Integration, Economies of Scale, and Transport Costs

In relatively small countries it will not be profitable to produce goods subject to large economies of scale. This could be because of lack of inputs or because the local market is

85

FIGURE 4.4

**Theil Concentration Indexes for Exports; Argentina, Rest of the World, and Mercosur**

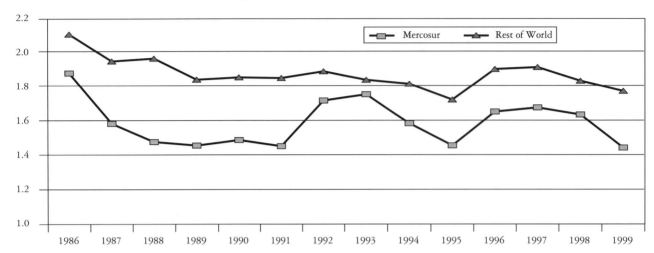

*Source:* Sanguinetti, Pantano, and Posadas 2001.

FIGURE 4.5

**Herfindahl Index for Exports, Uruguay**

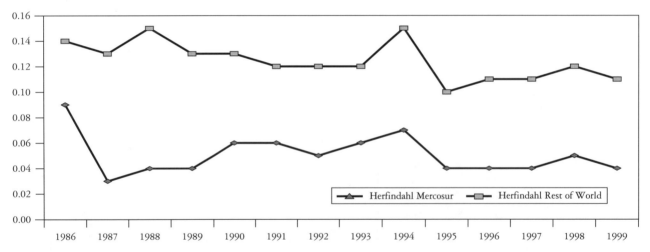

*Source:* Sanguinetti, Pantano, and Posadas 2001.

too small to achieve the required amount of sales to cover costs. Regional integration agreements (RIA) can help overcome this scale problem as local markets are pooled into a single larger market (see World Bank 2000 and Corden 1972). Thus, once countries form an RIA and the domestic market expands, new products subject to economies of scale will be produced.

The question that arises here is whether this inconvenience of smallness can also be overcome with general, nonpreferential trade liberalization. Under what circumstances is this argument about economies of scale stronger for

regional integration compared to unilateral trade liberalization? Three types of arguments can be made. First, unilateral liberalization does not ensure access to export markets, though it stimulates efficiency in domestic production, and in this respect it encourages exports. Reciprocity, on the other hand, is a key aspect of regional liberalization, and because of this it could be an effective tool to gain access to other markets.

A second related argument in favor of an RIA is that regional integration may enhance and protect market access. The multilateral trading system is still far from assuring market access. Contingent protection is pervasive throughout the world, and neither protection in the form of antidumping safeguards nor other border frictions can be completely avoided. Regional integration could provide a WTO-plus environment where free trade within the regional markets is more sustainable and less subject to this contingent form of protection. The case of the European Union with the Single Market Program of 1989 is a clear example of a regional integration scheme where deep integration has been pursued. Even Mercosur has established a WTO-plus environment in some areas of trade policy. For example, safeguard actions are not allowed within the region.[11]

Finally, another aspect in which an RIA can facilitate trade within the area, relative to that with the rest of the world, is by encouraging cooperation among countries in the area of physical integration. This could produce a significant reduction in transport costs, especially in the case where the countries that formed an RIA share common borders. For some products, this reduction may imply that these goods are traded within the region but not with third markets. Examples of these products are electricity, natural gas, and cement, all of which are typically subject to economies of scale in production.[12]

### Regional Tariff Preferences: Diversification through Trade Diversion

Regional integration will change relative prices in member countries. Imports from partners become cheaper due to the elimination of tariffs. This in turn affects import demand and as a consequence affects trade flows and production. As indicated previously, the presence of tariff preferences may foster local production and exports of products that could not have been exported under a nonpreferential liberalization. Thus part of the diversification of exports we observe may be a consequence of trade diversion. However, it is also possible that RIAs might become platforms for world exports under certain circumstances. This possibility and new empirical evidence is discussed in Box 4.4. The following paragraphs review empirical evidence concerning the question of whether Mercosur helps explain the export diversification trend experienced by Argentina in the 1990s.

### Empirical Evidence

Sanguinetti, Pantano, and Posadas (2001) present the statistical results for Argentina covering 1991 to 1995. The authors assessed the impact of Mercosur on export concentration. In this case the dependent variable is the change in Argentina's export shares to Brazil relative to Argentina's export shares to the rest of the world. This analysis focuses on whether Mercosur helped Argentina diversify by allowing exports of new products to Mercosur but not to the rest of the world, either through trade diversion or economies of scale. Thus it is qualitatively different from the analysis in Box 4.4, which focuses on whether Mercosur allowed its members to export new products to the world after exporting them to Mercosur. Additional exercises presented in Sanguinetti, Pantano, and Posadas (2001) considered alternative periods.

All the econometric evidence discussed by Sanguinetti, Pantano, and Posadas (2001) shows that tariff preferences had a significant effect on the share of Argentine exports to the region (Brazil) compared with the rest of the world. The net effect of tariff preferences on Argentine export shares to Brazil is positive and significant, while the same preferences have had a negative and significant effect on export share of the same items to the rest of the world. Thus, as expected, tariff preferences have encouraged exports of certain items to Mercosur markets relative to extra-Mercosur destinations.

The evidence concerning the role of economies of scale in Mercosur is more ambiguous, suggesting that, contrary to what was predicted by theoretical arguments, sectors subject to larger economies of scale have expanded their exports to the rest of the world relative to Mercosur. This result is nevertheless not robust to small changes in the period of analysis (1992 to 1995 and 1992 to 1996). Thus, we should interpret this result with caution.

Overall, we conclude that tariff preferences played a positive role in encouraging Argentine exports to the region. However, the empirical models, and in particular the tariff preference margins, explain a small proportion of the variation across exports of the share going to Mercosur relative to the rest of the world. Thus other factors not contemplated in the aforementioned empirical analysis may have played a key role. Within those, we suspect that transport costs are relevant.[13] In addition, most of the diversification of Argentina's and Uruguay's exports occurred within sectors. Hence the removal of the anti-export bias brought by the unilateral trade liberalization is probably the main driving force of trade diversification in these economies. Mercosur helped a bit, but the action was elsewhere.

BOX 4.4

## Mercosur as a Platform for World Exports: New Empirical Evidence

Supporters of regional integration often argue that the formation of a larger market may serve as a platform for exporters to world markets (Devlin and French-Davis 1999). The region can serve as a "classroom" for potential exporters, where they can learn "how to export" and create a reputation as reliable suppliers. The knowledge acquired in the regional market can then be used to penetrate more distant markets outside the regional agreement. The regional market not only allows for the exploitation of economies of scale and learning by doing, but information about customs procedures, required design of export products, foreign consumer tastes, and firm reputation are generated through exports to the regional market.

Nicita, Olarreaga, and Soloaga (2001) explore the effect that regional exports within Mercosur had on the ability of members to export manufacturing products to the rest of the world. From a policy perspective, the presence of platform effects may create sufficiently large gains to compensate for potential trade diversion associated with preferential market access.

Information flows to other countries on regional exporter performance in other Mercosur markets are captured by weighting the evolution of exporter market share in the regional market by the bilateral share of trade in newspapers and periodicals (for example, *Journal of Commerce*, *Export Channel*, *Made for Export*, *Gazeta Mercantile*) between Mercosur members and each rest-of-the-world potential market.

After controlling for potential information flows among rest-of-the-world countries on the export performance of Mercosur members in their respective markets, there is no evidence of a platform effect associated with the creation of Mercosur in 1991 at the aggregate level. However, in the case of the small members of Mercosur (Uruguay and Paraguay), there is evidence of export information spillovers in the regional markets, but also in the rest of the world, before and after the creation of Mercosur in 1991. This suggests that the tariff preferences granted from 1991 onward had little effect on their availability to penetrate other foreign markets. Exporters in

Paraguay and Uruguay benefited from export information spillovers, regardless of the creation of Mercosur.

On the other hand, at a more disaggregated level (SITC 1 digit), there is evidence of platform effects for all Mercosur member exporters. Argentina's exporters of chemicals (SITC 5) and machinery (SITC 7) have taken advantage of their increase in exports to the regional market, after the creation of Mercosur in 1991, to improve their performance in rest-of-the-world markets. The same is true for Brazilian and Paraguayan exporters of basic manufacturing (SITC 6: textiles, wood, paper, and leather) and for Brazilian and Uruguayan exporters of machinery.

Moreover, there is also evidence for the small members of Mercosur (Paraguay and Uruguay), both at the aggregate and disaggregated level, that they have benefited from other Mercosur member export performance in rest-of-the world markets. Since the creation of Mercosur, improvements of other Mercosur member export performance in rest-of-the-world markets has helped exporters in Paraguay and Uruguay increase their exports to the rest of the world in all industries, except for basic manufacturing in Uruguay and other manufacturing (SITC 8: apparel, footwear, instruments, and furniture) in Paraguay. For example, exporters of Uruguayan machinery to the rest of the world have therefore benefited from better export performance of Brazilian exporters of machinery in those markets.

In sum, although platform effects are not generally present across all industries for Mercosur exporters, there is evidence that exporters in different Mercosur countries have benefited from platform effects associated with the creation of Mercosur in at least some industries. Since 1991 exporters to the rest of the world in Paraguay and Uruguay have also benefited from large Mercosur member export performance in those markets. However, note that whether these platform effects dominate the trade-diverting effects associated with preferential access behind (high) external tariffs remains an open question.

*Source:* Nicita, Olarreaga, and Soloaga 2001.

## Brazil's Reforms, Manufacturing Productivity, and EMBRAER

As shown, the economic reforms undertaken in the past decades in Latin America had significant impacts on the productivity and export performance of the agricultural sector. This was also the case in manufacturing. In this section, we first review the evidence on the turnaround in Brazilian manufacturing productivity during the 1990s. We then look in detail at the case of EMBRAER, the Brazilian aircraft manufacturer that in recent years has become a commercial success.

### Productivity Growth in Brazilian Manufacturing: Review of the Evidence

Although estimates of productivity vary considerably with the specific methodologies adopted, and with the source and level of aggregation of the data, all the available studies indicate a considerable improvement in Brazilian productivity during the 1990s. At the aggregate level, studies performed at Brazil's Central Bank and Planning Ministry find increases of annual productivity growth from the 1980s to the 1990s of, respectively, 2.7 percent and 1.1 percent. World Bank estimates suggest an increase of 1.9 percent (see Teixeira da Silva 2001, Bonelli and Fonseca 1998, and Loayza 2001).

As expected, the improvements were even larger in the manufacturing sector, where exposure to import competition is greatest. Although the estimates also vary considerably depending on the level of aggregation of the data, studies performed on the basis of industry-level figures suggest increases of around 4.5 percent from the 1980s to 1990–97.[14] Also, the efficiency gains of Brazilian manufacturing firms were reflected in considerable reductions of their markups during the 1990s. From 1990 to 1995, the difference between real prices and costs fell by 21.1 percent in the Brazilian manufacturing sector, while another 5.3 percent reduction occurred during 1995–98 (see Moreira 2000).

The pressure to increase efficiency came from the unprecedented access of Brazilian consumers to imported goods, as nontariff trade barriers were mostly eliminated and tariffs were reduced to almost one fourth of their previous average. Also, as part of the successful inflation stabilization policy implemented in 1994, the real exchange rate experienced a significant appreciation during most of the decade, which further stimulated imports. In this context, cost-reducing and quality-increasing strategies became a necessity for the survival of Brazilian manufacturing firms. However, it is very important to remember that the real appreciation of the *real* was also associated with extremely high interest rates and with low aggregate economic growth rates. Thus, the real exchange rate appreciation was not good for the economy as a whole.

The opening of the economy also provided new means for efficiency improvement. After decades of limited access to state-of-the-art equipment, components, and technologies in general—whenever a product had a "national similar" its imports were automatically prohibited—Brazilian firms gained access to the same suppliers used by their foreign competitors. Thus, effective rates of protection diminished at an even faster rate than nominal tariffs, and imports of intermediate and especially capital goods reacted to the opening of the economy more rapidly than those of final products.

Although the timing of the productivity turnaround coincided with the adoption of trade liberalization, its underlying causes have still been the subject of some debate. Indeed, it has been argued that part of the productivity growth recovery could be associated with cyclical factors, particularly the deep recession that followed Brazil's failed attempts at stabilization during 1990 and 1991. This argument, however, has been overtaken by the fact that productivity increases have persisted during the periods of output growth after 1992. Moreover, the basic result of a significant turnaround in productivity growth appears to be robust to the use of different data sources and the particular approach adopted to measure the services of labor and capital—including therein different measures of capacity use, data on electricity consumption, corrections for unemployment, hours worked, and so forth.

Finally, econometric estimates confirm a positive impact of trade liberalization on the level and growth of manufacturing productivity. For instance, studies performed using firm-level data suggest that both the level and the rate of growth of TFP were significantly associated with reductions in tariffs and with real exchange rate appreciations (see Hay 1997 and Muendler, Sepúlveda, and Servén 2001).[15] Similar conclusions are obtained with data tabulated at the industry level, which also suggests a positive association between the degree of import penetration and the rate of industry TFP growth (see Rossi Júnior and Ferreira 1999).

## Brazil's EMBRAER

Chapter 2 discussed the recent evolution of the structure of Brazil's net exports.[16] It is clear that the country maintains a comparative advantage in a variety of products, ranging from tropical agriculture to capital-intensive manufactures. However, the behavior of net exports of machines since the early 1990s indicates that the only sector in which Brazil maintains a notable comparative advantage is in the export of transport equipment (excluding road vehicles), especially aircraft. The Brazilian company EMBRAER, the relatively successful firm that produces small airplanes, is an example.

In June 1999, at the Paris Le Bourget air show, EMBRAER announced sales of 200 commuter jets, with contracts totaling US$6.6 billion. During 1999, EMBRAER's sales of US$1.9 billion made it the fourth-largest aircraft manufacturer and the second-largest in the market for regional jets, with net revenue of US$230 million. The excellent recent performance of EMBRAER is even more impressive if one considers the fact that at the beginning of the 1990s the formerly state-owned Brazilian company was on the brink of bankruptcy.

In December 1994 the company was bought by a consortium led by a local financial conglomerate. The government assumed the company's debt and reduced its ownership to 6.8 percent. The new management implemented a thorough reengineering process, and gave full priority to the project of the ERJ-145, a 50-passenger jet that was already at the end of the development process, and the sales of which would later be responsible for the company's reversal of fortune. However, a complete explanation of the company's recent performance has to contain at least two other important dimensions.

First, EMBRAER benefited from substantial government support, including but going far beyond the export subsidies that are now the focus of an ongoing dispute between Brazil and Canada at the WTO. Second, the company's commercial success in the global market for regional jets cannot be dissociated from the knowledge and skills accumulated by EMBRAER over the years, related to the company's early foreign market exposure, associated with its export orientation and the coupling of high R&D investments with strategic partnerships with foreign manufacturers.

As for the government policies used to support EMBRAER, it must be emphasized that the company benefited from much more than the current subsidized credit lines. EMBRAER's initial projects, staff, and equipment were absorbed, at no cost, from other Air Force–related institutions. The government also designated to EMBRAER a fraction of the income tax paid by all companies established in the country, a transfer which amounted to US$500 million between 1969 and 1985.[17] Other benefits include the exemption of import, export, sales (ICM), and industrial products (IPI) taxes, import protection, large orders from Ministries of Aeronautics and Agriculture, government loans and grants, and the support of Brazilian diplomacy in international sales, especially in the military market.

It must be noted that in an oligopolistic market such as the one for commuter aircraft, governments may have incentives to pursue strategic trade policies, in order to shift profits from foreign to domestic firms. However, although there is evidence that this has in fact been a common practice in that market, welfare gains from government interventions of this type are not guaranteed, especially if possible retaliation is taken into consideration (see Baldwin and Flamm 1989).

As for EMBRAER's particular market strategies, one of the most important is the company's early focus on reaching foreign markets as opposed to concentrating on Brazil's protected local market, as many other manufacturing companies in that country did. For instance, EMBRAER's first important product, the 19-passenger turboprop EMB-110 or *Bandeirante*, was first delivered in 1973 to the Brazilian Air Force, and in 1979–82 it had already attained a 32 percent share of the U.S. market for 15- to 19-passenger aircraft. The *Brasilia*, a 30-passenger, twin-engine turboprop first delivered in 1985, reached market shares of 25 percent worldwide and 29 percent in the United States. Thus, in the early 1980s, EMBRAER's ratio of exports to production was already close to 50 percent, increasing to more than 60 percent at the end of that decade. After its recent comeback, EMBRAER's exports reportedly represent 95 percent of total sales.

EMBRAER also differed from the typical import-substitution-driven company in that it avoided any attempt to reach high degrees of local content in its products. This option, it must be noted, was not available to most Brazilian industries, which were subject to domestic content laws that forced them to use domestic suppliers for inputs.[18] During the 1980s, the ratio of imports to production was close to 50 percent, and it has increased in recent years, reaching 62.4 percent in 1999. In fact, almost all the key components and systems in EMBRAER's planes, such as engines and avionics, are purchased from foreign-based suppliers: 95 percent in the case of the ERJ-145 program and 85 percent for the ERJ-170/190 family of 70-to-108-passenger jets, whose initial deliveries are expected for 2002.[19]

As a consequence of EMBRAER's early focus on international sales, the company has been an important contributor to Brazilian exports. However, because of its intense use of foreign inputs, the company's net export performance has been less impressive, especially if one takes into consideration that its local suppliers also tend to have a large import-to-production ratio. For instance, it has been estimated that between 1975 and 1988, EMBRAER's net exports averaged US$123 million per year. But average net exports in that period shrink to less than US$20 million when an adjustment is made to consider imports by EMBRAER's suppliers (Dagnino 1993:54).

As for EMBRAER's technological strategies, one could distinguish three phases in its history of product development and manufacturing (Frischtak 1993, 1994). The first was characterized by the manufacturing of products developed outside EMBRAER, either by the Air Force's Centro Técnico da Aeronáutica (CTA) or by foreign companies. It is a period of intense learning in production technologies, and in the areas of marketing and customer technical assistance. A crucial role was played by the knowledge absorbed from foreign companies that partnered with EMBRAER during this period. Those important agreements, with Aermacchi, Northtrop, and Piper, were made possible by the intervention of the Brazilian government, which in practice used them as conditions to gain access to the Brazilian civil and military markets.

A second phase started in the late 1970s and lasted until the company's privatization in 1994. It was characterized by the development of in-house formal R&D activities, which generated a series of increasingly sophisticated planes. While EMBRAER still counted on government finance for the military planes, three of the five main projects of this period were targeted primarily at the civil market, and were financed with the company's own resources and commercial loans. Although all projects were the source of important internal spillovers, generating knowledge and skills on which successive planes would be based, only two of them were a clear commercial success—the *Tucano* and the *Brasilia*. The development of a sixth plane was started in the late 1980s—the EMB-145—but the company's excessive indebtedness, in addition to the commercial failure of some of

its products, and a softening of the international aircraft market, led to delays in the project.

Production of the EMB-145 began during EMBRAER's third phase, after its privatization. Among the changes introduced by the new management must be emphasized the shift from an engineering-driven to a market-driven strategy. Indeed, among the planes developed by EMBRAER, the three main commercial failures were characterized by being overpriced for their market segment, even though all were technical successes with good operational records. Moreover, especially during the late 1980s, the company opted for an expansion of its product line by engaging in technically sophisticated expensive development projects at a time when its financial structure was already fragile. This type of decision would probably not be made by the new private controllers, committed to the profitability and financial sustainability of their investments.

The new phase has also been characterized by the use of risk-sharing partnerships, four in the case of the EMB-145, and 10 in the case of the new ERJ-170/190 family.[20] Another important partnership was created in November 1999, when a French consortium including Aerospatiale-Matra, Dassault Aviation, Thompson-CSF, and Snecma bought a 20 percent stake in EMBRAER. Among other gains, this new partnership is expected to improve the company's access to international financial markets, and to contribute to its expansion in the military and in foreign markets in general. For the French companies, the partnership with EMBRAER could probably increase their odds of being selected as suppliers of the Brazilian Air Force in its forthcoming new round of equipment procurement (see Goldstein 2000 and Bernardes 2001).

It is important to note that a rigorous cost–benefit analysis of Brazil's commitment to the development of EMBRAER is hampered by the difficulties in quantifying the numerous benefits that the company received from the Brazilian government. However, it is clear that the total amounts involved are very large, because they cover a variety of government policies: the provision of specialized human resources, preference in government procurement to the company or its partners, direct transfers of tax revenues and capital injections in general, a variety of tax exemptions, subsidized credit, and import protection, among others.

The total opportunity cost of the above resources should be weighted against the social benefits derived from EMBRAER's establishment and growth, including the externalities or spillovers reaped by other companies, and EMBRAER's contribution to Brazil's balance of payments, given its focus on international sales. Although these benefits are difficult to quantify, the fact that EMBRAER has concentrated on system-integration activities and maintains a low degree of indigenous content in its products, suggests that at least in terms of *net* exports, and the development of specialized *local* suppliers, the company's contributions have been limited.

More indirect spillover effects were probably significant at the local level because EMBRAER, together with CTA and the Instituto Tecnológico da Aeronáutica (ITA), reportedly contributed to the transformation of São José dos Campos, from a relatively small city in the 1950s, to a prosperous industrial center with a population of a half-million today. It must be noted, however, that significant local investments by multinationals in the automobile and consumer goods industries had already taken place before the establishment of EMBRAER in 1969.

In sum, much of the current market success of EMBRAER is related to its early exposure to foreign markets, both through its export orientation, and in terms of its strategy of combining high R&D investments with imports of foreign inputs and know-how, and strategic partnerships with foreign companies. However, although EMBRAER successfully developed into a world-class manufacturer of technologically sophisticated products, the costs involved in its development were enormous, and we do not know whether the company could have succeeded without substantial government support. Moreover, it is not clear that the net present value of the public investments made in EMBRAER are positive, even considering its recent commercial success. For instance, due to the company's focus on system integration and its limited use of local suppliers of inputs and components—both important aspects of its market and technology strategies—EMBRAER's interaction with local industries has not been significant, so that knowledge and technology spillovers have probably been limited. Even if the company has been a significant contributor to Brazilian exports, its net exports have been much more limited due to the fact that EMBRAER's imports have also been considerable. Finally, it must be remembered that the effectiveness of credit or other types of subsidies directed at shifting profits from foreign firms to EMBRAER is limited by the possible retaliations that those measures may trigger.

## Exports and Foreign Investment in Central American Countries: Tax Incentives, Institutions, or Human Capital?

Over the last decade, Costa Rica and El Salvador experienced exceptional economic growth.[21] In both cases, the expansion of exports—in particular those from EPZs—suggests that foreign investment and exports played a major role in fostering growth. Nevertheless, the profile of exports and dynamic sectors differs substantially across the two countries, suggesting that their future development paths will be quite different. Most notably, the types of technologies being adopted are considerably distinct.

This case study examines the policies implemented in these countries, and the challenges that must be faced. The study starts by describing the recent economic performance of the two countries. It then investigates the determinants of the different composition of exports and foreign investments between Costa Rica and El Salvador during the 1990s. The much higher stock of human capital in Costa Rica seems to explain why the more technologically advanced foreign investments chose Costa Rica as opposed to other countries in the region. To explore this view, the study looks at the explanations provided by firms about their decisions to locate in Costa Rica.

### Exports and Growth during the 1990s in Costa Rica and El Salvador

Like all Central American economies, Costa Rica and El Salvador experienced dramatic events during the 1980s. Costa Rica initiated the decade with a balance-of-payments crisis triggered by large internal and external macroeconomic imbalances. The stabilization required a large devaluation, as well as fiscal and monetary tightening. The fixed exchange rate regime was abandoned, and a more flexible crawling peg was adopted, together with other structural adjustment measures.

In the 1990s, all the economies in Central America, starting at different times and at different rates, embarked on a process of liberalization of markets, reduction of import protection, reduction of the size of the public sector, and incentives to exports. With macroeconomic stability in place, the scenario was remarkably different, and long-term development objectives were again a top priority. Like in the 1960s and 1970s, policy focused on how to speed up growth. The goal was now sought through exports of new goods to new markets and through foreign investment.

Both Costa Rica and El Salvador grew remarkably fast during this period, with per capita GDP average annual growth rates of 6 percent and 7.7 percent, respectively. To put these numbers in perspective, Costa Rica expanded its GDP by 78 percent, and El Salvador doubled its GDP during the period. The yearly aggregate exports of both countries during the decade grew even more dramatically, doubling for Costa Rica and more than tripling for El Salvador. The ratio of exports to GDP for both countries grew significantly over time, most notably in the second half of the 1990s.

The expansion of exports was not concentrated in traditional goods, nor was it the result of favorable movements in world prices. On the contrary, the expansion of exports was concentrated in new sectors, which changed the configuration of the two economies. To illustrate how fast the change took place, Figures 4.6a, 4.6b, 4.7a, and 4.7b display the average composition of the exports during 1995–96 and 1999–2000 for both countries. Clearly, the importance of the traditional goods—coffee for El Salvador, and coffee and bananas for Costa Rica—decreased.

Though part of the decline in the share of traditional goods was due to new producers in the international markets and increased protection from developed countries, mainly the European Union, part was also the result of the development of EPZs. For El Salvador, the share of exports out of EPZs, mostly *maquilas*, increased from 41 percent to 54 percent in less than five years. For Costa Rica, this same share went from 27 percent to 58 percent.[22] For Costa Rica, such an impressive growth was in great part due to the initiation of operations of Intel and other high-tech firms in the country (Remec, Sawtec, Cinair, and Sensortronics, for example).

The rising importance of EPZs in both countries is illustrated in Figure 4.8, which displays total exports and imports of firms in EPZs, and Figure 4.9, which shows the fraction of the total gross and net exports generated by EPZs. Here, the net series is constructed by removing the imports made by firms in EPZs, that is, (Exports$^{EPZ}$ − Imports$^{EPZ}$)/(Total Exports − Imports$^{EPZ}$). The importance of EPZs in gross export and import flows accelerated at the end of the 1990s. Furthermore, EPZs were not simply increasing both gross exports and imports, since the ratio of net exports more than quintupled for Costa Rica and almost tripled for El Salvador, in less than five years.

There is little doubt that forces working throughout the period—such as the political and macroeconomic stabiliza-

FIGURE 4.6a

**El Salvador: Composition of Exports, 1995–96**

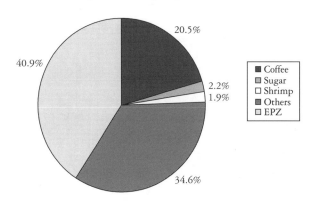

*Source:* Monge 2001.

FIGURE 4.6b

**El Salvador: Composition of Exports, 1999–2000**

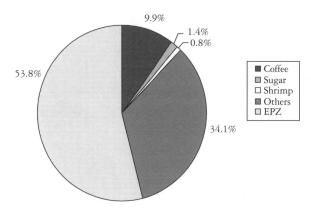

*Source:* Monge 2001.

tion in the region, the worldwide movement toward free trade, and the formation of trade blocks—would have increased the flows of foreign investment to the region, and the exports of *maquila* and other products. It should be noted that in several countries, notably in the Caribbean, rapid advances in information and communications technology have also added impetus to the development of new export activities in EPZs (see Box 4.5). However, governments in both Costa Rica and El Salvador actively promoted the development of EPZs.

### Tax Incentives in EPZs: Inevitable Reforms in the Future

Both Costa Rica and El Salvador provide significant benefits to the establishment of export-oriented firms in their

FIGURE 4.7a

**Costa Rica: Composition of Exports, 1995–96**

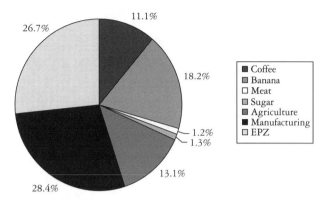

*Source:* Monge 2001.

FIGURE 4.7b

**Costa Rica: Composition of Exports, 1999–2000**

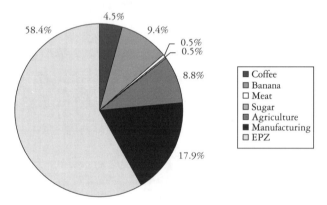

*Source:* Monge 2001.

territories. And, despite the fact that most of the established firms are foreign owned, this specific set of incentives is directed to exports, independently of nationality. Nevertheless, both countries also have incentives directly aimed at foreign investors. Table 4.5 compares the incentives provided by Costa Rica and El Salvador as of 2001. It is clear that the incentives are biased toward export-oriented markets, in sharp contrast with the incentives from the import-substitution schemes of the 1960s and 1970s.

Costa Rica and El Salvador offer similar incentives. There are no restrictions on the repatriation of profits or remittances, no import or exports taxes, and no sales taxes as long as the goods are sold abroad. However, there are important differences. On one hand, El Salvador is more generous with fiscal incentives. In every tax dimension explicitly mentioned, El Salvador offers either a larger benefit or a longer duration. Costa Rica, on the other hand, seems more proactive in terms of providing assistance with

training of the labor force. Also, in Costa Rica the benefits seem to target employment in underdeveloped regions, but those are additional benefits, not requirements.

While it is difficult to assess the actual effectiveness of these benefits, it would be extreme to think that they have been redundant. Figure 4.10 displays the FDI received by the two countries during the 1990s. It is obvious that they have grown dramatically. After a slow start, especially for El Salvador, the flows of FDI accelerated during the second half of the decade. Figure 4.10 also shows the large difference between Costa Rica and El Salvador in the volume of investments. Until 1996, FDI in El Salvador was negligible. Costa Rica, on the other hand, has consistently received large inflows and, apart from an expected slowdown during 1998–2000, the FDI flow increased steadily. Only in 1998 did El Salvador receive more FDI than Costa Rica, but even that cannot be taken as a signal of reversion because it was mostly due to the large privatizations taking place in El Salvador. In 1998 and 1999, El Salvador successfully privatized four electricity distribution companies, three thermal generation plants, and the national telephone company (which was split in two). The sum of these operations amounted to almost US$1 billion.

A common feature of the EPZs in these countries is the use of tax incentives to promote foreign investment. This is also true for EPZs in the Caribbean. In the case of the Dominican Republic, Law 8-90 permits a maximum of 20 percent of production to be sold in the local market. These types of export requirements will become illegal under the WTO framework by January 2003. Hence the aforementioned countries, as well as others in the LAC region, will need to make reforms to bring their incentive systems within the WTO's legal framework. Efforts are under way to raise the income-per-capita criteria used by the WTO to provide exemptions to this rule. But if these efforts fail, these countries will need to change their incentive structure.

More specifically, the relevant authorities should consider reducing corporate income tax rates to low levels for all firms, which should continue to attract FDI. This approach is now favored by Costa Rica. The main advantage of this solution is its simplicity, because the corresponding tax system is significantly simplified, thus reducing the costs (evasion, etc.) associated with complicated tax structures. On the other hand, this approach requires a substantial amount of regional coordination among Central American and Caribbean countries to prevent a race to the "bottom" in terms of tax rates, which could cause fiscal difficulties.

FIGURE 4.8

**Costa Rica and El Salvador: Exports and Imports from EPZs**

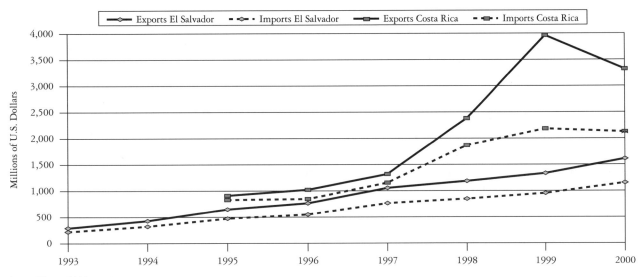

*Source:* Monge 2001.

FIGURE 4.9

**Costa Rica and El Salvador: Share of Exports from EPZs**

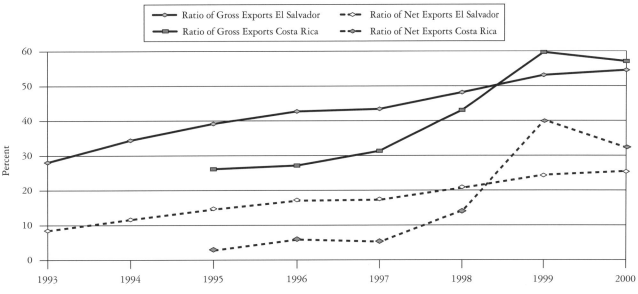

*Source:* Monge 2001.

Another alternative is to remove the export requirements and replace them with criteria permitted by the WTO, such as objectives for developing marginal geographic areas, or employment generation could also help stimulate future investments. The disadvantage of this set of incentives is that dynamic firms might not be attracted to those areas precisely because high-tech firms usually look for locations where there are other similar plants to take advantage of any knowledge externalities.

In the meantime, efforts at the regional level should coordinate the implementation of such changes to prevent investment diversion and a race to the bottom (in terms of providing more and more onerous fiscal incentives for firms) among LAC countries. We believe that making such a

BOX 4.5

## Information Services in Barbados and Jamaica

For the countries that manage to successfully participate in the new knowledge-based economy, the development of the ICT sector is the source of dynamic economic opportunities. With the development of the Internet and the dramatic reduction in telecommunications costs, the diffusion of ICT has accelerated.

Confronted with the persistent decline of their traditional primary exports, countries such as Barbados, Jamaica, and Trinidad and Tobago have visualized the ICT sector as the source of significant opportunities for export diversification, and for the attraction of FDI. Local authorities have made developing an export-oriented information services sector one of their top priorities, and have implemented a series of policies to that end.

Because comparative advantage in information services is crucially related to the availability of a labor force with the appropriate skills, and to a good telecommunications infrastructure, important efforts have been devoted to improving local conditions in those two areas. In addition, new policies have been implemented to advance the relevant institutional setup, including the creation of new investment promotion agencies, EPZs, and industrial parks; strengthening intellectual property rights; and establishment of venture capital funds directed at promoting new technology-based companies.

In education, measures have been taken at different levels to adjust the supply of skilled workers to the needs of the newly established sector. The measures include strengthening the information technology component of primary and secondary education, and making changes in the curriculum and degrees offered by graduate and undergraduate university programs, notably in Jamaica's University of the West Indies, which is considering establishing a science park.

Interestingly, some of the main initiatives in the area have been led by the private sector. In Jamaica, for instance, a successful in-house training program developed by a software firm, that was intended to prepare software programmers for the company, was eventually franchised to the island's second main university, the University of Technology. With this collaborative framework, supported by the government educational and export promotion agencies, the originally private training program will be applied in other institutions across Jamaica. Cooperative arrangements between universities and private companies are also found in Barbados, where the local University of the West Indies has had fruitful collaborative partnerships with information services firms.

In the field of telecommunications infrastructure, local governments have recognized the fact that the activities of businesses in the information technology sector increasingly rely on the movement of large amounts of data, so that the provision of modern and competitive telecommunication services is crucial for their development. Thus, both Barbados and Jamaica have embarked on telecommunications reform programs intended to assure the provision of competitive, state-of-the-art services such as low-cost broadband capacity at special rates for information services companies.

As a result of the attractive conditions offered to information services companies, some Caribbean countries have been able to attract a considerable number of investors in areas such as customized software development, industrial design, telemarketing, data entry, and multimedia. These firms comprise both foreign, but also increasingly domestic, firms. The number of such companies entering the offshore information services sector has grown exponentially, particularly during the 1990s. In 1997 they employed 3,000 workers in Barbados, or 2.5 percent of the work force. In Jamaica's Montego Bay Freezone, for example, in 2000 those companies employed 4,500 employees, surpassing employment in the declining manufacturing industry.

It is important to note that some characteristics of Barbados and Jamaica provide additional incentives for FDI that are not necessarily met in other Latin American or Caribbean countries. For example, these countries have some of the highest teledensities in the world; labor forces are literate and English speaking; labor costs are comparatively low, including benefits; and these countries have geographic proximity to the large North American market. However, in many respects the experience of these Caribbean countries is illustrative of the challenges and opportunities involved in the development of the information services sector.

*Source:* Brome 2001.

TABLE 4.5

## Costa Rica and El Salvador: Incentives for FDI

| TYPE OF INCENTIVE | COSTA RICA | EL SALVADOR |
|---|---|---|
| Income Tax | Exemption depending on the location. Ranges from 100% for 8 years and 50% for 4 other years to 100% for 12 years and 50% for 6 other years. | 100% exemption while the firm operates in the country. |
| Import Taxes and Tariffs | 100% exemption on materials, machinery and most equipment. | 100% exemption on materials, equipment and machinery. |
| Sales Taxes | 100% exemption for the entire period. | 100% exemption for the entire period. |
| Municipal Taxes | 100% exemption on estate taxes and taxes on net capital. | 100% exemption from taxes on assets. |
| Reinvestment | Exemption of 75% of income tax for 4 years. | Not mentioned. |
| Training and Research | Assistance from the National Institute of Learning (INA). | Not mentioned. |
| Employment | Tax exemptions assigned for firms based on underdeveloped regions. The exemptions are for 5 years, starting at 10% the first year ending in 2% the fifth year. | Not mentioned. |
| Other | Exemption from taxes to resale of estate. | Exemption of taxes to resale of estate. |
| | Exemption from export taxes. | |
| | No taxes or restrictions on repatriation of profits. | No taxes or restrictions on repatriation of profits. |
| | No taxes on remittances abroad. | No taxes on remittances abroad. |
| | Processing firms and service firms can sell up to 25% and 50% in local market | Free sale in the local market as long as import, income, sales and other taxes are paid. |
| | Developers and managers of the industrial parks have the same incentives. | Managers and developers of industrial parks are exempted from 100% of the income tax (for 10 years), taxes over net worth (for 15 years) and taxes on resale of assets (except the manager of the park). |
| | | Local governments can grant additional benefits. |

*Source:* Monge 2001.

transition should not be costly from a developmental viewpoint, because the main benefits of these zones for foreign investors are the establishment of transparent institutions safeguarding the property rights, and the geographic location and skills of the local labor force. Yet human capital played a key role in determining the structure of FDI in Costa Rica.

### FDI and High-Tech Firms in Costa Rica: The Roles of CINDE and Human Capital

In 1996, Intel decided to locate a plant in Costa Rica, and the plant was built in approximately two years. Why did Intel choose Costa Rica? The Costa Rican government offered an attractive set of incentives, such as subsidies on electricity and several tax exemptions. But other countries, such as Brazil, Chile, El Salvador, Indonesia, Mexico, the Philippines, and Thailand, competed with similar incentive packages. Indeed, at the beginning of the selection process by Intel executives, Costa Rica was not even considered a serious candidate. The usual argument is that the final decision was based on the combination of geographical proximity to the United States and internal labor market conditions—with political stability and the quality of the labor force being highlighted. While Intel is the most commonly mentioned high-tech firm installed in Costa Rica, it is not the only one. Recently, other technology firms, such as Procter and Gamble, Roche, and Abbott Laboratories, also started operations in the country.

It is true that Costa Rica has been more politically stable than most Latin American countries. However, it is not clear that high-tech firms are particularly vulnerable to expropriation or other forms of political risks. On the contrary, the high-tech sector seems to be less sensitive to the risk of expropriation, since the main source of value is the know-how and human capital of the managers.

An important factor that helped attract FDI to Costa Rica was the role of the CINDE, a private nonprofit orga-

FIGURE 4.10

**Costa Rica and El Salvador: Net FDI**

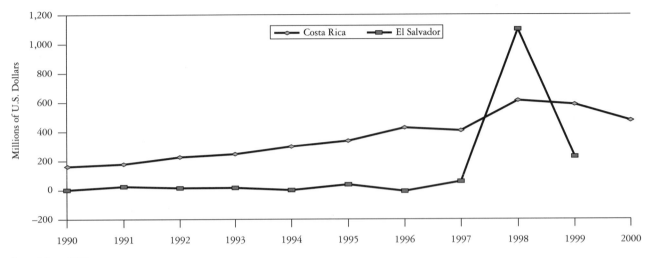

*Source:* Monge 2001.

nization. It was founded in 1983 by prominent business-people, supported by the Costa Rican government, and financed by grants from the United States Agency for International Development (USAID). Its broad mission was to help in the development of the economy, but the attraction of FDI was always one of its top priorities. In the early 1990s CINDE realized that the country was losing competitiveness in unskilled-labor-intensive industries to other members of the CBI and also due to the prospects for NAFTA, which would give Mexico better access to the U.S. market than beneficiaries of the CBI. At the same time, CINDE was losing the USAID funding it had enjoyed since its creation. Given these circumstances, it decided to focus its FDI attraction efforts on fewer sectors, choosing the ones that were a better match for Costa Rica's relatively high education levels (that is, skilled-labor-intensive industries).

For the strategic plan of 1993, CINDE focused on sectors associated with the electrical, electronic, and telecommunications industries. These sectors not only required more skilled workers, but were also experiencing fast growth in the United States, and strong competitive pressures were forcing companies to search for low-cost locations around the world. It was thought that these sectors were a particularly good match for Costa Rica, not only because of its high-quality public institutions, but also because of its supply of technicians and engineers at relatively low cost, and also because of the widespread knowledge of English. Moreover, there was a high quality of life, with good access to

health services, nightlife and cultural amenities, and natural resources (for which the country was increasingly better known, given the ecotourism boom). By 1995, several high-tech multinational corporations (DSC Communications Corporation; Sawtek, Inc.; Merrimac Industries; and Remec) had set up plants in Costa Rica.

When word got out in 1996 that Intel was shopping for a new site, CINDE played a key role in attracting attention to Costa Rica, and essentially managed to get the country on the list of candidates. Not only was CINDE important in convincing Intel to consider Costa Rica as a possible location for its plant, but it was also extremely helpful to Intel in conducting its research and obtaining the credible and consistent information it demanded. Moreover, its links to and credibility with the government allowed it to play a key role in arranging successful meetings between Intel executives and government authorities.

Besides its support of CINDE, the government was very diligent in responding to Intel's concerns in areas such as education, electricity, and taxes. The concessions made were not specific to Intel, but were generally applicable to other companies as long as they met the required conditions. In this sense, it could be argued that these were not concessions, but rather Intel-inspired reforms to improve the country's performance. For example, the "concessions" included the addition of a one-year certificate program of education focused on technical skills and physics or chemistry competency, and a one-year associate degree program focused on semiconductor manufacturing. These reforms came from recommendations made by a special committee that was created for this purpose and was composed of, among others, the Minister of Education and the Minister of Science and Technology. [23]

While the activities of the government and CINDE were key, in what follows we explore further the role of the qualified labor force. Box 4.6 conducts a further statistical analysis that shows that the levels of FDI across LAC countries can be explained by differences in the levels of human capital.

The results of a survey from the Association of American Chambers of Commerce in Latin America on the qual-

ity of the labor force asked firms located in various countries in Latin America to rate, on a scale from 0 to 10, several aspects of the labor force in each country. Figure 4.11 shows the results of the survey in terms of two variables: productivity and speed of learning. The actual numbers should be interpreted with caution, because different industries may be located in the different countries, and sample sizes may vary significantly. Yet, these responses make a strong case in favor of the hypothesis that the labor force in Costa Rica compares favorably with other countries, even with the most advanced ones, such as Argentina and Chile. The results should not surprise those who are aware of the fact that Costa Rica consistently ranks at the

---

BOX 4.6

## FDI and Human Capital in LAC

In our discussion of the determinants of the magnitude and composition of exports and FDI in Costa Rica and El Salvador, we argued that human capital played a major role. Our view is that the quality of the labor force in the different countries determines the attractiveness of the country to foreign investors. A highly skilled labor force attracts capital in more dynamic, knowledge-intensive sectors, thus sustaining export dynamism and enhancing the prospects for economic growth.

Here we systematically investigate the relation between FDI and human capital for a group of 21 Latin American countries. We look at the relation between the 1990 human capital level of a country and the amount of net FDI received by that country (as a share of GDP) in the subsequent years. To check the robustness of the results, we use different human capital indicators and different time frames for the FDI. We also analyze the determinants of the net FDI received specifically from the United States, to check whether it is in any way different from the general pattern observed. The human capital indicators come from the Barro and Lee dataset, and they are the following, all for the population above age 15: percentage of secondary school attained, average schooling years, average years of primary schooling, and average years of secondary schooling. The periods of FDI analyzed are 1985–98, 1990–98, and 1985–98. The first set of results refers to simple regressions of the average FDI for

these periods on the different indicators of human capital, and the second set includes additional controls in these regressions (the controls are output per worker and a CBI dummy variable). Results for the coefficients on the human capital indicators are summarized in Table 4.6.

The results show a consistent positive relation between initial levels of human capital and subsequent FDI. Most of the time, this correlation survives the inclusion of additional controls. The results imply, for example, that an increase of five years in the average level of education of the population above age 15 is usually associated with an increase in FDI of 3 percent of GDP. The results also suggest that the sensitivity of FDI to the initial level of human capital is even higher at higher levels of education (secondary), and that it increased significantly in the second half of the 1990s. The results for the United States share similar patterns, and FDI from this country seems to be even more sensitive to human capital levels. Overall, the evidence supports the point that human capital determines the amount of FDI received by a country. The role of education in spurring economic growth seems to go beyond the traditional view of enhancing productivity within given economic activities. Education can determine the prospects of the country in terms of access to technologies and development of new dynamic sectors.

TABLE 4.6

## FDI as a Percentage of GDP and Human Capital Indicators in LAC Countries: Econometric Results

### UNIVARIATE REGRESSIONS

| ALTERNATIVE INDICATORS OF HUMAN CAPITAL | 1985–98 | | | 1990–98 | | | 1995–98 | | | FLOWS FROM UNITED STATES: 1994–98 | | |
|---|---|---|---|---|---|---|---|---|---|---|---|---|
| | COEFFICIENT T-STATISTIC | R2 | | COEFFICIENT T-STATISTIC | R2 | | COEFFICIENT T-STATISTIC | R2 | | COEFFICIENT T-STATISTIC | R2 | |
| Percent Secondary Attainment | 0.071 | 0.2823 | | 0.0938 | 0.2857 | | 0.121 | 0.2039 | | 0.1634 | 0.2948 | |
| | 2.8737 | | | 2.8984 | | | 2.3191 | | | 2.9632 | | |
| Average Schooling | 0.4284 | 0.2367 | | 0.5633 | 0.2318 | | 0.7747 | 0.1877 | | 0.9208 | 0.2145 | |
| | 2.5522 | | | 2.517 | | | 2.2029 | | | 2.3495 | | |
| Average Primary Schooling | 0.5699 | 0.1732 | | 0.7291 | 0.1474 | | 0.953 | 0.1079 | | 0.9858 | 0.0932 | |
| | 2.0973 | | | 1.9057 | | | 1.5936 | | | 1.4694 | | |
| Average Secondary Schooling | 1.3716 | 0.3208 | | 1.7829 | 0.3495 | | 2.5182 | 0.2986 | | 2.9672 | 0.3853 | |
| | 3.1491 | | | 3.3592 | | | 2.9903 | | | 3.6281 | | |
| | N obs = | 21 | | N obs = | 21 | | N obs = | 21 | | N obs = | 16 | |

### MULTIPLE REGRESSIONS: INCLUDE OUTPUT PER WORKER AND CARIBBEAN BASIN DUMMY

| ALTERNATIVE INDICATORS OF HUMAN CAPITAL | 1985–98 | | | 1990–98 | | | 1995–98 | | | FLOWS FROM UNITED STATES: 1994–98 | | |
|---|---|---|---|---|---|---|---|---|---|---|---|---|
| | COEFFICIENT T-STATISTIC | R2 | | COEFFICIENT T-STATISTIC | R2 | | COEFFICIENT T-STATISTIC | R2 | | COEFFICIENT T-STATISTIC | R2 | |
| Percent Secondary Attainment | 0.0667 | 0.4581 | | 0.0715 | 0.376 | | 0.0921 | 0.2623 | | 0.1765 | 0.434 | |
| | 2.5909 | | | 2.0459 | | | 1.5852 | | | 3.1636 | | |
| Average Schooling | 0.4755 | 0.434 | | 0.4757 | 0.351 | | 0.6794 | 0.2608 | | 1.2491 | 0.4695 | |
| | 2.3521 | | | 1.7927 | | | 1.57 | | | 3.4762 | | |
| Average Primary Schooling | 0.5041 | 0.3577 | | 0.4756 | 0.2894 | | 0.6104 | 0.2006 | | 1.5193 | 0.3307 | |
| | 1.5428 | | | 1.0558 | | | 0.8362 | | | 2.2854 | | |
| Average Secondary Schooling | 1.5495 | 0.5241 | | 1.5821 | 0.4369 | | 2.3459 | 0.3485 | | 3.4523 | 0.5794 | |
| | 3.2485 | | | 2.6283 | | | 2.3712 | | | 4.5531 | | |
| | N obs = | 21 | | N obs = | 21 | | N obs = | 21 | | N obs = | 16 | |

*Note:* Dependent variables are average level of total net FDI/GDP for the periods indicated, and average level of net FDI/GDP from the United States (1994–98). Independent variables are indicators of human capital for 1990. Controls included in the multiple regressions are: dummy for countries in the CBI and output per worker. Countries included in the total FDI/GDP sample are Argentina, Bolivia, Brazil, Chile, Colombia, Costa Rica, the Dominican Republic, Ecuador, El Salvador, Guatemala, Haiti, Honduras, Jamaica, Mexico, Nicaragua, Panama, Paraguay, Peru, the República Bolivariana de Venezuela, Trinidad and Tobago, and Uruguay. Countries included in the U.S. FDI/GDP sample are Argentina, Barbados, Brazil, Chile, Colombia, Costa Rica, the Dominican Republic, Ecuador, Guatemala, Honduras, Jamaica, Mexico, Panama, Peru, the República Bolivariana de Venezuela, and Trinidad and Tobago.
*Source:* Estimates by A. Monge (Northwestern University).

top in the United Nations Development Programme's Human Development Index.

A survey on the labor market conditions faced by high-tech firms was conducted in 2000 by Promotora del Comercio Exterior de Costa Rica (PROCOMER), and asked 28 firms questions about the quality of managers, technicians, engineers, and skilled and unskilled labor, and questions on the quality of the training programs and curricula of existing educational institutions (technical and higher education). In general, the perception is favorable. Managers, engineers, technicians, and skilled and unskilled workers receive high marks in terms of productivity, speed of learning, and disposition to work variable shifts. Most notably, managers and engineers have the highest scores in terms of productivity, creativity, initiative, and speed of learning.

The scores are relatively lower, but still not bad (above 8 out of 10), in terms of specific knowledge and skills for engineers. In this last dimension, technicians and skilled and unskilled workers have a more modest score, just above 6. This is not surprising, because this new industry requires activities to be performed by workers who did not have any previous experience. Another aspect worth mentioning is the gap in terms of English proficiency. Consistently, firms indicate that employees at all levels are not quite as fluent in English as would be desirable. English proficiency, however, does not really seem to pose a long-term problem because the industry of English as a second language has bloomed in Costa Rica. English has also been introduced in the national curriculum of primary schools in the whole country.

FIGURE 4.11

**Perception of International Investors on Labor Force Quality**

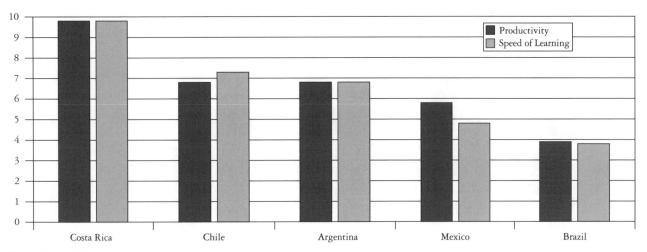

*Source:* Monge 2001.

The PROCOMER survey also suggests that wages of high-skilled labor are attractive to foreign firms. It is well known that labor costs in Costa Rica are higher than in other neighboring countries. But, for any economic decision, the relevant consideration is the price of effective labor, that is, the cost of labor per unit of time versus its productivity. Interestingly, the firms in the survey generally do not find the costs of different workers in Costa Rica to be high: only 4 percent make that claim for engineers and managers, 12 percent for administrative staff and technicians, and 20 percent for skilled and unskilled workers. The general pattern is that the relation of productivity to cost improves with the level of human capital of the employee. Indeed, the responses of the firms in the sector suggest that there are significant cost reductions by operating in Costa Rica as opposed to the United States.

The two main educational institutions, the University of Costa Rica and the Costa Rican Institute of Technology, also receive good evaluations. The survey asked about the perception of the firms in relation to quality and appropriateness of the programs for their needs. While the adequacy of the curriculum for their specific needs was questioned, the quality of the two institutions received very good reviews. Table 4.7 reports the scores, in ascending scale from 0 to 10. Private universities and the public national university obtained significantly lower marks. Moreover, few enterprises in the survey indicated that they had hired professionals from the public university.

This group of firms has also needed to train its workers because of both the specific tasks required for each job and the newness of the sector in the economy. Most of the firms use the local plant or the headquarters of the company for training, and only 46 percent and 39 percent, respectively, use public and private local institutions (see Figure 4.12). Yet the survey also indicates that there is room for improvement. On one dimension, the high-tech firms indicate that workers need to improve their discipline, especially toward following the safety requirements on the job. Also, as Table 4.7 makes

TABLE 4.7

**Perception of High-Technology Firms on the Education/Training in Costa Rica**
(On a Scale of 1 to 10)

| INSTITUTION | QUALITY OF EDUCATION | QUALITY OF TRAINING PROGRAMS |
|---|---|---|
| Technological Institute of Costa Rica | 9.33 | 9.00 |
| University of Costa Rica | 9.02 | 8.75 |
| National University | 7.75 | 6.80 |
| Private Universities | 6.67 | 6.40 |
| National Institute of Learning | 7.90 | 7.75 |
| Technical Secondary Schools | 8.30 | 8.00 |
| Other | 8.50 | 8.30 |

*Source:* Monge (2001) based on a PROCOMER Survey.

FIGURE 4.12

**Costa Rica: Fraction of Firms Using Training Programs**

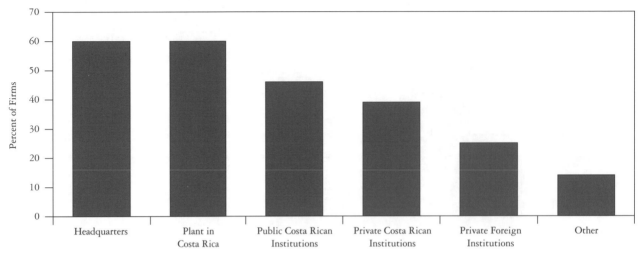

*Source:* Monge 2001.

clear, although the quality of the two main universities and technical schools is satisfactory, at least 70 percent of the respondents express concerns about the appropriateness of the short-term classes and training programs offered.

The operation of this new sector provides Costa Rica with an interesting opportunity, but also with serious challenges. If the sector is to grow, the country has to produce workers with the required skills. Figures 4.13, 4.14a, and 4.14b decompose the employment of the firms in the survey into different skill groups. In most firms, the largest share of employment is composed of production workers. But it is clear that, relative to any other sector, these firms are high-skill-intensive, since 25 percent of their labor force is composed of engineers and technicians, and 20 percent are skilled workers. Figures 4.14a and 4.14b decompose engineers and technicians into areas of expertise.

According to the survey, most of the firms indicated that they planned to increase their levels of operation. About 60 percent indicated that the growth will originate mainly from the expansion of existing lines, while 40 percent indicated that expansion will arise from new lines of production. The planned expansion is not small. The firms expect to hire approximately 2,100 new employees in 2001; 2,330 in 2002; and more than 2,600 in 2003. From their answers, it seems that the new demand will have a larger share of skilled than unskilled workers. Still, their projections include 500 engineers and technicians hired in 2001 alone. For the other two years the estimates are slightly lower.

The challenge for Costa Rica is to provide enough quantity and quality of professionals in those areas. Interestingly, the educational market seems to be catching up with the demands of the new sector. There is a significant increment in the areas of computation and information technology and in industrial engineering (Figure 4.15). At a lower level, the government and the market are also actively reacting to the new demand for skilled workers and technicians: in less than four years, enrollment increased by almost 10 percent in the technical colleges, reaching almost 44,000 students in 1999; the National Institute of Learning saw its student body increase from around 47,000 in 1994 to 124,191 in

FIGURE 4.13

**Costa Rica: Composition of the Workers in the High-Technology Firms**

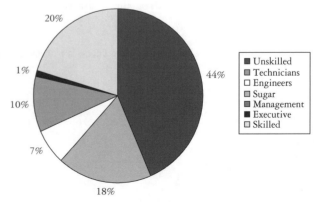

*Source:* Monge 2001.

102

FIGURE 4.14a

**Costa Rica: Composition of Engineers in the High-Technology Firms**

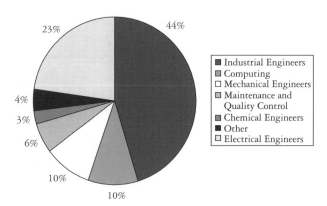

Source: Monge 2001.

FIGURE 4.14b

**Composition of Technicians in the High-Technology Firms**

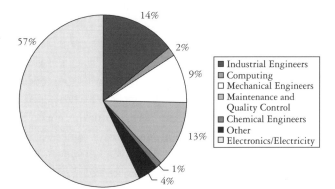

Source: Monge 2001.

1997; and the applications for *diplomados* and technicians (one- and two-year programs) in the Costa Rican Institute of Technology increased by almost 300 percent.

### Human Capital in Costa Rica and El Salvador

Combined with stable institutions, the skills of the Costa Rican labor force made it the leading candidate in LAC for the development of high-tech industries. To effectively create a basis of skilled workers, technicians, engineers, managers, and other professionals, any country needs to have a solid primary and secondary education. Table 4.8 compares the statistics for Costa Rica and El Salvador. Costa Rica is far ahead of El Salvador, not only in coverage for all levels, but also in terms of the efficiency of the educational system

(with the exception of pupils per tutor in secondary education). This observation becomes even more relevant once one realizes that El Salvador compares favorably with the other Central American countries (for example, Honduras and Nicaragua). Furthermore, these differences are the result of government policies. Figure 4.16 compares the expenditures on education in Costa Rica and El Salvador as fractions of GDP and government expenditures. Costa Rica spends much more in education, both because it is richer and because it spends a higher fraction of its income. The fractions declined during the 1980s, partly because of the fiscal imbalances and, in the case of El Salvador, increased military spending.

These differences show up, for example, in the degree of illiteracy in the population and its composition. El Salvador has a much higher illiteracy rate (28 percent compared to 5 percent in 1997), which is concentrated in the younger population. While the composition of the illiterate population in Costa Rica is becoming more concentrated in the elderly over time, the fraction of young individuals in the total illiterate population in El Salvador is high and increasing, reflecting the poor coverage of primary education and probably the impact of the war. This implies that, for long periods of time, El Salvador will have an active labor force with a high percentage of low-skilled workers.

### Summing Up: Different Paths of Development in the Future

Costa Rica and El Salvador are similar countries in terms of natural and geographic conditions and cultural aspects. Also, from a macroeconomic perspective, they had similar performances during the 1990s, driven by exports and foreign investment. Nevertheless, the Costa Rican economy, supported by a highly educated labor force, experienced an important transformation during the period. Several technology-intensive firms started operating in the country, thus changing the profile of its employment and exports. El Salvador, on the other hand, concentrated its expansion mainly in traditional labor-intensive sectors, mainly apparel.

The operation of the high-tech firms in Costa Rica has a two-way relation with the quality of the labor force. First, its introduction was determined precisely by the relatively high quality of the local labor force. Second, at the same time, its successful operation demands increasing amounts and quality of labor at different levels. The great challenge for the Costa Rican economy is to respond adequately to the increased demand, by improving the overall quality of

FIGURE 4.15

**Costa Rica: Supply of New Engineers in the Areas in Most Demand by New High-Technology Firms**

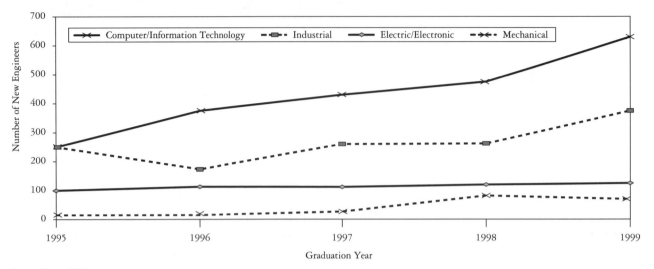

*Source:* Monge 2001.

universities and high schools, and education in rural areas. Besides, infrastructure reforms that have been lagging behind (such as telecommunications) can become a limiting factor if not dealt with in a timely fashion. If Costa Rica responds to these challenges, the possibility of attaining a sustained growth path—where investments in human capital reinforce growth, which feeds back into human capital accumulation—is an attractive and plausible development path.

El Salvador has a difficult task ahead: long-term growth could be limited by the quality of its labor force. A transition to more dynamic sectors is unlikely in such an environment. The demographic profile of the labor force in terms of the relation between ages and skills raises even more serious concerns about the long-term prospects. The

gains obtained from the development of the traditional industrial sectors should be partly directed to an aggressive policy of investments in human capital to improve the coverage and efficiency of basic education. Recent innovations in the education sector of El Salvador, such as increasing parental involvement in the management of schools, could provide avenues for future improvements in this area. The recent adjustments in terms of infrastructure and telecommunications are important advances. But with low human capital, those investments might not lead to dynamic growth in labor productivity.

## The Impact of NAFTA on Mexico's Trade Structure

In Chapter 2 we analyzed the evolution of Mexico's net export structure since the early 1980s. We noted that beginning in 1995, the country developed a clear comparative advantage in machine exports, especially in road vehicles, and office (data-processing) and telecommunications equipment. In the following subsections we take another look at Mexico's trade structure by comparing its structure within NAFTA to that observed with the whole world. After the analysis of the structure of trade, we turn our attention to the electronics industry, which includes the office equipment sector, including personal computers. The objective is to gain some understanding of whether Mexico's comparative advantage in these products has been transformed

TABLE 4.8

**Costa Rica and El Salvador: Human Capital Indicators**

|  | COSTA RICA | EL SALVADOR |
|---|---|---|
| Literacy Rate (1995) | 95.0 | 72.0 |
| Gross Enrollment Primary (1997) | 103.5 | 97.3 |
| Gross Enrollment Secondary (1997) | 48.4 | 36.8 |
| Gross Enrollment Tertiary (1997) | 30.3 | 17.8 |
| Pupils per Teacher Primary (1997) | 30.0 | 33.0 |
| Pupils per Teacher Secondary (1997) | 18.0 | 16.0 |
| Coeff. of Efficiency Primary UNESCO[a] (1995) | 80.0 | 63.4 |
| Years Input per Graduate Primary (1995) | 7.3 | 14.2 |

a. United Nations Educational, Scientific, and Cultural Organization.
*Source:* Monge 2001.

FIGURE 4.16

## Costa Rica and El Salvador: Public Expenditures in Education

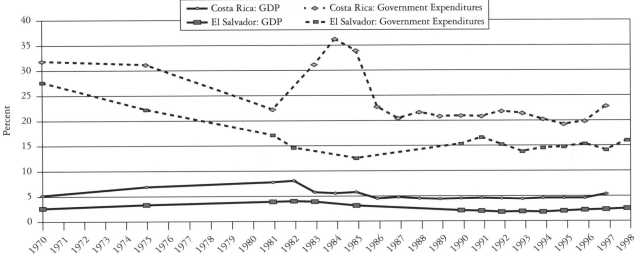

*Source:* Monge 2001.

from production processes driven by competitive labor costs or by the establishment of new industries driven by innovation and knowledge creation.

### The Structure of NAFTA Trade

Figure 4.17 shows the structure of Mexico's net exports to Canadian and U.S. markets during 1986–98. As with the structure of its net exports to the whole world, this chart shows a structural change toward the end of the period, when net exports of machines turned positive. This change was driven by exports of road vehicles, telecommunications equipment, and office and automated data-processing equipment. However, this change occurred in 1993 for exports to Mexico's NAFTA partners, while it appeared a year later in the structure of overall net exports. Hence it seems that change occurred in anticipation of the actual implementation of the agreement in January 1994. It is worth recalling that the United States had approved fast-track legislation for the negotiation of NAFTA in 1991. Thus it is quite likely that foreign and domestic firms made investment decisions to expand their operations in Mexico prior to the formal implementation of the agreement. This interpretation of the evidence is consistent with econometric evidence provided by Freund and McLaren (1999), who find anticipated structural effects of trade agreements throughout the world. However, we must acknowledge

that the exchange rate adjustment that took place in late 1994 might also have played an important role in stimulating exports of manufactures. But the fact that the structural change within NAFTA occurred earlier indicates that the negotiation of the agreement itself was an important force for change.

Figure 4.18 provides further descriptive evidence about the impact of NAFTA on Mexico's trade structure. The graph shows the evolution of the Grubel-Lloyd index of IIT introduced in Chapter 2, as well as Brulhart's (1994) index of marginal intra-industry trade (MIIT). The MIIT index measures the extent to which changes in trade structure are driven by IIT.

The graph contains the indexes constructed with data from Mexico's trade with the world and trade with its NAFTA neighbors. The data clearly show that all four indexes of IIT jumped after 1991, when the formal negotiations were launched. Indeed, the intra-NAFTA indexes are virtually indistinguishable from the overall indexes for most of the period. Consequently, we can safely conclude that Mexico's IIT is mainly driven by its North American trade. This is not surprising when one considers the fact that NAFTA merchandise exports rose from about 80 percent of total exports in 1991 to over 90 percent by early 2001. The share of merchandise imports originating in North America fluctuated around 75 percent during the last decade.

105

FIGURE 4.17

**Mexico: Structure of NAFTA Net Exports**

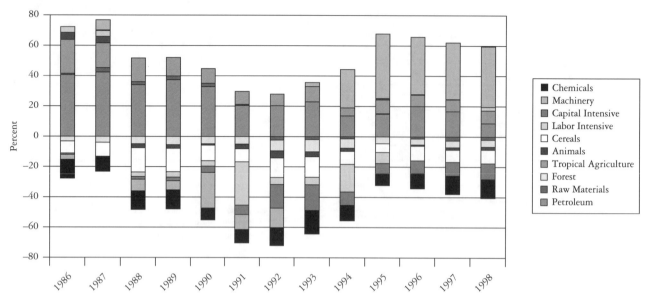

*Note:* To see this figure in color, refer to Figure A.12 in the Annex.

FIGURE 4.18

**Mexico's IIT with North America: NAFTA, IIT, and the MIIT Index**

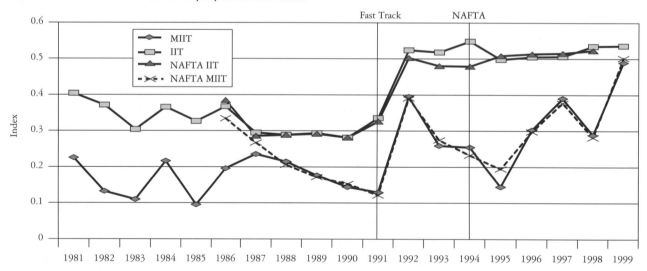

With this evidence in hand, it is difficult to deny that the negotiation of NAFTA had substantial structural effects on Mexican trade. The following subsection looks at the internal geographic distribution of FDI in Mexico. We attempt to understand how geography and some of the other "new" endowments such as human capital help explain the location of foreign firms within Mexico.

*FDI in Mexico: The Role of Geography
and Human Capital*

There are several important questions related to the role of geography and human capital in the determination of foreign direct investment in Mexico.[24] First, though the agglomeration of FDI on the border with the United States is well known, is distance the dominant factor, and hence are states or countries farther away at an insuperable disadvantage? Second, since Lucas (1979) showed that a human capital–augmented production function can generate radically different returns to capital than might be calculated on the basis of capital–labor ratios alone, how important is a well-educated work force to attracting FDI? Third, given the recent literature on agglomeration effects or infrastructure, how important is the concentration of economic activity in urban areas? Fourth, how much of a barrier to participating in FDI are language or cultural characteristics related to being members of indigenous groups? Put differ-

ently, is Chiapas marginalized because it is distant, poorly educated, rural, and heavily indigenous?

Figure 4.19 shows that most FDI per capita is concentrated on the northern border. However, there are important exceptions. First, the highest concentration is, in fact, in Mexico City, although this appears to result from the fact that companies with headquarters there might not register the actual location of their investments, but rather the location of headquarters. On the other hand, the states immediately around the capital also show high per capita rates, and the central region has, traditionally, been the

FIGURE 4.19

## Mexico: Geographic Distribution of Variables

Per Capita FDI (From 1994 to 2000)

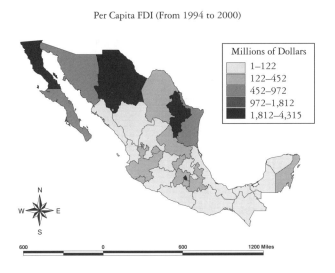

Schooling (in Years)

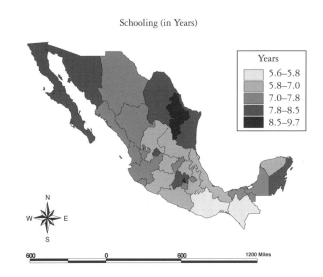

Degree of Urbanization

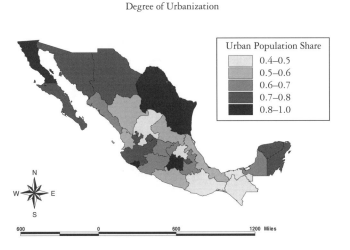

Percent Speaking Indigenous Languages

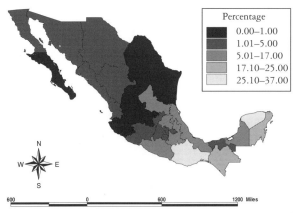

*Source:* Aroca and Maloney 2001.

center of industrial activity. Second, the region around Guadalajara in central Mexico is not particularly close to the border, yet receives substantial FDI, perhaps due to the presence of Hewlett-Packard and other transitional firms. Finally, Quintana Roo, in the Yucatan peninsula, also shows relatively high FDI per capita.

Schooling is more evenly distributed, although it shows, again, the highest levels along the border, the central region, and Quintana Roo, suggesting some correlation with FDI as well. The difficulty of isolating the influence of any particular social variable is highlighted by the fact that the degree of urbanization also seems highly correlated with both education and FDI. This complicates attempts to identify the influence of ethnicity since the highest concentration of indigenous-language speakers is in the south, which also tends to have lower levels of both urbanization and education.

Again, the high degree of correlation of these variables means that multivariate analytical techniques are necessary, and these are presented in Table 4.9. Columns A, B, and C suggest that distance, education, and urban population share enter with the expected signs, although it is difficult to identify the impact of the last two. The share of indigenous population does not enter significantly, suggesting that there is no effect independent of the fact that these communities tend to have lower education levels, live in rural areas with less infrastructure, and are concentrated in areas far from the United States. Column D generates a *positive* impact of the indigenous variable if we drop a dummy included to capture the fact that, although Yucatan and Quintana Roo

are very distant from the United States by road, they are very close to Miami by boat, and hence our distance measure is probably incorrect. The relatively high density of indigenous population appears to be correlated with relatively high FDI, given the road distance from the United States.

In sum, proximity to the United States, higher education, and more urbanized areas capturing perhaps agglomeration effects or infrastructure are positively correlated with FDI. However, areas with indigenous populations appear to receive less FDI only because they tend to also have lower education, are more rural, and are located farther from the United States. The following section explores in detail how geography and knowledge have affected the evolution of the electronics industry in Mexico.

### The Mexican Electronics Industry

Can labor-intensive offshore manufacturing activities evolve into skill-intensive, high-value-added operations? What is the role of government promotion policies in the context of an open trade regime? Although there are no general responses to these queries, the recent experience of the Mexican electronics industry does provide some clues to what the possible answers may be.

### Background and Facts

Between 1995 and 1998, Mexico's GDP grew at an average rate of 5.9 percent per year. This impressive performance, after a quick recovery from the effects of the 1994 devaluation, was partly due to the dynamism of the country's man-

TABLE 4.9

### Tobit Estimates

DEPENDENT VARIABLE: FDI PER CAPITA (TOTAL 1994–2000)

| VARIABLES | COEF. A | T | COEF. B | T | COEF. C | T | COEF. D | T | COEF. E | T | COEF. F | T |
|---|---|---|---|---|---|---|---|---|---|---|---|---|
| Education | 180.4 | 1.13 | | | 388.5 | 3.35 | 496.4 | 4.94 | | | | |
| Urban Population Share | 1343.3 | 1.67 | 2047.1 | 3.8 | | | | | | | | |
| Percent Indigenous Population | 364.6 | 0.28 | −88.2 | −0.07 | 230.5 | 0.17 | 1887 | 2.51 | −5885.5 | −2.7 | −2698.8 | −2.32 |
| Distance to the United States | −47.1 | −5.65 | −49.5 | −6.01 | −47.9 | −5.44 | −42.4 | −5.25 | | | | |
| Dummy | 468.2 | 1.09 | 545.5 | 1.25 | 656.4 | 1.48 | | | 1447.7 | 2.06 | | |
| Constant | −1086.1 | −1.14 | −178.9 | −0.35 | −1644.1 | −1.64 | −2629.5 | −3.15 | 509.4 | 3.71 | 413.2 | 3.11 |
| | | | | | | | | | | | | |
| Sample Size | 31 | | 31 | | 31 | | 31 | | 31 | | 31 | |
| LR chi2(df) | 51.4 | | 50.1 | | 48.8 | | 46.4 | | 10.7 | | 5.6 | |
| Pseudo R2 | 14.30% | | 13.90% | | 13.60% | | 12.90% | | 3.00% | | 1.60% | |
| Log Likelihood | −154.3 | | −154.9 | | −155.6 | | −156.8 | | −174.7 | | −177.2 | |

*Note:* FDI lower than US$50 per period of 1995–2000 set to zero leading to 9 left-censored observations at FDI<=0, 22 uncensored observations. The Federal District (Mexico City) was dropped from the sample. Education is measured in years. Percent indigenous variable is calculated as the percentage of the population of age five years or older or more that speaks a native language. Dummy equals 1 for Quintana Roo and Rucatan, and 0 otherwise.
*Source:* Aroca and Maloney 2001.

ufacturing sector, the annual rate of growth of which was 9.4 percent during the same period (see Lederman and others 2001a, 2001b). Manufacturing exports evolved from 43 percent of total exports in 1990 to 85 percent in 1999. Within manufacturing, no industry matched the growth of the Mexican electronics manufacturers. Between 1995 and 1998, for instance, output and exports in that industry grew at average annual rates of 25 percent and 31 percent, respectively.

Exports of electronic products totaled US$29 billion in 1998, representing 27.6 percent of manufacturing exports. Although imports have also increased significantly, net exports of electronics products have been positive since 1995, attaining almost US$5.6 billion in 1998. As in other manufacturing industries, the United States is Mexico's main trading partner in electronics, accounting for 93.8 percent of the country's exports and 83.5 percent of its imports.

Although NAFTA led to the elimination of tariffs in the bilateral trade between Mexico and the United States, it did not pose a threat to their respective electronics industries. Indeed, the United States already had a very low tariff on electronics products (below 5 percent), and the Mexican exports of electronics are complementary to those of its neighbor. Indeed, the main Mexican export products are consumer electronics and data-processing equipment, mainly TV sets and computers, whose shares in total electronics exports are 17 percent and 15 percent, respectively.[25] As for the Mexican imports, they consist largely of parts and components, notably semiconductors (20 percent) and cinescopes (11 percent).

In fact, the consumer electronics industry is even geographically integrated with the United States, with most manufacturers located in Mexico's northern states, especially near the border. The state of Baja California, in particular, has attracted 81.6 percent of the investments made in the electronics industry during 1995–98, which amounted to more than US$2.3 billion, and is the host of the main Korean and Japanese manufacturers of consumer electronic products. As for the computer and telecommunications equipment industries, they are mostly located in Jalisco, which ranked second in terms of investments in electronics, totaling US$394 million during 1995–98. Concentrated in the city of Guadalajara, the electronics industry established in Jalisco grew 52.6 percent between 1993 and 1997, increasing its share of the national production of computer and telecommunication equipment from 31.9 percent to 71.4 percent, mostly at the expense of the Mexico City met-

ropolitan area (see Casaneuva and Brown 2000). Among the main manufacturers of final products with plants in Jalisco are IBM and Hewlett-Packard, which established themselves in the 1970s, at the time when the Mexican policy for the informatics industry required foreign firms to produce locally in order to supply the domestic market. Other manufacturers with more recent investments include NEC, Unisys, Siemens, AT&T, Alcatel, Ericsson, and Motorola.

More than half of the manufacturers of electronic products operating in Mexico are *maquilas*. These are mostly foreign-owned companies that assemble imported components for re-export, benefiting from fiscal incentives and simplified administrative procedures. Although most *maquilas* are located near the U.S. border, the fraction of *maquila* employment located in nonborder states has increased from around 5 percent in 1986 to more than 22 percent in 2000.

The share of the *maquila* operations in total electronics industry employment increased from 38 percent in 1992 to 54 percent by 1998. Almost all the consumer electronics manufacturers operate as *maquilas*, and so do most makers of telecommunications equipment. The non-*maquila* segment of the industry operates under the same conditions as the rest of the manufacturing industry, and has stronger local ties, both in terms of markets and suppliers. In fact, until the opening of the economy to foreign trade during the late 1980s, the non-*maquila* electronics industries established in Mexico were oriented mainly toward the domestic market, in which they enjoyed considerable protection from import competition.

With trade liberalization, however, and particularly after the implementation of NAFTA, the outward orientation of the non-*maquila* sector has increased considerably. For instance, the ratio of exports to production in the non-*maquila* sector increased from 35.1 percent in 1989 to 60 percent in 1994 to 83.5 percent in 1996. In the specific case of the computer industry, it must be noted that the liberalization of trade only occurred in 1990, at least two years after the other subsectors of the electronics industry. Moreover, during three years computer manufacturers benefited from fiscal incentives that included tariff exemptions, in the context of a special regime that rewarded local technological development and the use of domestic parts and components.

With 637,000 workers in 1998, the electronics industry is a relatively large employer, responsible for 9 percent of the jobs in manufacturing. Within the electronics industry, the *maquilas* have shown the strongest performance in terms of employment generation, and they have been responsible for most of the new jobs created in the industry. Between 1992 and 1998 employment grew 94 percent in the *maquila* sector, as opposed to a meager 3 percent in non-*maquila* companies. This is due both to the comparatively larger growth in the number of *maquilas*, and to the fact that these types of companies perform assembly operations that are relatively more labor intensive.

### Factors Determining Location

As for the factors that explain the decision of foreign companies to locate production facilities in Mexico, it must be remembered that before the 1990s, and outside the *maquila* sector, the main motivation for setting up local plants was to gain access to the protected Mexican market. This motivation is no longer relevant, so the new foreign investors are driven, at least in part, by favorable local conditions relative to locations in other countries, in order to sell not only to the Mexican but also to the U.S. and other markets. Moreover, given the dramatic reductions in transport costs and the possibility of "fragmenting" the stages of the electronics manufacturing process, location decisions may now involve the fragmentation of those stages across different cities and countries.

The main motivation for setting up electronics manufacturing plants in Mexico has been the combination of low labor costs, geographic proximity to the United States and, particularly after NAFTA, trade preferences and certainty of access to the U.S. market. The role of geography and human capital in attracting foreign investment to Mexico has been analyzed in a previous section. The point here is that geography has been crucial in all segments of the electronics industry. However, among *maquilas* it has been coupled to a decision of locating only the labor-intensive assembly operations in Mexico, while using mostly imported parts and components. Although labor-intensive operations have also been the focus of non-*maquila* businesses, their range of products and operations has widened considerably toward more skill-intensive activities, and they have made a growing use of inputs produced locally by companies that have also been attracted to the country. This option has been favored among manufacturers of products with more dynamic technologies, computers for instance, who tend to supply the American market in a "made-to-order" regime.

As already mentioned, a very important factor in the decision to locate electronics manufacturing operations in Mexico is the possibility of exporting with zero tariffs to Canada and the United States, provided the NAFTA rules of origin are met. The possibility of the *maquilas* importing parts and components with zero tariffs has recently become restricted to imports from NAFTA partner countries, under a clause of the agreement signed in 1994. However, FDI has not been significantly affected, in part because the share of parts and components purchased within NAFTA has increased significantly, and because of the proliferation of free-trade agreements dropping the duties on imports from non-NAFTA countries. This is notably the case of the goods imported from the European Union, which will be tariff exempt under a free-trade agreement signed in 1999.

Moreover, for some Asian countries, a further incentive to establish *maquila* operations in Mexico is the fact that they face quantitative restrictions in the U.S. market. These aspects appear to compensate for the fact that manufacturing wages in Mexico are still higher than in several locations in Asia—China and Malaysia—and Central and Eastern Europe—Bulgaria, Hungary, and the Russian Federation. For instance, it has been estimated that the total landed cost (including inventory costs, tariffs, and shipping) of producing electronics products for the U.S. market is up to 5 percent lower in Mexico than in Malaysia (Merrill Lynch 2000).

Besides traditional cost considerations related to relative labor and capital abundance, a factor that has become crucial in the investment decisions of electronic companies is the feasibility of implementing efficient logistics structures for the relationships with both suppliers and customers. Indeed, because of the very fast rate of technological change in the electronics industry, with important technological "leaps" occurring with a frequency of less than two years, companies cannot afford to maintain sizable stocks of either final products or parts and components. For instance, it was indicated in interviews that a Pentium processor loses 10 percent of its value every month, which explains the need to maintain a strong integration among companies in the computer supply chain, mainly through the use of information technologies. In fact, the semiconductor industry is the one in which that type of integration appears to be most crucial (Mann 2001).

Although the need to produce "to order" derives to a great extent from the swift rate of technological obsolescence of electronics products, the high importance attributed to logistics is also related to the high degree of internationalization of the electronics industry. Particularly in recent years, due to widespread trade liberalization and plummeting transport costs, the production activities of electronics manufacturers have become increasingly fragmented across plants and countries. Thus, while total international trade grew 6.8 percent per year during the 1990s, trade in electronics products increased at an average annual rate of 15 percent.

The renewed importance of logistics implies a crucial role in location decisions for the availability of an appropriate transport infrastructure. In this respect, compared to other countries, Mexico benefits from the fact that products can be shipped by truck to the United States, reaching the border in less than 24 hours from many locations—18 hours from Jalisco to Texas, for example. Moreover, with the increased flow of airfreight between Guadalajara and the United States, the number of daily flights to and from several major cities in the United States has increased significantly—there was only one flight per day a few years ago. There are also a number of overnight airfreight companies such as DHL, Federal Express, and UPS that offer their services in Guadalajara (Merrill Lynch 2000).

### The Dynamics of Agglomeration

Good logistics are also easier to implement when the companies that perform different parts of the manufacturing process decide to set up plants at the same location. At least in Jalisco this has been increasingly the case in recent years, and this has further contributed to the attractiveness of the region as a potential location for electronics manufacturers. To better understand these recent developments, it is worthwhile to sketch the stages of a typical production process in that industry. There are four main stages: R&D, manufacture of electronic parts and components, assembly of printed circuit boards (PCBs), and final assembly.

The first stage, R&D, is performed by so-called original equipment manufacturers (OEMs), which in turn distribute these activities across various R&D centers, which are often specialized in certain types of products. Larger OEMs usually have R&D centers in different countries, with each specific location determined by corporate strategies and the local availability of trained scientists and engineers. In the case of Jalisco, this availability appears to have played a role in the decision of several companies to implement locally the development of some of their products. It must

be emphasized, however, that only after the advent of trade liberalization did those companies increase their investments in local R&D activities.

The requirements for the second-stage manufacturing activities vary according to the specific type of component. Although some components are relatively simple and their manufacturing processes are mostly labor intensive, the production of most of the inputs of the electronics industry is particularly capital- and knowledge-intensive, as is notably the case for semiconductors. Thus, in Mexico, most of the components used by the electronics industry are imported from the United States, and to a lesser extent, from Asia.

The two final stages of electronics manufacturing are the most labor intensive, and their location is determined mostly by cost and logistics considerations. Although the degrees of vertical integration vary by product and by corporation, most OEMs tend to focus on R&D and on final system-integration activities. They thus tend to rely increasingly on providers of electronics manufacturing services (EMS), which perform most of the third and fourth phases of the manufacturing process, and purchase their components from specialized suppliers. With the diffusion of "lean production systems" and "just-in-time" relationships between OEMs (or EMS providers) and their suppliers, a trend has developed in the direction of an increasing geographic concentration of integrated supply chains.

At least in Mexico, the regional agglomeration of electronics manufacturing activities has been led by the investments of OEMs, which, after being established in a particular location have, in some cases, attracted some of their suppliers of parts and components. This process has been relatively limited in the case of the *maquila* operations, which tend to purchase most of their inputs abroad. In the non-*maquila* sector, however, notably in the case of Guadalajara, the OEMs have been followed by manufacturers of some of their main inputs, including producers of components, PCBs, plastics, packing materials, and sheet metal, and electronics distributors. It is worth noting, however, that most of these companies are foreign, while domestic manufacturers are limited to activities with relatively low capital and knowledge intensity, such as packing materials, labels, and cleaning and maintenance services (Casaneuva and Brown 2000).

Recently, some of the leading EMS providers have also been attracted to the region by the OEMs to which they provide services elsewhere in the world. After the establishment in 1987 of the first major EMS provider in Guadalajara, at least seven other leading companies have set up local plants in recent years, mostly after 1997. Some of the main EMS companies already in the region are SCI systems, Flextronics, Jabil Circuit, NatSteel Electronics, and Soletron. Although some of these companies, as well as other EMS providers, have plants in other Mexican cities—Hermosillo, Monterrey, Puebla, and Tijuana—it is clearly in Guadalajara that the largest concentration of EMS providers is found (Merrill Lynch 2000).

Interestingly, the establishment of EMS providers in the region is attracting more manufacturers of parts and components to Guadalajara, which could in turn increase the competitiveness of manufacturers of final products, potentially attracting further OEMs and EMS providers. Moreover, some recent modifications in the scope of the product lines manufactured locally by these companies suggest that they have been upgrading the technological content of their manufacturing activities. Thus, at least some of the EMS providers have been widening their local product lines in the direction of increasingly sophisticated products, for instance from personal computers and peripherals to notebooks, servers, and network equipment. Complementarily, within each product line, those companies have evolved from performing locally only the assembly of PCBs, to also internalizing the final assembly of full systems (Merrill Lynch 2000).

Some EMS providers have offered incentives for the establishment of parts and component suppliers, for instance in the form of instant access to necessary manufacturing infrastructure in their industrial parks. However, it is worth noting that government incentives have played no role in the Jalisco agglomeration, except, as mentioned, in the early years after trade liberalization. This fact has led industry leaders to lobby for fiscal exemptions based on claims that Jalisco would be losing important investment projects to countries that do offer fiscal advantages to investors, particularly in Asia.

### The Role of Education and Knowledge Policies

As for the upgrading of the activities performed locally by EMS providers, in terms of their technological content, it has been stimulated in part by the local availability of skilled personnel. Indeed, the metropolitan area of Guadalajara has six universities and is the second most important educational center in Mexico. Although it is not clear what

role this played in the location decisions of the first OEMs established in Jalisco in the 1970s, interviews with industry leaders suggest that there are significant externalities derived from the availability of a skilled workforce in the region.

In particular, the presence of trained scientists and engineers partially explains the establishment of R&D centers by the main OEMs, which have developed locally some products—printers, for instance—that are now manufactured in other countries.[26] Moreover, one of the leading companies in the industry has decided to transfer from the United States to Guadalajara part of its strategic financial operations, a decision that also reveals the high quality of the local telecommunications infrastructure. There is also evidence of increasing collaboration between local universities and the electronics manufacturers established in Jalisco, although it has so far been mostly limited to the training of personnel and support for the establishment of new local R&D centers by OEMs (Casaneuva and Brown 2000). The growth of the development activities performed in these centers could in principle lead to spinoffs in the form of the appearance of new, technology-based companies that would take advantage of the availability of trained personnel, with work experience in the OEMs' R&D centers. As indicated in interviews, these types of incentives are behind the ongoing development of a local software industry.

### Summing Up

In recent years the electronics industry has been one of the most dynamic in the Mexican economy, both in terms of output and export growth. Particularly after the implementation of NAFTA, the differences between *maquila* and non-*maquila* companies in terms of outward orientation have been reduced, as the latter have considerably increased both their exports and imports. However, unlike the consumer electronics manufacturers, which operate mostly as *maquilas* in the northern border states, importing almost all of their inputs, the companies that manufacture computer and telecommunications equipment in Guadalajara have created strong ties to other companies established in the region. Indeed, they have been able to attract the providers of electronics manufacturing services and the suppliers of parts and components that they use in other locations throughout the world. These investments appear to be leading to the creation of integrated supply chains, which could lead to important gains in competitiveness, based on both lower costs and better logistics. These gains should attract new manufacturers, generating a virtuous circle in which the expansion of the industrial agglomeration generates externalities that contribute to further cost reductions, particularly through the improvement of logistics, and thus leads to the attraction of new investments.

Overall, the case of the electronics manufacturing companies in Jalisco highlights both the possibility of evolving from pure *maquila*-type assembly operations to skill-intensive manufacturing and R&D activities, successfully integrated into global networks. This case also illustrates the crucial role played by the externalities derived from a good education and transportation infrastructure, and the increasing returns associated with the establishment of integrated supply chains. Some of the first manufacturers were established in Jalisco at the time when protectionist policies required local production to access the Mexican market. However, it must be noted that such a chain of events would be improbable in smaller countries where the size of local market does not justify tariff jumping. Also, the development of integrated supply chains and the technological upgrading of the activities performed locally took place only during the period that followed trade liberalization, particularly after NAFTA. Finally, it is worth noting that the role of government policies has recently been very limited, with no fiscal incentives being granted to new investors outside the *maquila* sector.

## Tourism and Development in the Caribbean

Tourism is a critical export sector for many countries in the region.[27] For many economies in the Caribbean, tourist receipts are the majority of exports, and their share in GDP can rise above 40 percent (1998 data) (see Figure 4.20).

Further, tourism is a growth industry globally. The arguments that suggest that primary products will enjoy a decreasing share of world income apply in reverse as increasing incomes and more leisure time raise tourist expenditures proportionally more than income. This is suggested by Figure 4.21, which shows annual growth rates in real global tourist expenditures of over 3.8 percent for the last 20 years. Some economies in the region have been able to take advantage of this growth. In the Dominican Republic, for example, tourism has been a booming sector, rising from 9.1 percent of total exports during 1971–80 to 29 percent by 1991–2000. However, similar to commodities, the supply of alternatives also affects revenues. Tourist expenditures in Latin America have risen 0.51 percent over the comparable period, and the region has dramatically lost market share. This suggests growth opportunities for many countries of the region.

### Tourism and Development

The impact of tourism can be significant on the local economy, and both input–output and computable general equilibrium (CGE) analysis can reveal the magnitude and nature

FIGURE 4.20

**Tourism's Share of Exports and GDP**

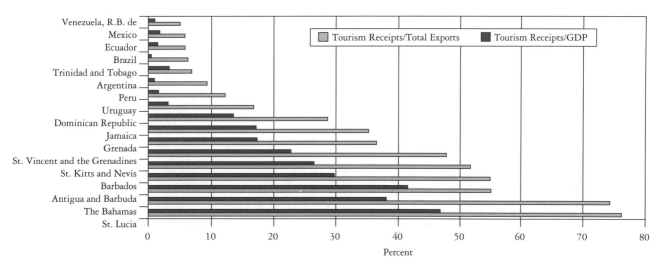

*Source:* Maloney and Montes Rojas 2001.

FIGURE 4.21

**LAC's Share and Rates of Growth**

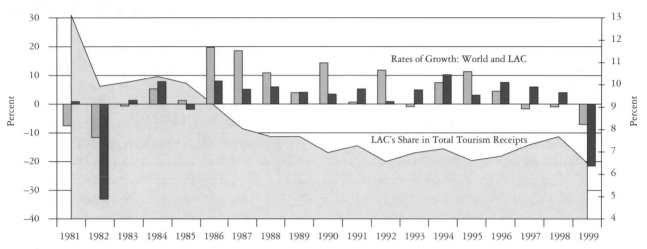

*Source:* Maloney and Montes Rojas 2001.

of linkages. As Table 4.10 shows, the GDP multiplier for Barbados is 1.4, close to the average calculated for other countries and at the high end of industry multipliers.[28]

Though more difficult to measure, the contribution to labor creation can be large. For the Windward Islands and Leeward Islands tourism directly and indirectly accounts for up to 24 percent of total employment, with direct employment accounting for 49 percent of the workforce in Anguilla. Employment multipliers range widely from 1.4 for Barbados to estimated magnitudes of 3 in the Windward Islands and the Dominican Republic.

Although it is difficult to generalize based on the available data, for Barbados the impact on government finances seems favorable. The state receives over 10 percent of tourist spending and the ratio of revenue to spending on infrastructure and other services exceeds 1.5. Finally, the impact of cruise ship arrivals is smaller along most dimensions. This is to be expected given the lower spending on housing and food that would have linkages to the rest of the economy.

In Barbados, this may be partially accounted for by the high foreign content of "shopping," which is estimated at 75 percent. Still, the contribution of cruise ship spending is

TABLE 4.10

**Results from a Limited Input–Output Model for Barbados**

|  | OVERNIGHT | CRUISE SHIP | TOTAL |
|---|---|---|---|
| *Contribution to GDP* | | | |
| Direct Contribution to GDP (at factor cost) | 12.9% | 1.3% | 14.2% |
| Direct and Indirect to GDP (at factor cost) | 18.4% | 1.5% | 19.9% |
| GDP Multiplier | 1.42 | 1.15 | 1.4 |
| Tourism-Related Imports/Tourism Spending | 31.2 | 39.8 | 31.9 |
| *Impact on Employment* | | | |
| Direct Employment | 17,634 | 1,427 | 19,061 |
| Indirect Employment | 6,133 | 202 | 6,335 |
| Direct + Indirect/Total Employment | 22.5 | 1.5 | 24.1 |
| Employment Multiplier | 1.348 | 1.142 | 1.332 |
| *Impact on Government Finances* | | | |
| Tourism-Related Government Revenue | 121,228,325 | 10,757,247 | 131,985,572 |
| Tourism-Related Government Spending | 78,942,311 | 8,771,368 | 87,713,679 |
| Revenue/Spending | 1.536 | 1.226 | 1.505 |
| Tourism Related Government Revenue/Tourism Spending | 11% | 12.2% | 11% |

*Source:* Caribbean Development Bank 1996.

not negligible. In the Galapagos, cruise ships owned by entities on the mainland generate 46 percent of the total value added on the islands, channeling income through crew wages and inputs supplied by the islanders. Locally based cruise ships accounted for 17 percent of gross island product, followed by fishing (8 percent), commerce (7.5), and farming (5 percent). In short, a small economy can be largely supported on the multiplier effects of cruise ship visitors.

### Possibilities for Growth

As Figure 4.22 suggests, revenues from tourism constitute a large fraction of both exports and GDP in many economies in the Caribbean. The natural question arises as to what the long-term potential for growth is. If at some point the number of tourists reaches the physical capacity of the environment, then how does income continue to rise?

We can think of the income per tourist resource (for example, beachfront, Mayan ruins) as

$$Income = \frac{L}{B} * \frac{V}{L} * \frac{S}{V}$$

where L is the capacity for lodging over the potential for total lodging dictated by the environment (beachfront, for example), and hence the first term measures the degree to which the natural tourist potential has been exploited physically. The second term is the "occupancy rate" of lodging potential, or the number of visitors over total potential visitors. The final term is the spending per visitor.

Increasing "productivity" of the value generated, given the tourist base, can occur along all three dimensions.

1. *Expand Capacity:* For long-established tourist destinations such as Barbados, the expansion of accommodation capacity is limited to replacing existing hotels with larger hotels or, alternatively, floating capacity offshore in the form of cruise ships. The second type of tourist, the cruise-ship tourist, tends to spend less overall, but given the expansion in the number of total tourists, they are desirable, and hence there is strong competition among islands to attract them.

2. *Reduce Vacancy Rates:* Room-occupancy rates in the Caribbean in 1999 averaged 65 percent, ranging from over 80 percent in Anguilla to 30 percent in Belize. Hence, there is room for using existing capacity more completely.[29] Economists at the CTO have suggested that local establishments adopt a system similar to that used by the airlines to ensure full booking.[30] These gains, although potentially large, are "one-off" and cannot be extended indefinitely.

3. *Increasing Value per Tourist:* Expanded capacity and reducing vacancy rates are fundamentally "extensive," and once exhausted, only increasing spending per tourist offers the potential for continued growth. Figure 4.22 suggests that high value added tourism can play a large role in a development strategy. For example, 50 percent of Bermuda's GDP comes from tourism, and the mean spending per tourist is very high—roughly US$200 per visitor day. The relationship with GDP could imply that raising value per

FIGURE 4.22

**Real Tourism Receipts per Tourist Day**

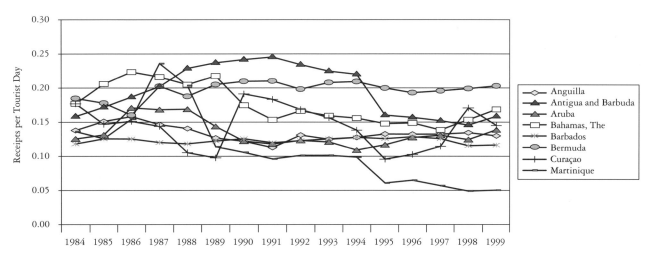

*Source:* Maloney and Montes Rojas 2001.

tourist has helped lead to higher income levels, or it may imply that in high-GDP countries, higher labor and land costs imply a higher-cost tourism product and hence higher spending per tourist. But it must also be the case that the product is proportionately better, and this highlights the need for continued innovation and differentiation of the tourism product. Bermuda and St. Martin can be more expensive only if a similar service cannot be easily found elsewhere. The question of substitutability is discussed later.

Has the Caribbean been increasing revenues by expanding the number of tourists, or by increasing the value of their product? Figure 4.22 suggests a very mixed answer. For Bermuda, Curaçao, and Barbados inflation-adjusted receipts per tourist have been stable or increasing, but in Antigua and Barbuda, the Bahamas, Aruba, and Martinique, the tendency over the last decade has been downward.

This may be partially due to the fact that "tourists" include both cruise passengers and overnight visitors. An increase in the relative proportion of cruise passengers could lead to an apparent decline in spending per visitor when, in fact, all we see is a desirable increase in lower-spending tourists. Table 4.10 suggests that it is highly likely that cruise ship receipts per person have decreased significantly—by about 5.5 percent per year—and that overnight stays may, optimistically, have increased by 1 percent. Decline or small gains could be due to two factors.[31] First, the rise of "all-inclusive" packages, while not necessarily decreasing the demand for goods and services of the host, does give large tour operators greater bargaining power with local providers.[32] Competition from other destinations, including within the United States, has also put downward pressure on prices.

The results are slightly more positive if we look at tourist receipts not in terms of how much one visitor buys in terms of a basket of U.S. goods, but in terms of the manufacturing unit value index used to compare the evolution of commodity prices. However, overall, we do not find tremendous gains in the value per tourist over time. This suggests that islands are overall not very mobile in the quality of their product. Further, it suggests that, without initiatives to find other ways for tourists to spend their money, the growth benefits will not be realized.

### Is Tourism Fickle?

Table 4.11 presents the standard deviation of growth rates of exports for several commodities that often complement tourism in island economies, particularly. What drives volatility separates tourism from the other commodities. Where price fluctuations are perhaps the larger concern for commodities, it is the sudden decline in tourist arrivals due either to recession in the country of origin or increased attractiveness of alternative destinations that causes more concern for tourism. But what is clear is that in virtually every case, tourism revenues are the least volatile. Only in Trinidad and Tobago do tourism revenues vary by more than the other commodities and, even then, by very little.

The central concern is that either a perceived similarity among islands or simply a fad will lead to a rapid redirection of tourists to other locales. Put more technically, the price elasticity of demand for tourism is very high. The only published study to date (Rosenzweig 1988) finds very high inter-Caribbean elasticities of over 2—a 1 percent rise in one island's prices will lead to a loss of 2 percent of its tourists, and an elasticity of 1 with respect to Mexico. Our findings,

TABLE 4.11

**Export Revenue Volatility**

(Standard Deviation of Growth Rate)

| COUNTRY | TOURISM | SUGAR | FRUITS | COFFEE | PETROLEUM AND GAS |
|---|---|---|---|---|---|
| Barbados | 0.08 | 0.17 | 0.33 | 0.96 | 3.61 |
| Belize | 0.36 | 0.11 | 0.21 | 0.69 | |
| Dominica | 0.11 | 2.55 | 0.91 | 0.48 | |
| Dominican Republic | 0.11 | 0.13 | 0.08 | 0.32 | 0.69 |
| Grenada | 0.17 | 2.39 | 0.49 | 0.27 | |
| Haiti | 0.13 | 2.79 | 1.09 | 0.71 | 1.65 |
| Jamaica | 0.09 | 0.23 | 0.15 | 0.13 | 2.66 |
| St. Kitts and Nevis | 0.11 | 0.37 | 0.91 | 1.82 | 0.94 |
| St. Lucia | 0.09 | 1.13 | 0.29 | 0.37 | |
| St. Vincent and Grenadines | 0.17 | | 0.30 | 0.47 | |
| Trinidad and Tobago | 0.29 | 0.23 | 0.22 | 0.28 | 0.24 |
| *Average*[a] | *0.4315* | *1.84* | *0.99* | *1.522* | *2.34* |

a. Includes all the countries.

although not strictly comparable, are much lower—about 0.4—and agree broadly with results from Spain and the Mediterranean.[33] This seems a bit more plausible for two reasons.

First, what determines the price responsiveness of tourism is, as with manufactures, product differentiation. If all destinations are identical beaches, then price elasticities should be very high. Similarly, as wages rise in such an economy over time, we would expect the tourism sector to contract over time and move to other locales. But we do not observe this in the case where a destination has something very particular to offer. France has very high wages and a booming tourist industry due to the fact that demand to see the Eiffel Tower is virtually vertical—double or triple the price and people will still go. However, the Dominican Republic, which has developed largely on mass-based tourism with little "product differentiation," is closer to the identical beach story. To date, the Caribbean islands have tended to offer a fairly differentiated product. British tourists charmed by the Barbados's air of "little England" are not likely to visit Bob Marley's stomping grounds in Jamaica because of small movements in prices. The French patronize their old colonies Guadeloupe, Martinique, and St. Martin, the Dutch Curaçao and St. Maarten, and they are not likely to be drawn to Cancun because of modest changes in prices.

Second, accommodation prices are keyed to the external market, and over the medium term changes in exchange rates or wages are likely to reflect more in profits than in prices. Over the longer term, we may expect more hotel building in areas with higher profit levels, such as Cuba.[34] This is probably not the case with large economies such as Brazil and Mexico, where a large share of what the tourist consumes is "interior," and hence would be more affected by exchange rate changes.

However, decreasing transport costs and the development of venues in Asia or even in the United States do offer alternatives that will increase this elasticity over time. Somewhat counterintuitively, Cuba's coming on line may have a salutary effect by calling more attention to the Caribbean Basin relative to other regions.

In sum, tourism remains a desirable sector with growth potential in the region. However, the same lessons apply to the tourism sector as to any other resource sector.

1. *Playing to Resource Strength.* Many of the economies of the region have the potential to tap into the tourism market: most obviously Costa Rica, Ecuador, and Trindad and Tobago increasingly find their niches as ecotourism destinations. Argentina and Chile have seen increases in tourism to their Patagonian extremities. Areas rich in natural beauty or simply beachfront, such as Brazil, could expand. Peru could follow Mexico with a more intensive marketing of its historical and cultural past.

2. *Increasing Value per Tourist.* For countries or islands with mature tourist industries, or in areas where environmental concerns prohibit further extensive development, improved "productivity" gains will come from providing more targeted and specialized tourist services. This can range from adventure tourism, such as shark or wall diving, to greater emphasis on cultural or historical tourism. In these cases, as with other natural resource–rich exports, there is a great possibility for applying human capital and know-how to add value to the basic resource. At the same time, relentless pursuit of product differentiation—for Trinidad and Tobago, perhaps a global steel pan competition; for Chile, the extremeness of the northern Atacama Desert; for Argentina, the Train of the Clouds—are the way to maintain market share and value as wages rise in the rest of the economy, and to reduce the fickleness of tourists.

3. *Going Online.* To use Mann's (2001) terminology, tourism is a very information technology–sensitive industry. Getting the message out, defining the image, facilitating arrangements, and engaging in differentiated pricing through the Internet will be the base level of competition over the next decades. Further, arrangements are increasingly being made electronically. Travel booking will generate US$3.1 billion by 2002 (Holder 2001).

4. *Increase Research.* Tourism represents another case where substantial R&D is essential to take advantage of market opportunities. The global market is evolving rapidly, and niches open for specialized products. Yet, at present, tourism statistics are not ideally suited to the types of analysis required; the Caribbean Hotel Association, the regional private sector tourism organization, has no research program; and the universities are not heavily invested in this area (Holder 2001).

## Notes

1. This section is based on Lederman and Soares (2001).

2. This section borrows heavily from Foster and Valdés (2001).

3. The last term in the decomposition of price movements is computed as a residual, combining changes in trade and price interventions and other possible changes in variables affecting the margins between domestic and border prices. The reader should also consider that, although the real exchange rate is equal for all products at any point in time, for each product the relevant domestic and border

prices and the exchange rate were computed at the harvest month corresponding to the product in question. For milk and beef, sold throughout the year, the exchange rates represent an annual average.

4. The data for domestic prices of apples are suspect.

5. In general, while the immediate reaction might be to consider this outcome a cost of adopting a certain market-oriented economic policy (to be balanced against corresponding benefits), upon reflection, it is not obvious that it has been or will be in the medium term a serious detriment to Chile. To the degree that Chilean agriculture can incorporate varieties and techniques developed elsewhere, there would be less to gain by replicating a system of taxpayer support for universities and other institutions specializing in agricultural research leading to beneficial but hard-to-internalize results. Even with respect to the human capital necessary to make use of the latest agricultural production and processing technologies, the benefits of absorbing the fixed costs of sustaining large agricultural research faculties are diminished in light of the access to foreign graduate programs, consultants, and scholars. The marginal dollars spent on a publicly funded, long-term, public good–oriented research project or educational institution specializing in agriculture might offer higher returns if used to give a potential Chilean agronomist or engineer the basic training and English proficiency necessary to take advantage of technical services or educational opportunities available elsewhere. This would be especially so if similar projects—leading to the same publicly accessible results—are already being conducted at the expense of foreign taxpayers who have been conveniently persuaded of their duty to support public research efforts and sophisticated graduate training programs.

6. This section is based on Sanguinetti, Pantano, and Posadas (2001a).

7. The Asuncion Treaty also stipulates far-reaching objectives in terms of coordination of policies in other areas, particularly, policies applied in the following sectors: agriculture, industry, public taxes and expenditures, monetary rules, exchange rates, capital market, services, transport, and communications.

8. The Herfindahl concentration index was discussed in Chapter 2.

9. The magnitude of the fall in the concentration indicator (the gain in diversification) depends on which index we use. For example, using the Gini Coefficient, export concentration falls about 10 percent, while using the Theil Coefficient, the fall is nearly 20 percent.

10. The commodity groups are the one-digit Harmonized System of Classification aggregates. Results do not change when using alternative groups.

11. On the other hand, antidumping actions are still permitted (as of mid-2001), although there was a compromise to eliminate them by the end of 2000. See Sanguinetti and Salustro (2000) for details about tariff and nontariff barriers in Mercosur.

12. This argument applies not only to goods subject to economies of scale.

13. Garriga and Sanguinetti (1995) present an early assessment of the effect of transport costs on the composition of total trade by destination in Mercosur.

14. See Bonelli and Fonseca (1998) and Rossi Júnior and Ferreira (1999). The recovery in manufacturing productivity is also supported by calculations performed on the basis of the available microlevel data, which are representative of medium and large but not of the supposedly more dynamic small firms. For instance, Muendler, Sepúlveda, and Servén (2001) find an increase of 1.8 percent in manufacturing productivity growth from 1987–90 to 1991–98.

15. It is worth noting that the problems of endogeneity related to reverse causality from productivity to trade openness are minimized in these studies because of the use of firm-level data.

16. This section is based on Fajnzylber (2001a).

17. See Dagnino (1993) for an account of the government benefits received by EMBRAER.

18. See Luzio and Greenstein (1995), for example, for an analysis of the price and performance practices of the Brazilian microcomputer industry, which until 1990 was subject to severe local content requirements and lagged international standards by at least three and as much as five years.

19. In this new family of jets, the number of suppliers is also expected to decline, from more than 400 to around 40, with "first line" suppliers becoming system integrators themselves. This should lead to a further reduction in the manufacturing and integration activities carried out within EMBRAER (see Bernardes 2001).

20. The risk-partnership arrangement was initiated when EMRAER was still a state-owned company, in order to pursue the EMB-145 project in the context of a severe shortage of resources faced by the company at the time. EMBRAER's share in the EMB-145 and EMB-170/190 projects is, respectively, 60 percent and 45 percent. In the case of the EMB-145, the support of Banco Nacional de Desenvolvimento Econômico e Social (BNDES) was also instrumental, because it financed US$100 million of the development costs (Bernardes 2001).

21. This section is based on Monge-Naranjo (2001) and Rodríguez-Clare (2001).

22. EPZs in Costa Rica include firms from the Zonas Francas and Perfeccionamiento Activo.

23. Briefly, the other reforms were the following: In the area of electricity, the rates were very high, so the government asked the regulator to establish a new lower rate for energy-intensive industrial facilities. In the area of taxes, there was an ambiguity in the applicability of a new tax to companies in the EPZ system, so the government requested a formal interpretation from the Attorney General, which turned out favorable to Intel and other companies then entering the EPZ system.

24. This section is based on Aroca and Maloney (2001).

25. In fact, Mexico is the largest supplier of TV sets for the U.S. market, and the second-largest supplier of electronics products in general, surpassed only by Japan.

26. On the role of human capital, see Box 4.5 and the section on the experiences of Costa Rica and El Salvador.

27. This section is based on Maloney and Montes Rojas (2001).

28. Aroca (2001) calculates multipliers for Chile of real estate 1.02, agriculture 1.14, construction 1.21, transportation and communication 1.27, mining 1.28, manufacturing 1.28, retail 1.31, fishing 1.35, business services 1.41, and utilities 1.66.

29. Caribbean Tourism Statistical Report 1999–2000.

30. Interview with Luther Miller, CTO (2001).

31. We regress total receipts on the number of overnight tourists (or overnight adjusted for reported average length of stay, or hotel occupancy rates times installed room capacity) and number of cruise ship visitors. Though a long-term cointegrative relationship might be expected, the results were much more stable in differences.

32. A study commissioned for the Caribbean Development Bank (1996) concluded that there was no evidence that all-inclusives consume fewer local goods and services than any other stay-over visitors.

Spending through one supplier, however, provides a stronger position with subcontractors. Hence these packages might have the same overall impact but different distributional implications.

33. We follow Arellano and Bond (1991) in running a dynamic panel specification in differences of number of tourists from five geographic areas to each island on the calculated purchasing power parity in each country relative to the principal competitor countries, and several measures of total tourist demand.

34. We are grateful to Mr. Luther Miller of the CTO for this point.

# CHAPTER 5

# How We Work:
# Job Quality in Emerging Sectors

T HE GOAL OF ALL TRADE POLICY IS TO IMPROVE THE QUALITY OF LIFE OF A COUNTRY'S citizens, and as one key dimension, the overall quality of jobs. To paraphrase the theme of this report, it's not what you do, but how you work. Yet over the last decade, concern has emerged that trade liberalization and the emerging patterns of trade have caused workers to lose ground.

This chapter argues that this is not the case. There have been major job dislocations of workers as firms adjust to more competition, but probably over the medium term, unemployment issues will not be the central problem. The quality of the jobs created will be. But here the evidence is generally encouraging. Wages in more open or resource-dependent sectors hold their own, or do better than others, perhaps due to more aggressive adoption of technologies and demand for high skill levels. Technological progress is also held largely responsible for the widening wage differentials observed throughout the region. This trend, though probably not permanent, is far preferable to the reverse. It implies that the new jobs being created are "good" in the sense of demanding more of workers in terms of human capital.

This chapter examines more closely one dimension of job quality that has drawn much attention: the increase in informality over the 1990s. It offers an alternative framework that argues that this trend has more to do with the macroevolution of the region's economies, and in particular the nontradeables booms of the

early 1990s. Again, increased informality does not appear to be a permanent feature of the region's labor market.

Finally, this chapter looks at several types of jobs that have emerged over the period of greater integration, including jobs in EPZs, tourism, teleservice industries, and nonagricultural exports.

## Employment

Several LAC countries experienced high unemployment in the 1990s. What is far less clear is how much unemployment can be attributed to greater openness, and how much is permanent.

To be sure, part of this unemployment must be laid at the door of increased international competition. As Figure 5.1 shows, the region has seen very substantial reallocations of its workforce. Argentina lost much of its automobile industry while seeing an expansion in more sophisticated

chemicals and capital- and labor-intensive manufactures. Brazil lost much of its cereals industry to Argentina under Mercosur, and its manufacturing industry suffered more generally. Mexico also experienced a large decline in cereal and animal production and substantial increases in all types of manufactures. Costa Rica lost much of its labor-intensive manufacturing processes to Mexico after NAFTA, but also saw a substantial increase in manufactures of computer chips. (See Box 5.1 for a review of the "original" NAFTA.) In each case, substantial numbers of workers lost their jobs, and some experienced either very long periods of unemployment, large wage losses, or both. The 2000 LAC regional publication, *Securing Our Future in a Global Economy*, made the case for why an improved safety net is necessary to moderate the high costs of these adjustments.

However, these dislocations, though extremely costly in human terms, are transitional, and do not imply perma-

FIGURE 5.1

**Composition of Labor Force (All Workers)**

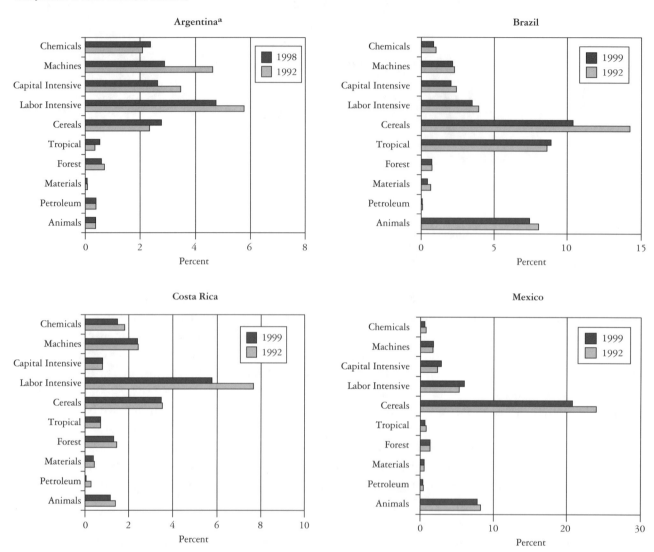

a. Urban workers only
*Source:* National Labor Force Surveys.

nently higher rates of unemployment. In the long term, equilibrating forces bring demand for workers in line with supply. Cross-country comparisons can be seen as approximating the "long term," and statistical analysis suggests that, globally, there is no relationship between openness and unemployment (see Figure 5.2).[1] Nor is there any relationship between resource intensity and unemployment (see Figure 5.3). Even within the region, as Table 5.1 shows, unemployment rates in many liberalizing economies are not high by historical standards (with the notable exception of Argentina). More specifically, Chile, the LAC country that is the most advanced and most integrated in the world econ-

omy, experienced double-digit rates of unemployment for several years following liberalization, but from 1986 to 1997 had among the lowest rates in the region until the Asian crisis severely depressed its export market in 1998. In fact, Figure 5.4 suggests that after a period of "shaking out" from the recession of the early 1980s, employment grew steadily from 1983 to 1995. Similarly, Mexico's present rate of unemployment is roughly at its traditional level, despite a dramatic integration with the United States.

Further, the observed high rates of unemployment in some countries partially reflect the unfinished business of macrostabilization. No one following the debate over

BOX 5.1

**Losers and Winners in the Original NAFTA**

The first North American Free Trade Area was established by the U.S. Constitution, signed in 1789, which forbade barriers to trade among states. Many of its signers were farmers who effectively unemployed their grandchildren. As an example, the town of Maynard, Massachusetts, was primarily agrarian at the turn of the 19th century, but its relatively poor and rocky soil made it no match for the imports from the new territories in the Midwest. Its economic base would be reborn in the form of textile manufacturing, which would again be subsequently overcome by cheaper imports from the southern states. Maynard is now better known as the birthplace of Digital equipment, which was one of the founders of the Rt. 128 technology boom and which made its headquarters in the old mill buildings.

In each reincarnation farmers went bankrupt, textile workers lost their jobs, and the subsequent dislocations caused untold human hardship. But in retrospect, would it have been good for Maynard workers to protect New England agriculture from "foreign" competition from other states of the Union?

whether Argentina should attempt a depreciation of its currency can attribute the present economic situation entirely or even primarily to liberalization. The challenge of bringing inflation down from triple-digit levels and establishing responsible and credible fiscal and monetary policies has led to multiple stabilization plans and striking volatility in wages and employment over the last 20 years in Argentina, Brazil, Mexico, and Peru. Nor can Colombia's present unemployment rates be attributed primarily to liberalization. The financial crisis, combined with ill-advised minimum-wage policies, has created unnecessarily high levels of unemployment, exacerbated by rapid migration from violence-torn rural areas. Again, the two countries that have gone the farthest in opening, and that have re-established solid macrofundamentals, Chile and Mexico, have shown normal rates of unemployment by historical standards.

Finally, unemployment is a function of both demand for workers and supply. As Table 5.2 suggests, supply has risen substantially in Argentina, Bolivia, and Chile—by around 3 percent—and if figures are to believed, in Peru—by almost 10 percent. Such increases require substantial increases in job creation to maintain constant unemployment rates. Further, the increase in women's participation was especially large, ranging from 5 to 10 percent across the 1990s, and across most household structures (Figure 5.5). The concomi-

FIGURE 5.2

**Unemployment and Openness, 1998**

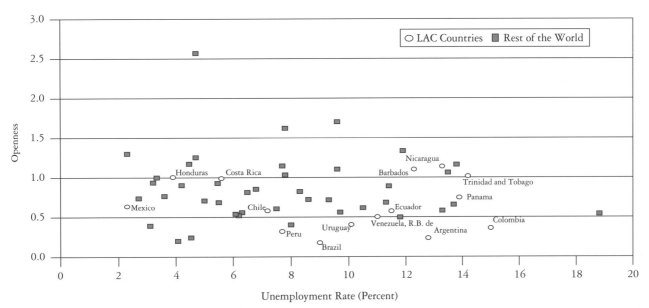

*Note:* Openness is measured as X + M/GDP.
*Source: World Development Indicators 2001.*

FIGURE 5.3

## Unemployment and Resource Intensity, 1998

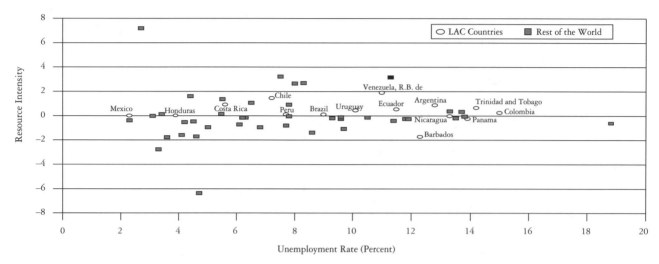

*Note:* Resource intensity is measured by net exports per worker of nonmanufactured goods.
*Source: World Development Indicators 2001.*

tant 5 percent average increase in women's wages relative to men's wages may reflect that their rising rates of participation have led them to be younger and their human capital on average to be of higher quality than that of men, and that there are fewer who became obsolescent during restructuring (Figure 5.6). However, as will be discussed in the last section, it may also be due to the booms in the industries that have emerged in the region that have tended to reward the characteristics associated with being female.

TABLE 5.1

## Average Unemployment Rates in LAC
(Percent)

| COUNTRY | 1970s | 1980s | 1990s | ENTIRE PERIOD |
|---|---|---|---|---|
| Argentina | 4.1 | 4.8 | 12.1 | 7.0 |
| Bolivia | 6.3 | 7.7 | 4.9 | 6.3 |
| Brazil | 6.6 | 5.4 | 5.6 | 5.9 |
| Chile | 10.5 | 14.4 | 7.1 | 10.7 |
| Colombia | 9.6 | 11.3 | 11.5 | 10.8 |
| Costa Rica | 5.0 | 6.9 | 5.3 | 5.7 |
| Guyana | 0.5 | 0.3 | — | — |
| Honduras | — | 4.5 | 5.8 | 5.1 |
| Mexico | 7.0 | 4.7 | 3.7 | 5.1 |
| Paraguay | 7.3 | 11.8 | 6.3 | 8.5 |
| Peru | 7.4 | 7.4 | 8.5 | 7.8 |
| Uruguay | 9.2 | 10.6 | 9.9 | 9.9 |
| Venezuela, R.B. de | 5.7 | 8.8 | 10.3 | 8.3 |
| *LAC—Mean* | 6.6 | 7.6 | 7.6 | 7.3 |
| *LAC—Median* | 6.8 | 7.4 | 6.7 | 7.0 |

— Not available.
*Source:* De Ferranti and others 2000.

## Wages and Distribution

As important as the number of jobs created is the quality of those jobs. The most straightforward measure is the wage a worker receives, both what it can buy and how it compares to other wages in the economy; that is, the wage distribution.

As Stallings and Peres (2000) and Weller (2000) note, real manufacturing wages grew strongly from 1991 to 1998 in Bolivia (37 percent), Brazil (24 percent), Chile (29 percent), Costa Rica (23 percent), and Jamaica (70 percent). The stagnation in Argentina (–2 percent) and Mexico (–2.5 percent) again must be largely blamed on difficulties in macrostabilization in the Argentine case, and the Tequila Crisis in Mexico. Overall, they see the reforms as having a positive impact on wages.

Looking at a sectoral level reveals two important findings.[2] First, though survey data on rural and natural resource sectors, especially mining, are often weak or unrepresentative, Figures 5.7 to 5.10 show both raw wages and wages adjusted for human capital and by Leamer categories. Some striking patterns emerge. Leamer's classification of manufactures by increasing sophistication—labor intensive, capital intensive, machinery, and chemicals—is reflected in increasing levels of wages, and wages adjusted for human capital. But equally important, it is not obviously true that these sectors offer higher wages than petroleum, mining, forestry products, or even tropical agriculture. This is prob-

124

FIGURE 5.4

## Chile: Steady Manufacturing Employment Growth after Reforms

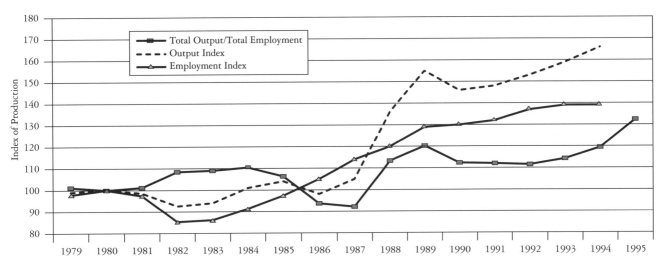

*Note:* 1,501 Chilean firms, 1979–95. For 1995, only employment index data were available.
*Source:* Chilean manufacturing survey.

TABLE 5.2

## Labor Force Participation Rates in the 1990s

(Percent)

| COUNTRY | PERIOD | FIRST YEAR | LAST YEAR | CHANGE |
|---|---|---|---|---|
| Argentina | 1991–97 | 59.8 | 62.6 | 2.8 |
| Bolivia | 1989–96 | 52.8 | 56.4 | 3.6 |
| Brazil | 1992–97 | 61.5 | 60.1 | –1.4 |
| Chile | 1990–96 | 51.6 | 54.4 | 2.8 |
| Colombia | 1988–95 | 56.8 | 58.1 | 1.3 |
| Costa Rica | 1990–96 | 53.5 | 52.2 | –1.3 |
| Jamaica | 1989–96 | 69.8 | 68.4 | –1.4 |
| Mexico | 1991–96 | 53.6 | 55.4 | 1.8 |
| Peru | 1991–97 | 58.0 | 67.8 | 9.8 |

*Source:* Weller 2000.

ably not too surprising. In the long term, labor mobility will equilibrate total remuneration among sectors, and those that cannot pay as well will shrink and lose workers. And, as Chapter 3 notes, natural resource–rich sectors have the potential to show productivity gains as high as those in manufacturing, and hence there is no reason for these sectors to be in decline or to pay less. Again, Australia and the Scandinavian countries still have large fractions of their workforces in primary product–intensive industries and enjoy extremely high standards of living. In sum, as a first cut, reorientation toward products with a higher natural resource content does not obviously imply worse jobs.

Further, exposure to global competition more generally increases wages. Figure 5.9 looks at wages in industries ranked by their degree of exposure to international competition. For each country, the bar on the extreme left represents the third of workers in import-competing industries that are most exposed, measured as the dollar value of imports per worker. The next bar captures the third of workers progressively less exposed, and so on. The right three bars capture increasing exports per worker moving right. The middle bar corresponds to workers in nontraded industries such as services or commerce. What jumps out immediately is a U or J pattern that emerges in Argentina, Brazil, Costa Rica, the Dominican Republic, and Mexico, where those industries most exposed to competition pay higher wages. Figure 5.10 shows that, even adjusting for levels of human capital, education, and experience, this pattern remains and in fact becomes more striking.

One explanation is consistent with the theme of this report: it is not only *what* is produced, but *how*. As Chapter 3 discussed, external competition stimulates the adoption of new technologies and these, in turn, require training and skill upgrading. As only one example, in Mexico the tripling of manufacturing exports observed during the 1990s has been associated with increased rates of adoption of modern production technologies, an acceleration of productivity growth, and a relative increase in the demand for skilled labor. Lopez-Acevedo (2001a) shows that between 1992 and 1999 the rates of increase in the adoption of modern manufacturing technologies were not only higher

FIGURE 5.5

**Change in Women's Labor Force Participation Rates by Household Structure**

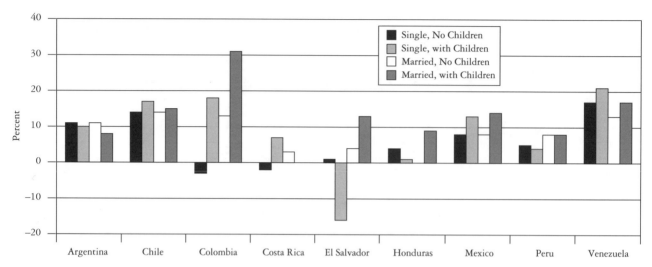

*Source:* Cunningham 2001.

FIGURE 5.6

**Change in the Ratio of Women's Wage to Married Men's Wage**

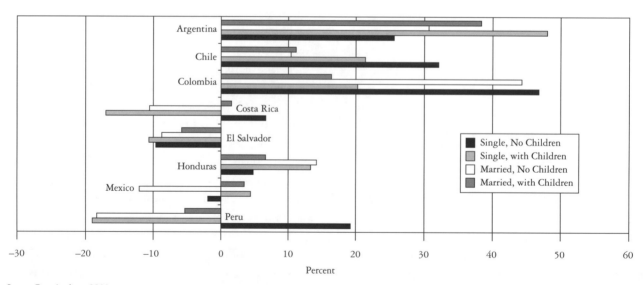

*Source:* Cunningham 2001.

among exporters than nonexporters, but also increased more rapidly. Audretsch and Lopez-Acevedo (2001) also show that the modernization of production processes during the 1990s was associated with an increase in employment, labor productivity and, at least during the second half of the decade, higher wages. Hallberg and Tan (1998)

also find higher rates of both human capital and skill building prior to entering export markets, and find a clear association between plant-level efficiency (TFP) and exporting. To the degree that these additional skills are not captured by the fairly standard and imprecise human capital variables, these more open industries will appear to pay higher

FIGURE 5.7

**Current Raw Wages by Leamer Category**

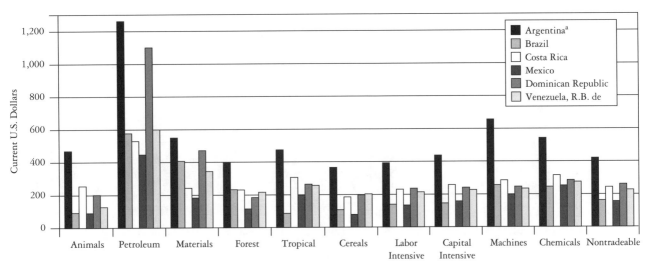

a. Urban workers only.
*Source:* National Labor Force Surveys.

FIGURE 5.8

**Wages by Leamer Category Adjusted for Human Capital**

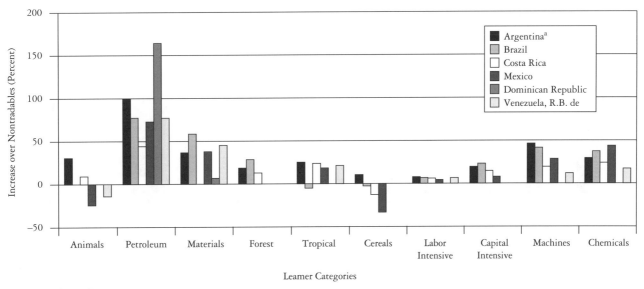

a. Urban workers only.
*Source:* National Labor Force Surveys.

wages. Further, these industries may also pay higher than market-clearing or "efficiency" wages to hold onto workers who they have trained.[3]

Again, these results are entirely consistent with the insistence of Swedish trade unions on maintaining an open trade regime and on constantly upgrading production tech-

nologies. In the long term this is the only possible path to increasing wages, and job quality more generally.

*Inequality*

The fact that more exposed sectors may be demanding higher skill levels is frequently cited as a possible explana-

FIGURE 5.9

**Current Raw Wages by Trade Exposure**

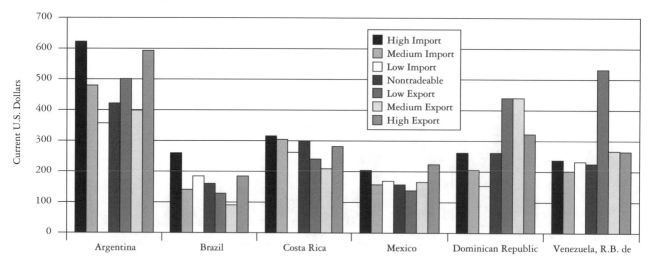

*Note:* Nonagricultural workers. Means by trade balance per worker centiles.
*Source:* National Labor Force Surveys.

FIGURE 5.10

**Wages by Trade Exposure Adjusted for Human Capital**

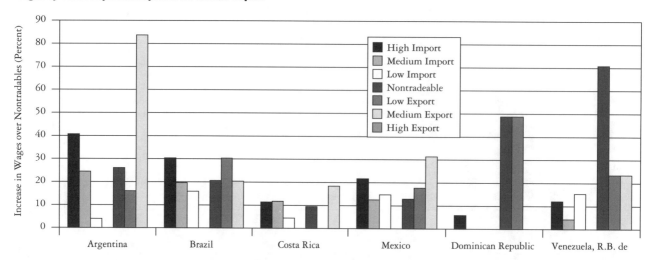

*Note:* Nonagricultural workers. Conditional on human capital.
*Source:* National Labor Force Surveys.

tion for the apparent trend toward greater wage inequality observed after liberalization in Argentina, Chile, Colombia, Costa Rica, Mexico, and Uruguay.[4]

These movements were not necessarily permanent. While the ratio of the wages of the highest- to the lowest-paid workers increased in the 1980s in Chile and the mid-1990s in Mexico, as Figure 5.11 shows, it had largely reverted by the early and late 1990s, respectively. Nonetheless, these movements immediately following reform run counter to what many expected. The Stolper-Samuelson theorem, one of the four central results of the Hekscher-Ohlin-Samuelson framework, suggests that trade liberalization would stimulate the production of goods that used Latin America's presumed abundant factor of production, unskilled labor, and raise its relative return. As Box 5.2 shows, the logic behind the Stolper-Samuelson theorem is very simple, and therein lies both its appeal and its many limitations.

FIGURE 5.11

**Wage Inequality Spread**

(90th over the 10th percentile)

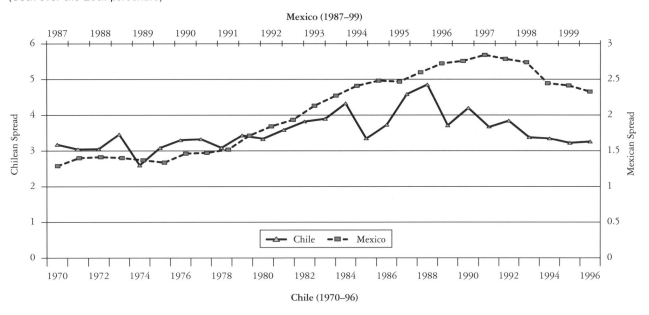

*Note:* Chilean openess began in 1973 but increased during the 1980s. Mexican liberalization began in 1985 and deepened with NAFTA (1994).

In particular, two assumptions do not correspond to LAC's reality. First, there are no intermediate factors or mobile factors of production in the Hekscher-Ohlin-Samuelson framework, yet one of the motivations of the trade reform was exactly to give firms access to better capital and intermediate goods. This could potentially have two important effects. First, as Jones (2000) argues, if factors of production are mobile, the traditional Stolper-Samuelson results can be overturned under reasonable conditions. But as important from the point of view of this report is that mobile capital, or the technology it embodies, may be skill biased, implying that it must be combined with higher skills, and this could also reverse the expected effect. Feenstra and Hanson (1995, 1996), for example, show that, though the United States moved their least-skill-intensive part of the production process to the Mexican *maquila* sector, nonetheless, these processes were skill intensive by local standards.

More generally, technological change, however induced, appears to increase the demand for skilled workers. Looking at Colombia, Mexico, and Taiwan (China), Tan and Batra (1997) find that firms that invest in research and development or training of workers tend to have wider spreads between skilled and unskilled workers than firms that do not. Consistent with studies of the OECD, Pavcnik (2000)

and Lopez-Acevedo (2001b) find that Chilean and Mexican firms with greater access to technology have, overall, a higher demand for skilled workers. Dramatic increases in skilled and unskilled labor in the industrialized world have been almost entirely attributed to technological progress and very little to trade. Sanguinetti and others (2001a, 2001b) find that import penetration increases inequality in Argentina, although Galiani and Sanguinetti (2000) find that this can account for only a small share of the increase. Santamaria (2000) find a similarly small effect for Colombia. Pavcnik, Blom, and Schady (2001) show that in Brazil, after controlling for workers' personal characteristics, wages rose in the industries where tariffs experienced larger reductions, but they do not find any correlation with inequality. Similarly, Sanguinetti and others find no connection in Uruguay. Most recently, Behrman, Szekely, and Birdsall (2001) find that for 18 Latin American countries during 1977–98, technological progress, rather than trade flows, appears to be a channel through which reforms affect wages (see Box 5.3).

These effects are, in reality, hard to separate. First, since Latin America is not a major source of technological innovation, most is "imported." Second, most authors acknowledge that any sector adjusting to increased trade exposure will displace workers to all other industries, not just those

BOX 5.2

**Stolper-Samuelson: Why We Thought Unskilled Workers Should Benefit from Liberalization**

The logic behind the Stolper-Samuelson theorem is simple. Suppose we have two goods—wine, where we use two units of labor for each unit of capital, and automobiles, where we use one unit of labor for each unit of capital. And suppose that before liberalization, cars were heavily protected and wine suffered negative rates of protection. This was more or less the case in Chile in 1967.

Now we liberalize, which lowers the price of cars and raises the price vintners get, reducing the productivity of cars and raising the production of wine. If we produce one less car, this frees up one unit of labor and one unit of capital. To produce one more bottle of wine takes that one unit of capital, but two units of labor. This means that there is excess demand for labor, and the wage must rise relative to capital. The logic is the same when the two factors are skilled and unskilled labor.

There are several reasons why the predicted result may not have occurred in LAC beyond the two discussed in the text. First, as Leamer has noted, and as has been documented in this report, Latin America does not export labor-intensive manufactures in general. Compared to the OECD, the region is unskilled-labor abundant, but compared to Asia, it is not, and hence the Stolper-Samuelson effect may simply be reflecting that the product whose price is rising is not a labor-intensive good, but a resource-intensive good.

Second, Stolper-Samuelson is fundamentally a long-term story where factors are fully mobile among industries. This leads to the counterintuitive finding that labor and capital should never be on the same side of a protection dispute: if capital is intensive in the industry, then more protection will help capitalists and hurt labor. Yet in real life we see both owners and unions resistant to lowering protection. This makes much more sense when we realize that in the short to medium term, both groups are tied to the sector, either by invested capital or specific skills, and hence are not mobile. Decreasing protection on existing unskilled-labor-intensive products will lead to a decline in their wages relative to other factors.

BOX 5.3

**Will Technological Progress Usher in a Golden Age of Equality?**

From a global perspective it is not necessarily obvious that, if technological progress tends to reward more skilled workers, then relatively unskilled Latin American workers continue to fall behind. Krugman (1999) argues (as does Landes [1998]) that, in other historical episodes, technology has displaced the relatively skill endowed as well, and he sees no reason why it should not be "college graduate" saving in the future.

"So here is a speculation. The time may come when most tax lawyers are replaced by expert systems software, but human beings are still needed—and well paid for such truly difficult occupations as gardening, house cleaning, and the thousands of other services that will receive an ever growing share of our expenditure as mere consumer goods become steadily cheaper. The high-skill professions whose members have done so well during the last 20 years may turn out to be the modern counterpart of the early 19th-century weavers, whose incomes soared after the mechanization of spinning, only to crash when the technological revolution reached their own craft.

I suspect, then, that the current era of growing inequality and the devaluation of ordinary work will turn out to be only a temporary phase. In some sufficiently long term the tables will be turned. Those uncommon skills that are rare because they are so unnatural will be largely taken over or made easy by computers, while machines will still be unable to do what every person can. In other words, I predict that the current age of inequality will give way to a golden age of equality. In the very long run, of course, the machines will be able to do everything we can. By that time, however, it will be their responsibility to take care of the problem."

*Source:* Krugman (1999: 203).

affected by trade, thereby muddying any statistical effect of trade.

What we can say, however, is that technological progress is desirable and hence, in the short term, there may be a short-term tradeoff between good jobs that are generated in modernizing industries, and wage distribution in economies with poorly educated work forces. Countries want to create jobs that require higher levels of schooling and hence the likelihood of training, continual career development, and worker satisfaction. As discussed above, even in the Mexican *maquilas*, the newly created jobs demand relatively higher levels of skill than that possessed by the workforce. Though no one would want to further "dumb down" *maquila* employment, this implies that relatively skilled workers will see a rise in their relative earnings. In fact, as Venables (2001) notes, the widening differentials appearing over the last decade offer the right market signal to young people to accumulate higher levels of human capital.

### Labor and Human Capital Supply: The Missing Link

In fact, the deficient supply of skilled workers in the workforce is a critical part of the distribution story and poses a major policy challenge to the region's governments. In Brazil, large shifts in educational composition have taken place in the last two decades and this has had an ambiguous, although large, impact on relative wages. The primary and secondary education system expanded substantially, increasing mean years of schooling from 4.8 in 1981 to 6.9 in 1999 and decreasing the Gini Coefficient of years of schooling from 0.49 to 0.37. However, the tertiary education system lagged

behind. This asymmetric push in education altered remuneration of education in the labor market in two ways. First, as illustrated in Figure 5.12, the wage of unskilled workers (defined as workers with no school diploma) experienced a relative wage increase compared to medium-skilled workers (defined as workers with complete primary or secondary education). The relative wage increase coincides with a stable decline in the relative supply of unskilled labor. Second, as depicted in Figure 5.13, the wage of highly skilled workers, defined as workers with tertiary education, increased.

Blom and Vélez (2001) estimate that around 60 percent of the increase of the skill premium to tertiary education can be attributed to the asymmetric expansion of the education system, and only 40 percent is due to a shift in labor demand toward highly skilled labor. Since they find no structural breaks in the behavior of demand over the last two decades, even this 40 percent appears unrelated to trade liberalization per se. Overall, the reduction of returns to secondary education drove the overall fall in inequality despite the offsetting effect of rising returns to a college education.[5]

Similarly, Vélez and others (2001) argue that during the 1990s, the increased participation by women was partially responsible for the worsening wage distribution in Colombia. Generally, women's skill levels tend to be lower than average and hence they depress earnings to lower-skilled workers. Given the large increases in female participation across the region, this is likely to be a more general phenomenon. However, it may also offer an explanation for the fact that there does not seem to be a corresponding increase

FIGURE 5.12

**Relative Labor Supply and Wage of Workers with No Schooling Compared to Workers with Lower Secondary Schooling in Brazil**

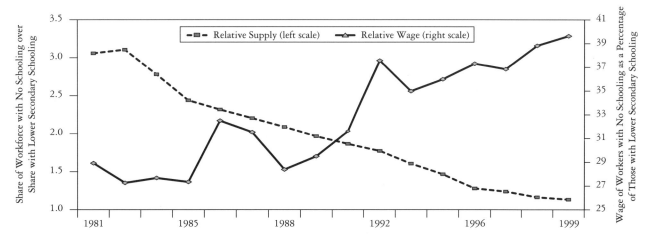

*Note:* Surveys were unavailable for 1984, 1991, and 1994.
*Source:* Velez and others 2001.

FIGURE 5.13

**Relative Labor Supply and Wage of Workers with Tertiary Schooling Compared to Workers with Upper Secondary Schooling in Brazil**

*Note:* Surveys were unavailable for 1984, 1991, and 1994.
*Source:* Velez and others 2001.

in *per capita household* inequality over the 1990s at the country or regional level (Wodon and Yitzhaki 2001; Stallings and Peres 2000). Though the rising participation of women helped worsen the wage distribution of *individuals* in Colombia, this represented an additional earner in poor households, and hence reduced overall inequality.

The issue of migration spans both international movements in factors and human capital supplies. Though the report does not examine the issue in any depth, Box 5.4 suggests some of the channels through which flows of remittances, which amount to large fractions of export revenues, affect both distribution and poverty.

*Sectoral Reallocation*

A final consideration that leads us into the next section is that the expansion of nontradeables sectors, and the concomitant expansion in self-employment in the 1990s, may also have had adverse impacts on measured inequality among income earners, although not necessarily wage earners. This could occur through two channels. First, the tradeables and nontradeables sectors may have differing demands for skills such that the shift toward nontradeables observed across the period would affect wage distribution. Sanguinetti and others (2001a) find that controlling for this shift lessens the direct impact of import penetration on the skill premium, but directly contributes to it in Argentina. They find no statistically significant effects for Uruguay.

Second, the nontradeables sectors have a higher fraction of the self-employed, and as Figure 5.15 shows, self-employed

earnings show roughly twice the inequality as those of salaried workers. This is due to the riskiness of self-employment (see Wodon, Maloney, and Barenstein 2000), and the higher measured returns to both education and experience among the self-employed.[6] This means that the increase in self-employment could also have an impact on measured inequality.

In sum, the emerging picture of the evolution of wages and distribution is not bleak. The sectors more exposed to trade appear to pay more than those in the less-exposed sectors. Further, the observed worsening distribution of wages seems largely due to the fact that firms are adopting technologies and more efficient modes of production and, in the process, are creating jobs that demand more from, but are also more satisfying to, workers.

**Informality**

An emerging preoccupation in the region is that trade liberalization has contributed to the rising number of "informal" workers—those unprotected by social security and health benefits. As Stallings and Peres (2000) of the Centro Estudios para America Latina (CEPAL) noted, in the 1990s six of every 10 jobs in the seven countries surveyed[7] were created in the informal sector, suggesting a substantial erosion of job quality.[8]

The channel through which the increased openness may have had this impact is not clear. At one extreme, those opposing greater integration into the global economy argue that global manufacturing networks seek to control costs

BOX 5.4
## Migration, Remittances, and Their Implications

In many countries, labor has become an important export, and its associated remittances amount to an important share of poor household income. In El Salvador, 23 percent of the work force is estimated to migrate, and in the Dominican Republic and Mexico the rates are above 12 percent. Remittances, which have been growing at double-digit rates, are equivalent to nearly one third of the region's foreign direct investment and exceed official development inflows. As shown in Figure 5.14, remittances account for 10 percent of GDP or 20 percent of exports in many countries. They exceed total coffee exports in Colombia and tourism in Mexico (López-Cálix 2001).

Remittances have profound effects on all elements of the receiving village. They constitute an important social safety net in natural disasters (Meyers 1998) and have important impacts on household budgets. In the late 1980s, a special survey by CEPAL found that in El Salvador, Guatemala, and Nicaragua, 4 to 8 percent was spent on children's health and education, 5 to 6 percent on investment, and the remainder on consumption (CEPAL 2001). A 1997 study by FondoMicro in the Dominican Republic reports that 84.9 percent of the received funds went toward expenses of the family, while 7.1 percent went toward the business, and 8 percent went toward other expenses. The impact on inequality can differ by region: Since those migrating from rural areas are often those with the highest human capital, inequality may increase, and the reverse is true in the urban areas (Gonzalez, Koning, and Wodon 2001a).

An often-overlooked source of investment capital for microenterprises are remittances from relatives working abroad. In Mexico, Woodruff and Zenteno (2001) find that within the 10-state migration region, more than a third of invested capital is sourced from family remittances, and that in total, remittances add to about a fifth of aggregate investment capital in urban Mexican microfirms. In El Salvador one-quarter of remittance receivers have established small businesses as a result of the availability of remittances (Lopez and Seligson 1990). Moreover, migration networks may act as a source of information, support, and cooperation that reduces risks and increases rewards. In this case, those with greater access to remittances are also likely to have greater access to formal credit and to significantly higher chances of firm entry, survival, and expansion.

Studies on the Dominican Republic and El Salvador also suggest that migration also affects consumption habits, and may create negative attitudes toward work. In both countries, most household remittance receivers (mainly composed of women, children, and parents) develop a dependent subsistence culture: they receive just enough money to provide for basic needs, but not enough for investment (Georges 1990; Lopez and Seligson 1990; and Funkhouser 1992).

FIGURE 5.14
## Remittances as a Share of GDP and Exports, 1999

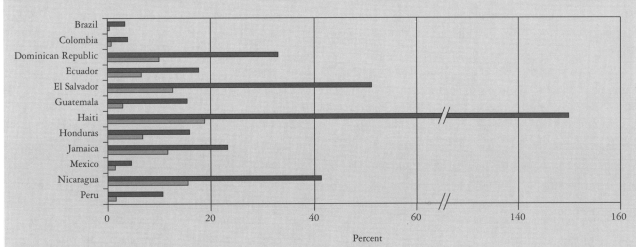

Percent

*Source:* López-Cálix 2001, World Bank 2001, and Meyers 2001.

133

FIGURE 5.15

**Earnings Inequality Decomposition for Salaried versus Self-Employed Workers, 1995**

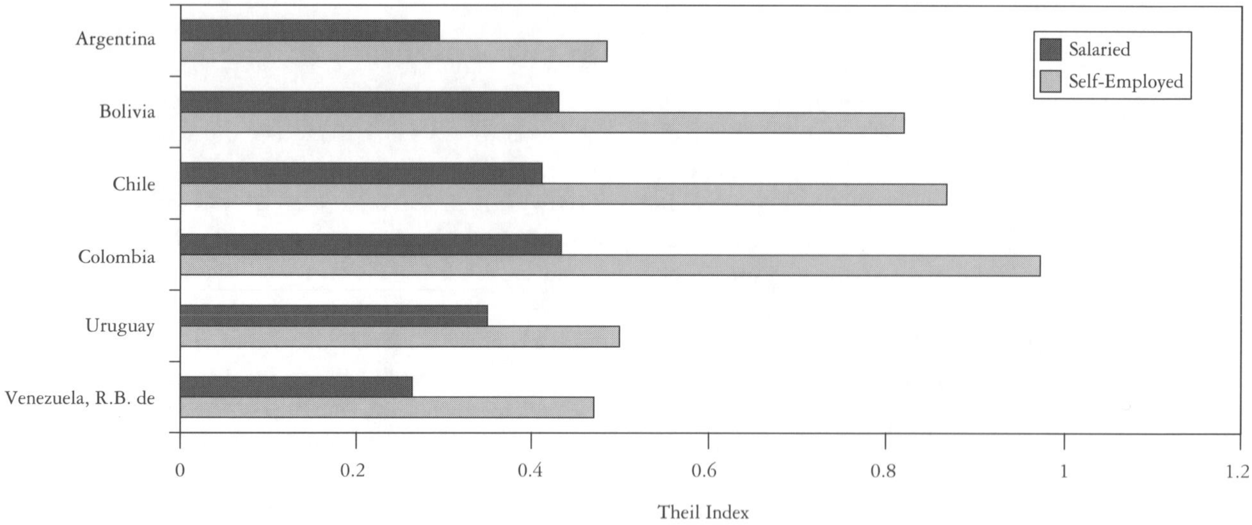

*Source:* Wodon, Maloney, and Barenstein 2000.

by reducing worker benefits: large- and medium-size firms facing international competition, or multinationals themselves, outsource production to informal small firms, including home-based and self-employed microentrepreneurs (Portes, Castells, and Benton (1989); Borrus and Zysman 1997). In a sense, this view takes the fragmentation of the production process down to the microfirm level, but with a very negative twist: informal firms get their comparative advantage by avoiding worker protections and taking on the risk associated with demand volatility.

The evidence offers little support for this view. This section argues that the increasing informalization of the region is not primarily related to trade liberalization per se, but rather to the increasing attractiveness of nontradeables employment, which itself was partially related to macrostabilization and capital inflows. In some cases it appears to result from increased rigidities in labor markets and tax regulations. Further, those few microfirms linked to larger firms either through subcontracting or other market transactions tend to be both better paid and more formal. Arguably, the larger challenge is how to reduce the isolation of informal microfirms and help them to take advantage of the emerging opportunities.

### The Nature of the Informal Sector: A Comprehensive Approach

A more general approach is necessary to understand the dynamics of the informal sector, which can incorporate three emerging stylized facts about the sector. First, as Box 5.5 suggests, the informal self-employed in Argentina, Mexico, and Paraguay report being largely voluntary. To say voluntary is not to say well-off or even happy, only that in a market without segmentation, this option was deemed better than any alternative job in the formal sector. Second, the vast majority of informal jobs, generally around 70 to 80 percent, operate in nontradeables sectors, such as commerce, transport, and services. Third, the sector is heterogeneous, including both voluntary members who would not be made better off in formal sector jobs, and involuntary members who are effectively "rationed" by higher than market-clearing wages due to minimum-wage laws or other rigidities.[9] This view encompasses both traditional dualistic views of segmented labor markets and newer views of integrated markets where the share of voluntary members is determined by how binding formal sector rigidities may be.

These features suggest that, as a first approximation, the informal self-employed could be considered to be unregulated entrepreneurs in the nontradeables sector. This, in turn, has implications for how we view the trends over the last decade. First, as Balassa (1964) noted, the size of the nontradeables sector is largely determined by its productivity compared with the tradeables sector. Productivity gains in the formal sector both increase the attractiveness of formal sector jobs relative to being self-employed, and raise the relative cost of nontradeable goods, reducing their demand. This relationship is borne out in Figure 5.17,

BOX 5.5
**Are Most Informal Sector Workers Voluntary?**

Evidence from Argentina, Mexico, and Paraguay suggests that most people in the informal sector are there voluntarily. In Mexico, 70 percent report entering the sector either because of more flexibility, higher wages, or simply the desire to be their own boss. Panel data suggest that of those workers who started in the formal salaried sector but moved into self-employed 15 months later, two-thirds report moving voluntarily, citing a desire for greater independence or higher pay as the principal motives (see Figure 5.16). These findings are consistent with the sociologists Balán, Browning, and Jelin's (1973) extensive interviews with Monterrey workers who state that being one's own boss was well regarded and that movements into self-employment from salaried positions often represented an improvement in job status. This is broadly consistent with interview data from Argentina: a small survey in the province of Jujuy revealed that 80 percent of the self-employed had no desire to change jobs, and under 18 percent viewed self-employment as a temporary activity before they found a "real" job. In Greater Buenos Aires, another survey found that while 36 percent would have preferred to work more hours, only 26 percent were looking for other work. In Paraguay, only 28 percent of those in the informal self-employed sector stated a desire to change occupations. Among those often thought to be the worst off, informal salaried workers, the percent rose only to 32 percent.

*Why Would Workers Prefer to Be "Unprotected"?*
There are several reasons why workers may be willing to voluntarily become "unprotected" and rely more on informal safety nets. First, developing-country microentrepreneurs may not be fundamentally different from their counterparts in the industrialized world who also take on responsibility for medical insurance or saving for retirement that was previously covered by their employers. Second, in a market with flexible wages, the cost of employer-provided benefits is partially passed down to workers in the form of lower wages. If workers do not value the benefits as much as the decline in wages, they will seek out jobs in the unregulated sector where remuneration is entirely monetary. This might happen if social security or health benefits provision is very inefficient, if there are very weak linkages between benefits and contributions, or if one member of the family is already formal and hence the rest of the family already receives benefits. Third, the interviews of Balán, Browning, and Jelin (1973) suggest that the very legislation that is thought to induce rigidities into the labor market in fact stimulates such turnover and encourages workers to leave salaried employment. The paucity of openings for promotion on the rigid *escalafon* and the ceiling on mobility opportunities for manual workers makes self-employment the remaining outlet for further advancement. These last two issues suggest that, in contrast to the usual view, the extant labor protections may make formal sector work less desirable rather than less attainable.

FIGURE 5.16
**Mexico—Reasons to Start a Microenterprise**

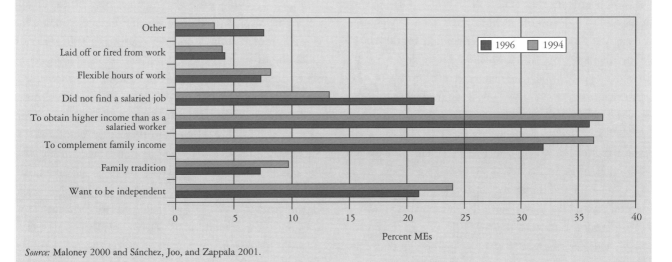

*Source:* Maloney 2000 and Sánchez, Joo, and Zappala 2001.

FIGURE 5.17

## Self-Employment versus Industrial Productivity

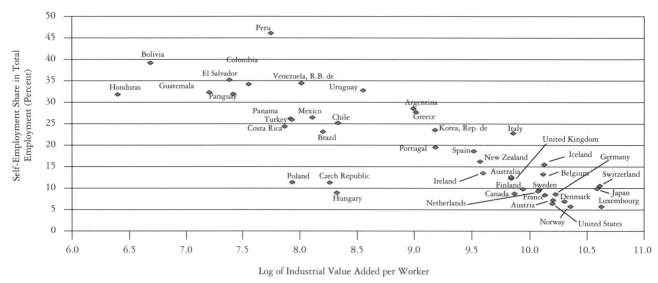

*Source:* Maloney 2001a.

which shows that the large size of the self-employed sector reflects low formal sector productivity, and hence lower wages of the region. As the relative attractiveness of formal sector work increases with the development process and productivity rises, the share of self-employment will fall.

Second, this characterization of the informal sector also implies that the short-term and long-term overall macrobehavior as captured in standard small economy or "Australian" models of the economy may offer important explanations for the increase in informality we observe in the region (Maloney 1997; Fiess, Fugazza, and Maloney 2001). Figure 5.18 plots the ratio of the number of formal sector workers relative to the number of informal workers, their relative incomes, and the real exchange rate for Argentina, Brazil, and Mexico, which together account for 60 percent of the regional population. Much of the regional trend is driven by Brazil, which showed a steep rise in the number of workers *sem carteira*, or without the signed work card that would give them access to benefits. In a traditional dualistic or segmented view of the informal sector, we would expect to see the two labor market variables move against each other: a rise in the formal sector wage, perhaps due to an increase in minimum wages, forces workers into the informal sector and drives down the informal wage relative to the formal. But what is striking is that in Argentina, Brazil, and Mexico, these series move together in the beginning of the 1990s, and at the same time that the exchange

rate is appreciating. This suggests that the dramatic rise in informality during this period was driven by increased opportunities in the nontradeables sectors that boomed in many countries of the region following the liberalization of the trade and capital accounts. The case is most suggestive in Brazil, where statistically the real exchange rate, the size of the informal self-employed sector, and the relative earnings can be shown to move together, suggesting that much of the large increase in informality is voluntary.[10]

Third, in the wake of these booms, there does seem to be evidence of an increase in informality concomitant with a decline in relative informal income in Mexico from 1992 to 1994, in Argentina post-1993, and in Brazil immediately before the 1998 depreciation, which suggests segmentation arising from nominal rigidities presenting difficulties in adjusting to further shocks. As an extreme case, Figure 5.19 shows a massive increase in relative informal self-employment in Colombia after the decline of the boom and onset of the crisis in 1998. Unfortunately, the data do not permit us to separate informal and formal salaried employees for long periods of time. However, the estimated wage distributions in Figure 5.20 suggest that in 1998 Colombia's minimum wage was far more binding in both the formal and informal salaried sectors than in the other three countries. Further, indexing it to overly pessimistic forecasts of inflation led to it rising another 6 percent in real terms in 1999, despite the worst crisis in the postwar period.

FIGURE 5.18

## Relative Formal/Informal Sector Sizes and Incomes and the Real Exchange Rate

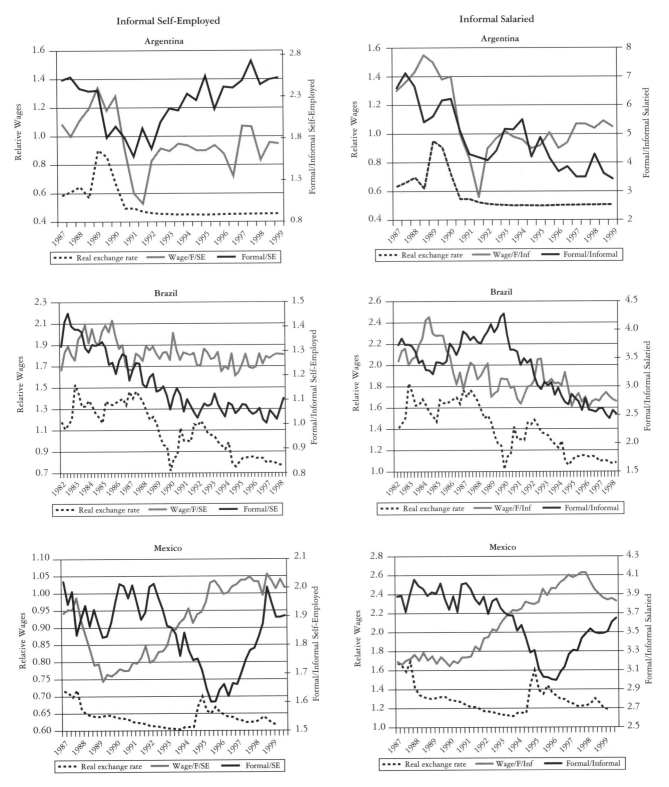

F: Formal
Inf: Informal salaried
SE: Self-employed
*Source:* Fiess, Fugazza, and Maloney 2001.

FIGURE 5.19

**Relative Formal/Informal Sector Sizes and Income and the Real Exchange Rate, Colombia (Informal Self-Employed/ All Salaried Workers)**

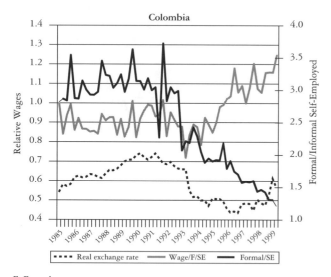

F: Formal
SE: Self-employed
*Source:* Fiess, Fugazza, and Maloney 2001.

In sum, a sizeable component of the observed rise in informality in the beginning of the 1990s may be due to the booms in the nontradeables sector and the necessary macroeconomic adjustments afterward.

### Does Trade Liberalization Impact Informality?

What is more difficult to establish is a direct link to greater integration in the global economy. It is worth noting that relatively open economies such as Belgium and Singapore, and resource-intensive economies such as Australia, Canada, Finland, Sweden, and the United States, are not especially informal. Nor is it obvious from Figures 5.21 and 5.22 that there is a tight correlation between either openness or particular types of exported goods. For Argentina, Brazil, and Mexico, the familiar U-pattern appears with more exposed industries having relatively more formal work forces. Figure 5.22 suggests that most of Leamer's export categories have higher rates of formality than nontradeables sectors, although animal and cereal production appears in general to be among the least formal. Certainly it would not be possible to argue that manufactured products, particularly labor-intensive goods, are uniformly more formal than the more resource-oriented sectors.

Nor is there much evidence that competitive pressures during liberalization have increased the amount of out-

sourcing or "gray" area workers. Most compelling is the case of Mexico. If any country were to be thought of as the low-skilled manufacturing appendage to global capitalism, it would have to be the United States' southern neighbor. Yet Figure 5.18 does not suggest a permanent rise in informality, either of self-employment or informal salaried workers. In the first case, we do see a sharp rise in informal salaried workers across the 1990s, but this is sharply reversed after the 1995 depreciation and crisis. Since many informal salaried workers are hired by informal microfirms, the boom at the beginning of the 1990s, and the resulting rationing during the crisis, can explain much of the increase. But the level of informality is clearly on trend to return to 1988 levels in the next year or two, and we see no secular trend either in total share of informal salaried workers, or their share in large-firm employment. The macroeconomic fluctuations driven by attempting to stabilize the peso are far more obvious than any long-term trend that might be attributed to NAFTA.

When we look more closely, we do not see strong evidence of linkages between informal microfirms and multinational and large firms. The fact is that the vast majority of microenterprise activity remains oriented toward the domestic consumer market. In the Dominican Republic and Mexico, almost 90 percent of microenterprises sell their goods and services primarily to individuals, with the remaining 10 percent selling to firms. Only a small fraction sell their goods or services to international markets, ranging from 1 percent in Mexico to 1.7 percent in the Dominican Republic to 4 percent in Ecuador. As Figure 5.23 illustrates, in the Dominican Republic the percentage of firms with business clientele that might possibly have linkages with foreign firms has increased but remains low, and in Mexico the number of microfirms claiming to be linked to such firms actually fell from 1994 to 1996. While this may reflect the temporary effects of the crisis, this nonetheless makes it even more difficult to argue that there has been an increase in outsourcing since NAFTA was passed. In fact, the higher rates of informality among microenterprises may be more due to a shift toward the nontradeables service areas, which usually show lower degrees of formality.

The difficulty in pinning the rise in informality on trade liberalization also appears in Argentina. In Figure 5.24 Gasparini plots the share of the informal work force relative to the formal. What is striking is not only the dramatic secular trend, but that the trend begins in the beginning of the 1980s, long before Mercosur or the opening of the

FIGURE 5.20

**Impact of Minimum Wages on the Distribution of the Wages of Informal and Formal Salaried Workers**

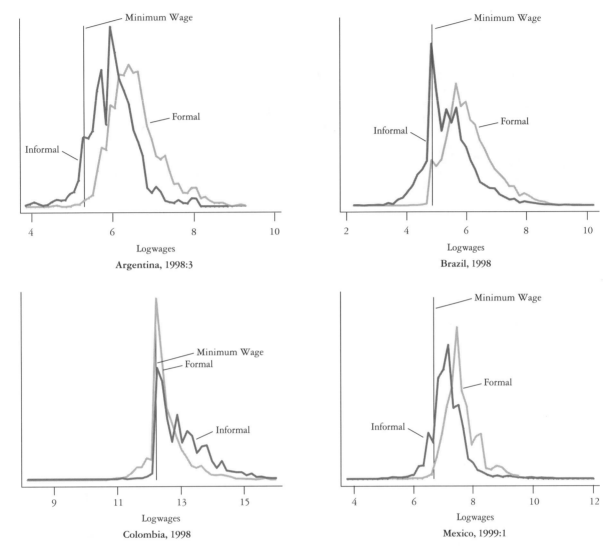

*Source:* Maloney and Nuñez 2000.

economy. Decomposing the changes observed, Gasparini is unable to attribute to increased openness the source of increased informality. Given Mexico's relative stability of informal share, it seems that Argentina's informalization may be more related to extraordinary macrovolatility combined with fairly rigid labor markets, and the rise in payroll taxes across the period. Figure 5.25 suggests that the increased informality has occurred across firms of all sizes. It is not, for example, a subcontracting out of processes to microfirms, but increased evasion at all levels.

Brazil is a central case, both because of the dramatic increase in informality and the size of the economy. In addi-

tion to the large increase in self-employment, which is responsible for much of the rise in informal salaried employment, Blom, Pavcnik, and Schady (2001) find a secular increase in informality in every major sector. However, employing the same technique discussed in analyzing the movements in income distribution, they are unable to find a direct link between a decline in tariffs by industry and the increase in informality. What is happening is general, and not specific to firms more open to trade. It, again, may be partly related to issues of stabilization or labor taxes.

This does not imply that insertion into the global economy does not somehow contribute, but the impact may not

FIGURE 5.21

**Formality Rates by Trade Exposure**

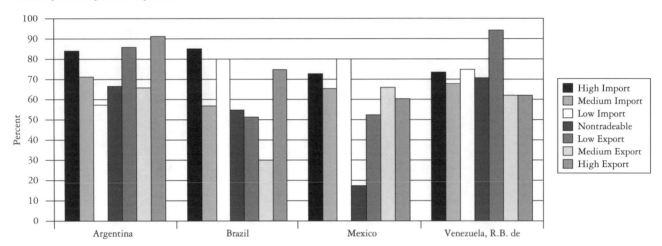

*Note:* Nonagricultural workers. Means by trade balance per worker centiles.
*Source:* National Labor Force Surveys.

FIGURE 5.22

**Formality Rates by Leamer Categories**

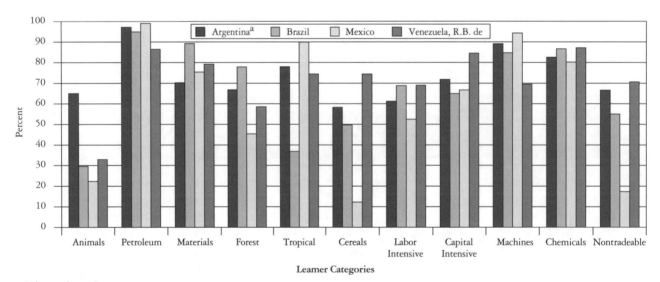

a. Urban workers only.
*Source:* National Labor Force Surveys.

be as direct as sometimes thought. Helfner and Castro de Rezende (2001) show that the increased exposure to competition, particularly from Argentina through Mercosur, had a devastating impact on wheat and other cereal production in the south of Brazil. This, combined with the appreciated exchange rate and cheaper imported fertilizer and machinery that raised the relative cost of labor 70 percent, meant a decrease in the rural workforce of around 4 percent, a large fraction of which would have migrated to cites and perhaps contributed to swelling the size of the informal sector.

In sum, an observer in 1995 would have seen a dramatic rise in informality in Argentina, Brazil, Colombia, and Mexico, four countries accounting for 75 percent of the region's population. But arguably much of this was voluntary and driven by demand pull to the nontradeables sector. And to an observer in 2001, much of the increase observed

FIGURE 5.23

**Domestic and Foreign Businesses as Microenterprise Clients, Mexico and the Dominican Republic**

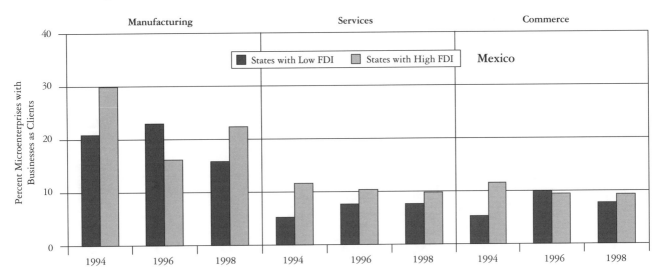

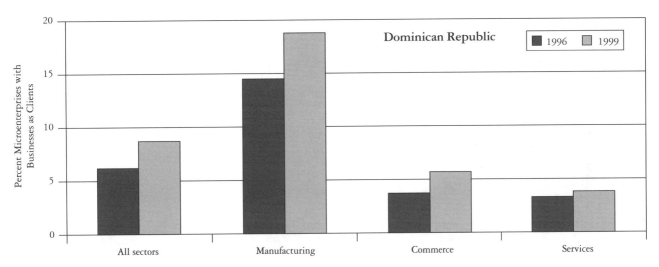

*Source:* Sánchez, Joo, and Zappala 2001.

in the second half of the 1990s could be attributed to standard difficulties in macroadjustment in the face of nominal rigidities. Neither looking across countries nor at one country across time suggests a tight link to greater integration in the world economy.

### Microenterprises: Improving How They Work in the Global Environment

This is not to say that greater openness has not had large impacts on the microfirm sector. In the Dominican Republic, for example, despite the fact that only 2 percent re-

ported selling their products to foreign individuals or businesses, 16 percent of owners said that trade liberalization had left them better off than before, compared to 24 percent who said they were worse off. The impact was even greater within individual sectors: 60 percent of those in commerce reported being better off, while half of those in textiles reported being hurt.

On the other hand, for firms that have been able to connect with larger firms, the overall impact has probably been positive. Male-headed microfirms whose clients are small or large firms, or those located in areas with high FDI, earned

FIGURE 5.24

**Informality Rate for Salaried Workers in Greater Buenos Aires, 1980–99**

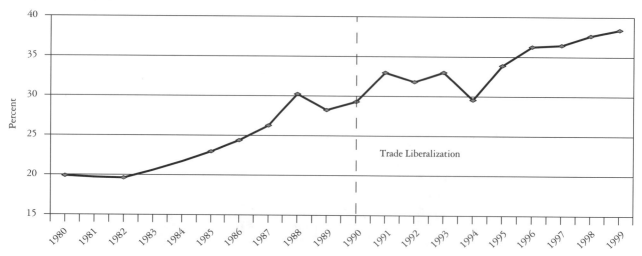

*Source:* Gasparini 2000.

FIGURE 5.25

**Share of Informal Workers in Greater Buenos Aires**

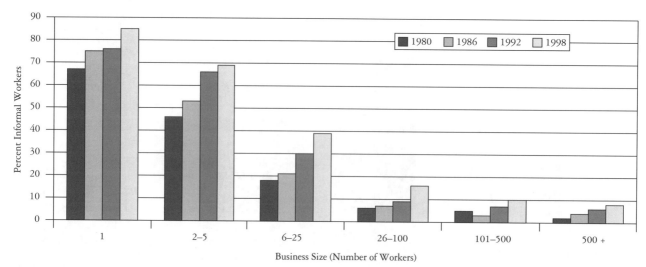

*Source:* Gasparini 2000.

roughly 25 percent more than their comparable counterparts, and for female-headed firms the numbers are even higher (Figure 5.26). Moreover, there is no evidence that these entrepreneurs enjoy fewer social security benefits.

There are also clear benefits from improving access to the supply of inputs and raw materials. In the Dominican Republic, microfirms in commerce, which account for 47 percent of microfirms, stressed the greater variety and quality of the inputs available, resulting in increased sales. In addition, imports in the form of equipment and technology as factor

inputs can be particularly valuable for growth and efficiency improvements (Yusuf 2001). Again, Figure 5.26 suggests that Mexican microfirms with large suppliers do better than comparable firms by roughly 10 percent. (For a discussion of home-based work and the informal microfirm, see Box 5.6.)

### The Real Problem: Isolation from Domestic and Global Markets

In fact, though the data to date are scarce, it is probably the case that microfirms suffer more from isolation from prod-

FIGURE 5.26

**Premium on Reported Profits of Mexican Microfirms with Firms as Clients Compared to Other Microenterprises**

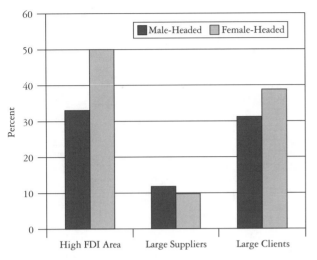

*Source:* Sánchez, Joo, and Zappala 2001.

uct, financial, and technology markets than from excessive integration. This is the theme of the bulk of the literature on microenterprises that focuses on difficulties in acquiring information and technology or insufficient access to finance, and it applies equally well as microfirms attempt to meet the challenges and opportunities of openness.[11]

Ironically, the largest barrier may exactly be that microfirms remain largely "informal," operating outside laws and regulations. While being informal is often seen purely as evasion of taxes or labor benefits, Levenson and Maloney (1998) argue that formality, conceived as participating in the institutions of society, is a necessary input for business growth. Entrepreneurs may choose to comply with specific norms and regulations because of potential benefits, such as access to financing, contract systems, and risk-pooling mechanisms. In their study on the barriers to technological adoption, Parente and Prescott (2000) cite de Soto's (1989) work on Peru, in which he finds that the high "costs of formality" present obstacles to adoption of new technologies and hence to growth.

One of the principal barriers to becoming formal is the high fixed costs of business registration and the ongoing cost of formalization, resulting from inflexible tax and labor legislations. To register a firm, microentrepreneurs typically face a process that can take up to hundreds of days, as shown in Table 5.4, and require several hundred

dollars in "official fees," ranging from US$420 in Mexico to US$1,755 in Argentina.

The second major barrier is the misalignment of the contributions to and benefits from state social programs (Maloney 1998). At the level of individual benefits, Roberts' (1989) interviews in Guadalajara, Mexico, found that many informants cited the deductions made for welfare as a disadvantage of formal employment, since the services they received were poor.

Entrepreneurs may also lack the ability to assimilate new techniques or knowledge. This may arise from deficient understanding of where their operating problems really lie, but there are clearly supply bottlenecks as well. A World Bank review found that in Jamaica most microfirms lack proper information on where to find supplier and market opportunities outside of their immediate areas, and how to exploit them. Linkages to businesses through marketing, management, technical, financial, and design assistance, within value chains or with anchor firms, could be effective channels of learning and productivity for these microbusinesses. Furthermore, traditional forms of networking that have been largely personal and informal will continue to play an important role.

Finally, although awareness of the benefits of information and communications technology is still low, they are also a promising strategy for microenterprises to pursue for a number of reasons, particularly if built into an integrated approach to development. Some pilot projects offer examples of how both for-profit and nonprofit organizations are promoting handmade crafts and artwork of microfirms from around the world on their Web sites. The fact that microfirms face significant logistic and managerial limitations in selling through the Internet suggests the need for linkages through intermediary organizations. Also, pilot projects of business development centers plan to use the Internet as a resource for information on how to reduce transaction costs, become more efficient, expand networks, access new markets, and receive better information about prices and markets.[12] Some business development strategies that use information technology have the potential to facilitate the successful integration of microfirms through the provision of Internet access and consulting, training, and computer services (see Box 5.7).

Poor access to finance and the high cost of financing are cited throughout the region and across firm sizes as a barrier to growth and expansion into domestic and foreign markets (see Figure 5.28). Generally speaking, microfinance is largely

BOX 5.6
### Home-Based Work: Exploitation or Flexible Work Arrangement?

A particular modality of the informal microfirm that has received increasing attention is that of home-based work. Numerous authors (Arriagada 1998; Prugl 1997; WIEGO 2000) tend to see the subcontracting of these workers as a way for large firms to maintain flexibility, quality, and global profitability by both avoiding benefits and transferring the risks of demand volatility to workers. The absence of an internationally accepted definition of home-based work, among other problems, means that the reported shares of the workforce, ranging from 1.5 percent to 20 percent (Table 5.3), are probably not comparable (Chen, Sebstad, and O'Connell 1999).

TABLE 5.3
### Home-Based Workforce
(Percent)

| COUNTRY | ESTIMATED PROPORTION | PROPORTION FEMALE | YEAR OF ESTIMATE |
|---|---|---|---|
| Algeria | 3.3 | 97 | 1989 |
| Australia | 2.9 | — | 1989 |
| Brazil | 5.5 | 74.8 | 1999 |
| Ecuador | 17.3 | 73.6 | 1999 |
| India | 2.5 | — | 1981 |
| Japan | 1.6 | 93.5 | 1988 |
| Mexico | 4.4 | 64.4 | 1999 |
| Philippines | 23.0 | — | 1980s |
| Peru | 10.5 | — | 1987 |
| United Kingdom | 2.3 | 70 | 1981 |
| United States | 7.53 | — | 1985 |

— Not available.
*Sources:* ILO 1995 and Cunningham and Ramos 2001.

Though some very famous firms, such as Italy's Benneton, started as a cluster of home-based workers, it is questionable how important international linkages really are. As with informal microenterprises more generally, the fraction that report working as contract workers, perhaps for large companies, rather than selling their work directly in the local market, is generally reported as less than 0.7 percent in Brazil, 1.2 percent in Ecuador, and 1.6 percent in Mexico. What does seem to emerge is that the sector is largely comprised of women, often over 75 percent, and of those whose personal characteristics make outside work inaccessible (ILO 1995; Carr 2000; Tomei 2000; Cunningham and Ramos 2001). The concern is that employers may take advantage of the situation of those whose work options are limited to the home by subjecting home-based workers to lower remuneration and labor standards than workers who can compete in the larger labor market

FIGURE 5.27
### Hourly Wage Premium to Working outside the Home Compared to Home-Based Work

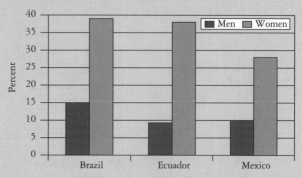

*Source:* Cunningham and Ramos 2001.

(Krawczyk 1993; WIEGO 2000). Though anecdotal evidence suggests this may occur, statistical studies have yet to document it as a widespread phenomenon.

Home-based workers do earn lower wages than other workers. Controlling for higher skill levels in the sector, salaried workers earn 28.9 percent, 39.6 percent, and 22.8 percent more than home workers in Brazil, and Ecuador, and Mexico, respectively (Cunningham and Ramos 2001) (see Figure 5.27). These lower wages may reflect the price of work-shift flexibility that allows juggling other household responsibilities, of not having to travel to the worksite, or other benefits that accrue to homecare providers. This is partially borne out by the fact that home-based workers spend an average of 30 hours in productive activities each week, compared to more than 40 hours weekly among non-home-based workers (Cunningham and Ramos 2001; Tomei 2000), a result largely driven by women, especially those with young children, a spouse, or both. Home-based work may thus be a preferred work arrangement for those who have both home and market duties (Prugl 1999; Tomei 2000; Arriagada 1998). Women with more young children, a spouse, or both are more likely to engage in home-based work than are those without such household constraints, and less than half are household heads, with the large proportion being spouses or dependent children (Cunningham and Ramos 2001). Interviews with female home-based workers who have children reveal that these women hope to work outside the home once their children have left home (Jelin, Mercado, and Wyczkier 2001).

TABLE 5.4

**Business Registration in Selected Countries and by Region**

| COUNTRY/REGION | NUMBER OF STEPS | TIME (BUSINESS DAYS) |
|---|---|---|
| Argentina | 12.0 | 71.0 |
| Bolivia | 20.0 | 82.0 |
| Chile | 12.0 | 78.0 |
| Colombia | 17.0 | 55.0 |
| Ecuador | 12.0 | 141.0 |
| Mexico | 15.0 | 112.0 |
| Uruguay | 9.0 | 105.0 |
| Venezuela, R.B. de | 15.0 | 124.0 |
| Latin America average | 13.5 | 92.7 |
| Africa region average | 12.0 | 83.0 |
| Europe region average | 9.3 | 59.5 |
| Asia region average | 10.0 | 71.1 |
| United States | 4.0 | 7.0 |

*Source:* Jansson and Chalmers 2001, as reported by Djankov and others 2000.

ineffective at reaching the large, densely poor markets (Christen 2000). Together Argentina, Brazil, Mexico, and the República Bolivariana de Venezuela serve fewer than 150,000 clients among them. In Mexico, for example, the percentage of urban microenterprises receiving credit from any source has remained stable at around 13 percent since 1992, in spite of the emergence in the country of very successful microfinance lenders, such as Compartamos.

These low uses of credit raise concerns about how to increase the supply of financial services for microenterprises, particularly in macrocontexts where credit has been contracting or at least experiencing slow growth across all spheres of economic activities. Microfirms retain their traditional handicaps: the characteristics of the financial services demanded (for example, a very small loan amount, short-term maturity, uncollateralized loans) make extending credit expensive for formal financial intermediaries, and the characteristics of the clients make lending risky. In the Dominican Republic microenterprise access to finance has improved in the 1990s, with 54 percent reporting receiving credit from any source in 1999, up from 21 percent in 1993. Commercial bank penetration increased to 4.5 percent in 1999, partly through the creative use of credit cards now used by 13.3 percent of microenterprises.[13] Importantly, Clarke and others (2001) find that privatization and the entry of foreign banks have not obviously led to decreased services to microentrepreneurs.[14]

In sum, the evidence is not strong that the increasing integration of the region has been driving the increase in informality. Much of the observed movement was driven by

nontradeables booms related more to stabilization policies, financial liberalization, and the resulting capital inflows. Since in many cases the increasing size of the informal microenterprise sector was correlated with an improvement in earnings relative to formal sector employment, it is hard to dismiss the possibility that these movements were welfare improving. The sector is very heterogeneous and, without question, there are workers who would prefer formal sector jobs. Still, the sector is probably best viewed as an unregulated microenterprise sector that offers relatively attractive jobs for unskilled workers. Though the data to date are very thin, and more methodical research is essential, even for home-based workers it is hard to reject the idea that this modality of work offers a desirable combination of income with flexibility for many workers. In some countries, there is evidence of excessively high minimum wages and other labor market rigidities that correspond to the more traditional dualistic view of informality, but this does not seem to be the dominant explanation.

Certainly there is a striking absence of any statistical evidence of significant outsourcing from large exporting firms. In fact, arguably, it is the *isolation* from markets more generally, and from public institutions, that is the larger problem. The roots of this isolation lie in the low human capital of the entrepreneurs, the high barriers to participation in formal sector institutions, the low efficiency and quality of social security systems, weak property rights, and information asymmetries. Progress in institutional, capital market, and labor market reforms, along with a creative introduction of new information technologies, offer the hope that microentrepreneurs can take advantage of emerging opportunities.

## New Jobs from Trade: Opportunity or Exploitation?

New export industries have created new types of jobs, some of which have proved controversial. This section looks at four types of jobs in *maquilas* or EPZs: the teleservice industry, nontraditional agriculture, and tourism. The chosen sectors are not necessarily new—there is a long tradition of tourism in the region—but they correspond either to the sectors discussed in Chapter 4, or those that have received particular attention in the literature. Several conceptual issues guide the discussion.

First, the benchmark of job quality is not a similar job in the industrialized world, but rather other opportunities

BOX 5.7

**Promoting International Linkages for Artisans**

Microenterprises are overcoming obstacles and finding ways to bring their products to the export market. With the help of a link to international markets, there is now hope for many microenterprises to experience growth and sustainability by selling their products abroad. As seen in the case of handicraft artisans, a focus on increasing social capital through traditional methods such as cooperatives, and nontraditional methods such as electronic business development services and e-commerce, is assisting microenterprises to integrate into the global economy.

**Ten Thousand Villages** is a nonprofit organization operated by the Mennonite Central Committee (MCC) of Akron, Pennsylvania. Originating in 1946 under the name SELFHELP Crafts of the World, Ten Thousand Villages and partner organizations operate 180 retail stores across the United States and Canada. Using a traditional approach, the organization purchases handicrafts from artisan groups in 30 countries (nine in Latin America) for sale in their retail stores. Purchases have increased from US$3.5 million in fiscal year 1997 to US$5.2 million in 2001. The organization benefits some 60,000 craftspeople.

Artisan groups are comprised of cooperatives and associations of artisans living in developing countries who promote employee participation in decisionmaking and ownership. While artisan groups are required to produce high-quality goods, local MCC offices and partner organizations serve as an additional layer of quality control by making recommendations to Ten Thousand Villages before orders are placed. In most cases, Ten Thousand Villages purchases items directly from the artisan groups. The groups receive half of the payment when orders are placed, with the second half paid upon receipt of shipment. In addition, Ten Thousand Villages buyers informally offer advice to artisan groups on such areas as product design and development, marketing, diversification of products, and expansion of markets.

Ten Thousand Villages stores typically employ a store manager and sometimes an assistant manager; however, to keep overhead costs low, all other workers are volunteers.

**PEOPLink**, a nonprofit corporation formed in 1996, uses a less-traditional method by employing the Internet to promote the sale of artisan handicrafts. The system's 92 Trading Partners (TPs) serve as contact points for artisans to gain exposure to the international market. TPs (six in Latin America) are development organizations representing hundreds or thousands of artisans in a particular region or country. PEOPLink provides TPs with a "toolkit" consisting of a video camera and computer, onsite installation of hardware, and Internet training to upload images of crafts.

PEOPLink then places the images on the Web site for retail and wholesale buyers in industrialized countries. Orders are filled from the headquarters in Maryland, with future plans for shipping from the country of origin. Funding consists of retained income, donations, and loans and grants from the Organization of American States, the Inter-American Foundation, Aid to Artisans, the John D. and Catherine T. MacArthur Foundation, U.S. Agency for International Development, the World Bank, and the Inter-American Development Bank. PEOPLink expects to cover operating expenses by sales and donations alone by 2001.

**Novica**, an online marketer for crafts from around the world, also uses the Internet as its primary mode of operation. The Web site was launched in 1998. Novica's philosophy, "Artists make more—collectors pay less—the power of the Internet," has attracted 1,700 artisans worldwide, with 5,000 expected by the end of 2002. Novica employs 200 people in 11 regional offices (six in Latin America) to review potential products and ship orders abroad. Artisans present their products to Novica's local staff, and if the goods meet certain quality standards the products are added to the Web site at no charge.

The artisans can raise or lower their prices and remove their items from the site at any time. Although most orders are filled from the regional offices, some are shipped from the headquarters warehouse in Los Angeles. Products are available for shipping worldwide. Novica secured The National Geographic Society as a strategic partner in December 2000. Financing has been provided by Chris Burns, Rust Capital, and Scripps Ventures. Novica is expected to go public in the near future.

**Artisan Enterprise Network (AEN)**, started in 2000, has taken an altogether different approach to assisting with the promotion of artisan exports. Unlike the direct sales involvement of the previous organizations, AEN was designed with the emphasis on providing information and training to artisan entrepreneurs. Through the Web site www.artisanenterprisenetwork.org, artisans interested in exporting their products can find product trend reports for the United States, a database of U.S. importers, wholesalers, and retailers of handmade products, information on trade shows, financing, con-

tract preparation, product development, freight forwarding, and low-priced sources for raw materials and equipment. For business owners and training-of-trainers programs, AEN offers the Artisan Entrepreneur Curriculum, a course on small-business planning and management skills. The pilot phase will take place in Peru, and will expand to other countries.

*Source:* Sánchez, Joo, and Zappala 2001.

FIGURE 5.28

**Microenterprise Access to Finance**

(Use of Credit Services by Type of Lender)

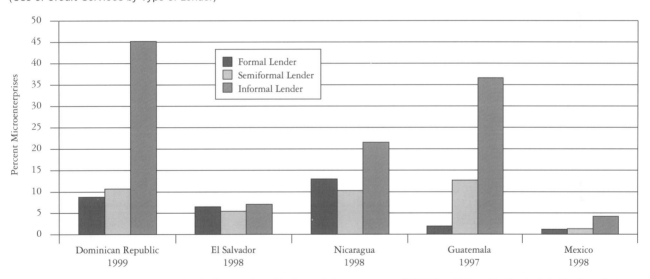

*Note:* Formal lenders include private and public banks, semi-formal lenders include cooperatives and NGOS, and informal lenders include friends & relatives, moneylenders, and supplier credit.
*Source:* Microenterprise surveys in various countries.

available to the worker. (See Table 5.5 for the characteristics of *maquila* free trade zones.) Though perhaps not the best jobs when viewed from afar, many newly created jobs must be considered good for the unskilled workers who are likely to take them when they compare them to existing alternatives. In the case of the often-maligned assembly work in the Dominican Republic or Mexico, the evidence suggests that these jobs pay better than comparable work in those countries, and that they do pay benefits. The work may be repetitive, but young women in Guadalajara, Mexico, appear to prefer them to more traditional jobs such as domestic servants. Some cases, such as migrant farmwork-

ers working in nearby Sayula, offer apparently difficult dilemmas. Working and living conditions are hard. Nonetheless, the indigenous peoples who return yearly know what to expect and, by returning, vote with their feet: they want these jobs. Comparing these jobs to those lost from increased import competition is impossible. What we can say is that, as the first section noted, liberalization appears to have had a positive impact on real wage growth, and that the jobs reviewed here are competitive.

Second, the possible improvements over the short term are circumscribed by some very basic economic relations. Most of these new jobs tend to be in industries with a high

TABLE 5.5

**Characteristics of Maquila/Free Trade Zones**

| CHARACTERISTICS | MEXICO (1997) | COSTA RICA (1997) | DOMINICAN REPUBLIC (1998) | EL SALVADOR (1997) |
|---|---|---|---|---|
| Maquila Proportion of Exports | 41% | 58% | 51.1% | 54% |
| Value of Exports | 1.5% of GDP | 31.2% of GDP | — | 13.4% of GDP |
| Proportion of Total Employment | 3.1% | 3.3% | 6.3% | 1.3% |
| Main Assembly Industries | Electronics, transportation equipment, textiles | Textiles, electronics, other manufacturing, machinery metal | Textiles | Textiles, footwear |

— Not available.

*Sources:* UNIFEM 2000, Fleck 2001, Lizardo and Guzmán 2001, and Monge 2001.

degree of global competition, and the simple Marshall's factor demand relation described in Box 5.8 presents some unpleasant arithmetic that cannot be ignored, no matter how much we wish it were otherwise. Though obviously humans cannot be equated with machines or natural resources, Marshall's simple point is that how much employment in an industry falls with respect to a rise in wages, benefits, or working conditions depends on how easily labor is replaced by other factors, how large a fraction of total costs wages constitute, and how competitive the product market is. If local producers face a high degree of global competition, even modest changes in labor costs can lead to a large decline in employment. Over the longer term, better-paying jobs in better conditions can be achieved only by increasing the skills of the workers, labor productivity, and by encouraging some degree of product differentiation.

Finally, as discussed in the previous chapters, who winds up employed or benefiting from these new jobs to some degree depends on the characteristics of the individual worker. People, like nations, trade based on their comparative advantage. In case after case the striking fact emerges that women have dominated the workforce in emerging industries. This is a pattern that was observed in the industrialized countries as well a century ago, and to some degree it arises because most men were already working, and hence women were the "free agents." But in the EPZs, teleservices, and tourism industries, a range of gender-linked characteristics ranging from dexterity to reliability, and lower incidence of alcoholism, appear to motivate employer choices. This opens the door to wide-ranging discussions of reinforced gender stereotyping and changing

family dynamics as a result of newfound purchasing power that this report can only hint at. The bottom line, however, seems to be that, for the most part, female-dominated jobs tend to represent opportunities, and may have social repercussions beyond the purely economic.

### EPZ Work

Export processing sectors have generated high rates of employment growth and now account for over 6 percent of the workforce in the Dominican Republic, although that percentage is substantially less in Costa Rica, El Salvador, and Mexico.[15] Although EPZ jobs have generated controversy in some countries, the overall impression is that they are good jobs for people with modest skill levels. Fleck (2001) finds that in 1998 *maquila* hourly earnings were 2.6 percent lower than Mexican wage workers in other sectors, but benefits averaged 8 percent more, leaving *maquila* workers ahead. More recently, Brown (2001) finds that women and men who work in *maquilas* earn 38 percent and 31 percent, respectively, more than their counterparts in non-*maquila* manufacturing. Although relative wage data are difficult to find in the Dominican Republic, the Dominican Republic *maquila* workers are in the middle of the income spectrum—neither very rich nor very poor, but with lower rates of extreme poverty than elsewhere (see Figure 5.29).[16] As Box 5.9 suggests, surveys of workers confirm that these are among the better options for these kinds of workers.

The high degree of homogeneity of product, and the strong competition with Asia means that Marshall's fundamental law of labor demand holds ferociously in this indus-

BOX 5.8

## Alfred Marshall Meets Juan Valdez (and Burro)

Beginning from a simple and standard model of how firms work, in 1894 Alfred Marshall derived a simple "fundamental law of factor demand" that describes the relation between employment and the cost of labor:

$$\Delta L = \alpha \Delta w + \eta \, \frac{w * L}{P} \, \Delta w$$

The first term on the right-hand side simply measures the ease of substitution with other factors—machinery, for example. But the second term measures how much a rise in the wage translates into a rise in the cost of the finished product through labor's share in the price of the good. Then $\eta$, the product elasticity of demand, tells by what percent output falls with a 1 percent rise in product price and, hence, proportionally how much demand for labor would fall. When a firm sells a very common object that many people sell—tomatoes, nondescript textiles, or even basic computers, for example—it faces perhaps an almost infinite $\eta$. This means even very small rises in labor costs cause a very large fall in employment.

Two important findings emerge from this. First, in a very competitive industry, efforts to raise labor or environmental standards are either passed down to workers as lower wages, a tradeoff which may or may not be desir-

able, or total labor costs rise and there are large losses in employment. Although Rodrik (1997) argues that trade liberalization, by increasing product elasticities, would exacerbate these effects, Fajnzylber and Maloney (2000) found no impact in Chile and Colombia, and only a small rise in Mexico. This may be because liberalization has not been as complete as thought. But it also might be that Latin American products will find a lower elasticity when exported, and the impact on imported inputs could also lower nontradeables elasticities.

Second, this implies that, over the long term, countries want to find a market niche that gives brand recognition and some differentiation from other products. This lowers $\eta$ so that if their price rises, they do not lose their entire market, or have their footloose leave. Developing brand loyalty is precisely the aim of Juan Valdez and his burro, who are the trademarks of Colombian coffee. Similarly, Brazilian shoes have not yet reached the degree of product differentiation of Italy's Ferragamo or Bruno Magli, but Nine West is now "branded," as are the Mexican beers Corona and Dos Equis. Similarly, if you can convince tourists that "It's better in the Bahamas," an increase in the cost of a tourist package will not send them all running to the neighboring islands.

FIGURE 5.29

## Dominican Republic: Earnings Distribution by Sector; Selected Sectors

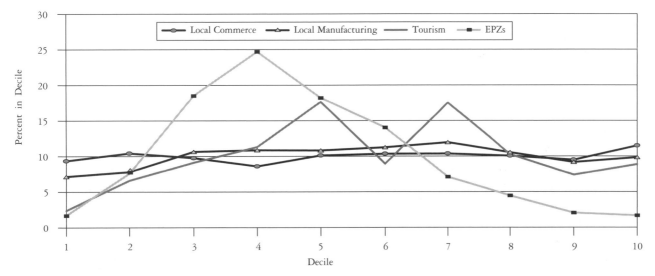

*Source:* Lizardo and Guzmán 2001.

BOX 5.9
**Voices from the Maquila: Is This Exploitation or a Choice?**

To identify the motivations of workers to work in the *maquila* sector, organizational behavior professor John Sargent interviewed 59 production-level workers in Ciudad Juárez and Ciudad Chihuahua in Mexico.

His findings: 74 percent reported the ease of attaining *maquila* work, particularly for those with little education and the lack of attractive opportunity in non-*maquila* jobs; 15 percent replied that they joined because of the indirect benefits, specifically medical insurance; 13 percent cited the better working conditions relative to other options, particularly construction; 30 percent cited *maquila* policies, in particular free Saturdays and Sundays.

Workers were then asked how they rated their jobs relative to their friends and family. His findings: 23 percent said the *maquila* job was better, 56 percent said it was of

similar quality, and 21 percent said that it was worse. A less-skilled worker, however, might still envy jobs that he or she is not qualified to attain. A better measure of true alternatives, then, is a comparison with previous jobs held. These included cashiers, street vendors, construction workers, golf caddies, fieldhands, domestic servants, truckers, and hair cutters. Among women, 65 percent had worked only in *maquilas* compared to 15 percent of men; 57 percent reported that their *maquila* job was better than their previous job, 26 percent said it was the same, and 17 percent said it was worse. In short, for 73 percent of those interviewed, the *maquila* job was as least as good as the alternative.

*Source:* Sargent and Mathews 1999.

try. A very high elasticity of product demand means there is relatively little latitude for raising wages. Electronics producers in Guadalajara report a very slim margin (3 percent including transport) over Malaysia in electronics assembly, and the source of their comparative advantage lies in the ability to respond quickly to customize machines within days, which the Asian manufacturers cannot do. Costa Rica lost many of its low-skilled assembly industries to Mexico's greater proximity and NAFTA. It is not clear that great increases in wages or benefits are feasible in the short term.

But a process of skill upgrading over time seems likely. Again, as mentioned earlier, Feenstra and Hanson (1996) attribute a large fraction of the rising wage dispersion in Mexico to the fact that the parts of the production process being transferred south of the border are skill intensive relative to the jobs already there. Hallberg, Tan, and Koryukin (2000) and Lopez-Acevedo (2001c) suggest that export-oriented firms have been those most likely to adopt new technologies and advances in sophistication in Mexico, and this, in turn, tends to be associated with higher training. The experiences of Costa Rica and Mexico illustrate the potential for deepening and moving into more sophisticated technologies. The fact that Costa Rica has the highest software exports per capita in the region, and that Intel is establishing a center to develop software, suggests that the technological sector will have "roots" in a way that pre-

vious assembly did not. Further, there can be no question that in both Costa Rica and Guadalajara, these jobs, firmly dependent on an open economy, are absolutely good jobs.

It is also clear in both cases that the sine qua non of working at this level is a very educated work force. In Chapter 4 Monje shows that the perception of international investors is that Costa Rica's labor force is far more able than those of other countries in the area. Both he and Rodriguez-Clare (2001) stress the importance of an existing university system with a strong technological focus. This also appears to have greatly influenced the choice of Guadalajara, which, in terms of distance from the border, is not the most obvious choice.

### Who Works in EPZs?

*Maquila* workers tend to be young, slightly better educated than the workforce in general, with some secondary schooling.[17] In both the Dominican Republic and Mexico, workers have roughly a year more education than average, and in the Dominican Republic they have higher literacy rates. In Mexico they also tend to be young, more educated than the labor force in general, and without dependents.

What emerges in this report as a recurring characteristic of new industries is that the *maquila* sector began disproportionately female. The Mexican *maquila* began at 80 percent female, and even having declined to 53.4 percent, is still far above the economywide average share of female employment of 34 percent (see Figure 5.30). In the Dominican Republic the share of female employment in the free trade zone fell from 58 percent in 1994, again compared to an economywide female share of 37 percent. This high participation rate reflects, as always, a combination of demand and supply factors. There was not always an obvious translation of household skills to the industry. Although in the interior of both Mexico and the Dominican Republic, women dominate the textile industry, on the Mexican border women are found in footwear, chemical, machinery, electronics, toys, other manufacturing, and services *maquila* industries. Perhaps of greater relevance is the perception of employers that the temperaments of women are more suited to *maquila*-type work.[18]

On the supply side, the literature suggests several considerations. First, women may prefer *maquila* work because of the combination of relative security (Fussell 2000) and flexibility when needed. High turnover is a result of voluntary exits, not firing, the work shift is unchanging, and workers typically have weekends free (Sargent and Matthews 1999). For working women, especially those with children, this secure source of income and free time, combined with flexibility to enter and exit the industry (UNIFEM 2000) without specialized skills or contacts, allows them to allocate time to both the home and the market, and gives them a rapid source of autonomy (Chant 1991; Sargent and Matthews 1999).[19] This is supported by Brown (2001), who finds a growth in *maquila* participation among women

with young children, which is less observed among men or women in non-*maquila* manufacturing. Second, women may select *maquila* work because it offers higher welfare when taking into consideration all the benefits. There are many additional sources of income or in-kind benefits that workers might value: bonuses for punctuality and two meals daily (UNIFEM 2000). Furthermore, they enjoy sports activities, an onsite nurse, transportation, and other nonwage benefits (Sargent and Matthews 1999; UNIFEM 2000).

Consultations with women's NGOs for this report confirmed the impression that these *are not* considered "bad" jobs, and in fact the concern was raised that the defeminization represented men crowding out women for good jobs. This is difficult to prove or disprove without on-the-ground observation, but Figure 5.31 suggests it is probably not true. There is no correlation between sectors where wages are increasing most rapidly (one measure of job quality) and where women's participation is decreasing. It is more likely that the 80 percent participation rates were simply not sustainable as the industries grew, when average participation rates for women are only around 43 percent compared to 83 percent for men (Fleck 2001). As one supportive anecdote, in Guadalajara desirable jobs in the electronic *maquilas* have grown such that it is essentially impossible to contract domestic help. The traditional reservoir of unskilled labor— young single women—is therefore largely dry.

At the same time, it may be the case that the rise in relative quality of *maquila* jobs to the status of "career" jobs rather than jobs for young, single women may be more

FIGURE 5.30

**Total Maquila Employment and Women's Share in Mexico**

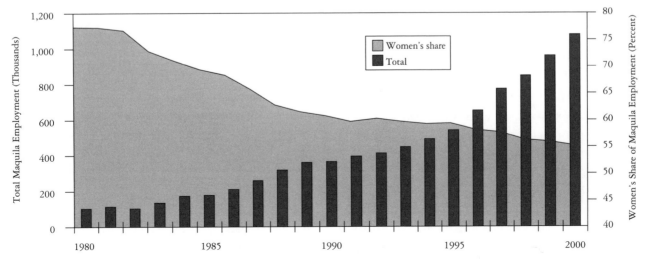

FIGURE 5.31

**Mexico: Change in Wages and Women's Share of Employment in the Maquila Sector, 1980–98**

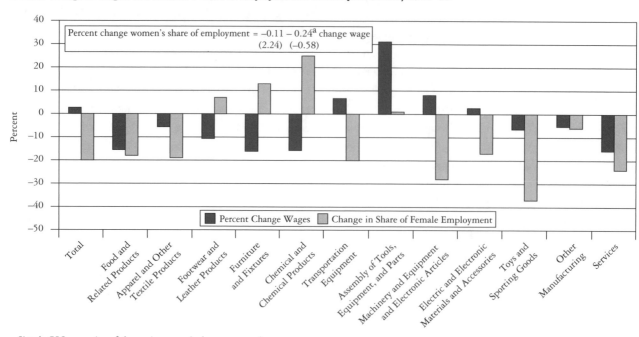

a. Simple OLS regression of change in women's share on wage changes.

attractive to men now than in the past. Increasingly, men with spouses are entering this sector, perhaps because it offers more earnings stability, which breadwinners must offer their families. On the demand side, Kopinak (1995) suggests that employers are shifting their perception of the ideal worker away from young, single women (although their employment in the sector continues to grow) toward men and women with families, who are thought to take their jobs more seriously due to their family responsibilities (UNIFEM 2000). This would be consistent with a greater need for employee stability to train for more sophisticated processes.

*Teleservice Industries*

Data on the emerging long-distance service industries are also sparse, although Pearson (1997) offers a window into the Jamaican data-processing firms. Similar to *maquila* industries, the jobs are low skilled with few options for additional training, a flat promotion structure, and tedious work, thus limiting the jobs as potential careers for all but the small portion who do advance up the narrow job ladder. However, data processing does offer advantages that the more traditional assembly jobs or agriculture do not. First, workers receive some training in technology-related areas, lasting from two weeks to three months, which can be

applied to work in other industries. Second, wages are higher in this sector than in other typically female jobs, such as textile manufacturing, and comparable to manufacturing wages. Since the work is visibly located in offices with a sizeable work force, the workers generally receive all the benefits that accrue to formal sector work.

Processing firms, which compete for contracts on pricing, prefer to hire young women, who constitute 90 percent of the workforce. They tend to have low levels of education, to be young (18 to 19 years old), able to type, and have an aptitude for dealing with technology and the stress of high workloads. Again, Pearson (1997) finds that employers appear to assume that women are more patient, dexterous, and flexible in learning new skills, and hence are more productive at secretarial-type work, and this has led to a high demand for female labor. Furthermore, the high levels of concentration and short turnaround times require young women who do not have household constraints that may limit their time and productivity. However, as demand grows, employers are starting to hire older women.

*Tourism*

Data on job quality in tourism are not easily accessible. Lizardo and Guzmán (2001) find that in the Dominican

Republic far fewer workers are found in the bottom quintiles, most are solidly in the middle of the distribution, and overall the skill level of the industry is high: 32 percent of workers have completed secondary school and 21 percent have completed college, compared to 25 percent and 16.4 percent, respectively, for the economy as a whole. The study of Barbados in Chapter 4 suggests comparable wages in tourism and nontourism sectors. Further, the collected numbers may not include tips, which further push up the relative wage. In addition, it seems possible that over the longer term, wages and job quality can improve. Industrialized countries and wealthy islands, such as Bermuda, have large tourism sectors paying industrialized-country wages. The key, again, however, is to have a sector that offers a differentiated product that attracts travelers, even as the wage, and hence, the cost of the product, rises.

As found in the *maquila* and agricultural sectors, women are often overrepresented in the industry. Chant (1991) finds for Mexico that women's participation in tourism jobs exceeds their overall participation rate by 10 percentage points. Again, as Box 5.10 suggests, jobs may be allocated according to the perceived comparative advantage, which may affect long-term career progress. The relative dominance of women also appears in the Dominican Republic, although men's employment in tourism has been increasing, from 64.4 percent in 1994 to 70 percent by 1999. The roots of the decreasing feminization of the industry are not clear, but the story may be similar to that for the other sectors: where the industry starts with above-average rates of female participation, perhaps due to the availability of untapped female labor, a rapidly expanding industry may almost by definition eventually progressively employ more men.[20]

Tourism employment is also affected by continuing concerns over the environmental sustainability of the industry. The Galapagos Computable General Equilibrium (CGE) model discussed in Chapter 4 also highlights the hard choices implicit in environmental preservation: Reducing tourism by 10 percent would reduce the income of those presently on the island by 7 to 9 percent, with a potentially large increase in poverty.

Finally, unlike other products, tourism is consumed within the host country, and this can generate a microcosm of global income disparities and a sense of being a second-class citizen in one's own country.[21] In the long term, this contradiction is not necessary: Parisians may feel overwhelmed by summer tourists, but they do not feel like aliens in France.

Nonetheless, in the short term, tourism offers a particularly visible reminder of the intrinsic randomness and injustice of the global distribution of wealth and opportunity.

## Nontraditional Agricultural Exports

As discussed in the previous section, concerns about low productivity growth in the nontraditional agricultural exports (NTAE) sector are probably unfounded. However, it is in this area that among the most serious concerns are raised about workers' rights, labor standards, and discrimination. Rural workers have traditionally been among the worst paid, they have lived in the most severe poverty, and social relations retained a feudal flavor well into the 20th century. Employment progress has not always been as fast as would be desired, and work conditions are difficult, as is often the case in the rural areas.[22]

But again, the comparison must be to *alternative* jobs in the local areas, and here the evidence seems to suggest that, overall, the growing NTAE sector offers opportunity. Wages in NTAEs tend to be higher than other wages in rural areas. Women in the flower export sector in Ecuador earn 40 percent more than other rural women, while men earn one-third more than their counterparts in other agricultural work. Further, two-thirds of men and women cite the low risk in terms of wages and employment as an attraction of the sector, and 13 percent of women highlight the benefit of having their own wage (Newman 2000). Similarly, in Chile, both men and women in the fruit-exporting industries earn approximately 50 percent more per day than do workers in non-NTAE jobs in the same locality (Jarvis and Vera-Toscano 2001). These differentials are smaller during the off-season, but the premium to NTAE work largely persists across the production cycle.

This picture seems hard to square with, for instance, the situation of migrant workers in Guadalajara, Mexico, described in Box 5.11, where working conditions are indeed harsh. But again, what is clear is that workers do consider these jobs to be better than their best alternative. Further, as Box 5.11 suggests, it is not clear how much latitude there is for large increases in worker protection or quality. The tomato market is highly competitive and Marshall's law appears strongly binding.

What is missing from such analysis is a total economy view of the impact on the rural poor. Carter, Barham, and Mesbah (1997) study three agricultural export booms and find very different impacts dependent on three factors: (a)

BOX 5.10

**What Do Employers Look For? What Do They See?**

A window into the nature of the demand for labor in the tourism industry is offered by sociologist Sylvia Chant (1991), who studied the tourism industry in Puerto Vallarta, Mexico. She found employers very clear on their perceptions of men's and women's skills and how they fit into their industry (Table 5.6). The hotel industry, virtually by definition, has a high demand for skills traditionally found in the household; hence women tended to work as chambermaids, laundrywomen, and cashiers in small food establishments, and as clerks in souvenir shops, while men tended to work as clerks in more upscale shops, and bellhops, bartenders, doormen, chefs, and waiters in more upscale establishments where strength was more valued and which were more in the traditional domain.

Though this allocation to jobs according to perceived "comparative advantage" has a certain logic, Chant argues that it works against women in two ways. First, the types of jobs that women are in are those without opportunities for vertical or horizontal movement. A chambermaid may become promoted to head maid, but that is the end of her job ladder, while a bartender may become a waiter, a head waiter, and eventually a maître d'. Second, men are in more visible jobs, so that although the legal minimum wages for men's activities such as bellboy, general cleaner, groundsman, or bar attendant were roughly 75 percent of that earned by cooks, chambermaids, or laundryworkers, tips and commissions could dramatically reverse this.

*Source:* Chant 1991: 103.

TABLE 5.6

**Perceptions of Male and Female Employees in the Tourism Sector (in Order of Most Cited)**

| MEN | WOMEN |
|---|---|
| POSITIVE | |
| Greater work experience | Docility |
| Greater physical strength | Reliability |
| Foreign language skills/experience | Punctuality |
| Willingness/ability to work overtime | Flexibility (additional tasks) |
| | Willingness to take orders |
| | Domestic skills |
| | Diligence |
| | Patience |
| | Cooperative disposition |
| NEGATIVE | |
| Drunkenness on the job | Neurotic/temperamental |
| Greater rates of absenteeism (due to idleness/heavy drinking) | Greater rates of absenteeism (due to family problems/pregnancy) |
| Troublemaking (union activity) | Unwillingness/inability to work overtime |
| Dishonesty | Lack of education/experience |
| Impatience | Physical weakness |
| Inflexibility (extra tasks) | Lack of authority (as manager) |
| Unwillingness to do demeaning/female work | |
| Demanding (higher wages) | |
| Resistant to authority (especially female supervisors) | |

*Source:* Chant 1991.

whether small-scale units participate in producing the export crop and can enjoy higher incomes, (b) whether the crop induces a pattern of structural change that systematically improves or worsens the poor's access to land, and (c) whether agricultural exports absorb more or less labor of landless and part-time farming households. In Guatemala

the latest boom in winter-vegetable exports followed an inclusive path. Smallholders took on the production of broccoli and snow peas, and primary export crops were not obviously less labor absorbing than displaced traditional crops. Further, they observe land transferred from larger to smaller farmers that adopted new agricultural products. At

BOX 5.11

### We Don't Want Those Bad Jobs. Or Do We?

Sayula, Jalisco, Mexico lies roughly an hour from Guadalajara, Mexico's Silicon Valley, and it is a major center for the growing tomato export industry. It also offers an important example of the difficulties in raising job quality in an industry where products lack differentiation, capital is easy to move, and hence small increases in labor costs may lead to major declines in employment (see Box 5.8).

In 1999, the Jalisco human rights commission sued Chajoma Industries for human rights violations and won a large settlement against them. Migrant workers were literally housed in old chicken coops and sanitation and health conditions were extreme. However, rather than raising worker conditions, within months Chajoma had left Jalisco. It is reasonable to think, as one human rights worker remarked, that "We don't want those bad jobs anyway."

But the issue is complex. The System for the Integral Development of the Family, jointly with the National Autonomous University of Mexico, interviewed 728 migrant families in the Sayula area as to their reasons for leaving their home areas in Veracruz, Guerrero, and Oaxaca, three of the poorest states in Mexico. Fifty-three percent said they lacked good work; 27 percent said that they needed money; 15 percent wanted to travel to other

places; and 3 percent had no, bad, or contested land. But, importantly, only 1 percent said they were deceived by the contractor who brought them to Jalisco. This, combined with the recurrent seasonal nature of the jobs and well-developed information networks, suggests that migrants knew about the conditions they would find and were so poor as to choose to take the jobs anyway. Losing these jobs arguably worsened their poverty.

The relationships between human rights workers and the remaining plants are cooperative and progress has been made as a result. Firms like Bonanza 2000 have better, although still very basic, facilities, and they forbid the families to put their children in the field. Wages are still low and educational facilities largely absent. But the margin for maneuver is small. Bonanza has extreme competition, not only from other states, but from countries where wages are lower. And the migrants have voted with their feet. They want these jobs. In the long term, the best hope is to raise the skill level of the migrants and make them qualified for better jobs, such as those emerging in the technology industry in Guadalajara. In the short term, the ethical tradeoff is harsh.

*Source:* Jalisco 2000.

the other extreme, small farmers faced severe credit constraints that prohibited them from participating as owners in Paraguay's wheat and soy boom, and the large farms absorbed relatively little labor. The net effect has been largely exclusionary. Finally, participating in Chile's fruit boom also required large capital investments with long gestation periods, factors that precluded small farmers with limited access from participating in the boom. Many small parcel holders, faced with high prices for land and squeezed in traditional crops, simply sold out. On the other hand, the overall employment impact of the boom was large and appears to have largely offset the first impact. Carter, Barham, and Mesbah's (1997) conclusion is twofold. First, there is nothing intrinsically beneficial or harmful to the poor about expanding export-oriented crops. It depends substantially on the crop and the local context. Second, addressing the barriers to credit and information could ensure a more inclusive development of these sectors.

### Women in NTAEs

The agribusiness labor force began as highly feminized and continues to be today. Women make up more than 80 percent of the NTAE work force worldwide (Carr 2000), and Latin America is no exception. Women constitute over two-thirds of the flower-sector workers in Ecuador (Newman, Larreamendy, and Maldonado 2000), more than 50 percent of the temporary workers in the Chilean fruit business, over 80 percent of the Colombian flower sector, 70 percent of Brazilian grape production, and over half of the NTAEs in Costa Rica, Guatemala, and Honduras (Barrientos and others 1999). In Chile, as in the Mexican *maquila* sectors, women were perceived as possessing the dexterity suited to specialized agriculture, and as having experience with household agriculture. They were also perceived as less militant and thus less likely to oppose the new organization of work (assembly line) developed by agribusiness. As a result, women tend to work in caring for plants, harvesting, and preparation for shipping, while men tend to specialize in heavy field work, fumigation, and physically transporting the agricultural products throughout the growth, preparation, and export process (Newman, Larreamendy, and Maldonado 2000; Barrientos and others 1999).[23] But perhaps as important as this comparative advantage, as Jarvis (2001) argues, the growth of the sector was so rapid, and more employment alternatives existed for men in the rural labor markets than for women, so women were the source of available labor for the emerging industries.

Perspectives differ on whether to view often backbreaking and repetitive jobs as providing opportunity for women, or simply a new modality of exploitation. But again, interviews with workers in the Ecuadorian flower industry suggest reasons for working there that are similar to those heard in the *maquila* sector in many ways. Thirty-six percent of interviewed workers felt that the industry offered a stable, dependable income, while 30 percent cited ease of entry (low job-search costs) (Newman, Larreamendy, and Maldonado 2000) in locations where jobs were few and the alternatives for women were local commerce or migration to the city to work as domestic servants and in construction, transport, or small-scale agriculture for men (Newman, Larreamendy, and Maldonado 2000). Additional benefits mentioned were medical services and transportation to the work site, and women cited the benefit of the development of new skills in nondomestic-type activities.

Gender wage differentials are smaller in the NTAEs than in the general rural labor market, but some persist, perhaps due to gender segregation of jobs within the NTAE industry. For example, in the Ecuadorian flower industry, women earn 2 percent less than men per hour, but in the general labor market, they earn only half of men's wages. The existing differential in the NTAEs is attributed to men's segregation in more skilled jobs, such as operating tractors. On the other hand, in the Chilean fruit industry women earn approximately 10 percent more than men, while women working in non-NTAEs earn approximately 10 percent less than men. The higher daily earnings of women is attributed to the high value placed on preparation of the product for market, which is usually done by women, who are assumed to be more cautious with the fruit (Barrientos and others 1999) (see Box 5.12). Finally, as Jarvis (2001) shows, where piecework is the primary form of payment, women actually earn more than men, perhaps because they have longer experience in the sector (seven years compared to four years for men), and they work longer hours.[24]

## Indigenous Groups: How Do They Integrate?

The impact of trade liberalization on indigenous peoples and racial minorities is important, because they are among the poorest in Latin America.[25] The Sayula case highlights, in particular, the relationship between indigenous communities and jobs in the new economy. From the time of the conquest, indigenous groups of the region have suffered discrimination and exploitation. But even if this were not the case, it is doubtful that these communities would be well positioned to take advantage of opportunities that a more open economy might offer. On one hand, there is some room for exploiting a comparative advantage in "cultural" goods. There can be no doubt that access to international markets has vastly expanded demand for traditional products, and almost certainly reduced their product elasticity of demand. Nonetheless, it is also clear that exploiting these global niche markets has not been sufficient to lift these communities out of poverty, and this is partly due to factors which give them a comparative disadvantage in the emerging industries. At the most basic level, only 55 percent of the migrants to Jalisco discussed earlier spoke Castilian; the vast majority speak Nahuatl or Huastelo, and this makes coordination difficult even in the tomato business. As with other indigenous groups, they have among the lowest level of literacy, and the need to put their children in the fields perpetuates low educational attainment. There is simply no possibility that they would have sufficient human capital to work in the Hewlett-Packard or IBM *maquilas* only an hour away from the Jitomate fields.

Nor is it likely that firms will relocate to their home areas, which are often distant, poorly served by infrastructure and schooling facilities, and distant from markets. Viewing indigenous communities as any other "country" seeking to trade, we know from Chapter 2 that these characteristics are unlikely to generate a dynamic modern economy. But further, theory tells us that when factors of production can migrate, it is possible for regions to have "no comparative advantage" and not produce anything for "trade." A study done by the Bolivian Vice-Ministry for Indigenous Affairs of the Ministry of Sustainable Development and the World Bank (1999) applied Porter's "diamond" evaluation strategy to identify the competitiveness of indigenous communities. Despite the possibility of building on biodiversity products, as Figure 5.32 shows, measured along standard dimensions, no pueblo was very competitive, 23 percent were competitive, and 77 percent were either not competitive at all or were only slightly

BOX 5.12

### New Jobs, New Gender Roles

Interviews with men and women working in full-time (Ecuadorian flower NTAEs), seasonal (Chilean fruit NTAEs), and home-based (Guatemalan specialty agriculture) industries suggest that access to new jobs gives women increased bargaining power in the household and alters relations vis-à-vis men, but the degree of change is subject to the permanence of the job.

Interviews with 123 workers in three Ecuadorian flower NTAE zones showed that the steady, well-paid jobs were changing the roles and expectations between men and women, but the changes were at times difficult. In particular, focus groups discussed that at the household level, women with a steady source of income have more decisionmaking power, ranging from how to spend money to the feeling that they have exit options should their spouse or partner treat them badly. Domestic violence is lower in communities where a high percentage of the workforce is in the NTAE sector, and responsibility for reproductive health is higher. However, it should be noted that the propensity to actually leave a spouse or partner is not higher in NTAE regions than non-NTAE regions. In addition, the long work shifts, particularly of women who can work late into the night due to electricity in the packing plants, unlike men in the field who quit when the sun goes down, has shifted some of the domestic burden to men. Those men who also work in the NTAEs share more of the homecare duties with their wives than do men who work elsewhere. They were more likely to see women as equals (though this transformation is incomplete due to the high segregation of jobs by gender in the sector). At the individual level, women who work can better protect their interests. The money earned by women is allocated more toward women's needs and priorities—both expenditures for the household, such as food, clothing, children's needs, and also for herself (Newman 2000).

However, the self-esteem gained through working is partially offset by the feeling of failure to fulfill the role of a woman (Newman 2000). In particular, women and men still feel that women's role is in the household, and some women are unhappy and uncomfortable delegating childcare responsibilities to a relative or a paid daycare center. In fact, 35 percent of women in NTAEs who choose not to work cite "care of the household and children" as the rationale behind their decision.

In contrast, interviews with women and men in the seasonal Chilean fruit-packing NTAE industries reveal that responsibilities in the household and women's decisionmaking power changed less than among full-time Ecuadorian NTAE workers. Although women did make decisions about how to spend the money they earned, often on labor-saving appliances that allow them to work more efficiently in the household, Barrientos (1999) suggests that the home sphere has not evolved in terms of women's new roles and responsibilities as quickly as the market has, and that women's empowerment in the home is questionable because women still work the double shift (although Newman [2000] does not find evidence of a double shift) and identify with a traditional female identity.

Finally, among women working in contract farming, since most work with their husbands (Katz 1995), there is not a notable change in gender roles. Instead, this organization of farming is an extension of the unpaid farming that they did when the farms were not contracted, such that work time, decisionmaking power, and even the decision to work is still decided by the husband. The primary gender impact of this form of farming was that older girls had more household responsibilities so their mothers could work in the fields, but this may be a general trend when there are work opportunities rather than specific to contract farming.

competitive, with scores of under 1.5 on a scale of 3. The challenges are not only of bringing up the level of education and infrastructure. The fact that 75 percent of pueblos were only slightly or not competitive in the use of their primary factor of production, land, also implies a long-term

tradeoff between development and retaining the anchor of traditional society, land.

There are cases where indigenous communities have been able to extensively take advantage of the global market. Indigenous communities in the south of Mexico have

FIGURE 5.32

### Bolivian Highlands: Exports Determinants

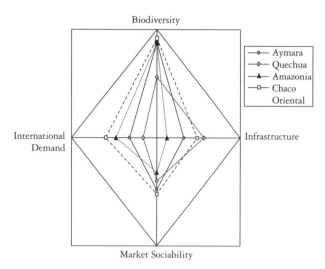

*Note:* Indigenous people of Bolivia. Average of communities index.
*Source:* World Bank 1999.

made progress in developing environmentally sound means of both cultivating and selling coffee on the international market that offers a medium-term horizon for development based precisely on their traditional factor of production.

Nonetheless the obstacles are daunting. As has been shown, despite the vast inflow of FDI in Mexico, virtually none of it has gone to the states with the highest indigenous population, and there is a statistically negative relationship between the percent of the population that speaks an indigenous tongue and FDI. However, if we also compensate for shipping distance to the United States, level of education, and level of urbanization, the indigenous character of the region proves unimportant. It is not being indigenous per se, but the locale and level of education that are important—again, the community's comparative advantage. In fact, Yucatan and Quintana Roo, which are on the Yucatan Peninsula and have ready access by sea to U.S. markets, have higher-than-predicted FDI, suggesting that indigenous language or culture need not be a barrier to participating in emerging industries.

Ironically, these same barriers may have buffered communities somewhat from the heat of international competition. For example, NAFTA and related initiatives call for a gradual (15-year) phaseout of price supports for corn staples. Studies using aggregate computable general equilibrium (CGE) models concluded that, since these products

are not to the comparative advantage of Mexico, a reduction in the government-supported price of corn would decrease rural incomes, employment, and wages, and stimulate a sharp increase in rural outmigration. However, these negative impacts of agricultural policy reforms have not materialized. Despite an 18 percent real drop in the support price for white corn between 1994 and 1997, corn output declined only slightly, from 18.13 million metric tons to 18.02 million metric tons (according to the Mexican Ministry of Agriculture). There is no evidence that rural workers suffered disproportionately from structural reforms in Mexico, or that Mexico-to-U.S. migration increased above its (rising) trend of recent years.

Taylor (2001) argues that the reason for the low impact of the falling prices was precisely that rural *campesino* communities are much more diversified than previously thought, and face very high transaction costs getting their crops to market, making prices locally and not internationally determined. In a sample of 196 households in the central Mexican state of Michoacan, a number of surplus-producing farmers sold their excess production locally, rather than selling to the government at the higher guaranteed price. When asked why, most responded that it was too costly to transport their harvest to the nearest government (Compañía Nacional de Subsistencias Populares, CONASUPO) purchase point, approximately 40 miles away. Others cited cases in which neighbors had paid to transport their maize, only to have it rejected on the grounds that the quality was not sufficiently high or the silo was already full. This added marketing uncertainty, discouraging farmers from selling unless there was a sufficient price spread to cover not only transportation, but also an implicit marketing risk premium. Some farmers complained that, lacking their own vehicles, they would have had to sell to intermediaries at a price below the guaranteed price (reflecting the high transaction costs and marketing risks in this region).

Both diversification and transaction cost effects can be analyzed in a village-level CGE model that, when adjusted to reflect the characteristics of his sample, explains what happened (see Box 5.13). When perfect product integration with the national, and hence international, market was assumed, a massive decline in output of 26 percent appeared, and migration to the United States increased 4 percent. But when prices were determined locally, production actually increased, due to the impacts on consumption of the transfer from the Programa de Apoyos Directos al Campo (PROCAMPO).

BOX 5.13
## Mexico Village-Town CGE Model

The village-town CGE model for Michaocan, Mexico, is really two models—one for the town and the other for the three villages. These two models are linked to each other, especially through trade. Each model has five components: (a) household-farm production, (b) household-farm income, (c) expenditures, (d) a set of general equilibrium closure equations, which ensure that either local markets clear or the village-town is a net buyer ("importer") from or seller ("exporter") of marketed surplus to outside markets, and (e) a price-determination component, which sets village-town prices equal to outside market prices for tradeables. For nontradeables (that is, goods or factors for which high transaction costs isolate the village-town from regional or national markets), local prices are endogenous "equilibrium" prices, at which local supply and demand are in balance. The component behavioral equations are estimated from the village data and the simulations done under two assumptions: that corn prices are determined in national (international) markets, or that transaction costs imply that they are determined locally.

TABLE 5.7
### Estimated Percentage Effects of a 10 Percent Decrease in Grain Prices and Compensating Income Transfer

| VARIABLE | STAPLE PRICE NATIONALLY DETERMINED | STAPLE PRICE LOCALLY DETERMINED (TRANSACTION COSTS) |
|---|---|---|
| Basic Grain Prices | −10.0 | 0.2 |
| Output | | |
|   Staple | −25.7 | 0.7 |
|   Other Crop | 3.5 | −0.1 |
|   Livestock | 4.3 | −0.1 |
| Mexico–U.S. Migration | 0.4 | 0.1 |
| Labor Factor Demand | −1.3 | 0.3 |
|   Wage | −0.1 | 0.0 |
| Village Real GDP | −2.5 | 0.2 |
| Household Real Income | | |
|   Commercial | 0.5 | 1.6 |
|   Subsistence | 1.1 | 0.8 |
| Capital Investment | −0.5 | 1.1 |
| Marketed Surplus | 247.7 | — |

— Not available.

*Source:* Taylor 2001 and Yúnez-Naude and Dyer 1999.

The lesson is, then, that the poor infrastructure, geographical distance, and even cultural norms that often isolate indigenous communities prevent ready access to the new opportunities offered by the global marketplace, but also gives them time to adjust to competition on the import side. This time can be used to both raise the quality of education and to think through appropriate strategies of growth that maintain, to whatever degree possible, cultural integrity.

## Conclusion: How Can We Continue to Raise Job Quality?

Over the short term many observers have focused on the issue of labor standards. This is a complex issue that this report can only touch on by noting some of the parameters of the debate and what the available evidence suggests about their impact on trade patterns. As has been stressed throughout, the ability to raise job-quality wages, benefits, and job environment is circumscribed by the productivity of workers and Marshall's law of labor demand. The labor standards debate overlaps greatly with the debate examining the impact of other labor market distortions or rigidities.

On the second point, the evidence is highly ambiguous. Mah (1997) shows that developing countries that ratify International Labour Organisation conventions have lower exports as a share of GDP than those that do not. He then interprets this as evidence that these developing countries lose part of their comparative advantage as they become more similar to their industrialized trading partners. Van Beers (1998) somewhat counterintuitively concludes that strict labor standards, such as those prevalent in OECD countries, disproportionately affect skilled labor by reducing skilled-labor-intensive exports. Rodrick (1996) shows that more rigid regulation increases the cost of labor and therefore diminishes a country's comparative advantage in labor-intensive goods. As numerous authors have noted, such results are hard to interpret anyway since there is often a correlation between high labor standards and other interventions, such as industrial policies or other distortions. (See Rama and Tabellini 1992 and Kuruvilla 1996.)

Having said this, however, it is important to point out that, with the exception of Rodrick (1996), the studies discussed above use exports as a share of GDP or some other macroeconomic measure as their dependent variable.[26] This implies that, while we can conclude that stricter labor standards have little effect on the overall trading performance of developing countries, this tells us little about the effect that they may have on other variables of interest.

Probably of more relevance is the emerging literature on the employment impacts of various labor market interventions. Numerous studies in the region suggest that labor market interventions have costs—those benefiting do better, but jobs may be lost. As only one example, recent work on minimum wages by Fajnzylber (2001a) in Brazil and Maloney and Nunez (2001) in Colombia, does find important negative employment effects of raising minimum wages. Pages and Heckman (2000), for example, also find adverse employment effects of firing restrictions. In a world where labor-cost differences across competing developing countries are fairly small (for example, the difference in labor costs between Malaysia and Mexico is a mere 3 percent), a moderate increase in labor costs may lead firms to substitute labor for capital, or to substitute across different types of labor in order to maintain their competitive edge.

Where the interest in labor standards goes beyond simple analysis of labor market interventions is in the debate about whether they should be set globally. Some of the sentiment in favor of global standards arises from highly publicized cases of treatment of workers in export processing plants. On average, this appears to be overstated. As this chapter suggests, for example, EPZs do not pay below comparable wages in the country and tend to pay benefits. As Box 5.14 suggests, this appears to be more the rule than the exception in much of the world. The related concern, however, is that transnational firms can play one country off another to reduce wage and benefits costs. At some level, this is not a

problem. Below some total package of remuneration, firms cannot attract workers. It may be more of an issue where labor protections force total remuneration above market clearing and the transnational bargaining undermines insider benefits. More generally, this concern has manifested itself through the idea that the large informal sectors are, de facto, workers stripped of these benefits. As this chapter suggests, this very commonly cited scenario is not, in fact, prevalent in the region.

Of greater concern is who gets to set the labor standards. Latin American governments have been suspicious of labor side clauses to trade agreements. This is because higher legislated workplace quality or benefits that do not cause unemployment necessarily diminish the fraction of total remuneration paid in wages. There is no guarantee that regionally or globally set standards about the composition of benefits will reflect local worker or local preferences. More fundamentally, however, the concern is the potential for abuse as trade barriers in the industrialized countries.

In any case these proposed measures can make only marginal changes in worker welfare. Historically, the only way to raise living standards in a sustained fashion is through

---

BOX 5.14

**Labor Standards in EPZs**

It is commonly argued that labor standards are most likely to be ignored in EPZs to increase competitiveness. However, Romero (1995) points out that EPZs generally pay higher wages and offer better working conditions than the rest of the economy because (a) they pay productivity incentive bonuses (for example, piece rates) and overtime; (b) they tend to be larger, and usually pay scales and working conditions are correlated with firm size, perhaps because large firms are easier to monitor and regulate than smaller ones; (c) most foreign-owned firms apply their domestic "best-practice" codes in all their branches; and (d) the government often regulates higher minimum wages for firms in this sector.

Exceptions, nevertheless, can occur in those cases where monitoring procedures are lax or union rights restricted. This opens the case for government monitoring and international coordination.

*Source:* Romero 1995.

increasing labor productivity—workers can be paid more if they produce more. As this report has argued, the challenge of raising productivity is a multidimensional one involving measures to accelerate capital formation, innovation, and the adoption of foreign technologies, and those to increase the human capital of the workforce. Swedish labor unions understand the fundamental fact that Swedish forestry workers earn more than those in Brazil and Chile not because of labor legislation, but because of a higher degree of mechanization combined with dynamic knowledge clusters that encourages constant innovation and increasing labor productivity. The process of raising job quality is thus the process of development.

## Notes

1. In LAC, we can find a slightly positive correlation between unemployment and openness, but it is highly dependent on just a few small, open economies such as Barbados, Trinidad and Tobago, and Nicaragua, and is sensitive to specification. For example, if we adjust openness for the fact that small countries are inherently more open, the relationship reverses.

2. This section is based on Maloney and Montes Rojas (2001).

3. See Abuhadba and Romaguera (1993) for Brazil, Chile, and the United States; Marquez (1990) for the República Bolivariana de Venezuela; and Krebs and Maloney (1999) for Mexico.

4. See Galiani, Arim, and Pantano (2001) for Argentina; Santamaria (2000) for Colombia; Robbins (1994) for Chile; Robbins and Gindling (1999) for Costa Rica; Cragg and Epelbaum (1996) for Mexico; Acosta and Montes Rojas (2001), and Sanguinetti and others (2001b) for Uruguay.

5. The reduction of wage differentials of medium-skilled to completely unskilled workers dominates the unequalizing effect of tertiary education and produced a net reduction of 2.5 points of the Gini between 1988 and 1996. If the returns to tertiary education had remained at the 1988 level (that is, 19 percent instead of 23.9 percent), the total reduction of wage inequality due to changes in returns to education would have been 2 more percentage points of the Gini. Moreover, if returns to education had fallen to U.S. levels (13 percent), the additional reduction in wage inequality due to change in returns would have been twice as large.

6. The arguments from the small-firm-dynamics literature suggest a higher variance or volatility of earnings among the self-employed (businesses can be driven out of the market). The selection process for survival in the self-employed sector typically leads to a broader distribution of earnings for any given level of human capital, compared to what would be obtained if workers were all salaried with non-stochastic and smoothly increasing wages. This leads to higher levels of inequality in the self-employment sector. It also implies that standard wage regressions will have less explanatory power in the self-employment sector, as found by Rees and Shah (1986) and Bor-

jas and Broners (1989). In fact, Rees and Shah in the United Kingdom find no significant relationship between self-employed earnings and human capital variables. Their regressions included far more than the basic human capital variables, which prevents a straightforward comparison of their explanatory power in the various sectors.

7. The countries included were Argentina, Brazil, Chile, Colombia, Costa Rica, Mexico, and Peru.

8. Conceptual and statistical definitions of the informal sector are not as clear-cut as one might expect because of its characteristically diverse and complex nature. In this section, the informal sector includes three groups of workers: (a) employers who hire at most 15, or in most cases less than five, paid workers, with or without apprentices; (b) self-employed workers who own and operate one-person businesses alone or with the help of unpaid workers, generally family members, and apprentices; and (c) employees in these microfirms regardless of their degree of protection. Alternative definitions of the informal sector focus on the issue of "protectionism," and thus include owners or workers in firms of fewer than 15 employees who do not have social security or medical benefits.

9. Cunningham and Maloney 2001 employ cluster and factor analysis to identify a typology of informal microentrpreneurs in Mexico.

10. Fiess, Fugazza, and Maloney (2000) use a multivariate Johansen approach (Johansen 1988) to explore cointegration relationships in relative earnings, relative sector size, and the real exchange rate, and formulate hypotheses to identify the degree of segmentation in the labor market in Brazil, Colombia, and Mexico. Positive comovements between relative wages and sector sizes is attributed to segmentation, while negative comovements of relative wages and sector sizes is classified as integration. Different labor market regimes are empirically identified with the LR-test on the coefficients of the cointegration vectors. The period under consideration runs from 1985:Q1 to 1999:Q2 for Colombia, from 1987:Q1 to 1999:Q1 for Mexico, and from 1992:Q1 to 1998:Q2 for Brazil. For Mexico the test of integrated markets cannot be rejected prior to 1995. For Brazil, the hypothesis of integration cannot be rejected and the hypothesis of segmentation is rejected at the 1 percent level. For Colombia, the hypothesis of segmentation cannot be rejected, while the hypothesis of integration can be. In all three cases, however, tests of the stability of the cointegration space suggest the possibility of different relationships in different subperiods. This finding is consistent with the argument that rigidities in the formal sector may bind in some periods and not in others, depending on the macroeconomic environment.

11. These strategies include augmentation of the diversity of products and innovation; reduction of the costs of inputs, labor, raw materials, and other supply goods; networking and forming linkages horizontally or vertically; switching product lines; training employees to be more efficient and managers to be more effective; marketing; and increasing the quality and customization of services (product differentiation).

12. Barton and Bear (1999) advocate business models that provide basic sets of standardized services to a broadly targeted market that can be augmented at relatively little additional cost; such models can be commercially viable and cost-effective, and increasingly

profitable as more consumers become aware of the gains of telecommunications and information services.

13. Lack of detailed microdata on firms is probably a major reason why banks have not developed large portfolios of small-firm loans. First, developing credit information registries, which provide rapid access to standard information on borrower behavior from a variety of sources, such as lenders and utility companies, and making borrower credit history available to all lenders, allows sorting potential borrowers at low cost and reduces adverse selection problems (Galindo and Miller 2001). Credit registries may provide additional incentives for timely repayment because they allow borrowers to create a "reputation collateral" in credit markets as good credit risk. Using credit-scoring technologies, banks can take advantage of such information to assess the risk and profitability of microfirm loans. In the United States, credit scoring is already allowing large banks to expand into small-business lending (Mester 1997). Second, a potentially important step would be reforming aspects of the legal and institutional framework. Movable assets (equipment, machinery, inventories, livestock, and accounts receivable), which constitute the bulk of microfirm capital, had very limited capacity to carry debt. These assets represented most of the aggregate value of assets of Mexican microfirms, for example. However, present legislation unduly restricts the use of movable assets to secure credit transactions (Holden 1996; Fleisig 1995). Further, in some cases, microfirm owners cannot pledge land and buildings as collateral because of unclear property rights.

14. Using bank data, Clarke and others (2001) find that during the 1990s in Argentina, Chile, Colombia, and Peru, lending by all types of banks to small businesses generally shrank. However, after controlling for other factors that might affect lending, large foreign banks actually appear to lend more to small businesses (as a share of total lending) than large domestic banks in two of the four case study countries, Chile and Colombia. Finally, one of the most interesting findings of the authors is that public banks do not appear to surpass private banks in the extent to which they lend to small businesses, suggesting that privatization of public banks would not obviously hurt small businesses.

15. Employment in the *maquila* sector is growing, but less rapidly than employment in non-*maquila* manufacturing. Between 1980 and 1990, when the *maquila* industry experienced its highest employment growth in both countries, *maquila* employment grew by 273 percent in Mexico and 692 percent in the Dominican Republic. This compares to non-*maquila* manufacturing employment growth of 780 percent in Mexico. Employment growth slowed to 101 percent by 1990–97 in Mexico, and 40.2 percent in the Dominican Republic, but non-*maquila* manufacturing growth in Mexico was 237 percent over the same period.

16. Only 4.4 percent of all workers in EPZs and tourism come from poor households, while this number is 18 percent for those in other sectors. Due to the lack of information on household income net of the worker's wage, or on whether the worker is the primary earner in the family, we need to be cautious in interpreting this difference in poverty rates as a result of employment in EPZs and tourism. Lizardo and Guzmán (2001) show that this relationship

holds econometrically. They also point out that areas with a relatively strong presence of EPZs and tourism exhibit lower unemployment and illiteracy rates.

17. Literacy rates are higher—only 3 percent of *maquila* workers in the Dominican Republic are illiterate, compared to 14.6 percent of workers in the rest of the economy. On average, workers have some secondary education in both countries, and approximately one more year of education than workers in the rest of the economy. Most of the difference is in the lower incidence of workers with no education—only 1.3 percent compared to 9.4 percent for the economy as a whole—and lower rates of college graduation—7.6 percent compared to 16 percent for the economy overall. Primary and secondary education are correspondingly higher.

18. In their interviews, Sklair (1989) and Tiano (1994) found that employers perceived women as "docile and dexterous," and that these traits were more suitable to a highly competitive, repetitive assembly process.

19. The industries that women dominate are not necessarily the lowest paying. Assembly of tools is the highest-paying industry, especially for men, who are overrepresented in the sector, especially in the nonborder areas. However, machinery, transportation, and electronics also pay well, all industries where women dominate. Furthermore, 65 percent of working women are in these industry groups. The lowest-paying industries are food and textiles, where women dominate in the nonborder region, with over 50 percent of women in these categories, but it is mixed on the border, where only 8 percent of women work in these industries. Regardless of the industry, though, men earn more than women (Figure 5.31). The differential is greatest in the tools industry, with an average of 92 percent for the whole *maquila* industry.

20. The decreasing share of women in tourism is a double-edged sword, though. On one hand, these jobs reinforce women's stereotypes, since they are highly domestic and provide fewer labor market opportunities for women than do production jobs, where there are promotion ladders. On the other hand, the seasonality of the jobs and the lack of discrimination based on household structure may give women flexibility to work in both the market and the home. Furthermore, any income earning by women (in any industry) will increase their decisionmaking powers (Chant 1991).

21. See, for example, "Alien" lyrics by Rohan Seon, sung by the Mighty Pep (1994 Saint Lucia Carnival King Winner).

22. In the Ecuadorian flower industry, for example, nearly 70 percent of male workers complain of the danger of the insecticides that are heavily used on the crops, both during the planting season and for shipping. Women in the same industry recognize the danger of men's work with chemicals (64 percent), but they themselves primarily complain of repetitive tasks and remaining on their feet throughout the work shift, which can last up to 16 hours. Similar complaints are heard in the Chilean fruit industry. However, some workers say they prefer the cleanliness and orderliness of the packing plants to alternative job arrangements (Barrientos and others 1999).

23. The assignation of tasks by gender is a natural extension of the work done on the home farms and in the domestic sphere. For

example, Katz (1995) likens the training of vines to weaving, thus making this task a feminine task.

24. It is not clear whether men or women have a comparative advantage in NTAEs. Although the sector started out being heavily represented by women, the change in land policies and the fewer options available for rural employment (except migration) have led to an increase of men in this employment. Since men and women are sorted into tasks in NTAEs based on physical characteristics (such as strength), assumed characteristics (such as dexterity), and gender biases (such as employing men only in chemicals), only the first, which is a small group of NTAE jobs, points toward a clear comparative advantage. It is hard to document that, in fact, women are indeed more careful and thus better able to prepare fruit for export, for example. However, as long as this bias exists, women will have a comparative advantage in the well-paid Chilean fruit industry. However, the organization of production is highly constraining for women (long, exhausting shifts, nowhere to care for children, unable to go home for lunch) who still have home duties, making further partici-pation in these jobs difficult for women, even as men are taking over some of the homecare burdens.

25. Using household-level data for several countries, Wodon and others (2001a) show that belonging to an indigenous population leads to a reduction in per capita income, even after controlling for other household characteristics. In Guatemala, the negative impact of being indigenous represents about 15 percent of per capita income. In Bolivia, households not speaking Spanish or a foreign language also tend to be poorer. This is the case for Quechua and Aymara speakers, but the impact is not significant for rural households speaking Guarani. In Brazil, black (Preta) and ethnically mixed (Parda) groups face a reduction in income of about 10 to 20 percent when compared to otherwise similar white households. These results suggest that there may be some level of discrimination in labor markets against indige-nous populations or specific ethnic groups depending on the country, so that assessing the impact of trade liberalization on these groups is all the more important since they are already at a disadvantage.

26. Rodrick (1997) uses labor cost per worker in manufacturing.

# Bibliography

The word *processed* describes informally reproduced works that may not be commonly available through libraries.

Abuhadba, Mario, and Pilar Romaguera. 1993. "Interindustrial Wage Differentials: Evidence from Latin American Countries." *Journal of Development Studies* 30 (1): 190–206.

Acosta, Pablo, and Gabriel V. Montes Rojas. 2001. "Trade Reform, Technical Change and Inequality: The Case of Mexico and Argentina in the 90's." World Bank, Washington, D.C.

Amsden, Alice H., and Takashi Hikino. 1994. "Staying Behind, Stumbling Back, Sneaking Up, Soaring Ahead: Late Industrialization in Historical Perspective." In William J. Baumol, Richard R. Nelson and Edward N. Wolff, eds., *The Convergence of Productivity, Its Significance, and Its Varied Connotations*. Oxford and New York: Oxford University Press.

Arellano, Manuel, and Stephen Bond. 1991. "Some Tests of Specification for Panel Data: Monte Carlo Evidence and an Application to Employment Equations." *Review of Economic Studies* 5: 277–97.

Armington, Paul S. 1969. "A Theory of Demand for Products Distinguished by Place of Production." *International Monetary Fund Staff Papers* 16 (1): 159–78.

Aroca, Patricio. 2001. "Impacts and Development in Local Economies Based on Mining: The Case of the Chilean II Region." *Resource Policy* 27: 119–34.

Aroca, Patricio, and William F. Maloney. 2001. "A Note on the Determinants of FDI in Mexico: Distance, Education and Ethnicity." World Bank, Washington, D.C. Processed.

Arriagada, Irma. 1998. *The Urban Female Labour Market in Latin America: The Myth and the Reality*. Serie Mujer y Desarrollo #21. Economic Commission for Latin America and the Caribbean, Chile.

Baer, Werner. 1969. *The Development of the Brazilian Steel Industry*. Nashville, Tenn.: Vanderbilt University Press.

_____. 2001. *The Brazilian Economy. Growth and Development*. 5th Edition. Westport, Conn.: Praeger Publishers.

Balán, Jorge, Harley L. Browning, and Elizabeth Jelin. 1973. *Men in a Developing Society. Geographic and Social Mobility in Monterry, Mexico*. The Institute of Latin American Studies. Austin and London: University of Texas Press.

Balassa, Bela. 1964. "The Purchasing Power Parity Doctrine: A Reappraisal." *Journal of Political Economy* 72 (December): 584–96.

_____. 1989. "'Revealed' Comparative Advantage in Japan and the United States." *Journal of International Economic Integration* 4: 8–22.

Balassa, Bela, and Luc Bauwens. 1988. *Changing Trade Patterns in Manufactured Goods: An Econometric Investigation*. Amsterdam: North-Holland.

Baldwin, Richard, and Harry Flam. 1989. "Strategic Trade Policies in the Market for 30–40 Seat Commuter Aircraft." *Weltwirtschaftliches Archiv* (125): 484–500.

Barham, B., M. Clark, E. Katz, and R. Schurman. 1992. "Nontraditional Agricultural Exports in Latin America." *Latin America Research Review* 11 (26): 43–82.

Barrientos, Stephanie, Anna Bee, Ann Matear, and Isabel Vogel. 1999. *Women and Agribusiness: Working Miracles in the Chilean Fruit Export Sector*. London: Macmillan Press.

Barro, Robert J., and Xavier Sala-i-Martin. 1995. *Economic Growth*. New York: McGraw Hill, Inc.

Barton, Clifton, and Marshall Bear. 1999. "Information and Communications Technologies: Are They the Key to Viable Business Development Services for Micro and

Small Enterprises?" Microenterprise Best Practices Project, USAID, www.mip.org/pubs/mbp/ict.htm. Washington, D.C.

Basu, K. 1998. "Child Labor: Cause, Consequence and Cure, with Remarks on International Labor Standards." World Bank Policy Research Working Paper No. 2027. Washington, D.C.

Baumol, William J., Richard R. Nelson, and Edward N. Wolff, eds. 1994. *The Convergence of Productivity, Its Significance, and Its Varied Connotations.* Oxford and New York: Oxford University Press.

Becker, Gary S., and Kevin M. Murphy. 1992. "The Division of Labor, Coordination Costs, and Knowledge." *The Quarterly Journal of Economics* 106 (4): 1137–60.

Behrman, Jere, Miguel Szekely, and Nancy Birdsall. 2001. "Economic Reforms and Wage Differentials in Latin America." Paper presented at the Poverty and Applied Micro Seminar Series. World Bank, Washington, D.C.

Bergman, Edward M., and Edward J. Feser. 2001. *Industrial and Regional Clusters: Concepts and Comparative Applications.* Regional Research Institute, West Virginia University, West Virginia.

Berlinski, J. 1998. *El Sistema de Incentivos en Argentina.* Instituto Torcuato Di Tella, Serie Documentos de Trabajo. Buenos Aires, Argentina.

Bernard, A., and C. I. Jones. 1996. "Productivity Across Industries and Countries: Time Series Theory and Evidence." *Review of Economics and Statistics* 78 (1): 135–46.

Bernardes, Roberto. 2001. "Redes de Inovação e Cadeias produtivas Globais: Impactos da Estratégia de Competição da Embrear no Arranjo Aeronáutico da Região de São José dos Campos." Fundação SEADE, São Paulo. Processed.

Bils, Mark. 1984. "Tariff Protection and Production in the Early U.S. Cotton Textile Industry." *Journal of Economic History* 44 (4): 1033–45.

Blom, Andreas, and Carlos Eduardo Vélez. 2001. "The Dynamics of the Skill-Premium in Brazil; Growing Demand and Insufficient Supply?" Background paper to World Bank report on Inequality in Brazil. Washington, D.C.

Blom, Andreas, Dorte Verner, and Holm-Nielsen. 2001. "Education, Earnings and Inequality in Brazil 1982–1998; Implications for Education Policy." World Bank Policy Research Working Paper. Washington, D.C.

Blom, Andreas, Pinelopi Koujianou Goldberg, Nina Pavcnik, and Norbert Schady. 2000. "Trade Liberalizations and Industry Wage Differentials in Brazil." Dartmouth College and World Bank, Washington, D.C. Processed.

Blomström, Magnus, and Ari Kokko. 2001. "From Natural Resources to High-Tech Production: The Evolution of Industrial Competitiveness in Sweden and Finland." Stockholm School of Economics. Stockholm, Sweden. Processed.

Blomström, Magnus, and Patricio Meller. 1991a. *Diverging Paths: Comparing a Century of Scandinavian and Latin American Development.* Washington, D.C.: Inter-American Development Bank.

———. 1991b. "Issues for Development: Lessons from Scandinavia—Latin Comparisons." In Magnus Blomström and Patricio Meller, eds., *Diverging Paths: Comparing a Century of Scandinavian and Latin American Development.* Washington, D.C.: Inter-America Development Bank.

Bond, Eric. 2001. "Trade Structure and Development: The Role of Logistics Costs in Latin American Countries." Department of Economics, Penn State University. University Park, Penn. Processed.

Bonelli, Regis, and Renato Fonseca. 1998. "Ganhos de produtividade e de eficiência: novos resultados para a economia brasileira." *Pesquisa e Planejamento Economico* (Brazil), 28 (2): 273–314.

Borjas, George J., and Stephen G. Bronars. 1989. "Consumer Discrimination and Self-Employment." *Journal of Political Economy* 97 (3): 581–605.

Borrus, Michael, and John Zysman. 1997. "You Don't Have to Be A Giant: How the Changing Terms of Competition in Global Markets are Creating New Possibilities for Danish Companies." Danish Research Unit for Industrial Dynamics Working Paper No. 97-5. Aalborg, Denmark.

Bouzas, Roberto. 1996. "Mercosur y Liberalización Comercial Preferencial en América del Sur: Resultados, Temas y Proyecciones." In Richard G. Lipsey and Patricio Meller, eds., *Western Hemisphere Trade Integration: A Canadian–Latin American Dialogue.* International Political Economy Series. New York: St. Martin's Press.

Brome, Pearson. 2001. "Information Services: Integrating into the World Economy." University of the West Indies. Processed.

Brown, Cynthia J. 2000. "The Impact of Foreign Direct Investment on Small Business and Employment Formation in Mexico." Unpublished dissertation. University of Texas Pan American, Edinburg, Tex.

_____. 2001. "Gender in Mexico's Maquila Industry." World Bank, Washington, D.C. Processed.

Brown, Drusilla K. 2000. "International Trade and Core Labor Standards. A Survey of the Recent Literature." Medford, Mass.: Tufts University. Processed.

Brown, Drusilla K., Alan V. Deardorff, and Robert M. Stern. 2000. "U.S. Trade and Other Policy Options and Programs to Deter Foreign Exploitation of Child Labor." Tufts University, Working Paper. Medford, Mass.

Brulhart, Marius. 1994. "Marginal Intra-Industry Trade: Measurement and Relevance for the Pattern of Industrial Adjustment." *Weltwirtschaftliches Archiv* 130 (3): 600–13.

Buffington, Robert M., and William French. 1999. "The Culture of Modernity." In Michael C. Meyer and William Beezley, eds., *The Oxford History of Mexico*. Oxford: Oxford University Press.

Burki, S. Javed, and Guillermo E. Perry. 1997. *The Long March: A Reform Agenda for Latin America and the Caribbean in the Next Decade*. Washington, D.C.: World Bank.

Burki, S. Javed, Guillermo E. Perry, and Sara Calvo, eds. 1997. "Towards Open Regionalism." World Bank, Washington, D.C.

Cárdenas, Enrique. 1997. "A Macroeconomic Interpretation of Nineteenth-Century Mexico." In David Canning, 1999, "Infrastructure's Contribution to Aggregate Output." Policy Research Working Paper No. 2246. World Bank, Washington, D.C.

Carr, Marilyn, Martha Chen, and Jane Tate. 2000. "Globalization and Home-Based Workers." *Feminist Economics* 6 (3): 123–42.

Carter, Michael R., Bradford L. Barham, and Dina Mesbah. 1997. "Agricultural Export Booms and the Rural Poor in Chile, Guatemala and Paraguay." *Latin American Research Review* 31 (1): 33–65.

Casanueva Reguart, Cristina, and Flor Brown Grossman. 2000. "Globalization and Industrial Restructuring in Mexico: The Cases of the Automobile and Electronic Industries." Mexico: Instituto Tecnológico y de Estudios Superiores de Monterrey. Mexico City Campus, Mexico. Processed.

Chant, Sylvia. 1991. *Women and Survival in Mexican Cities*. Manchester: Manchester University Press.

Chen, Martha, Jenifer Sebstad, and Leslie O'Connell. 1999. "Counting the Invisible Workforce: The Case of Home-Based Workers." *World Development* 27 (3): 603–10.

Christen, Robert P. 2000. "Commercialization and Mission Drift: The Transformation of Microfinance in Latin America." Consultative Group to Assist the Poorest. Occasional Paper. World Bank, Washington, D.C.

Clark, Don P., and Denise Stanley. 1999. "Determinants of Intra-Industry Trade Between Developing Countries and the United States." *Journal of Economic Development* 24 (2): 79–94.

Clarke, George, Robert Cull, Maria Soledad Martinez Peria, and Susana M. Sánchez. 2001. "Bank Lending to Small Businesses in Latin America: Does Bank Origin Matter?" Paper to be presented at the Latin America and the Caribbean Economic Association 2001.

Clert, C., and Quentin Wodon. 2001. "The Targeting of Government Programs in Chile: A Quantitative and Qualitative Assessment." *Cuadernos de Economia*.

Collier, Paul, and Anke Hoeffler. 1998. "Greed and Grievance in Civil War." World Bank Policy Research Paper No. 2355. Washington, D.C.

Conning, Jonathan. 2001. "Latifundia Economics." Department of Economics, Williams College. Williamstown, Mass. Processed.

Cooper, David P. 2001. "Innovation and Reciprocal Externalities: Information Transmission via Job Mobility." *Journal of Economic Behavior & Organization* 45: 403–25.

Cord, C., and Quentin Wodon. 2001. "Do Mexico's Agricultural Programs Alleviate Poverty? Evidence from the Ejido Sector." *Cuadernos de Economia*, 114: 239–56.

Corden, W. Max. 1972. "Economies of Scale and Customs Union Theory." *Journal of Political Economy* 80 (3): 465–75.

Cortes Conde, Roberto. 1985. "Some Thoughts on the Industrial Development of Argentina and Canada in the 1920s." In D. C. M. Platt and Guildo di Tella, eds., *Argentina, Australia and Canada: Studies in Comparative Development, 1870–1965*. London: MacMillan Press, 149–60.

Cragg, Michael Ian, and Mario Epelbaum. 1996. "Why Has Wage Dispersion Grown in Mexico? Is It the Incidence of Reforms or the Growing Demand for Skills?" *Journal of Development Economics* 51 (1): 99–116.

Cuddington, John T., Rodney Ludema, and Shamila A. Jayasuriya. 2001. "Prebisch-Singer Redux." Georgetown University/World Bank. Washington, D.C. Processed.

Cunningham, Wendy. 2000. "Latin America and the Caribbean Gender Database." Forthcoming.

Cunningham, Wendy, and William F. Maloney. 2001. "Heterogeneity Among Mexico's Micro-Enterprises: An Application of Factor and Cluster Analysis." Policy Research Working Paper No. 1999. World Bank, Washington, D.C.

Cunningham, Wendy, and Carlos Ramos. 2001. "The Home as the Factory Floor." Draft. World Bank, Washington, D.C.

Dade, Carlo. 2001. "Approaches to Increasing the Productive Value of Remittances." Inter-American Foundation, Washington D.C.

Dagnino, Renato. 1993. "Competitividade da Indústria Aeronáutica." ECIB–Estudo da Competitividade da Indústria Brasileira." Nota Técnica Setorial. Available at: http://www.mct.gov.br/publi/Compet/Default.htm.

De Ferranti, David, Guillermo Perry, Indermit S. Gill, and Luis Servén, with Francisco H. G. Ferreira, Nadeem Ilahi, William F. Maloney, and Martin Rama. 2000. Securing Our Future in a Global Economy. Washington, D.C.: World Bank.

de Soto, Hernando. 1989. The Other Path: The Invisible Revolution in the Third World. New York: Harper and Row Publishers.

Deardorf, Alan V. 1994. "Exploring the Limits of Comparative Advantage." Weltwirtschaftliches Archiv 130 (1): 1–18.

_____. 1984. "Testing Trade Theories and Predicting Trade Flows." Chapter 10 in R. W. Jones and P. B. Kenen, eds., Handbook of International Economics, Volume 1, International Trade. Amsterdam: North Holland.

Dehem, Robert. 1962. "The Economics of Stunted Growth." Canadian Journal of Economics and Political Science 28: 502–510.

Devlin, Robert, and Ricardo French-Davis. 1999. "Towards an Evaluation of Regional Integration in Latin America in the 1990s." World Economy 22: 261–90.

Di Tella, Guildo. 1985. "Rents, Quasi Rents, Normal Profits and Growth: Argentina and the Areas of Recent Settlement." In D. C. M. Platt and Guildo di Tella, Argentina, Australia and Canada: Studies in Comparative Development, 1870–1965. London: MacMillan Press, pp. 19–37.

Djankov, Simeon, Rafael La Porta, Florencio Lopez-de-Silanes, and Andrei Shleifer. 2000. "The Regulation of Entry." National Bureau of Economic Research Working Paper No. 7892. Cambridge, Mass.

Dollar, David, and Edward N. Wolff. 1997. "Convergence of Industry Labor Productivity Among Advanced Economies, 1963–1982." In Edward N. Wolff, ed., The Economics of Productivity 2: 39–48.

Duncan, Tim, and John Fogarty. 1984. Australia and Argentina: On Parallel Paths. Carlton, Victoria, Australia: Melbourne University Press.

Engerman, Stanley L., Stephen H. Haber, and Kenneth L. Sokoloff. 1999. "Inequality, Institutions, and Different Paths of Growth Among New World Economies." Cambridge, Mass.: National Bureau of Economic Research. Processed.

Engerman, Stanley L., and Kenneth L. Sokoloff. 1997. "Factor Endowments, Institutions, and Differential Paths of Growth Among New World Economies: A View from Economic Historians of the United States." In Stephen H. Haber, ed., How Latin America Fell Behind: Essays on the Economic Histories of Brazil and Mexico, 1800–1914. Stanford, Cal.: Stanford University Press.

Fajnzylber, Pablo. 2001a. "Aircraft Manufacturing in Latin America? Notes on Brazil's EMBRAER." World Bank, Washington, D.C.: Processed.

_____. 2001b. "Minimum Wage Effects Throughout the Wage Distribution: Evidence from Brazil's Formal and Informal Sectors." Centro de Planejamento Regional – Universidade Federal de Minas Gerais (CEDEPLAR – UFMG), Working Paper No. 151. Belo Horizonte, Brazil.

Fajnzylber, Pablo, and William F. Maloney. 2000. "Labor Demand and Trade Reform in Latin America." Policy Research Working Paper No. 2491. World Bank, Washington, D.C.

Feenstra, Robert C., and Gordon H. Hanson. 1995. "Foreign Investment, Outsourcing and Relative Wages." Working Paper No. 5121. National Bureau of Economic Research, Cambridge, Mass.

_____. 1996. "Globalization, Outsourcing, and Wage Inequality." Working Paper No. 5424, National Bureau of Economic Research, Cambridge, Mass.

Feldstein, Martin, and Charles Horioka. 1980. "Domestic Saving and International Capital Flows." *The Economic Journal* 90: 314–29.

Fiess, Norbert M., Marco Fugazza, and William F. Maloney. 2001. "Real Exchange Rates, Labor Market Rigidities, and Informality." World Bank, Washington, D.C. Processed.

Findlay, Ronald, and Ronald W. Jones. 2001. "Input Trade and the Location of Production." *American Economic Review* 91: 29–33.

Fleck, Susan. 2001. "A Gender Perspective on *Maquila* Employment and Wages in Mexico." In Maria Correia and Elizabeth Katz, *The Economics of Gender in Mexico.* Washington, D.C.: World Bank.

Fleisig, Heywood. 1995. "The Power of Collateral." Public Policy for the Private Sector, Note No. 43. World Bank, Washington, D.C.

Foster, William, and Alberto Valdés. 2001. "Has Reform Failed Latin American Agriculture? A Review of Argentina, Chile and Colombia." World Bank, Washington, D.C. Processed.

Freund, Caroline L., and John McLaren. 1999. "On the Dynamics of Trade Diversion: Evidence from Four Trade Blocs." U.S. Board of Governors of the Federal Reserve System. International Finance Discussion Papers, 637: 1–51.

Frischtak, Claudio R. 1993. "Development of the Brazilian Electronics Industry: A Study of the Competitiveness of Four Subsectors." In Bjorn Wellenius, Arnold Miller and Carl J. Dahlman, eds., *Developing the Electronics Industry.* World Bank Symposium, Washington, D.C. pp. 181–207.

_____. 1994. "Learning and Technical Progress in the Commuter Aircraft Industry: An Analysis of Embraer's Experience." *Research Policy* (Netherlands) 23: 601–12.

Funkhouser, Edward. 1992. "Mass Emigration, Remittances and Economic Adjustment: The Case of El Salvador in the 1980s." In George Borjas and Richard Freeman, eds., *Immigration and the Work Force: Economic Consequences for the United States and Source Areas.* Chicago: University of Chicago Press.

Fussell, Elizabeth. 2000. "Making Labor Flexible: The Recomposition of Tijuana's Maquiladora Female Labor Force." *Feminist Economics* 6 (3): 59–79.

Galiani, S. and P. Sanguinetti. 2000. "Wage Inequality and Trade Liberalization: Evidence from Argentina." Universidad Torcuato Di Tella, Buenos Aires, Argentina. Processed.

Galindo, Arturo, and Margaret Miller. 2001. "Can Credit Registries Reduce Credit Constraints? Empirical Evidence on the Role of Credit Registries in Firm Investment Decisions." Paper prepared for seminar, *Towards Competitiveness: The Institutional Path.* Inter-American Development Bank, Washington, D.C.

Gallup, John Luke, Jeffrey D. Sachs, and Andrew D. Mellinger. 1998. "Geography and Economic Development." Working Paper Series No. 1856. Harvard Institute of Economic Research, Cambridge, Mass., pp. 1–57.

Garces-Diaz, Daniel. 2001. "Was NAFTA Behind the Mexican Export Boom (1994–2000)." Banco de México. Processed.

Garriga, Marcelo, and Pablo Sanguinetti. 1995. "Es el Mercosur un Bloque Natural?: Efectos de la politica Comercial y la Geografía sobre el Comercio Regional." *Estudios Económicos.* Revista de la Fundación Mediterranea, Abril/Junio. Buenos Aires, Argentina.

Gasparini, Leonardo C. 2000. "La Informalidad Laboral en la Argentina: Evolución y Caracterización." La Economía Oculta en la Argentina. Fundación de Investigaciones Económicas Latinoamericanas, Argentina, pp. 162–223.

Gaytan Hernández, and Ana Isabel. 2000. "Tirar los pesticidas a flor de piel. Percepciones del riesgo, cuerpo y salud en fumigadores del jitomate." Master's Thesis in Social Anthropology. Centro de Investigaciones y Estudios Superiores en Antropología Social. Guadalajara, Jalisco. Processed.

Georges, Eugenia. 1990. *The Making of a Transnational Community: Migration, Development and Cultural Change in the Dominican Republic.* New York: Columbia University Press.

Glick, Reuven, and Andrew K. Rose. 2001. "Does a Currency Union Affect Trade? The Time Series Evidence." National Bureau of Economic Research Working Paper No. 8396. Cambridge, Mass.

Goldberg, Pinelopi Koujianou, and Nina Pavcnik. 2001. "Trade Protection and Wages: Evidence from the Colombian Trade Reforms." National Bureau of Economic Research, Cambridge, Mass. Processed.

Goldstein, Andrea. 2000. "The Political Economy of High-Tech Industries in Developing Countries: Aerospace in Brazil, Indonesia and South Africa." Organisation for Economic Co-operation and Development, Development Centre, Paris. Processed.

Gonzalez Koning, G., and Quentin Wodon. 2001a. "Remittances and Inequality." World Bank, Washington, D.C. Processed.

_____. 2001b. "Remittances, Education, and Child Labor." World Bank, Washington, D.C. Processed.

Griliches, Zvi. 1986. "Economic Data Issues." In *Handbook of Econometrics*, Volume 3, pp. 1466–1514. New York: Elsevier Science.

Grossman, Gene M., and Elhanan Helpman. 1991. *Innovation and Growth in the Global Economy*. Cambridge, Mass.: MIT Press.

Grubel, Herbert G., and P. J. Lloyd. 1975. *Intra-Industry Trade: The Theory and Measurement of International Trade in Differentiated Products*. New York: John Wiley & Sons.

Guasch, J. Luis, and Joseph Kogan. 2001. "Inventories in Developing Countries: Levels and Determinants: A Red Flag for Competitiveness and Growth." Policy Research Working Paper No. 2552. World Bank, Washington, D.C.

Gylfason, Thorvaldur. 1999. "Natural Resources and Economic Growth: A Nordic Perspective on the Dutch Disease." Working Papers No. 167, the United Nations University, World Institute for Development Economic Research, Finland.

Haber, Stephen H. 1992. "Assessing the Obstacles to Industrialization: The Mexican Economy, 1830–1940." *Journal of Latin American Studies* 24: 1–32.

_____. 1997a. "Financial Markets and Industrial Development: A Comparative Study of Governmental Regulation, Financial Innovation, and Industrial Structure in Brazil and Mexico, 1840–1930." In Stephen H. Haber ed., *How Latin America Fell Behind: Essays on the Economic Histories of Brazil and Mexico 1800–1914*. Stanford, Cal.: Stanford University Press.

_____. 1997. "Introduction: Economic Growth and Latin American Economic Historiography." In Stephen H. Haber, ed., *How Latin America Fell Behind: Essays on the Economic Histories of Brazil and Mexico 1800–1914*. Stanford, Cal.: Stanford University Press.

Hadass, Yael S., and Jeffrey G. Williamson. 2001. "Terms of Trade Shocks and Economic Performance 1870–1940: Prebisch and Singer Revisited." National Bureau of Economic Research, Working Paper No. 8188. Cambridge, Mass.

Hakura, Dalia S. 2001. "Why Does HOV Fail? The Role of Technological Differences within the EC." *Journal of International Economics* 54: 361–82.

Hall, Bronwyn, and John Van Reenen. 2000. "How Effective Are Fiscal Incentives for R&D? A Review of the Evidence." *Research Policy* 29: 449–69.

Hall, Robert E., and Charles I. Jones. 1999. "Why Do Some Countries Produce So Much More Output Per Worker Than Others?" *Quarterly Journal of Economics* 114 (1): 83–116.

Hallberg, Kristin, Hong Tan, and Leonid Koryukin. 2000. "Export Dynamics and Productivity: Analysis of Mexican Manufacturing in the 1990s." World Bank, Washington, D.C. Processed.

Hansen, Roger D. 1971. *The Politics of Mexican Development*. Baltimore: The Johns Hopkins University Press.

Harrigan, James, and Egon Zakrajsek. 2000. "Factor Supplies and Specialization in the World Economy." International Research Department. Federal Reserve Bank of New York. Processed.

Hay, Donald. 1997. "The Post-1990 Brazilian Trade Liberalization and the Performance of Large Manufacturing Firms." Instituto de Pesquisa Económica Aplicada. Texto para Discussao 523.

Heckman, James. 1976. "The Common Structure of Statistical Models of Truncation, Sample Selection, and Limited Dependent Variables and a Simple Estimator for Such Models." *The Annals of Economic and Social Measurement* 5: 475–92.

_____. 1979. "Sample Selection Bias as a Specification Error." *Econometrica* 47: 153–61.

Helfner, Steven M., and Gervásio Castro de Rezende. 2001. "Brazilian Agriculture in the 1990s: Impact of the Policy Reforms." Paper prepared for delivery at the XXIV International Conference of Agricultural Economists, August 13–18, 2000, Berlin.

Hirschman, Albert O. 1958. *The Strategy of Economic Development*. New Haven, Conn.: Yale University Press.

Hjalmarsson, Lennart. 1991. "The Scandinavian Model of Industrial Policy." In Magnus Blomström and Patricio Meller, eds., *Diverging Paths: Comparing a Century of Scandinavian and Latin American Development*. Washington, D.C.: Inter-American Development Bank.

Holden, Paul. 1996. "Collateral without Consequence: Some Causes and Effects of Financial Underdevelopment in Latin America." The Enterprise Research Institute of Latin America, Washington, D.C.

Holder, John S. 2001. "Some Ideals for Tourism Change in a Changing World." Secretary General. Caribbean Tourism Organization, Barbados.

Hummels, David. 1999. "Toward a Geography of Trade Costs." Processed. Purdue University.

Hveem, Helge. 1991. "Developing an Open Economy: Norway's Transformation 1845–1975." In Magnus Blomström, and Patricio Meller, eds., *Diverging Paths: Comparing a Century of Scandinavian and Latin American Development.* Washington, D.C.: Inter-American Development Bank.

Imbs, Jean, and Romain Wacziarg. 2000. "Stages of Diversification." London Business School, London, England, and Stanford University, Stanford, Cal. Processed.

Innis, Harold. 1933. *Problems of Staple Production in Canada.* Toronto: University of Toronto Press.

International Labour Organization. 1995. *World Employment.* Geneva: ILO.

Irwin, Douglas. 1996. *Against the Tide: An Intellectual History of Free Trade.* Washington, D.C.: The American Enterprise Institute.

———. 2000. "How Did the United States Become a Net Exporter of Manufactured Goods?" National Bureau of Economic Research Working Paper No. 7638. Cambridge, Mass.

Jansson, Tor, and Geoffrey Chalmers. 2001. "The Case for Business Registration Reform in Latin America." Inter-American Development Bank, Washington, D.C. Processed.

Jarvis, Lovell S. 1992. "Cambios en los roles de los sectores publico y privado en el desarrollo tecnologico: lecciones a partir del sector fruticola chileno." *Colección Estudios CIEPLAN* 36: 5–39.

Jarvis, Lovell, and Esperanza Vera-Toscano. 2001. "Seasonal Adjustment in a Market for Temporary Agricultural Workers: Fruit Workers in Chile." Draft. Washington D.C., World Bank.

Jeanneret, Teresa. 1972. "El sistema de protección a la industria chilena." In *Proceso a la industrialización chilena.* Centro de Estudios de Planificación Nacional. Santiago, Chile: Ediciones Nueva Universidad.

Jelin, Elizabeth, Matilde Mercado, and Gabriela Wyczykier. 2001. "Home Work in Argentina." Boosting Employment Through Small Enterprise Development (SEED) Working Paper No. 6. *Series on Homeworkers in the Global Economy.* International Labour Organization, Geneva.

Jones, Ronald W. 2000. *Globalization and the Theory of Input Trade.* Cambridge, Mass.: MIT Press.

Jones and Kierzkowski. 1990. "The Role of Services in Production and International Trade: A Theoretical Framework." In R. Jones and A. Krueger, eds., *The Political Economy of International Trade.* Oxford: Basil Blackwell, pp. 31–48.

Katz, Elizabeth. 1995. "Gender and Trade Within the Household: Observations from Rural Guatemala." *World Development* 23 (2): 327–42.

Katz, Jorge. 2000. "Cambios estructurales y productividad en la industria latinoamericana, 1970–1996." *Revista de la CEPAL* 71 (agosto): 65–84.

Katz, Lawrence F., and Kevin M. Murphy. 1992. " Changes in Relative Wages, 1963–1987: Supply and Demand Factors. *Quarterly Journal of Economics* 107 (1): 35–78.

Kearns, Allan, and Frances Ruane. 2001. "The Tangible Contribution of R&D-Spending Foreign-Owned Plants to a Host Region: A Plant Level Study of the Irish Manufacturing Sector (1980–1996)." *Research Policy* 30: 227–44.

Keller, Wolfgang. 2001. "The Geography and Channels of Diffusion at the World's Technology Frontier." National Bureau of Economic Research Working Paper No. 8150. Cambridge, Mass.

Key, Nigel. 1999. "Contract Farming, Smallholders, and Rural Development in Latin America: The Organization of Agropocessing Firms and the Scale of Outgrower Production." *World Development* 27 (2): 381–401.

Kopinak, Kathryn. 1995. "Gender as a Vehicle for the Subordination of Women Maquiladora Workers in Mexico." *Latin America Perspectives* 22: 30–48.

Kraay, Aart, and Jaume Ventura. 2001. "Comparative Advantage and the Cross-Section of Business Cycles." National Bureau of Economic Research Working Paper No. 8104. Cambridge, Mass.

Kraay, Aart, Norman Loayza, Luis Servén, and Jaume Ventura. 2000. "Country Portfolios." National Bureau of Economic Research Working Paper No. 7795. Cambridge, Mass.

Krebs, Tom, and William F. Maloney. 1999. "Quitting and Labor Turnover. Microeconomic Evidence and Macroeconomic Consequences." Policy Research Working Paper No. 2068. World Bank, Washington, D.C.

Krueger, A. 1996. "Observations on International Labor Standards and Trade." National Bureau of Economic Research Working Paper No. 5632. Cambridge, Mass.

Krugman, Paul R. 1979. "Increasing Returns, Monopolistic Competition and International Trade." *Journal of International Economics* 9: 469–479.

_____. 1999. *Pop Internationalism*. Cambridge, Mass.: MIT Press.

Kuruvilla, S. 1996. "Linkages Between Industrialization Strategies and Industrial Relations–Human Resources Policies: Singapore, Malaysia, the Philippines and India." *Industrial and Labor Relations Review* 49 (4).

Lagos, Gustavo. 1997. "Developing National Mining Policies in Chile: 1974–96." Resources Policy 23 (1/2): 51–69.

Landes, David S. 1998. *The Wealth and Poverty of Nations: Why Some Are So Rich and Some So Poor.* New York and London: Norton.

Lane, Philip R., and Aaron Tornell. 1999. "The Voracity Effect." *American Economic Review* 89: 22–46.

Leamer, Edward E. 1984. *Sources of International Comparative Advantage: Theory and Evidence.* Cambridge, Mass.: MIT Press.

_____. 1987. "Paths of Development in the Three-Factor, n-Good General Equilibrium Model." *Journal of Political Economy* 95 (5): 961–99.

_____. 1995. "The Heckscher-Ohlin Model in Theory and Practice." Princeton Studies in International Finance No. 77. Department of Economics, Princeton University, Princeton, N.J.

Leamer, Edward E., and Jerome Levinsohn. 1995. "International Trade Theory: The Evidence." Chapter 3 in G. M. Grossman and K. S. Rogoff, eds., *Handbook of International Economics*, Volume 3. Amsterdam: North Holland.

Leamer, Edward E., Hugo Maul, Sergio Rodriguez, and Peter K. Schott. 1999. "Does Natural Resource Abundance Increase Latin American Income Inequality?" *Journal of Development Economics* 59: 3–42.

Lederman, Daniel. 2001. "The Political Economy of Protection: Theory and Chilean Experience." Ph.D. Dissertation. The Johns Hopkins University, Baltimore.

Lederman, Daniel, Ana María Menéndez, Guillermo Perry, and Joseph Stiglitz. 2001a. "Mexican Investment after the Tequila Crisis: Basic Economics, 'Confidence Effects' or Market Imperfections?" *Journal of International Money and Finance.*

_____. 2001b. "Mexico: Five Years after the Crisis." In *Annual Bank Conference on Development Economics, 2000.* Washington, D.C.: World Bank.

Lederman, Daniel, and Lixin Colin Xu. 2001. "Comparative Advantage and Trade Intensity: Are Traditional Endowments Destiny?" World Bank, Washington, D.C. Processed.

Lederman, Daniel, and Rodrigo Reis Soares. 2001. "A Note on the Impact of Economic Reforms on the Performance of the Agriculture Sector in Latin America." World Bank, Washington, D.C. Processed.

Levenson, Alec R., and William F. Maloney. 1998. "The Informal Sector, Firm Dynamics, and Institutional Participation." Policy Research Paper No. 1988. World Bank, Washington, D.C.

Levy, Santiago, and Sweder Van Wijnbergen. 1995. "Transition Problems in Economic Reform: Agriculture in the North American Free Trade Agreement." *The American Economic Review* 85 (4): 738–54.

Lewis, Karen. 1999. "Trying to Explain Home Bias in Equities and Consumption." *Journal of Economic Literature* 37: 571–608.

Lewis, P., W. Martin, and C. Savage. "Capital and Investment in the Agricultural Economy." *Quarterly Review of the Rural Economy* 10 (1): 48–53.

Li, Hongyi, Lixin Colin Xu, and Heng-Fu Zou. 2000. "Corruption, Income Distribution, and Growth." *Economics and Politics* 12 (2): 155–82.

Linbeck, Assar. 1974. *Swedish Economic Policy.* Berkeley and Los Angeles: University of California Press.

Lizardo, Magdalena, and Rolando M. Guzmán. 2001. "Patrones de integracion a la economía global: ¿Qué comercializa América Latina? ¿Qué hacen sus trabajadores? El Caso de la República Dominicana." World Bank, Washington, D.C. Processed.

Loayza, Norman. 2001. "Growth in Brazil." World Bank, Washington, D.C.

Lopez, Jose R., and Mitchell Seligson, 1990. *Small Business Development in El Salvador: The Impact of Remittances.* Report of the Commission for the Study of International Migration and Cooperative Economic Development. Washington D.C.: Government Printing Office.

Lopez-Acevedo, Gladys. 2001a. "Technology and Firm Performance in Mexico." World Bank, Washington, D.C. Processed.

_____. 2001b. "Technology and Skill Demand in Mexico." World Bank, Washington, D.C. Processed.

_____. 2001c. "Determinants of Technology Adoption in Mexico." World Bank, Washington, D.C. Processed.

López-Cálix, José R. 2001. "LAC Migration and the New Patterns of Integration." World Bank, Washington, D.C. Processed.

Lucas, Robert E. B. 1979. "Sharing, Monitoring, and Incentives: Marshallian Misallocation Reassessed." *Journal of Political Economy* 87 (3): 501–21.

Lumenga-Neso, Olivier, Marcelo Olarreaga, and Maurice Schiff. 2001. "On 'Indirect' Trade-Related R&D Spillovers." World Bank Development Economics Research Group, Washington, D.C. Processed.

Luzio, Eduardo, and Shane Greenstein. 1995. "Measuring the Performance of a Protected Infant Industry: The Case of Brazilian Microcomputers." *Review of Economics and Statistics* 77: 622–23.

Maddison, Angus. 1994. "Explaining the Economic Performance of Nations, 1820–1989." In William J. Baumol, Richard R. Nelson and Edward N. Wolff, eds., *Convergence of Productivity.* New York: Oxford University Press, pp. 20–60.

Mah, J. 1997. "Core Labour Standards and Export Performance in Developing Countries." *World Economy* 20 (6).

Mahler, Sarah. 2000. "Migration and Transnational Issues." Working Paper No. 4. Hamburg: Institut fur Iberoamerika-Kunde. Germany.

Maloney, William F. 1997. "Chile." In Laura Randall, ed. *The Political Economy of Latin America in the Postwar Period.* Austin: University of Texas Press.

_____. 1999. "Does Informality Imply Segmentation in Urban Labor Markets? Evidence from Sectoral Transitions in Mexico." *The World Bank Economic Review* 14 (2): 275–302.

_____. 2000. "Informality Reconsidered." World Bank, Washington, D.C. Processed.

_____. 2001a. "Self-Employment and Labor Turnover in Developing Countries: Cross-Country Evidence." In Shantayanan Devarajan, F. Halsey Rogers, and Lyn Squire, eds., *World Bank Economists' Forum*, Volume 1. Washington, D.C: World Bank.

_____. 2001b. "Dealing with Dependency: A Comparative View." Washington, D.C.: World Bank. Processed.

_____. "Technical Capacity and Development: Australia, Latin America and Scandinavia." World Bank, Washington, D.C. Processed.

Maloney, William F., and Rodrigo Acevedo. 1995. "Trade Reform, Uncertainty and Export Promotion: Mexico 1982–88." *Journal of Development Economics* 48: 67–89.

Maloney, William F., and Gabriel V. Montes Rojas. 2001. "Demand for Tourism." World Bank, Washington, D.C. Processed.

Maloney, William F., and Jairo Nuñez, with Wendy Cunningham, Norbert Fiess, Claudio Montenegro, Edmundo Murrugarra, Mauricio Santamaria, Corinne Siaens, and Claudia Sepúlveda. 2001. "Measuring the Impact of Minimum Wages: Evidence from Latin America." World Bank Policy Research Working Paper No. 2597. Washington, D.C.

Mamalakis, Markos. 1976. *The Growth and Structure of the Chilean Economy: From Independence to Allende.* New Haven: Economic Growth Center, Yale University Press.

Mann, Catherine L. 2001. "Implications of Global Internet Commerce for Trade Competitiveness: A Consideration for Selected Latin and Asian Countries. *Chile, Mexico, Peru; Korea, Thailand, Vietnam.*" Institute for International Economics/World Bank, Washington, D.C. Processed.

Mariscal, Elisa, and Kenneth L. Sokoloff. 2000. "Schooling, Suffrage, and the Persistence of Inequality in the Americas, 1800–1945." In Stephen Haber, ed., *Political Institutions and Economic Growth in Latin America. Essays in Policy, History, and Political Economy.* Stanford University, Stanford, Cal.: Hoover Institution Press.

Marquez, Gustavo. 1990. "Wage Differentials and Labor Market Equilibrium in Venezuela." Ph.D. dissertation. Boston University, Department of Economics, Boston, Mass.

Martin, Will, and Devashish Mitra. 2001. "Productivity Growth and Convergence in Agriculture and Manufacturing." *Economic Development and Cultural Change* 49 (2): 403–22.

Martin, Will, and Peter G. Warr. 1993. "Explaining the Relative Decline of Agriculture: A Supply-Side Analysis for Indonesia." *World Bank Economic Review (International)* 7: 381–401.

Matsuyama, Kiminori. 2000. "A Ricardian Model with a Continuum of Goods under Nonhomothetic Preferences: Demand Complementarities, Income Distribution, and North-South Trade." *Journal of Political Economy* 108 (61): 1093–1120.

Meller, Patricio. 2001. "Chilean Copper: Facts, Role and Issues." Universidad De Chile Facultad De Ciencias Fisicas y Matemáticas Departamento de Ingenieria Industrial/World Bank, Washington, D.C. Processed.

Meredith, David. 1995. "The Role of Education and Health Services in the Economic Development of Australia and Argentina 1880–1940." School of Economics Discussion Paper, the University of New South Wales.

Merrill Lynch. 2000. "Emerging as an Electronics Manufacturing Hub for North America." New York. Processed.

Mester, Loretta J. 1997. "What's the Point of Credit Scoring?" *Business Review.* Philadelphia: Federal Reserve Bank of Philadelphia.

Meyers, Deborah. 1998. "Migrant Remittances to Latin America: Reviewing the Literature." Inter-American Dialogue, Washington D.C.

_____. 2001. "The Regional Map: Flows and Impact of Remittances in LAC." Washington, D.C.: World Bank. Processed.

Micco, Alejandro, and Natalia Perez. 2001. "Maritime Transport Costs and Port Efficiency." Inter-American Development Bank, Washington, D.C. Processed.

MIF/IDB. 2001. "Remittances to Latin America and the Caribbean: Comparative Statistics." Washington, D.C. Processed.

Monge, Alexander. 2001. "Exports and Foreign Investment in Costa Rica and El Salvador During the 1990's." Department of Economics, Northwestern University/ World Bank, Washington, D.C. Processed.

Moreira, Maurício Mesquita. 2000. "A Indústria Brasileira nos Anos Noventa: o que já se pode dizer?" São Paulo: *Banco Nacional de Desenvolvimento Econômico e Social* (BNDES). Processed.

Muendler, Marc, Claudia Sepúlveda, and Luis Servén. 2001. "Productivity Growth in Brazilian Industry." World Bank, Washington, D.C. Processed.

Murphy, Kevin. M., Andrea Shleifer, and Robert. W. Vishny. 1993. "Why is Rent-Seeking So Costly to Growth?" *American Economic Review* May: 409–14.

Nelson, R., ed. 1993. *National Innovation Systems: A Comparative Analysis.* New York: Oxford University Press.

Newman, Constance, Pilar Larreamendy, and Ana María Maldonado. 2000. "Mujeres y Floricultura: Cambios y Consecuencias en el Hogar." Draft. World Bank.

Nicita, Alessandro, Marcelo Olarreaga, and Isidro Soloaga. 2001. "The Region as a Platform to the World." World Bank, Washington, D.C. Processed.

North, Douglass C. 1955. "Location Theory and Regional Economic Growth." *Journal of Political Economy*: 243–258.

O'Rourke, Kevin H., and Jeffrey G. Williamson. 1999. *Globalization and History. The Evolution of a Nineteenth-Century Atlantic Economy.* Cambridge, Mass.: MIT Press.

Pages-Serra, Carmen, and James Heckman. 2000. "The Cost of Job Security Regulation: Evidence from Latin American Labor Markets." *Economia, Journal of the Latin American and Caribbean Economics Association* 1 (1).

Palacios, Marco. 1979. *El café en Colombia (1850–1970): Una historia Económica, Social, y Política.* Bogotá, Colombia: Editorial Presencia Ltda.

Parente, Stephen L., and Edward C. Prescott. 2000. *Barriers to Riches.* Cambridge, Mass.: MIT Press.

Pavcnik, Nina. 2000a. "Trade Liberalization, Exit, and Productivity Improvements: Evidence from Chilean Plants." National Bureau of Economic Research Working Paper No. 7852. Cambridge, Mass.

_____. 2000b. "What Explains Skill Upgrading in Less Developed Countries? National Bureau of Economic Research Working Paper No. 7846. Cambridge, Mass.

Pavcnik, Nina, Andreas Blom, and Norbert Schady. 2001. "Trade Liberalization and Industry Wage Differentials in Brazil." Dartmouth College and World Bank, Washington, D.C. Processed.

Pearson, Ruth. 1997. "Gender and New Technology in the Caribbean: New Work for Women?" In Janet Momsen, ed., *Women and Change in the Caribbean: A Pan-Caribbean Perspective.* Kingston: Ian Randle Press.

Pinto Santa Cruz, Aníbal. 1959. *Chile, un caso de desarrollo frustrado.* Editorial Universitaria. Santiago, Chile.

Porter, Michael E. 1990. *The Competitive Advantage of Nations.* New York: Free Press.

Portes, Alejandro, Manuel Castells, and Lauren A. Benton, eds. 1989. *The Informal Economy.* Baltimore: The Johns Hopkins University Press.

Prebisch, Raul. 1959. "Commercial Policy in the Under-developed Countries." *The American Economic Review, Papers and Proceedings* 49 (2): 251–73.

Pritchett, Lant. 1996. "Measuring Outward Orientation in LDCs: Can It Be Done?" *Journal of Development Economics* 49: 307–35.

Prugl, Elisabeth. 1997. "Microentrepreneurs and Home-workers: Convergent Categories." *World Development* 25 (9): 1471–82.

_____. 1999. *The Global Construction of Gender: Home-based, Work in the Political Economy.* New York: Columbia University Press.

Puga, D., and A. J. Venables. 1999. "Agglomeration and Economic Development; Import Substitution Versus Trade Liberalization." *Economic Journal* 109: 292–311.

Pindyck, Robert. 1988. "Irreversible Investment, Capacity Choice and the Value of the Firm." *American Economic Review* 78: 969–985.

Rama, M., and G. Tabellini. 1997. "Endogenous Distortions in Product and Labor Markets." Centre for Economic Policy Research, Discussion Paper No. 1143. London: Cambridge University Press.

Ramos, Joseph. 1998. "A Development Strategy Founded on Natural Resource-Based Production Clusters." *CEPAL Review* 66 (December): 105–27.

Reardon, Thomas, Julio Berdegué, and Germán Escobar. "Rural Nonfarm Employment and Incomes in Latin America: Overview and Policy Implications." *World Development* 29 (3): 395–409.

Rees, Hedley, and Anup Shah. 1986. "An Empirical Analysis of Self-employment in the U.K." *Journal of Applied Econometrics* 1 (1): 95–108.

Riera i Tuébols, Santiago. 1993. "Industrialization and Technical Education in Spain, 1850–1914." In Robert Fox and Anna Guagnini, eds., *Education, Technology and Industrial Performance in Europe, 1850–1939.* Cambridge: Cambridge University Press.

Robbins, Donald J. 1994. "Relative Wage Structure in Chile, 1957–1992: Changes in the Structure of Demand for Schooling." *Estudios de Economica* 21: 49–78.

Robbins, Donald, and T. H. Gindling. 1999. "Trade Liberalization and the Relative Wages for More Skilled Workers in Costa Rica." *Review of Development Economics* 3 (2): 140–54.

Roberts, Bryan R. 1989. "Employment Structure, Life Cycle, and Life Chances: Formal and Informal Sectors in Guadalajara." In Alejandro Portes, Manuel Castells and Lauren A. Benton, eds., *The Informal Economy.* Baltimore: The Johns Hopkins University Press.

Rodríguez, Francisco, and Jeffrey D. Sachs. 1999. "Why Do Resource-Abundant Economies Grow More Slowly?" *Journal of Economic Growth* 4: 277–303.

Rodríguez-Clare, Andrés. 2001. "Costa Rica's Development Strategy Based on Human Capital and Technology: How It Got There, the Impact of INTEL, and Lessons for other Countries." Paper written for the Human Development Report 2001. San José, Costa Rica. Processed.

Rodrik, D. 1996. "Labor Standards and International Trade: Do they Matter and What Do We Do About Them." In R. Z. Lawrence, D. Rodrik and J. Whalley, eds., *Emerging Agenda for Global Trade: High States for Developing Countries.* Baltimore: The Johns Hopkins University Press.

_____. 1997. "Has Globalization Gone Too Far?" Institute for International Economics, Washington, D.C.

Romer, P. 1990. "Endogenous Technological Change." *Journal of Political Economy* 98: 71–102.

Romero, T. 1995. "Labor Standards and Export Processing Zones: Situation and Pressure for Change." *Development Policy Review* 13.

Rosenzweig, Jeffrey A. 1988. "Elasticities of Substitution in Caribbean Tourism." *Journal of Development Economics* 29: 89–100.

Rossi Júnior, José Luiz, and Pedro Cavalcanti Ferreira. 1999. "Evolução da produtividade industrial brasileira e abertura comerical." *Pesquisa e Planejamento Economico* 29 (1): 1–35.

Ruffin, Roy J. 1999. "The Nature and Significance of Intra-Industry Trade." *Economic and Financial Review, Federal Reserve Bank of Dallas* Q4: 2–9.

Sachs, Jeffrey, and Andrew M. Warner. 1995a. "Natural Resources and Economic Growth." National Bureau of Economic Research Working Paper. Cambridge, Mass.

_____. 1995b. "Economic Reform and the Process of Global Integration." In William Brainard and George Perry, eds., *Brookings Papers on Economic Activity – V1 1995 – 25th Anniversary Issue.* Washington, D.C.: The Brookings Institution.

_____. 1997. "Natural Resources and Economic Growth." Revised version. Harvard Institute for International Development, Cambridge, Mass.

———. 1999. "The Big Push, Natural Resource Booms and Growth." *Journal of Development Economics* 59: 43–76.

Safford, Frank. 1976. *The Ideal of the Practical: Colombia's Struggle To Form a Technical Elite.* Austin and London: University of Texas Press.

Sánchez, Susana M., Anna Joo, and Cara Zappala. 2001. "Constrained Global Integration: A Note on Micro-enterprises in Latin America." World Bank, Washington, D.C. Processed.

Sanguinetti, Pablo, and Miguel Salustro. 2000. "El Mercosur y el sesgo regional de la política comercial: aranceles y barreras no tarifarias." CEDI, Buenos Aires, Argentina. Processed.

Sanguinetti, Pablo, Juan Pantano, and Josefiina Posadas. 2001. "Trade Liberalization and the Dynamics of the Trade Structure in Argentina and Uruguay." World Bank, Washington, D.C. Processed.

Sanguinetti, Pablo, Rodrigo Arim, and Juan Pantano. 2001. "Changes in Production and Employment Structure and Relative Wages in Argentina and Uruguay." Universidad Torcuato di Tella/World Bank, Washington, D.C. Processed.

Santamaria, M. 2000. "External Trade, Skill, Technology and the Recent Increase of Income Inequality in Colombia." Dissertation. Georgetown University, Washington, D.C.

Sapir, A. 1996. "The Effects of Europe's Internal Market Program on Production and Trade: A First Assessment." *Weltwirtschafliches Archiv.*

Sargent, John, and Linda Matthews. 1999. "Exploitation or Choice? Exploring the Relative Attractiveness of Employment in the Maquiladoras." *Journal of Business Ethics* 18: 213–27.

Schott, Peter K. 2000. "Do Countries Specialize?" Yale School of Management, New Haven, Conn. Processed.

Servén, Luis. 1998. "Macroeconomic Uncertainty and Private Investment in LDCs: An Empirical Investigation." World Bank Policy Research Working Paper No. 2035. World Bank, Washington, D.C.

Singer, Hans W. 1950. "The Distribution of Gains Between Investing and Borrowing Countries." *The American Economic Review* 40 (2): 473–485.

Sistema para el Desarrollo Integral de la Familia. 2000. "Perfil Socieconomico de Jornaleros Migrantes en Sayula, Jalisco Mexico." Jalisco, Mexico. Processed.

Sklair, Leslie. 1989. *Assembling for Development: The Maquila Industry in Mexico and the United States.* Winchester, Mass.: Unwin Hyman.

Smith, Adam. 1776. *An Inquiry into the Nature and Causes of the Wealth of Nations.* Oxford: Clarendon Press.

Stallings, Barbara, and Wilson Peres. 2000. *Growth, Employment and Equity, The Impact of the Economic Reforms in Latin America and the Caribbean.* Economic Commission for Latin America and Caribbean. Washington, D.C.: The Brookings Institution Press.

Stern, Scott, Michael E. Porter, and Jeffrey L. Furman. 2000. "The Determinants of National Innovative Capacity." National Bureau of Economic Research Working Paper No. 7876. Cambridge, Mass.

Stone, Joe A., and Hyun-hoon Lee. 1995. "Determinants of Intra-Industry Trade: A Longitudinal, Cross-Country Analysis." *Weltwirtschaftliches Archiv* 131 (1): 67–85.

Summerhill, William. 1997. "Transport Improvements and Economic Growth in Brazil and Mexico." In Stephen H. Haber, ed., *How Latin America Fell Behind: Essays on the Economic Histories of Brazil and Mexico 1800–1914.* Stanford, Cal.: Stanford University Press.

Tabor, S. R. 1995. "Structural Adjustment and Institutional Change." In S. R. Tabor, ed., *Agricultural Research in an Era of Adjustment.* Washington, D.C.: World Bank.

Tan, Hong, and Geeta Batra. 1997. "Technology and Firm Size–Wage Differentials in Colombia, Mexico, and Taiwan (China)." *World Bank Economic Review* 11 (1): 59–83.

Taylor, J. Edward. 2001. "Microeconomics of Globalization: Evidence from Mexico, China, El Salvador, and the Galapagos Islands." World Bank, Washington, D.C. Processed.

Teixeira da Silva Filho, Tito Nícias. 2001. "Estimando o produto potencial brasileiro." Banco Central do Brasil. Trabalhos para Discussao 17.

Terra, I. 1998. "Uruguay en el MERCOSUR: Perspectivas del Comercio Intraregional." Centro Estudios para America Latina (CEPAL).

Thom, Rodney, and Moore McDowell. 1999. "Measuring Marginal Intra-Industry Trade." *Weltwirtschaftliches Archiv* 135 (1): 48–61.

Tiano, Susan. 1994. *Patriarchy on the Line: Labor, Gender, and Ideology in the Mexican Maquila Industry.* Philadelphia: Temple University Press.

Tomei, Manuela. 2000. "Home Work in Selected Latin American Countries: A Comparative Overview." International Labour Organization, Geneva. Unpublished.

Torres, Gabriel. 1997. "La Fuerza de la Ironía." El Colegio de Jalisco y Ciesas, México.

Trefler, Daniel. 1995. "The Case of the Missing Trade and Other HOV Mysteries." *American Economic Review* 85 (5): 1029–46.

Umali, D. 1991. *Public and Private Sector Roles in Agricultural Research: Theory and Evidence.* Washington, D.C: World Bank.

UNIFEM (United Nations Development Fund for Women). 2000. *El Impacto del TLC en la Mano de Obra Femenina en México.* New York: United Nations.

Urrutia, Miguel. 1979. *Cincuenta años de desarrollo económico colombiano.* Bogotá: La Carreta.

Vaillant, M. 2000. "Limits to Trade Liberalization: A Political Economy Approach." Ph.D. Thesis. University of Pompeu Fabra.

Valdés, Alberto. 1986. "Impact of Trade and Macroeconomic Policies on Agricultural Growth: The South American Experience." In *Economic and Social Progress in Latin America, 1986 Report.* Washington, D.C: Inter-American Development Bank.

Van Beers, C. 1998. "Labor Standards and Trade Flows of OECD Countries." *World Economy* 221 (1).

Vanek, Jaroslav. 1968. "The Factor Proportions Theory: The N-factor Case." *Kyklos* 21 (4): 749–56.

Vélez, Carlos Eduardo, Jose Leibovich, Adriana Kugler, Cesar Boulillón, and Jairo Núñez. 2001. "The Reversal of Inequality Trends in Colombia, 1978–1995: A Combination of Persistent and Fluctuating Forces." Inter-American Development Bank and World Bank, Washington, D.C. Processed.

Venables, Anthony J. 2001. "Trade, Location, and Development: An Overview of Theory." London School of Economics and CEPR/World Bank, Washington, D.C. Processed.

Venezian, E., and E. Muchnik. 1994. "Structural Adjustment and Agricultural Research in Chile." Briefing Paper No. 9, International Service for National Agricultural Research. The Hague, Netherlands.

Villalobos, Sergio, ed. 1990. "Historia de la Ingenieria en Chile." Insituto de Ingeneiros de Chile, Ediciones Hachette. Santiago, Chile.

Viner, Jacob. 1952. *International Trade and Economic Development.* Glencoe, Ill.: Free Press.

Watkins, Melville. 1963. "A Staple Theory of Economic Growth." *The Canadian Journal of Economics and Political Science* 29: 141–158.

Weller, Jürgen. 2000. *Reformas económicas, crecimiento y empleo: los mercados de trabajo en América Latina y el Caribe.* Santiago, Chile: Fondo de Cultura Económica/Comisión Económica para América Latina y el Caribe.

Wheatly, Jeffrey J. 1999. *World Telecommunication Economics.* Exeter, England: Short Run Press Ltd.

WIEGO. 2000. "Women in Informal Employment: Globalizing and Organizing." *Women in the Informal Economy.* www.wiego.org.

Will, Robert Milton. 1957. "Some Aspects of the Development of Economic Thought in Chile (circa 1775–1878)." Unpublished doctoral dissertation, Duke University.

Wodon, Quentin. 1999. "Migration and Poverty in Latin America and the Caribbean." World Bank, Washington, D.C. Processed.

———. "Income Mobility and Risk During the Business Cycle." *Economics of Transition* 9 (2): 449–61.

Wodon, Quentin, with contributions from Robert Ayres, M. Barenstein, Norman Hicks, K. Lee, William Maloney, Pia Peeters, Corrine Siaens, and S. Yitzhaki. 2000. *Poverty and Policy in Latin America and the Caribbean.* World Bank Technical Paper No. 467. World Bank, Washington, D.C.

Wodon, Quentin, and G. Gonzalez Koning. 2001. "Do Cash Transfers to Farmers Reduce Migration? Procampo in Mexico." World Bank, Washington, D.C. Processed.

Wodon, Quentin, G. Gonzalez Koning, and Corinne Siaens. 2001. "Remittances and Housing, World Bank." World Bank, Washington, D.C. Processed.

Wodon, Quentin, and M. Minowa. 2001. "Training for the Urban Unemployed: A Reevaluation of Mexico's Probecat." In S. Devaradjan, F. Hasley and L. Squire, eds., *World Bank Economists' Forum.* World Bank, Washington D.C.

Wodon, Quentin, and S. Yitzhaki. 2001. "Evaluating the Impact of Government Programs on Social Welfare: The Role of Targeting and the Allocation Rules Among Program Beneficiaries." World Bank, Washington, D.C. Processed.

Wodon, Quentin, R. Castro-Fernandez, G. Lopez-Acevedo, Corrine Siaens, Carlos Sobrado, and Jean-Philippe Tre. 2001a. "Poverty in Latin America: Trends (1986–1998) and Determinants." *Cuadernos de Economia* 114: 127–154.

Wodon, Quentin, William Maloney, and Matias Barenstein. 2000. "Self-Employment as an Explanation for High Inequality in Latin America." World Bank, Washington, D.C. Processed.

Wood, Adrian. 1994. "Give Heckscher and Ohlin a Chance!" *Weltwirtschaftliches Archiv* 130 (1): 20–48.

Woodruff, Christopher. 2001. "Remittances and Microenterprises in Mexico." Monterrey: Monterrey Institute of Technology and Graduate Studies. Processed.

Woodruff, Christopher, and Rene Zentano. 2001. "Remittances and Microenterprises in Mexico." University of California, La Jolla, Cal., and Monterrey Institute of Technology, Guadalajara, Mexico. Processed.

World Bank. 1995. *World Development Report.* Washington, D.C.

_____. 2000. *Trade Blocs.* New York: Oxford University Press.

_____. 2001. *Global Economic Prospects and the Developing Countries 2002.* Washington, D.C.

Wright, Gavin. 1999. "Can a Nation Learn? American Technology as a Network Phenomenon." In Naomi R. Lamoreaux, Daniel M. G. Raff and Peter Temin, eds., *Learning by Doing in Markets, Firms and Countries.* Chicago: National Bureau of Economic Research and University of Chicago Press.

_____. 2001. "Resource Based Growth, Then and Now." Stanford University/World Bank, Washington, D.C. Processed.

Wylie, Peter J. 1990. "Indigenous Technological Adaptation in Canadian Manufacturing, 1900–1929." *Canadian Journal of Economics* 23: 856–72.

Wynia, Gary W. 1990. "Opening Late-Industrializing Economies: Lessons from Argentina and Australia." *Policy Sciences* 23: 185–204.

Yeats, Alexander J. 1998. "Does Mercosur's Trade Performance Raise Concerns About the Effects of Regional Trade Arrangements?" *World Bank Economic Review* 12 (1): 1–28.

Yusuf, Shahid. 2001. "Globalization and the Challenge for Developing Countries." World Bank, Washington, D.C. Processed.

ANNEX

# Selected Figures from Chapters 2, 3, and 4

FIGURE A.1

## Average LAC Net Exports per Worker by Commodity Groups, 1982–97

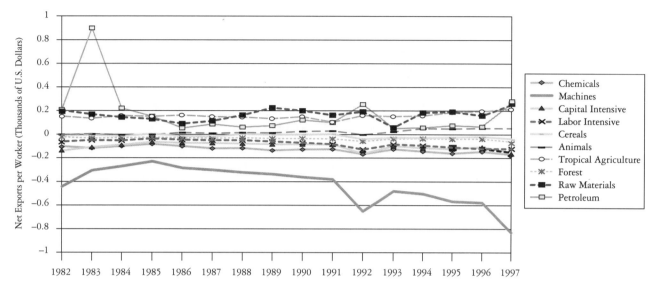

*Note:* Sample of 22 countries: Argentina, Barbados, Belize, Bolivia, Brazil, Chile, Colombia, Costa Rica, Ecuador, El Salvador, Guatemala, Honduras, Jamaica, Mexico, Nicaragua, Panama, Paraguay, Peru, the República Bolivariana de Venezuela, Suriname, Trinidad and Tobago, and Uruguay.

FIGURE A.2

## Argentina: Structure of Net Exports, 1980–99

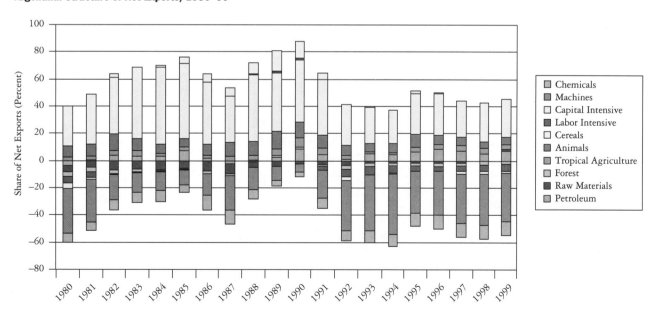

FIGURE A.3

## Brazil: Structure of Net Exports, 1981–99

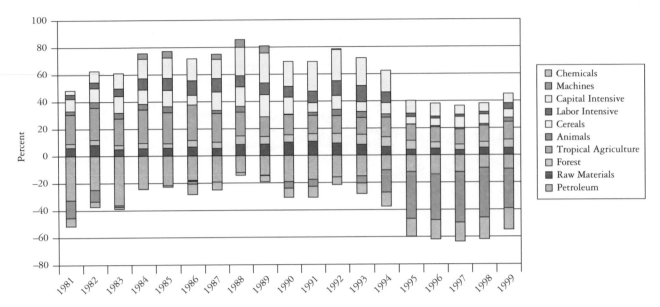

FIGURE A.4

## Chile: Structure of Net Exports, 1981–98

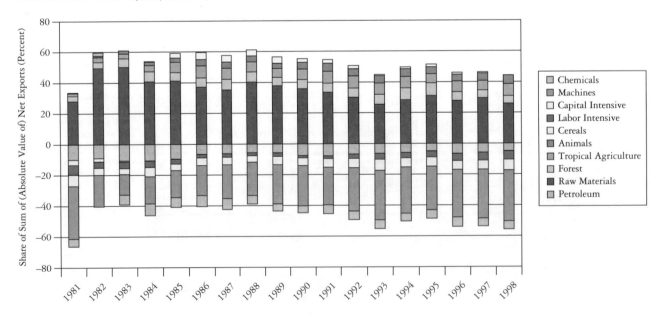

FIGURE A.5

## Costa Rica: Structure of Net Exports, 1981–99

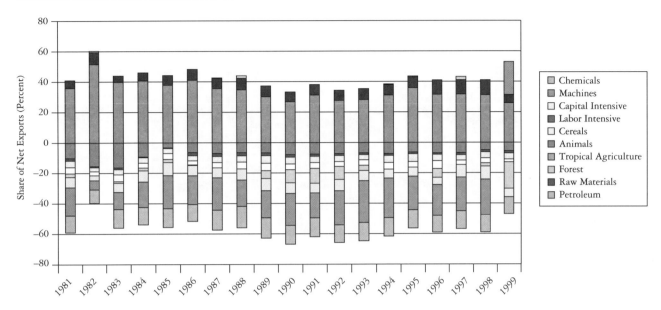

FIGURE A.6

## Dominican Republic: Structure of Net Exports, 1981–99

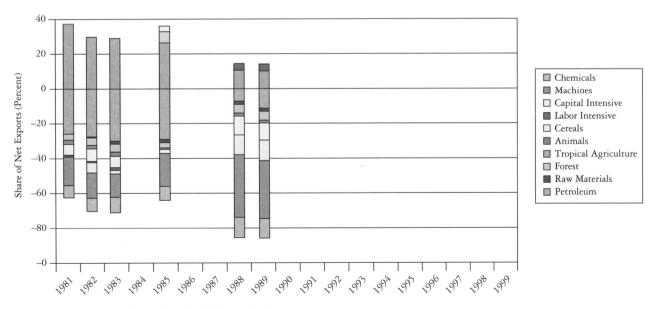

*Note:* Data were not available for 1984, 1986, 1987, and 1990–99.

FIGURE A.7

**Mexico: Structure of Net Exports, 1981–99**

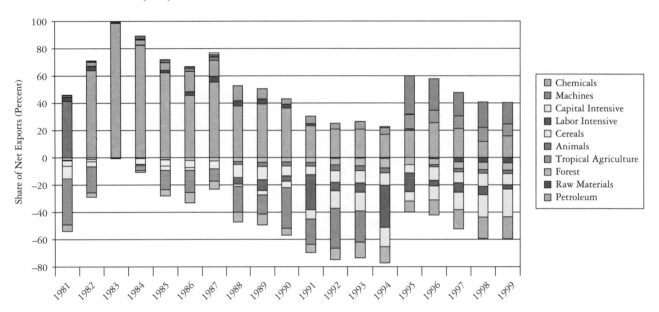

FIGURE A.8

**Australia: Structure of Net Exports in Selected Industrialized Countries**

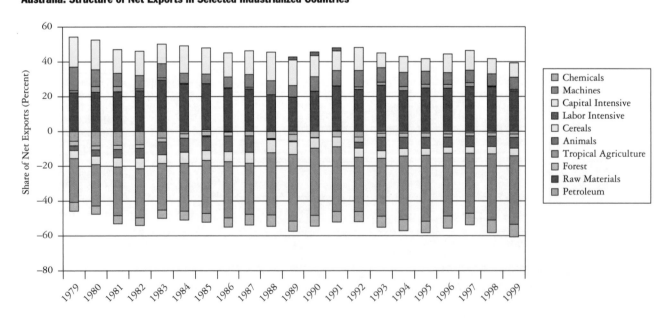

FIGURE A.9

**Canada: Structure of Net Exports in Selected Industrialized Countries**

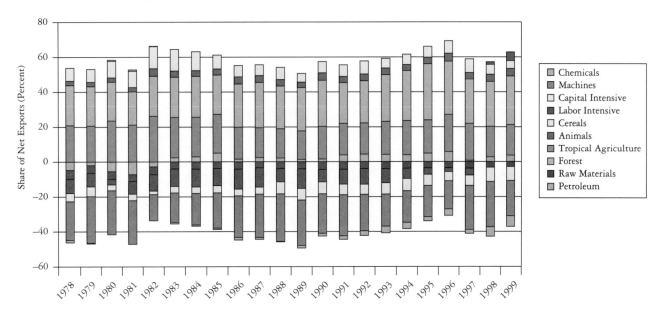

FIGURE A.10

**Finland: Structure of Net Exports in Selected Industrialized Countries**

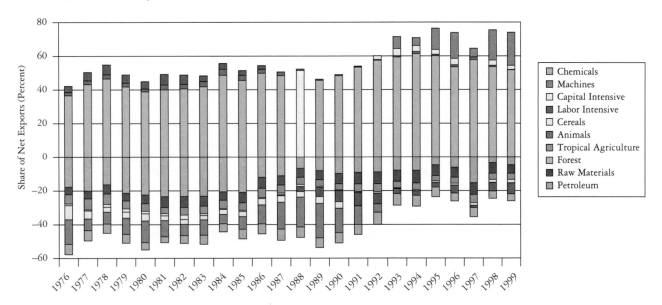

FIGURE A.11

## Sweden: Structure of Net Exports in Selected Industrialized Countries

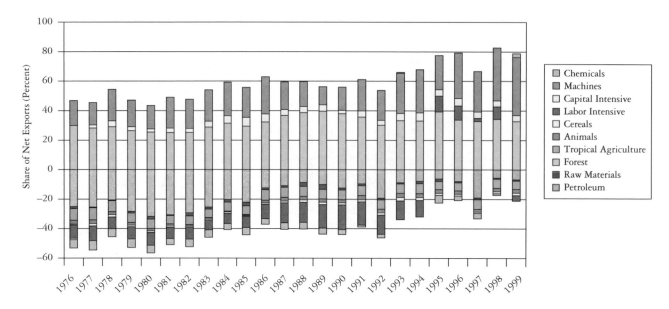

FIGURE A.12

## Mexico: Structure of NAFTA Net Exports

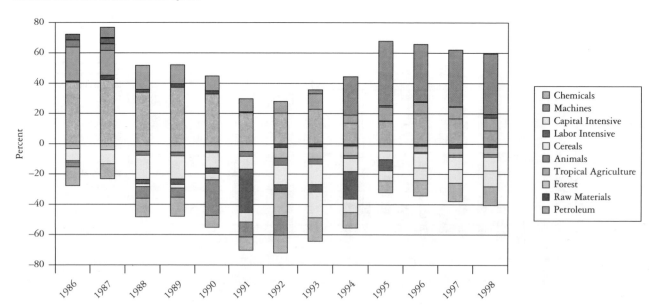